Cold Harbor to the Crater

Cold Harbor to the Crater

THE END OF THE OVERLAND CAMPAIGN

Edited by

Gary W. Gallagher *&* Caroline E. Janney

The University of North Carolina Press *Chapel Hill*

Publication of this book was supported in part by a generous gift from Catherine Lawrence and Eric Papenfuse.

The paper in this book meets the guidelines for permanence and durability of the Committee on Production Guidelines for Book Longevity of the Council on Library Resources.

The University of North Carolina Press has been a member of the Green Press Initiative since 2003.

Cover illustration: Thomas Nast, "The Campaign in Virginia: 'On to Richmond!'" *Harper's Weekly*, June 18, 1864 (Library of Congress, Ben and Beatrice Goldstein Foundation Collection)

Library of Congress Cataloging-in-Publication Data
Cold Harbor to the Crater : the end of the Overland Campaign /
edited by Gary W. Gallagher and Caroline E. Janney.
pages cm. — (Military campaigns of the Civil War)
Includes bibliographical references and index.
ISBN 978-1-4696-2533-1 (cloth : alk. paper)
ISBN 978-1-4696-2534-8 (ebook)
1. Overland Campaign, Va., 1864. 2. Cold Harbor, Battle of, Va., 1864.
3. Petersburg Crater, Battle of, Va., 1864. 4. Petersburg (Va.)—History—
Siege, 1864–1865. 5. United States—History—Civil War, 1861–1865—
Campaigns. I. Gallagher, Gary W. II. Janney, Caroline E.
E476.52.C65 2015   973.7′36—dc23
2015010513

For historians of the National Park Service,
major contributors to the field of Civil War history

⊰ CONTENTS ⊱

Introduction

⇥ GARY W. GALLAGHER & CAROLINE E. JANNEY ⇤

A French diplomat visited the battlefield at Cold Harbor shortly after the armies departed. Federal assaults had failed there on June 3, 1864, leaving a nightmarish landscape. "One sees on this ground," wrote Alfred Paul to superiors in Paris, "only entrenchments, rifle pits, chevaux-de-frise, scattered tree branches, corpses in putrefaction badly covered with a little ground almost carried away by the latest rains." Heat and moisture had left the air "foul, polluted by the exhalations of these human remains, and the flies rise from beneath the step of the horses as black clouds that poison the atmosphere." Two months later, a teenaged girl in Fredericksburg, Virginia, reacted to news of the battle of the Crater, which she called "the Yankees last new plan to exterminate our soldiers lives . . . by blowing our men high sky." Confederate counterattacks had sealed the Union breakthrough on July 30 and then restored the line. "In the pit which they had dug for us," recorded Mary G. Caldwell in her diary, "there were about 300 negroes and whites killed. It is said that our men just closed around this pit and killed them. How little did they think when they made the mine to blow our men open that it would be their own fate."[1]

Paul's and Caldwell's accounts deal with events that define the chronological framework for *Cold Harbor to the Crater*. Between the end of May and the beginning of August, Lt. Gen. Ulysses S. Grant and Gen. Robert E. Lee oversaw the transition between the Overland campaign—a remarkable saga of maneuvering, digging, and brutal combat—and what became a grueling, eight-and-one-half-month investment of Petersburg that eventually compelled Confederates to abandon Richmond. We consider the initial assaults at Petersburg on June 15–18 to be the last phase of the Overland campaign, an opportunity to earn a quick Union success that almost certainly would have doomed the Rebel capital. Until the U.S. failure at the Crater almost six weeks later, a protracted siege at Petersburg was far from certain—after it, few observers on either side expected anything else. In choosing this model, we depart from one that sees Grant's crossing of the James River on June 12–15 as the close of the Overland campaign and the fighting on the 15th–18th, when Maj. Gen. William F. "Baldy" Smith's Eighteenth Corps and Maj. Gen. Winfield Scott Hancock's Second Corps attacked Gen. P. G. T. Beauregard's badly outnumbered forces, as the start of the siege of Petersburg.[2]

The narrative of these operations is familiar. On May 20–21, following more than two weeks of combat and 60,000 combined Union and Confederate casualties at the Wilderness and Spotsylvania, U. S. Grant once again attempted to place his army between Lee and Richmond, angling to get around the Rebels' right flank. Lee anticipated the move and took up position behind the North Anna River, where fighting continued on May 23–26. By the end of the month, after additional action at Totopotomoy Creek and Bethesda Church, the Army of the Potomac and Army of Northern Virginia found themselves on nearly the same ground where Maj. Gen. George B. McClellan had faced Lee two years earlier during the Seven Days' battles. On June 1–3, near a crossroads just northeast of Richmond called Cold Harbor, Federals attacked their heavily entrenched enemy. Storied frontal assaults by the Union Second, Sixth, and Eighteenth Corps, together with other fighting on the 3rd, resulted in 4,500 Union and 1,500 Confederate casualties (the former figure far lower than innumerable treatments of the action would have it), and overall Grant lost approximately 14,000 and Lee 8,500 men between May 23 and June 3.[3]

Dubbed a "butcher" by many Confederate newspapers and the Copperhead wing of the Democratic Party, the Union general in chief remained focused on the task at hand. Holding Lee's attention with part of his army, Grant pulled the majority of his troops out of the trenches at Cold Harbor and sent them across the James River to threaten Petersburg, a key road and rail junction twenty-five miles south of the Rebel capital. This maneuver, which one perceptive Confederate later praised as "the most brilliant stroke in all the Federal campaigns of the whole war," included construction of an impressive 2,100-foot-long pontoon bridge. Fooled by Grant, Lee delayed three days in sending reinforcements to Petersburg, leaving Beauregard with only 2,500 soldiers on June 15 to contend against roughly seven times that number in the Union Second and Eighteenth Corps. But despite losing their initial line of well-prepared works, the Confederates held on for four days, abetted by a combination of lethargy, confusion, and exhaustion on the Federal side. Lee's veterans began to reinforce Beauregard on the 18th, and by the end of that day a priceless opportunity for Grant had slipped away. In the course of the four days, regiments of United States Colored Troops (USCT) saw action (notably on the 15th), while some white units, grown weary of assaulting entrenched Confederates for many weeks, refused to advance.[4]

Although Richmond and Petersburg remained in Confederate hands, Grant had created the situation Lee most feared—the Army of Northern Virginia immobilized behind fortifications. A year before, just after Chancellorsville, Lee had argued for an offensive into the United States so the Army of the Potomac could not "take its own time to prepare and strengthen itself to renew its advance upon Richmond, and force this army back within the entrenchments of that city. . . . I think it is worth a trial to prevent such a catastrophe." Lee reaffirmed this fear in early June 1864. "We must destroy this army of Grant's before he gets to James River," he told Lt. Gen. Jubal A. Early; "if he gets there, it will become a siege, and then it will be a mere question of time." Grant knew what he had accomplished. Originally hopeful that he could take Petersburg in one bold stroke, he telegraphed Chief of Staff Henry W. Halleck on June 14: "Our forces will commence crossing James River today. The Enemy show no signs of yet having brought troops to south side of Richmond. I will have Petersburg secured if possible before they get there in much force." A week later, he accepted the need for a longer effort but remained optimistic because he had cornered his opponent. "Our work progresses here slowly," he informed his wife in a letter inviting her to spend the summer at Fort Monroe, "and I feel will progress securely until Richmond finally falls."[5]

Popular understanding of the military situation at Petersburg in late June and July deviated from what Grant and Lee knew to be the truth. In the Confederacy, civilians maintained a strong belief in Lee, who had parried Grant's thrusts during the Overland campaign and seemed well positioned to defend Richmond over the long term. Continued stalemate, they believed, would hurt Lincoln and the Republicans in the fall 1864 elections and perhaps open the way for negotiations leading to Confederate independence. Morale in the United States, in contrast, sagged. Not only had Grant failed to capture Richmond, but an ancillary effort by Maj. Gen. David Hunter in the Shenandoah Valley also ended with his repulse at Lynchburg on June 18, after which the victorious Confederates under Jubal Early marched down the Shenandoah Valley, crossed the Potomac River, and on July 11 reached the outskirts of Washington. The spectacle of Rebel artillery shelling the outer defenses of the capital created a sensation in the loyal states. Early's approach temporarily discomfitted Lincoln, who on July 10 nervously requested that Grant personally bring a major part of the Army of the Potomac to deal with Early—though he also "should provide to retain your hold" at Petersburg. Grant replied to Lincoln in a reassuring telegram that evening, making the obvious point that "it would have a bad effect for me to leave here." Lincoln calmed down and Early soon retreated back into the lower Shenandoah Valley, but the episode highlighted how unsettled it had become on the Union home front.[6]

Grant's best chance to avoid prolonged operations at Petersburg came as civilian morale in the United States descended toward its wartime nadir. The idea originated with Lt. Col. Henry Pleasants of the 48th Pennsylvania Infantry and eventually made its way up the chain of command to army headquarters. The final plan involved tunneling 510 feet from behind Union lines to a position under part of the Confederate works, placing four tons of black powder in galleries at the end of the shaft, and literally blowing a hole in Lee's position. Infantry would exploit the break, seize high ground overlooking Petersburg, and force Lee's retreat. Work commenced on June 25, and on July 30, Federals detonated the powder, destroying the better part of one South Carolina regiment and some artillery. Ensuing assaults by the four divisions of Maj. Gen. Ambrose E. Burnside's Ninth Corps dissolved in confusion and ended in utter defeat at a cost of nearly 4,000 soldiers, many of them USCT men given no quarter as Confederate counterattacks wreaked havoc around the great hole created by the explosion. Grant famously termed the fiasco "the saddest affair I have witnessed in this war. Such opportunity for carrying fortifications I have never seen and do not expect again to have." His prediction proved accurate, and after what came to be called the battle of the Crater, the armies settled into siege operations.[7]

Cold Harbor to the Crater is the tenth volume in the Military Campaigns of the Civil War series. It completes coverage of the Overland campaign begun in *The Wilderness Campaign* (1997) and *The Spotsylvania Campaign* (1998).[8] Readers familiar with the series know that its titles provide neither full strategic and tactical coverage nor assessments of all important commanders. For detailed narratives of various parts of the fighting and biographies of leaders on each side, readers can consult the bibliographical essay at the end of this book. These ten essays, as in all earlier volumes in the series, seek to illuminate specific elements of the operations, highlight ties between military affairs and the home fronts, and explore longer-term resonance and ramifications. The essays take variant analytical positions and emphasize different aspects of topics. Readers will also find no precise consensus regarding the complex and often frustratingly imprecise exercise of reckoning casualties.

Gary W. Gallagher's opening essay focuses on Grant and Lee, who occupied singular positions in their respective nations. Both were compared to George Washington, a sure indication that fellow citizens invested substantial emotional capital in their leadership. As the Overland campaign ground toward its conclusion, with escalating losses and no clear indication that either side was winning, Grant and Lee came under intense scrutiny from newspapers, civilians, soldiers in their armies, and foreign observers. This essay assesses why Grant received harsher critiques, exploring, among other factors, the different political environments in the two nations, how previous operations affected civilian perceptions, and the relationships between Grant and Lee and their soldiers.

Robert E. L. Krick's essay surveys the assimilation of new troops into the Army of Northern Virginia following the heavy losses sustained throughout May. The army, in effect, had to be rebuilt on the move by siphoning strength from other parts of Virginia and elsewhere in the Confederacy. These units, many of which came from areas that had seen only limited military action, little resembled the battle-hardened regiments that had fought with the army in 1862 and 1863. Although the reinforcements buoyed the spirit of the veteran commands and indicated the government's commitment to Lee, many of them faced difficulties in getting to the front, demonstrated uneven effectiveness in battle, and encountered problems in forging a relationship with the army's veterans. Despite such problems, Krick explains, the Davis government's conscientious effort to keep the Army of Northern Virginia at roughly its pre-Overland campaign strength enabled Lee to hold Grant's forces at bay.

Kathryn Shively Meier widens the lens to soldiers in both armies in her essay. In 1887, Confederate general Evander M. Law famously described the battle of Cold Harbor as "not war" but "murder." Since that time, veterans and historians alike have characterized the battle as exceptionally violent, bloody, and crippling to soldier morale and willingness to fight. Meier departs strikingly from this conception of Cold Harbor while placing the battle within the wider scope of operations in May and early June. Despite the relentless pace of the campaign and the high casualty figures, she explains, the vast majority of volunteers endured and responded to circumstances ranging from lack of provisions and harsh summer heat to endless hours spent in the trenches by resorting to self-care strategies. Adapting techniques they had employed in previous campaigns, such as stealing away for a bath in a nearby river, volunteers remained functioning soldiers during and after Cold Harbor.

As the soldiers in Meier's essay knew only too well, increasingly sophisticated fieldworks became a notable feature of operations in May–July 1864. By the time of the fighting outside Petersburg on June 15–18, many Union soldiers had reached a breaking point in terms of their willingness to attack entrenched Rebels. Keith S. Bohannon examines Confederate engineering efforts during the campaign, as well as the attitude among men in the ranks toward the new type of warfare. General Lee, an accomplished engineer himself, fully grasped the role engineering would play in the campaign, and his men came to prize the value of earthworks—most of which they built—as much as Grant's infantrymen dreaded orders to attack them. In their eagerness to establish strong defensive positions, southern soldiers sometimes started digging before engineers had time to lay out their preferred line of defense. At Cold Harbor, the advantage conveyed by well-constructed works stood out in especially sharp relief.

Volumes in Military Campaigns of the Civil War always have featured one or two biographical essays, and Joan Waugh's portrait of Brig. Gen. Francis Channing Barlow continues that tradition. Hailed as a fiercely brave "boy general," Barlow had won acclaim for his leadership at Fair Oaks, Antietam, and elsewhere. But he was not known for his courage alone. His strict training regime and discipline simultaneously made him unpopular with his own men and one of Maj. Gen. Winfield Scott Hancock's most trusted division commanders in the Second Corps during the Overland campaign. Waugh's essay explores the arc of Barlow's Civil War, from enlistment as a private in April 1861 through his promotion to major general in 1865. She argues that he can be understood through the prism of his background—a Republican born in New York, reared in Massachusetts, and educated at Harvard. Cynical, pessimistic, and often critical of his commanders, Barlow sometimes doubted Union victory though he devoted himself completely to the cause, suffering two potentially career-ending wounds. By the summer of 1864, Waugh observes in analysis that offers counterpoint to some of Meier's findings, both mental and physical fatigue had taken their toll, leaving Barlow at his lowest point as the Army of the Potomac settled in for the siege of Petersburg.

Barlow's division was among those that disengaged from Lee at Cold Harbor to cross the James River and approach Petersburg. Gordon C. Rhea's essay takes a fresh, and somewhat revisionist, look at Grant's celebrated movement. Describing the withdrawal from Cold Harbor as well planned and executed, Rhea nonetheless believes many historians have praised it too fulsomely. Logistical elements of the movement could have been better, and Grant should have made the initial effort against Petersburg with more than two corps and provided better overall leadership—either his or George G. Meade's—when fighting began on June 15. Because of lapses at the moment of truth, the striking accomplishment of crossing the James before Lee knew what was happening achieved only meager results.

The next two essays engage Confederate topics. M. Keith Harris examines morale among soldiers in the trenches around Petersburg. Despite common perceptions among later historians that the siege marked the beginning of an inevitable slide toward Appomattox, Harris shows that many Rebels remained quite upbeat through the summer. Reading forward in evidence from 1864, rather than backward with full knowledge of the war's outcome, reveals surprising optimism in Confederate accounts. Harris concedes a degree of war weariness but identifies countervailing forces that bolstered morale. Among these were a belief that soldiers in the Army of Northern Virginia, under Lee's leadership, could hold off the enemy at Petersburg, that Confederate armies in Georgia and the Shenandoah Valley could win victories, and that Union military failures could undo Lincoln and his party in November.

Caroline E. Janney's essay directs attention away from the battlefront to the civilian experience during the siege. Giving full attention to conditions in June and July 1864, Janney also extends her analytical range beyond 1864 to the last spring of the war. She demonstrates that Petersburg's white residents, in the line of fire and wanting for food and materials for the better part of nine months, believed they were experiencing total and indiscriminate warfare. They bitterly concluded that both besieging Union soldiers and civilians on the northern home front approved of shelling Confederate churches and private homes—a bombardment that maimed many people and killed several civilians, black and white. Yet the siege failed to undermine the white population's faith in the Rebel cause. On the contrary, the fortitude with which civilians built bomb shelters and endured privations strengthened the resolve of Confederates within and beyond the Cockade City.

Confederates resented the Union's deployment of black soldiers in combat at Petersburg, using their presence to rally additional support for the Confederacy. Kevin M. Levin's essay touches briefly on that phenomenon while probing the larger story of African American troops at the Crater. Debates within the Union high command about how best to use USCT units, conflicting opinions about black comrades among white officers and troops, tactical details regarding fighting at the Crater on July 30, and competing postwar accounts of the battle all fall within Levin's purview. Perhaps most obviously, this essay underscores the degree to which history and memory can diverge.

Stephen Cushman extends Levin's coverage, and closes the volume, with an examination of the Crater in recent fiction and film. Using Charles Frazier's best-selling *Cold Mountain* (1997), Anthony Minghella's cinematic version of the novel (2003), Duane Schultz's *Glory Enough for All* (1993), and Richard Slotkin's *The Crater* (1980), Cushman, who is a poet and a historian, explores stylistic choices, differences between written and spoken language in the nineteenth century, the challenge and potential reward of mining historical sources to create fictional treatments, and the importance of audience. Cushman's discussion of Slotkin's handling of black characters and interweaving of historical, literary, and political sensibilities has implications far beyond the topic and texts of the essay.

Resuming publication in Military Campaigns of the Civil War after a nine-year hiatus raises the question of what remains to be done. The focus always has been, and will remain, on the Eastern Theater.[9] We envision a second volume on Petersburg that carries forward to Appomattox and also, to complete all major operations in the East, a pair on First and Second Bull Run—all on no particular timetable.

WE WISH TO THANK all the authors in this collection, half of whom wrote essays for earlier volumes in the series and all of whom showed great good humor in doing everything we asked. As in all the previous volumes, the contributors include public and academic historians. Both of us have worked extensively with historians at the National Park Service and other nonacademic scholars, and we are deeply indebted to them. We firmly believe that conversations with and among these historians and the interested public are integral to the study of the Civil War, something we hope this series demonstrates.

Notes

1. Dispatch 92, Alfred Paul to Foreign Minister Drouyn de Lhuys, June 25, 1864 (translation kindly made available by Dr. Donald E. Witt); Russell P. Smith, ed., "'I should look forward to the future.' The Diary of Mary G. Caldwell," pt. 2, *Fredericksburg: History & Biography* 12 (2013), 43–44 (entry for August 15, 1864).

2. For examples of treating the change of base as the end of the Overland campaign, see Noah Andre Trudeau, *Bloody Roads South: The Wilderness to Cold Harbor,*

May–June 1864 (Boston: Little, Brown, 1989); Mark Grimsley, *And Keep Moving On: The Virginia Campaign, May–June 1864* (Lincoln: University of Nebraska Press, 2002); and Alfred C. Young III, *Lee's Army during the Overland Campaign: A Numerical Study* (Baton Rouge: Louisiana State University Press, 2013).

3. Figures for casualties come from Gordon C. Rhea, *Cold Harbor: Grant and Lee, May 26–June 3, 1864* (Baton Rouge: Louisiana State University Press, 2002), 359–62, 392, and Young, *Lee's Army during the Overland Campaign*, 238–40.

4. The praise for Grant's movement is from Edward Porter Alexander, *Fighting for the Confederacy: The Personal Recollections of General Edward Porter Alexander*, ed. Gary W. Gallagher (Chapel Hill: University of North Carolina Press, 1989), 419–20. Alexander termed the pontoon bridge "the greatest bridge of boats since the time of Xerxes" and applauded the Federal engineers who built it. On participation by USCT troops and white regiments that would not attack, see Thomas J. Howe, *The Petersburg Campaign: Wasted Valor, June 15–18, 1864*, 2nd ed. (Lynchburg, Va.: H. E. Howard, 1988), 33–37, 130–33.

5. Robert E. Lee to Secretary of War James A. Seddon, June 8, 1863, in Robert E. Lee, *The Wartime Papers of R. E. Lee*, ed. Clifford Dowdey and Louis H. Manarin (Boston: Little, Brown, 1961), 504–5; Jubal A. Early, *The Campaigns of Gen. Robert E. Lee. An Address by Lieut. General Jubal A. Early, before Washington and Lee University, January 19th, 1872* (Baltimore: John Murphy, 1872), 41–42; Ulysses S. Grant, *The Papers of Ulysses S. Grant*, ed. John Y. Simon and others, 32 vols. to date (Carbondale: Southern Illinois University Press, 1967–), 11:45 (Grant to Halleck, June 14), 110 (Grant to Mrs. Grant, June 22) (set hereafter cited as *PUSG*).

6. Lincoln to Grant, July 10 (2:00 P.M.), 11, 1864, in Abraham Lincoln, *The Collected Works of Abraham Lincoln*, ed. Roy P. Basler, 9 vols. (New Brunswick, N.J.: Rutgers University Press, 1953–55), 7:437–38; Grant to Lincoln, July 10 (10:30 P.M.), 1864, in *PUSG*, 11:203. For a good narrative on Early's operations, see Frank E. Vandiver, *Jubal's Raid: General Early's Famous Attack on Washington in 1864* (New York: McGraw-Hill, 1960). Early's own account is in *A Memoir of the Last Year of the War for Independence, in the Confederate States of America* (Lynchburg, Va.: Charles W. Button, 1867), 35–62.

7. Grant to Henry W. Halleck, August 1, 1864, in *PUSG*, 11:361–62. See the bibliographical essay at the end of this book for titles on the Crater.

8. Volumes in the series did not address campaigns in chronological order. Those on Antietam, the Richmond campaign of 1862, the 1862 Valley campaign, and the 1864 Valley campaign were published between 1999 and 2006.

9. The Civil War Campaigns in the Heartland series, edited by Steven E. Woodworth and Charles D. Grear, has made an excellent start on operations west of the Appalachians and promises to continue with other battles in the Western Theater. To date, Southern Illinois University Press has published volumes on Shiloh (2009), Chickamauga (2010), Chattanooga (2012), and Vicksburg (2013).

Cold Harbor to the Crater

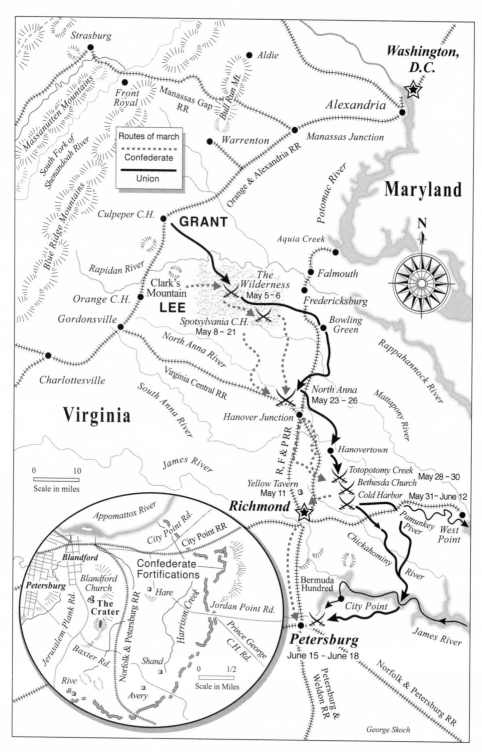

Theater of Operations, May–July 1864

The Two Generals Who Resist Each Other
Perceptions of Grant and Lee in the Summer of 1864

⊰ GARY W. GALLAGHER ⊱

Ulysses S. Grant and Robert E. Lee occupied singular positions in the spring of 1864. Each was the leading popular symbol of his respective cause, the person in whom fellow citizens invested the most emotional and political trust. Presidents Abraham Lincoln and Jefferson Davis, as well as other prominent soldiers such as Maj. Gen. William Tecumseh Sherman and Gen. Joseph E. Johnston, also received considerable public attention as the war entered its fourth year, but none matched Grant and Lee as rallying points of national hope. Between the opening of the Overland campaign in the Wilderness on May 5, through battles such as Spotsylvania and Cold Harbor, and into the post-Crater reality that Petersburg faced a protracted siege after August 1, Grant and Lee came under intensive scrutiny. Newspaper editors, Union and Confederate soldiers and civilians, and foreign observers, almost all of whom believed armies would decide the fate of the warring republics, rendered judgments. The contrast in opinions, with Grant subjected to far harsher treatment than Lee, illuminates the different political environments in the two nations, the impact of previous campaigns on civilian perceptions, and the nature of the commanders' pre-1864 reputations.

The primacy of the two men in early 1864 stood out in how they were linked to George Washington. Americans North and South had looked to Washington as their greatest national hero during the antebellum years, and the Confederacy followed that tradition by placing an equestrian image of him on its Great Seal. A public figure of unrivalled accomplishment, Washington impressed Americans as a remarkable republican patriot who, unlike Julius Caesar or Oliver Cromwell or Napoleon, willingly relinquished military and political power after the Revolution and again following his second term as president. Because citizens in the United States and the Confederacy almost never placed political or military figures alongside Washington, their doing so with Grant and Lee carried great weight.[1]

Abraham Lincoln offered the most notable instance of tying Grant to Washington. In a short speech delivered to the general in front of members of the cabinet and a few others on March 9, 1864, Lincoln addressed Grant's promotion to the rank previously held only by Washington. "The nation's appreciation of what you have done, and its reliance upon you for what remains to do, in the existing great struggle," remarked the president, "are now presented with this commission, constituting you Lieutenant General in the Army of the United States. . . . I scarcely need to add that with what I here speak for the nation goes my own hearty personal concurrence." In responding to the unprecedented gesture, Grant thanked Lincoln "for the high honor conferred," pledging that "with the aid of the noble armies that have fought on so many fields for our common country, it will be my earnest endeavor not to disappoint your expectations. I feel the full weight of the responsibilities now devolving on me and know that if they are met it will be due to those armies, and above all to the favor of that Providence which leads both Nations and men."[2]

Support for Grant's promotion to Washington's rank crossed political boundaries, in part because no one knew for certain whether the conqueror of Vicksburg was a Democrat or a Republican. The *Philadelphia Daily Evening Bulletin*, a Republican newspaper, anticipated Lincoln's action a week before the ceremony at the White House. "Ever since the question of the appointment of a Lieutenant-General has been mentioned in the present Congress," read the article, "the people have thought only of Ulysses S. Grant as the man for the post. The President could not, if he would, have appointed anyone else; and we do not believe that he would if he could. The Senate would have confirmed no one else, and the people would have been dissatisfied with anyone else." Shortly after the opening of the Overland campaign, the *New York Herald*, a Democratic-leaning sheet, called for Grant to emulate George Washington's ascension to the presidency: "We expect his election to be as unanimous as that of General Washington and as beneficial to the welfare of the republic." A few days later, the *Herald* added, "Never since Washington and Jackson, has any man so nobly earned the right to be President."[3]

Well before the spring of 1864, Lee assumed a position in the Confederate struggle for independence roughly equivalent to Washington's during the Revolutionary War. At the Virginia secession convention on April 23, 1861, John Janney, the presiding officer, evoked "Light-Horse Harry" Lee's famous words about Washington in bestowing the state's highest military rank on Harry's son Robert: "We pray God most fervently that you may so conduct the operations committed to your charge, that it will soon be said of you, that you are 'first in peace,' and when that time comes you will have earned the still prouder distinction of being 'first in the hearts of your countrymen.'"[4]

Given command of the Army of Northern Virginia in early June 1862, Lee rapidly achieved the kind of public renown and affection to which Janney referred. Four pieces of evidence, two each from 1862 and 1864, illustrate this phenomenon. In October 1862, a correspondent for the *Columbus (Ga.) Times* reported that Lee "has much of the Washingtonian dignity about him, and is much respected by all with whom he is thrown." Two months later, an Atlanta newspaper averred of Lee that, "Like Washington, he is a wise man and a good man, and possesses in an eminent degree those qualities which are indispensable in the great leader and champion upon whom the country rests its hope of present success and future independence." Denominating Lee the "grandson of Washington, so to speak," the author of this article hoped "the mantle of the ascending hero has fallen upon the wise and modest chief who now commands the army of Northern Virginia." In early 1864, Col. Clement A. Evans of the 31st Georgia Infantry aptly summed up the relationship between Lee and his soldiers. "General Robt. E. Lee is regarded by his army as nearest approaching the character of the great & good Washington than any man living," Evans wrote in a diary entry covering the period January 18–28: "He is the only man living in whom they would unreservedly trust all power for the preservation of their independence." The *Richmond Daily Dispatch*, which had the widest circulation of the capital's several newspapers, published a glowing sketch of Lee in March 1864 that found in him "a closer resemblance to George Washington than we had supposed humanity could ever again furnish."[5]

The presence of the war's preeminent soldiers fueled great anticipation regarding the Virginia campaign, and optimism predominated on both sides of the Potomac River.[6] People in the United States relished the thought that their hero would crush Lee, whose reputation had suffered little or no diminution after Gettysburg and who remained a bogeyman to the loyal American citizenry. "Each day brings us nearer to the great battle of the war which must soon be fought in Virginia," stated the *Chicago Tribune* in late April, "—a battle which we believe will be one of the most terrible ever recorded in history. Both Grant and Lee are massing their forces for the shock. . . . McClellanism is rooted out of the army. . . . It has confidence in the commanding General, and he takes the field unhampered with interference from any quarter. Upon the skill and prestige of success, we anticipate a victory which shall give the rebellion the finishing blow." The *New York Times*, like the *Tribune* a Republican newspaper, developed a common theme: "The Southern rebels, as well as some folks in the North, are fond of shaking their heads in view of Lieut.-Gen. Grant's approaching campaign in Virginia, with the remark that though Grant had heretofore been successful in beating the rebel Generals, he has never yet encountered *Gen. Lee*. That is true enough. But do these people ever think that, if it be true that Grant has never fought Lee, it is equally true that Lee has never met *Grant*?" The *New York Herald*, with earlier Union failures in the Eastern Theater obviously in mind, judged Grant a soldier who would not be "McClellanized" and whose "object is to crush the main armies of Jeff. Davis, and, first of all, the rebel army of Virginia, which is the life and soul of the rebellion."[7]

For their part, Confederates worried about Grant's superiority in manpower but doubted he could prevail against Lee. "Their army is twice as large as ours," Capt. Charles Minor Blackford, who served in Lt. Gen. James Longstreet's First Corps, informed his wife just before the Overland campaign opened, but Lee's "officers and men are confident of success." Blackford seconded that confidence while also confessing fears regarding "the force of numbers." From the Confederate capital, Judith Brockenbrough McGuire braced herself for renewed slaughter. "The enemy threatens Richmond," she wrote in her diary on April 25, "and is coming against it with an immense army." The Yankees prophesied success by the end of the summer, but the Confederate government "is making every effort to defeat them. I don't think that anyone doubts our ability to do it; but the awful loss of life necessary upon the fights is what we dread."[8]

Many Confederates deprecated Grant's western triumphs and savored the prospect of his encountering Lee. Toward the end of March, the *Richmond Daily Dispatch* attributed Grant's success in the Western Theater to "overwhelming numbers and the weakness and imbecility of our own resistance" and, in mid-April, assured readers that "his performances bear no comparison whatever to those of Gen. Lee. . . . The latter has always fought against immense odds, and has always been victorious." At Lee's headquarters, Lt. Col. Walter H. Taylor similarly insisted that Grant enjoyed an inflated reputation gained at the expense of Lt. Gen. John C. Pemberton, the much maligned officer who had lost Vicksburg: "He will find, I trust, that General Lee is a very different man to deal with & if I mistake not will shortly come to grief if he attempts to repeat the tactics in Virginia which proved so successful in Mississippi." Catherine Ann Devereux

GARY W. GALLAGHER

Edmondston, a keen diarist living in eastern North Carolina, mocked a northern newspaper's assertion that in Grant "We have found our hero!" Summoning a full measure of sarcasm, Edmondston observed on April 18, 1864, "This is the seventh *Hero* that the Yankees have found!" Then she listed all the army commanders who had come to grief against Lee.[9]

Judith McGuire's prediction of an "awful loss of life" proved accurate as the armies bludgeoned one another during the Overland campaign. A look at casualties, with numbers rounded to the nearest 500, will help frame analysis of reactions to Grant's and Lee's conduct of operations. At the outset, Grant fielded 119,000 and Lee 66,000 soldiers, which meant the Confederates mustered just more than 55 percent of their opponent's strength. Between May 5 and June 18, Grant received 48,000 reinforcements and Lee 30,000, bringing the overall numbers involved to 167,000 and 96,000, respectively, and raising the Rebels to 57 percent of Union strength over the entire period.[10] United States forces suffered nearly 65,000 casualties, with 54,500 killed or wounded and more than 10,000 captured or missing; Confederates lost 34,500, with 23,500 killed or wounded and 11,000 missing or captured. Grant's casualties approached 40 percent of his 167,000 men, with killed and wounded accounting for 33 percent; Lee's casualties fell just short of 36 percent of his 96,000, with killed and wounded totaling 24.5 percent. Grant thus lost nearly twice as many men overall as well as a higher percentage of his army.[11]

It has become a commonplace that previously unseen and unimaginable carnage marked the armies' track from the Rapidan River to the outskirts of Petersburg. Similarly, Grant's willingness to accept huge casualties to gain victory—twisted by some at the time and in subsequent generations into an image of him as "a butcher"—has colored many comparative estimates of the two great antagonists. Both of these subjects require some attention.[12]

Regarding the scale of casualties, the Overland campaign figured differently in Union and Confederate experiences. For the Army of the Potomac, it did represent a significant departure. Losses in the army's major campaigns prior to the spring of 1864—the Peninsula, Seven Days, Second Bull Run, Antietam, Fredericksburg, Chancellorsville, Gettysburg, Bristoe, and Mine Run—totaled 118,000, more than a third of which came at Chancellorsville and Gettysburg in a period of nine weeks. In several campaigns, significant parts of the army saw little action. For example, the First and Fifth Corps lost 1,000 men combined at Chancellorsville, and the Sixth Corps fewer than 250 at Gettysburg. Perhaps most notoriously, the Fifth

Corps, commanded by Maj. Gen. Fitz John Porter, avoided significant action at Antietam. In forty-five days under Grant, casualties soared to 55 percent of the total for the previous twenty-five months. That gruesome statistic aside, Grant's overall career had not featured huge losses. His operations in the Western Theater—Belmont, Forts Henry and Donelson, Shiloh, Vicksburg, and Chattanooga—yielded four striking successes at a cost of fewer than 35,000 casualties.[13]

The Confederate ledger tells a very different story. Before Grant arrived, the Army of Northern Virginia had suffered 102,500 casualties, 10,500 of them on the Peninsula before Lee took charge on June 1, 1862. Lee's effort against Grant between May 5 and June 18, 1864, resulted in casualties numbering almost exactly one-third of the previous total, a far lower percentage than in the Army of the Potomac. In other words, the Overland campaign represented a heavy but scarcely unprecedented level of loss for the Army of Northern Virginia—a force that, unlike its opponent, never had experienced the luxury of waging a battle without full commitment of virtually all units. Although Lee always commanded fewer men than his Federal opponents (far fewer at Antietam, Fredericksburg, and Chancellorsville; only at the Seven Days did he enjoy almost equal numbers), his losses approached 87 percent of theirs. Lee's 92,000 pre–Overland campaign casualties dwarfed those of Grant. Divided into different periods, the pre–Overland campaign casualties break down as follows: Peninsula through Seven Days, 12 weeks, 30,450 casualties; Seven Days through Chantilly, 9 weeks, 30,500; Second Bull Run through Antietam, 5 1/2 weeks, 23,500; Seven Days through Antietam, 11 weeks, 43,500; Chancellorsville through Gettysburg, 8 weeks, 40,500. By the spring of 1864, in sum, Confederates inside and outside the army had come to expect massive losses in the Eastern Theater, something that must be factored into the price of Lee's successful leadership.[14]

Behind the lines in the United States, the Overland campaign put faith in Grant to a severe test, extinguishing hopes that final victory would come by summer's end yet leaving most of the loyal citizenry clinging to the idea that eventually he would vanquish Lee. Politics in a two-party system certainly came into play. Democrats proved more willing than Republicans to criticize Grant, and the Copperhead wing of the Democratic Party, a minority within a minority of the voting populace, mounted a no-holds-barred assault on the new general in chief as part of an effort to discredit the Lincoln administration. Speculation about the upcoming presidential election intensified the partisan reaction to casualties, and the Republican

"The Campaign in Virginia: 'On to Richmond!'" Thomas Nast's stirring, and optimistically titled, tribute to Grant and soldiers in the Army of the Potomac reached readers of *Harper's Weekly* at the end of the Overland campaign. *Harper's Weekly*, June 18, 1864, 392–93.

national convention in Baltimore on June 7–8 made headlines as the armies glared at one another near Cold Harbor. Before the battle at that place on June 3, some Copperheads had decried Grant as a butcher responsible for casualties deemed unacceptable even in a conflict to save the cherished work of the founding generation. Overall, a sense of resignation spread across much of the North—acceptance of the prospect of a siege at Richmond and Petersburg as the likely, and potentially lengthy, route to success against the redoubtable Rebel army under Lee.

Support for Grant remained steady from mid-June through early August in most of the mainstream northern press. On June 18, *Harper's Weekly*, with its national circulation of more than 100,000, conveyed a sense of military progress in a double-page woodcut by Thomas Nast titled "The Campaign in Virginia: 'On to Richmond.'" The illustration featured a resolute Grant on horseback amid a mass of advancing Federals, pressing forward behind a tattered national flag to engage a much smaller number of Confederates. The same issue contained "Public Confidence," a short piece that applauded Grant's honesty in reporting about his operations against the Army of Northern Virginia. "It is easy to see that the work would have been easier could he have beaten Lee upon the Rapidan or at Spottsylvania," conceded *Harper's*, "because then he would have been spared the necessity of besieging Richmond. Yet great and difficult as the task is, there is a public tranquillity which springs from profound confidence in him and in the ultimate success of the cause." A week earlier, *Harper's* had run a cartoon showing Grant whipping Lee as well as an article that declared, "There is but one prayer in the great multitude of American hearts today. God bless President Lincoln and General Grant!"[15]

Horace Greeley's *New York Tribune* applauded Grant's tenacity, while consistently avoiding discussion of casualties, and urged everyone in the United States to match his determination. The *Tribune*'s treatment of Cold Harbor—by any reasonable standard a Union fiasco—reveals how the partisan press functioned. That awful repulse, in the *Tribune*'s view, accomplished "nothing decisive" but "to some extent was a success." Most important, it did not deflect the Army of the Potomac from its purpose: "Gen. Grant goes steadily toward Richmond, and his army finds encouragement in every step of progress." The paper also detected something positive in the unsuccessful Federal assaults at Petersburg on June 15–18. "The failure may point the way to the success of another attempt or to the adoption of a different plan," its rather opaque coverage explained, "but it does not suggest for a moment anything like a serious interruption to offensive operations." Although indecisive battles, or even defeats, might lie ahead, "there will never be a disaster overwhelming enough to shake the purpose of the indomitable soldier who carries with him the fortunes of the Republic."[16]

Other major Republican newspapers took similar positions, calling for resolute support in a war that would not end soon. Philadelphia's *Daily Evening Bulletin* mentioned how intense the fighting had been at Cold Harbor before quoting "informants" who reported, with an eye toward earlier failed commanders, "that the army is in the best possible condition and spirits. . . . The whole army fairly worship Gen. Grant, and say that he is the only man who has given them a chance to fight." Joseph Medill's *Chicago Tribune* sought to play down the cost and effect of Cold Harbor, characterizing it as "a reconnaissance" that resulted in "ten minutes of fighting." Like Greeley, Medill predicted "rough blows" ahead, to be given and taken by the Army of the Potomac. Turning to the northern public, the paper, in effect, issued a challenge: "Gen. Grant's operations are making good progress. . . . There is no occasion for disheartenment, and if you are disappointed that the end is not more nearly reached, the blame is your own, and the origin thereof a misapprehension of the magnitude of the undertaking." Open maneuvering had come to an end, patience would be essential, and the payoff would be worth the effort because the "fall of Richmond, when it comes, will stand on record with earth's great sieges, and such are not worked out in a night."[17]

The *New York Times* adopted a more measured tone in reviewing Grant's work through the middle of June. He had won some successes, but none could be labeled decisive. Like many other Republican newspapers, the *Times* tried to finesse Cold Harbor, the most obvious Union failure: "All that matchless valor directed by consummate skill could do, was done; but it was in vain." Grant had lost on average five men to Lee's three, a ratio that over the long term would erode the Union edge in manpower, making it "an equality, and presently an inferiority." All "hope of *crushing* the rebel army," Grant's original intention according to the *Times*, should be put aside. A new kind of campaign might soon commence. "If Lee allows himself to be shut up within Richmond," concluded the article with a measure of forced optimism, "the problem reduces itself to a repetition of Vicksburgh over again. Will he do it? There is a question."[18]

The Democratic press divided over Grant's conduct during the Overland campaign. The *New York Herald*, which sometimes took positions at odds with the party's mainstream, held a consistently positive stance though acknowledging, and trying to place in context, the enormous Union casualties. The general's "extraordinary genius" made him "the most consummate general of the age," gushed the paper on June 3. Two days earlier, in language sure to prompt at least some readers to think of George Washington, the editors had raised the possibility of a political future for the general in chief: "This is a man of whom it may be truly said that the Presidency seeks him, instead of his seeking the Presidency." During the first week of June, the paper also promoted—and then enthusiastically covered—a mass meeting in Union Square to express the nation's gratitude to Grant. Some Republicans questioned the paper's political motives in supporting the meeting, though George Templeton Strong, whose famous diary includes fierce denunciations of Democrats and their newspapers, noted that the event was "reported to have been large, earnest, and grave." Throughout June, the *Herald* flew a more partisan flag in denouncing what

The Two Generals Who Resist Each Other

it termed Lincoln's interference with Grant's plans. "Military genius," it commented, "is useless—the dreadful carnage of a month of battles is useless—if a politician in Washington may nullify all that is done simply to further a party scheme."[19]

Its faith in Grant notwithstanding, the *Herald* closed the month of June with a gloomy forecast. Grant's deft maneuvering and his army's effective fighting during the Overland campaign had not broken the Rebels, who seemed ready to defend their capital to the last ditch. All the Union army's bloody work had merely set the stage for a standoff at Petersburg "likely to continue for days, and maybe months." Striving to be upbeat, the editors did not "believe that Grant will fail" nor "that our hope for the fall of Richmond must be relinquished." But that hope, it had become apparent, "must be again deferred; and hope so many times deferred may sicken a nation as bitterly as it will the heart of any single person in it."[20]

New York's *Sunday Mercury*, a Democratic weekly that claimed as many national readers as *Harper's Weekly* and *Frank Leslie's Illustrated Newspaper*, echoed the *Herald* in praising Grant and condemning Lincoln. On June 5, an editorial blamed Lincoln for forcing Grant into an overland advance against Richmond "because the better route had been pointed out by McClellan" in 1862. Lincoln's "obstinacy" cost "about 60,000 men" and grew out of his fear that Grant might emerge as a political rival. "Great generals may become popular candidates for the Presidency," wrote the editors; "all opposition candidates must be made way with, even if the Republic goes down in the whirlpool of popular commotions." On July 17, the *Mercury* levied a darker accusation against Lincoln. The president had ignored Grant's warnings to protect the capital, allowing a small force under Jubal Early to reach the city's outskirts on July 11–12. Lincoln willfully risked extending the war because "peace would be ruin to his rich friends, the contractors," if Grant captured Petersburg and compelled the evacuation of Richmond. "To counteract such Union successes," concluded the editorial, "Lincoln left the back-door of the Capital open to the Rebel cavalry."[21]

The image of Grant as a butcher arose in, and remained confined to, the Copperhead wing of the Democratic Party.[22] The origins had everything to do with politics and very little with the Overland campaign. Well before the scale of fighting had become well known, Copperheads assailed Grant in an effort to discredit Lincoln's management of the war prior to the November elections. On May 11, less than a week after Grant and Lee collided at the Wilderness, the *Washington (Pa.) Reporter* quoted a Copperhead who predicted George B. McClellan's election "if the defeat of the Army of the

Potomac can be secured; if the butcher Grant can be snubbed in the South; if the beast Butler can be roasted in Norfolk." Less than a week later, while the armies lay at Spotsylvania, the *San Francisco Daily Evening Bulletin* disparaged a Copperhead who "took occasion to allude to Gen. Grant as a savage butcher—a man utterly reckless of the lives of his men—very different from McClellan." The *Ashland (Ohio) Union* announced on June 22 "a Federal defeat with the loss of an entire division of the butcher's army," linking Grant to the president "as just the man the administration has been looking for, to command the Potomac army. He can let more blood, and lead more innocent white men to the Lincoln slaughter pens than any other General in the army."[23]

The Old Guard, a Copperhead journal published in New York City, launched a bare-knuckled assault on Grant. Editor C. Chauncey Burr, who specialized in hyperbolic invective, slammed Lincoln, the Republicans, and Grant in one brutal passage: "What is the difference between a *butcher* and a *general*? A butcher kills animals for food. A general kills men to gratify the ambition or malice of politicians and scoundrels." Burr invited readers "to abhor the general whose business is to slaughter thousands of innocent men." The Republicans' war mocked the idea of civilization and left "monuments of shame" everywhere Union forces campaigned. Anyone unwilling "to lie outright" knew "Gen. Grant has not obtained a single victory in battle since he crossed the Rapidan. . . . He has destroyed the best part of his veteran army, and has fearfully demoralized what is remaining of it." As for Grant's future reputation, prophesied Burr, "Curses will follow his head to his grave. . . . Never more can he go into a town or village in the whole North where his name will not excite horror in the breasts of numberless widows and orphans. He is the death's head of a whole people."[24]

The Overland campaign undoubtedly took a grievous physical and mental toll on Grant's soldiers, though morale did not reach the crisis portrayed in *The Old Guard* and other Copperhead sources. A majority of the soldiers certainly shared feelings of loss over slain and maimed comrades, frustration at repeatedly being ordered to attack entrenched Confederates, and disappointment that the war promised to continue for many months. The fact that thousands of men whose three-year enlistments ran out in May and June refused to reenlist attests to weariness in the ranks. Yet from Cold Harbor through the end of July, most Federals also recognized how badly they had damaged the Army of Northern Virginia and believed Grant would sustain the pressure necessary for final victory at Petersburg and Richmond.[25]

The Two Generals Who Resist Each Other

Five well-known accounts reveal common attitudes within the army. Charles S. Wainwright, an artillery officer in the Fifth Corps, noted the widespread disillusionment with frontal assaults. "Whoever was responsible for the extended mode of attack," he wrote the day after the fighting on June 3 at Cold Harbor, "is getting no military credit, nor the love of the men who are being used up by it." The botched offensives at Petersburg on June 15–18, which included examples of units that refused to participate, elicited a similar entry. "The attack this afternoon was a fiasco of the worst kind," recorded Wainwright on the 18th; "I trust it will be the last attempt at this most absurd way of attacking entrenchments. . . . It has been tried so often now and with such fearful losses that even the stupidest private now knows that it cannot succeed, and the natural consequence follows: the men will not try it." Newspapers ascribed to Grant responsibility for the attacks, but Wainwright did not. "Here we see nothing of Grant," he remarked, "I hardly heard his name mentioned." Lt. Col. Theodore Lyman, a member of army commander George G. Meade's staff, famously quoted Maj. Gen. Gouverneur K. Warren's reaction to the campaign's carnage: "For thirty days now, it has been one funeral procession, past me; and it is too much!" Lyman's own opinion, rendered in his journal on June 4, was that "there has been too much assaulting this campaign! . . . The best officers and men are liable, by their greater gallantry to be first disabled; and, of those that are left, the best become demoralized by the failures, and the loss of good leaders; so that, very soon, the men will no longer charge entrenchments and will only go forward when driven by their officers."[26]

Others articulated a grim sense of progress. Elisha Hunt Rhodes, whose 2nd Rhode Island Infantry served in the Sixth Corps, called Cold Harbor "a terrible battle" for other units but not for the 2nd. "Perhaps because so many men go home tomorrow," he speculated, the regiment "has been kept in reserve." One of 326 men remaining with the 2nd after 265 comrades departed at the end of their enlistments on June 6, Rhodes, who began the war as a private, took charge of the regiment. "General Grant means to hold on," he wrote after Cold Harbor, "and I know he will win in the end." Col. Robert McAllister, whose 11th New Jersey Infantry served in the Second Corps, termed the area along the Chickahominy River "one vast graveyard—graves everywhere, marking the track of the army." Both sides now dug in at every opportunity, McAllister related to members of his family on June 6; he saw the future as "work by sieging" but still expected "we will have to charge sometimes." As for General Grant, he "understands his business and will eventually succeed. Everyone has confidence in him."

GARY W. GALLAGHER

12

Nine days later, after the army had crossed the James River, McAllister acknowledged losses but credited Grant with "weakening Lee's forces and destroying all the railroads in his course. We will soon be in the rear of Richmond. It is not worth while to speculate, but I will add: all is right."[27]

Grant's relationship with the men of the Army of the Potomac never approached that of Lee to his soldiers. Grant began the campaign a stranger to his troops and never earned their unqualified affection. He did win respect, as first evidenced when soldiers who realized he would continue the offensive after the battle of the Wilderness cheered him on May 7. He was different, a general who held out the chance to prove they could defeat Lee's army—unlike McClellan at the Seven Days and Antietam, Hooker at Chancellorsville, and Meade after Gettysburg—even if it cost many thousands of casualties. The rank and file never bestowed on Grant an affectionate nickname—no "Marse Robert," as Lee's men preferred, or "Uncle Billy," as did Sherman's, or "Little Mac," as longtime veterans of the Army of the Potomac called McClellan. Frank Wilkeson shed light on this topic in his excellent postwar memoir. A gunner in a New York battery, Wilkeson recalled how many Federals compared Grant to McClellan after the last attacks at Petersburg on June 18. They loved the latter but knew Grant had greater substance. "And the general opinion among them was," summarized Wilkeson, "given Grant in command of the army in 1862, and the rebellion would have been crushed that year." Yet the common soldiers held back with Grant, at least according to Wilkeson. "The enlisted men, who put down the slaveholders' rebellion," he concluded, "felt and talked and lived in hopes long deferred and never fulfilled, of the coming of a great commander whose military talent would command our unqualified respect. He never came."[28]

Grant always held the confidence of the most important person in the United States. Throughout May and early June, amid news of escalating casualties, significant opposition within his own party, and the steady drumbeat of Democratic criticism, Abraham Lincoln stood firmly with Grant. On June 3, in declining an invitation to attend the rally honoring Grant in New York City's Union Square, he affirmed, "My previous high estimate of Gen. Grant has been maintained and heightened by what has occurred in the remarkable campaign he is now conducting." Renominated on June 8 to run for a second term, Lincoln spoke eight days later at Philadelphia's Great Central Sanitary Fair. Grant "and the brave officers and soldiers with him," the president told an exuberant crowd, had gained "a position from whence he will never be dislodged until Richmond is taken."

Lincoln did fret about the pace of progress in Virginia, and he met with Grant at Petersburg on June 21–22. Back in Washington on the 23rd, "sunburnt and fagged but still refreshed and cheered," according to John Hay's diary, Lincoln reported "the army in fine health good position and good spirits" and "Grant quietly confident." The general had told his chief that "it may be a long summer's day before he does his work but that he is as sure of doing it as he is of anything in the world." Secretary of the Navy Gideon Welles, who thought "intense anxiety" about the Petersburg front prompted the presidential visit, concluded the time with Grant left Lincoln "in very good spirits."[29]

The president's high regard for Grant may not have impressed Mary Todd Lincoln. According to Elizabeth Keckley, the first lady's dressmaker and companion, "Mrs. Lincoln could not tolerate General Grant. 'He is a butcher,' she would often say, 'and is not fit to be the head of an army.'" When President Lincoln answered that Grant won victories, wrote Keckley in her early postwar memoir, he received a retort that might have appeared in the Copperhead press: "Yes, he generally manages to claim a victory, but such a victory! . . . According to his tactics, there is nothing under the heavens to do but to march a new line of men up in front of the rebel breastworks to be shot down as fast as they take their position, and keep marching until the enemy grows tired of the slaughter. Grant, I repeat, is an obstinate fool and a butcher." It is worth noting that nothing in Mary Todd Lincoln's own hand supports Keckley's account. To the contrary, Mrs. Lincoln wrote of Grant in August 1865, "He makes a good general, but I should think, a very poor President."[30]

Two foreign perspectives will complete this review of reactions to Grant's leadership. The British and French took an active interest in the North American war, and key observers representing each government reached similar conclusions as the siege of Petersburg commenced. Lord Lyons served as the ranking British diplomat in the United States and sent hundreds of dispatches each year from Washington to London. In early July 1864, he transmitted a pessimistic analysis of Union prospects to Lord John Russell, the British foreign secretary. Confederates continued to baffle Grant's grand plan "to cut off the Confederate Capital from all communications, and by this means not only to reduce the City but also to capture the whole of the Army of General Lee." That failure had created a crisis in the United States, where "the confident hopes of the Public have been succeeded by despondency." The Overland campaign, in the thinking of many loyal citizens, "must be considered as virtually ended, and that siege operations against Petersburg will only be continued until an excuse can be found for the abandonment by General Grant of his present position." On August 1, Lyons followed up with a report on the battle of the Crater, which fit a pattern for Grant's operations: "It would seem that the great losses sustained by the Federal Forces in the numerous hopeless assaults which they have made on Confederate entrenchments during the present campaign have very much damped their ardour."[31]

The French consul in Richmond similarly kept his superiors in Paris informed of events in America. Alfred Paul prepared detailed dispatches for Foreign Minister Drouyn de Lhuys, including one on June 11 that estimated "around 100 thousand men, Federals and Confederates, have been disabled in Virginia, within the space of one month without any real and decisive advantage that can be verified on one side or the other." So long as Confederates held Richmond, Grant would be reckoned a failure. "But this General is a stone's throw from the Capital," which heard "the din of the battle each day." Labeling Grant "the personification of obstinacy," Paul speculated that "perhaps the siege of Richmond barely begins." A month later Paul composed a much more pessimistic evaluation of Union military operations that had "produced nothing yet this year beyond devastation and carnage." Paul thought the Confederacy would "gain much in the dissensions that begin to stir the Northern populace on the point of the elections, unless General Grant . . . finishes by getting into the Capital of the Confederate States." With the Army of the Potomac "exhausted, obviously weakened," Paul believed "in the North that the situation becomes alarming for the country and almost humiliating for the men placed at the head of the army . . . who came and shattered their reputation against the walls of this place."[32]

Alfred Paul's summary of the campaign included a passage describing Richmond as "ably and heroically defended"—words that mirrored the overwhelming reaction in the Confederacy to Lee's performance. Newspapers offered almost universal praise, and soldier and civilian accounts also tended to be strongly favorable. Even northern newspapers often included positive observations about Lee as a general, evidence of a grudging admiration utterly absent in the southern press's coverage of Grant. This is not to say every Confederate celebrated Lee—that certainly cannot have been the case when talking about a large population. Still, the difference between responses to Lee and Grant is quite striking. Grant understood all this and discussed it perceptively, if somewhat testily, in his *Memoirs*. "To be extolled by the entire press of the South after every engagement, and by a portion of the press North with equal vehemence," wrote Grant of his opponent, "was calculated to give him the entire confidence of his troops and to make him feared by his antagonists." Although Grant ignored the degree to which Lee's reputation, in both the Confederacy and the United States, rested on solid military success rather than mere press puffery, he correctly underscored that "General Lee . . . was a very highly estimated man in the Confederate army and States."[33]

Two factors help explain the absence of much negative Confederate reaction to Lee in his operations against Grant. First, the absence of a two-party system meant there was no institutional opposition to the Davis government equivalent to the Democratic Party in the United States, and especially nothing like the Copperhead movement to use criticism of Lee's actions to harm the president. Moreover, the Confederates were not in the midst of a major national election—something that raised the stakes in the United States for Lincoln and Grant. Tremendous political strife did sweep through North Carolina in the spring and summer of 1864, with peace candidate William Woods Holden opposing Gov. Zebulon B. Vance, who presented himself as a staunch supporter of the war effort in seeking a second term. As Copperheads did with Lincoln, Holden focused his attention on what he and his followers considered the Davis administration's violations of civil liberties and state rights. Lee logically might have become a target for the Holden camp—after all, he supported conscription and virtually all other policies that increased central power in pursuit of a more effective war effort, and North Carolinians fell in profusion during the Overland campaign. But Holden never went down that path. Vance actively aligned himself with Lee, even visited the Army of Northern Virginia to rally North Carolina units to the national cause. Holden won less than a quarter of the overall vote in the summer balloting, and his proportion among North Carolinians in uniform fell far below that anemic percentage.[34]

Second, Lee entered the campaign with a towering reputation built on almost two years of success at the head of his veteran army in the Eastern Theater. In the absence of good news from major armies and generals in other theaters, Confederates naturally had turned their gaze increasingly toward Lee. Jefferson Davis laid out the situation in a letter to his brother Joseph in May 1863. Lee had just triumphed against double his numbers at Chancellorsville, marveled the president, and might replicate that success in the next campaign. But Confederate commanders elsewhere fell short. "A *General* in the full acceptation of the word is a rare product," affirmed

Davis with Lee obviously in mind, "scarcely more than one can be expected in a generation but in this mighty war . . . there is need for half a dozen." This attitude, prevalent in all parts of the Confederacy, meant Lee had nothing to prove to his men or to the civilian population, whereas Grant, in a new position and a different arena commanding soldiers unfamiliar with him, remained something of an unknown quantity and thus more vulnerable to criticism.[35]

A few representative examples show how most Confederates interpreted Lee's generalship. The press, whether supporting or opposing the Davis administration, closed ranks in lauding the general. On June 1, just before Lee's victory at Cold Harbor, the *Richmond Daily Dispatch* printed a hagiographical piece: "The confidence in Lee and his army is not confined to the ranks of that army and to our fellow citizens. It is as extensive as the Confederacy itself. It pervades every neighborhood and every family circle. There are few who do not feel it, and bless God when they acknowledge it, for sending us so great a General to lead so brave an army." Two weeks later, just before the siege of Petersburg began, the *Confederate Union* of Milledgeville, Georgia, stated that "Gen. Lee has been so often successful, that we should as soon expect a man to deny his own existence, as to express a doubt of Gen. Lee's ability to cope with the adversary on any field." Charleston's *Mercury*, an anti-Davis paper, consistently emphasized that Grant's numbers could not overcome Lee. On June 10, the *Mercury* assured its readership that "Richmond was never safer, nor the Confederate cause on higher or firmer ground." Grant's two-to-one advantage in men had proved insufficient "to overcome the invincible army of Lee."[36]

The Confederate press readily embraced the image of Grant as a butcher. Far more than in any but Copperhead newspapers in the North, this became a staple of coverage that allowed editors to create a brutish foil for Lee and his gallant band of brothers. The *Richmond Dispatch* praised what it termed Lee's "economy of his men's lives" while insisting that Grant's "men were butchered, slaughtered, immolated, after a fashion never known before since the invention of gunpowder." Another editor referred to Grant as "the unfortunate butcher" who persisted despite "the slaughter of his troops," and a third anticipated the vicious language C. Chauncey Burr later deployed in *The Old Guard*. "There are butchers of humanity," wrote this Georgian, "to whom the sight of their fellow-creature's blood affords an intoxicating pleasure; they are indifferent whose blood it is, so that it does not come from their own veins; and Grant is one of those charming individuals."[37]

The Two Generals Who Resist Each Other

Diaries and letters from inside and outside the Army of Northern Virginia include a lode of comparable evidence. FitzGerald Ross, an English-born Scot who served in the Austrian Hussars, traveled widely in the Confederacy before spending time in the North after April 1864. He wrote a number of letters between late April and June that, as he explained it, showed "views taken at that time of passing events by partisans of the South, with whom I almost exclusively associated." On May 22, he parroted the Copperhead line: "Grant's soldiers are getting tired of him and call him the butcher, and won't fight." After Cold Harbor, Ross remarked that "Lee seems to have his own way everywhere, though it is impossible to get at the exact truth, as Southern accounts are suppressed with wonderful success." Wherever Grant tried to overwhelm the Rebels, "he has been very badly beaten." Ross complained that people in the North lacked trustworthy information about Grant's movements, though by June 14 he considered it "pretty well understood that his active campaign has come to an end. He has certainly succeeded in spoiling a large army with greater celerity than any other general of modern times." Far to the south and three days earlier, Catherine Edmondston had scorned "Grant, 'butcher Grant' as his men call him," who, foiled north of the James River by Lee, was rumored to be changing base to the south side of the river.[38]

In reaching positive conclusions about Lee, Confederate accounts often grossly underestimated his losses and inflated Union casualties. John B. Jones, the famous "rebel war clerk" in Richmond, wrote in his diary on June 15, 1864: "Grant has *used up* nearly a hundred thousand men—to what purpose? . . . Our army is intact: Lee's losses altogether, in killed and wounded, not exceeding a few thousand." The chaplain of the 3rd Arkansas Infantry reported action "more or less every day for one entire month, and still the fighting continues. . . . Gen. Lee, by the blessing of God, has not been driven from any position he has taken." This clergyman estimated that Federals lost "four or five times as many men as we have" and pronounced "the inhumanity of Gen. Grant to his own men, well, wounded, and killed . . . beyond question." Lee's men, in contrast, faced the enemy "in good spirits and never more confident of success." Walter Taylor, who may have related ideas prevalent at Lee's headquarters, feared things had gone so well "our great danger is that we may become too self-reliant and boastful." The army was "in excellent trim—even in fine spirits—and ready for a renewal of the fight whenever the signal is given." A second lieutenant in the 26th Virginia put it more succinctly: "The 'Esprit du Corps' of his army is good whilst Grant's is destroyed. . . . I feel confident of success."[39]

A member of the 11th North Carolina Infantry, part of Maj. Gen. Henry Heth's division in the Third Corps, wrote just after Spotsylvania that "Grant is twice as badly whipped now as was Burnside or Hooker but he is so determined he will not acknowledge it, but I think before he gets through with Lee he will have to own up." As the army prepared to shift to the south side of the James in mid-June, the North Carolinian remained upbeat: "Grant is going to try Richmond from that side, he'll not find it any easier than he did on this." This veteran emphasized the difference between attacking and defending and clearly preferred battles where Lee's army had the advantage of breastworks. The Yankees "begin to see the folly of charging works protected by Rebs, . . . already we have saved thousands of lives by sticking to the works and letting the enemy do the charging."[40]

Far from thinking Lee had lost too many men, some Confederates urged more aggressive tactics. Three subordinates made the point in late May. "The strength of the army has been husbanded in a manner, which would astonish the oldest soldier," wrote Brig. Gen. John Gregg of the Texas Brigade: "I think, by losing greatly more, and taking the offensive, Genl Lee might have put Grant to flight before this." Col. Thomas H. Carter, an artillerist in the Second Corps, cheerfully noted that Grant's army had lost 50,000 troops since the campaign opened but groused that "Genl Lee talks of fighting another defensive battle. We will never do anything with Grant until we attack him." That complaint notwithstanding, Carter assured his wife, "We will whip Mr Grant in a week or more." The prospect of assuming the offensive animated officers of lower rank as well, among them Edgeworth Bird of Brig. Gen. Henry H. Benning's brigade. "Lee's army is now greatly strengthened," Bird wrote on June 1, "and it is probable he will resume the offensive. . . . Grant has before him an impossible task. He cannot take Richmond, and I hope and believe is destined to a more hopeless defeat than fell to the lot of McClelland."[41]

Brig. Gen. Gabriel C. Wharton developed themes widely repeated in other Confederate sources. A brigade commander in Maj. Gen. John C. Breckinridge's division, which had reinforced Lee's army just before Cold Harbor, Wharton sent frequent letters to his wife accentuating Lee's dominance on recent battlefields, gruesome Union losses, high Confederate morale, and deteriorating political and economic conditions in the North. The easy repulse of Federal attacks on June 3 left Grant in no "condition to attack again for a week or more," believed Wharton, who foresaw a Confederate counteroffensive: "Genl Lee will pitch into him as soon as the proper occasion arises." Certain that "Genl Lee has troops enough here

The Two Generals Who Resist Each Other

to manage," wrote Wharton from near Cold Harbor after a conversation with the army commander, ". . . our men are in the finest spirits & perfectly confident, whilst the Yankees are demoralised & whipped." More hopeful than ever before about prospects for Confederate victory, he stressed that "Grant *will not* take Richmond. Virginia *will not be abandoned.*" By early July, reports that Secretary of the Treasury Salmon P. Chase had resigned from Lincoln's cabinet and other evidence of political roiling in the United States joined the continuing "failures of Grant around Petersburg" to raise Wharton's already high spirits.[42]

The vital connection between Lee's operations and the presidential canvass unfolding in the United State resonated in the Confederacy. Mary Greenhow Lee of Winchester linked the two in her diary on June 17, 1864. An inveterate monitor of news and rumors, Mrs. Lee noted that "Grant was at Bermuda Hundred on the 14th, expecting to commence crossing to the South of the James that day." She understood this likely marked "the last move in the great game" that had begun the first week of May and affirmed, "I doubt not Lee is prepared to check-mate him speedily." Meanwhile, with "political dissensions at the North becoming more violent each day" and "opposition to Lincoln being so great," it seemed "probable all other factions will unite at the Chicago Convention & present [a] formidable rival, in either [John C.] Fremont or McClellan."[43]

In the United States, newspapers across the political spectrum buttressed Lee's reputation as an accomplished foe. Three examples—one Democratic and two Republican—underscore the degree to which the Rebel chieftain continued to bedevil the northern psyche. On June 6, the *New York Herald* criticized southern newspapers for saying Lee had bested Grant, but only six days later its own pages referred to "the great army of the Confederacy," which under Lee's guidance "certainly presented to the world a rare instance of human genius accomplishing much in a bad cause." The *New York Times* sought to explain the absence of a decisive Federal victory in Virginia in part because "Lee's army is an army of veterans; it is an instrument sharpened to a perfect edge." From Chicago, Joseph Medill added a western voice to this chorus: "Lee is a tough customer, physically, and in a military sense, and it is a pity that so much tenacity and power should be exerted in so bad a cause. But it is destined to give way sooner or later."[44]

Lee also inspired admiring coverage across the Atlantic. The *Illustrated London News*, by far the most widely distributed British periodical with

HARPER'S WEEKLY.

A JOURNAL OF CIVILIZATION

VOL. VIII.—No. 392.]   NEW YORK, SATURDAY, JULY 2, 1864.   [$4.00 FOR FOUR MONTHS.
$5.00 PER YEAR IN ADVANCE.

GEN. ROBERT EDMUND LEE.

GEN. SHERMAN'S CAMPAIGN.

THE REBEL GENERAL ROBERT EDMUND LEE.

Robert E. Lee on the cover of *Harper's Weekly*. Unlike the Confederate press's treatment of Grant, the northern press often admitted a grudging admiration for Lee. *Harper's Weekly* got Lee's middle name wrong (Edmund rather than Edward) but called him a "consummate master of the art of war." *Harper's Weekly*, July 2, 1864, 417.

sales of 300,000 copies a week, featured a full-length portrait of Lee on its front page during the first week of June. The accompanying article equaled any Confederate paper in its eagerness to position Lee among the world's celebrated captains. As "one of the greatest soldiers of this age," Lee had shown "his consummate mastery of the art of war" during three years of campaigning. Connected by marriage to George Washington, the Virginian, as an official of high rank observed, "was trusted by his Government, had the hearts of his soldiers, and possessed the entire confidence of his country"—all Confederates "relied implicitly upon his patriotism and genius." Modest in dress and utterly averse to self-promotion, Lee nonetheless cut an "imposing appearance" and remained "in the prime and vigour of manhood." Opponents "owned his superiority to all the successive generals of the Federal army." Not since the Duke of Wellington and Napoleon strutted on the early-nineteenth-century martial stage had the world witnessed, "in high perfection, that peculiar combination of moral and intellectual qualities which fits a man for military command."[45]

Parisians could form impressions of Lee through the pages of *Le Temps*, an Orleanist newspaper with a pro-Union editorial slant. Between the end of May and the end of August, Lee appeared in *Le Temps* as, among other things, "a very remarkable man of war" and a general in chief of "remarkable talent" whose victories showcased "the courage and energy of the Confederate troops." Yet most of the articles predicted Union triumph until mid-July (the factor of travel across the Atlantic before the final telegraphic cable had been laid must be kept in mind regarding timing of news), largely because of faith in "the military capacity, but especially in the tenacity and the character of Grant." After Union failure at the Crater and the onset of a real siege, *Le Temps* adopted a more ambivalent stance. "Whatever will be the denouement of this campaign in Virginia," observed Edouard Hervé in a piece that treated Lee and Grant as equals, "it will remain a testimony of the indomitable tenacity of the two armies and the two generals who resist each other for so long a time without any perceptible advantage on either side."[46]

The stalemate between Grant and Lee described by Hervé affected the contending nations, as well as the two commanders, in very different ways. As summer deepened into August, morale eroded significantly in the United States. The lack of movement at Petersburg and Richmond buoyed Democrats and troubled Republicans. Concern among the latter reached the point that Lincoln, in his famous blind memorandum to the cabinet dated August 23, pronounced it "exceedingly probable that this Administration will not be re-elected." Had the Republicans depended entirely on Grant's efforts against Lee, the president's gloomy reading of the electorate's mood well might have proved correct. Neither he nor anyone else could know in late August that over the next two months William Tecumseh Sherman and Philip H. Sheridan, executing elements of Grant's overall strategic blueprint in Georgia and the Shenandoah Valley, would reorient the political situation completely.[47]

Grant remained unchallenged as the Union's preeminent soldier, but his reputation had lost some luster. He had pummeled the Rebels, pinned their best army down, and denied Lee the opportunities for maneuver that paid such dividends for Confederates in 1862 and 1863—all of which anyone who paid close attention to the Eastern Theater well understood. But he had not beaten Lee unequivocally or captured Richmond, the two outcomes most loyal citizens had anticipated, and craved, at the beginning of the Overland campaign. Moreover, those failures had been accompanied by casualty rates previously unknown in the Army of the Potomac, a dimension of the operations Copperheads exploited relentlessly. At war's end, Grant stood alongside Lincoln as a coequal savior of the republic but never entirely escaped the shadow into which peace Democrats and Confederates assiduously labored to cast him. More than ninety years after Cold Harbor, Winston Churchill echoed the unsparing critiques, from both north and south of the Potomac, orchestrated in the summer of 1864. "Grant's tactics of unflinching butchery," sputtered Britain's redoubtable war leader, severely compromised performances between May and July that, "although they eventually gained their purpose, must be regarded as the negation of generalship."[48]

Closer to the events, Benjamin Brown French traced the decline of optimism as people in the United States realized Grant would not end the war with a dramatic military flourish. The commissioner of public buildings in Washington and a supporter of Lincoln, French kept a voluminous and revealing diary. Shortly after Spotsylvania, he recorded that "news from the Army does not amount to much lately, and I begin to imagine that Grant is not going to beat Lee so easily as everybody seemed to suppose. . . . I do hope we shall overpower the infernal villains soon." About six weeks later, in an entry devoted to the battle of the Crater, he exuded disappointment. "Grant blew up a fortification in front of Petersburg last Saturday (a week)," French wrote on August 7, "&, but for the bungling way in which it was done, the result might have been glorious. As it was, it was a failure." Shocked by what he deemed technical ineptitude on the part of the Federals, French manifested numbed acceptance: "But the thing is over—we were defeated, & all I hope is 'better luck next time.'"[49]

No diminution of reputation plagued Lee in the wake of the Overland campaign. If anything, he emerged with more impressive support among fellow countrymen and countrywomen. As in the United States, Confederates focused on the fact that Richmond remained a Rebel city and very well defended by the Army of Northern Virginia. Facing a less onerous task than Grant, Lee had blocked and bloodied his opponent at a cost most Confederates did not interpret as excessive. Vexed by no political faction resembling the Copperheads who yapped at Grant's heels, Lee inspired an almost universal admiration that also strengthened resolve not to capitulate to, or even negotiate with, Lincoln and Yankee emancipationists. Like George Washington, he seemed to many Confederates a good candidate to combine military and at least a measure of political power. As Col. William Ransom Johnson Pegram, a young artillerist in Lt. Gen. A. P. Hill's Third Corps, assured one of his sisters in Richmond in September, all would be well "if the President will only give everything into Genl. Lee's hands."[50]

Mary G. Caldwell of Fredericksburg, Virginia, typified those whose belief in Lee grew during the Overland campaign. "I am learning [to] place unbounded confidence in Gen. Lee," she wrote in her diary on July 25, "not that I ever did not put confidence in him, but, before this, I have always said Jackson was Lee's superior, but now I will say Lee is the best general we have. Oh, I should like to know him so much." Within another week, she expressed strong opposition to rumors of possible peace negotiations with the United States. "Are we to go to them," she asked rhetorically, "to make peace after all we have suffered through them? I should say not. I am very sorry for our poor soldiers and would like to have peace more for them than anyone else. But, as we have been trying to fight it out, I should say end it that way unless the Yankees recognize us people of the Southern Confederacy." General Lee and Jefferson Davis—it is telling that Caldwell mentioned Lee first—would never concede anything to the Yankees because the general and president were "fully aware what is due to their country and themselves." By mid-August, Caldwell took heart from reports that the armies might be heading northward, away from Petersburg and Richmond. "The North will now probably have the advantage of seeing a fight," she observed with retributive emphasis, "and have their land desolated like ours has been."[51]

On June 5 and 6, 1864, George G. Meade wrote two letters that encapsulate what happened to Grant and Lee during the Overland campaign.

The Army of the Potomac had compelled Lee "to draw in towards Richmond" but had failed "to overcome, destroy or bag his army." Lee's success lay "in preventing us from doing the above." With a tinge of satisfaction rooted in a painful history of campaigns against the Army of Northern Virginia, Meade continued, "I think Grant has had his eyes opened, and is willing to admit now that Virginia and Lee's army is not Tennessee and Bragg's army. Whether the people will ever realize this fact remains to be seen." But Union prospects remained encouraging as the armies prepared for the "great struggle . . . yet to come off in the vicinity of Richmond." Lee and his army benefitted from "advantages of position, fortifications, and being concentrated at their centre," which meant Grant and the Union army would "have to move slowly and cautiously, but I am in hopes, with reasonable luck, we shall be able to succeed." Meade's letters get at why Grant's reputation slipped a bit, why Lee's did not, and how popular perceptions often differed from military reality. Reality eventually would be complete success for Grant and failure for Lee. But the road to that end, far from clear to people in the United States and the Confederacy in August 1864, would be longer and more winding than Meade or most others could envision.[52]

Notes

1. For an excellent brief treatment of the establishment and growth of Washington's reputation, see François Furstenberg, *In the Name of the Father: Washington's Legacy, Slavery, and the Making of a Nation* (New York: Penguin, 2006), esp. chap. 1. "One surprising aspect of the Washington commemorations was their general lack of interest in Washington as general or president," writes Furstenberg: "They skipped quickly over everything that made Washington a great military and political figure, to dwell at length on his willingness to give up power" (65). On the Confederate Great Seal, see "Seal of the Southern Historical Society," in J. William Jones and others, eds., *Southern Historical Society Papers*, 52 vols. (1876–1959; reprint, with 3-vol. index, Wilmington, N.C.: Broadfoot, 1990–92), 16:418–22. The depiction of Washington on the seal was based on Thomas Crawford's equestrian statue dedicated in 1858 on the Capitol grounds in Richmond. "Washington has been selected as the emblem for our shield," wrote Confederate senator Thomas J. Semmes of Louisiana, "as a type of our ancestors, in his character of *princeps majorum*" (420).

2. Abraham Lincoln, *The Collected Works of Abraham Lincoln*, ed. Roy P. Basler, 9 vols. (New Brunswick, N.J.: Rutgers University Press, 1953–55), 7:234; Ulysses S. Grant, *The Papers of Ulysses S. Grant*, ed. John Y. Simon and others, 32 vols. to date (Carbondale: Southern Illinois University Press, 1967–), 10:195. Congress voted to revive the rank of lieutenant general on February 29, 1864, and Grant's promotion took effect on March 10.

3. *Philadelphia Daily Evening Bulletin*, March 2, 1864; *New York Herald*, May 16, 28, 1864.

4. George H. Reese, ed., *Proceedings of the Virginia State Convention of 1861*, 4 vols. (Richmond: Virginia State Library, 1965), 4:370–71.

5. (Atlanta) *Southern Confederacy*, October 31 (quoting a dispatch dated October 11 from a correspondent for the *Columbus (Ga.) Times*), December 5, 1862 (signed "P.W.A.," this was written by Peter W. Alexander and reprinted in "Confederate Chieftains," *Southern Literary Messenger* 35 [January 1863]: 34–38); Robert Grier Stephens Jr., ed., *Intrepid Warrior: Clement Anselm Evans, Confederate General from Georgia; Life, Letters, and Diaries of the War Years* (Dayton, Ohio: Morningside, 1992), 342–43; *Richmond Daily Dispatch*, March 19, 1864.

6. On expectations in the spring of 1864, see Brooks D. Simpson, "Ulysses S. Grant, the Northern Press, and the Opening of the Wilderness Campaign," and Gary W. Gallagher, "Our Hearts Are Full of Hope: The Army of Northern Virginia in the Spring of 1864," both in Gallagher, ed., *The Wilderness Campaign* (Chapel Hill: University of North Carolina Press, 1997), 1–65.

7. *Chicago Tribune*, April 30, 1864; *New York Times*, April 21, 1864; *New York Herald*, April 21, 1864.

8. Charles Minor Blackford to Susan Leigh Blackford, May 3, 1864, in Susan Leigh Blackford and Charles Minor Blackford, eds., *Memoirs of Life In and Out of the Army in Virginia during the War Between the States*, 2 vols. (1894; reprint, Lynchburg, Va.: Warwick House, 1996), 2:189; James I. Robertson Jr., ed., "Diary of a Southern Refugee during the War, June 1863–July 1864: Judith Brockenbrough McGuire," in William C. Davis and Robertson, eds., *Virginia at War, 1864* (Lexington: University Press of Kentucky, 2009), 189.

9. *Richmond Daily Dispatch*, March 26, April 13, 1864; Walter H. Taylor to Bettie Saunders, March 15, 1864, in Walter H. Taylor, *Lee's Adjutant: The Wartime Letters of Colonel Walter Herron Taylor, 1862–1865*, ed. R. Lockwood Tower (Columbia: University of South Carolina Press, 1995), 139; Catherine Ann Devereux Edmondston, *"Journal of a Secesh Lady": The Diary of Catherine Ann Devereux Edmondston, 1860–1866*, ed. Beth Gilbert Crabtree and James W. Patton (Raleigh: North Carolina Division of Archives and History, 1979), 547–48.

10. Gordon C. Rhea, *The Battle of the Wilderness, May 5–6, 1864* (Baton Rouge: Louisiana State University Press, 1994), 34; Alfred C. Young III, *Lee's Army during the Overland Campaign: A Numerical Study* (Baton Rouge: Louisiana State University Press, 2013), 218–19, 232–34; U.S. War Department, *The War of the Rebellion: A Compilation of the Official Records of the Union and Confederate Armies*, 127 vols., index, and atlas (Washington, D.C.: Government Printing Office, 1880–1901), ser. 1, 36(3):665–66.

11. Young, *Lee's Army*, 242–43 (for reinforcements, I combined Young's figures for "Reinforcements" [25,495] and "New and Returning Personnel" added to units already with the army [4,565]); Noah Andre Trudeau, *Bloody Roads South: The Wilderness to Cold Harbor, May–June 1864* (Boston: Little, Brown, 1989), 341; Thomas J. Howe, *The Petersburg Campaign: Wasted Valor, June 15–18, 1864* (Lynchburg, Va.: H. E. Howard, 1988), 136, 175 n. 1; Andrew A. Humphreys, *The Virginia Campaign of '64 and '65: The Army of the Potomac and the Army of the James* (1883; reprint, Wilmington, N.C.: Broadfoot,

1989), 224. Lee's losses on June 17–18, when part of his army helped P. G. T. Beauregard's units defend Petersburg, are estimated at 1,000.

12. For representative discussions of the scale of slaughter, see Charles P. Roland, *An American Iliad: The Story of the Civil War*, 2nd ed. (Lexington: University Press of Kentucky, 2004), 176–77; Michael Fellman, Lesley J. Gordon, and Daniel E. Sutherland, *This Terrible War: The Civil War and Its Aftermath*, 2nd. ed. (New York: Pearson Longman, 2008), 272–74; and David Goldfield, *America Aflame: How the Civil War Created a Nation* (New York: Bloomsbury Press, 2011), 328–30.

13. Calculating casualties for Civil War operations defies precision. The figure of 118,000 for the Army of the Potomac relies on numbers given in Stephen W. Sears, *To the Gates of Richmond: The Peninsula Campaign* (New York: Ticknor and Fields, 1992), 355; E. B. Long, *The Civil War Day by Day: An Almanac, 1861–1865* (Garden City, N.Y.: Doubleday, 1971), 250, 258 (Second Bull Run), 266 (South Mountain), 296 (Fredericksburg); Stephen W. Sears, *Landscape Turned Red: The Battle of Antietam* (New York: Ticknor and Fields, 1983), 295–96; Stephen W. Sears, *Chancellorsville* (Boston: Houghton Mifflin, 1996), 477, 484, 492, 501; Sears, *Gettysburg* (Boston: Houghton Mifflin, 2003), 496, 498; Adrian G. Tighe, *The Bristoe Campaign: General Lee's Last Strategic Offensive with the Army of Northern Virginia, October 1863* (n.p.: n.p., 2011), 474, 477; and Frances H. Kennedy, ed., *The Civil War Battlefield Guide*, 2nd ed. (Boston: Houghton Mifflin, 1998), 259 (Mine Run). For Grant's casualties in the West, see Long, *Civil War Day by Day*, 136 (Belmont), 172 (Fort Donelson), 195 (Shiloh), 438 (Chattanooga), and Kennedy, *Civil War Battlefield Guide*, 157–58, 164–67, 170–71 (Vicksburg campaign).

14. For Confederate casualties, see the sources in n. 13 above. Lee's losses as a percentage of the Federals' is calculated using his 92,000 and Union casualties during the period beginning with the Seven Days. Joseph T. Glatthaar notes in his careful study of the Army of Northern Virginia that Lee's soldiers "had some of the toughest fighting and incurred some of the greatest losses in American history. . . . Almost three of every four soldiers who ever served in the Army of Northern Virginia were killed, died of disease, wounded, captured, or discharged for a disability" (Glatthaar, *General Lee's Army: From Victory to Collapse* [New York: Free Press, 2008], 468–69).

15. *Harper's Weekly*, June 18, 1864, 392–93 (woodcut), 386, and June 11, 1864, 384 (cartoon), 370. *Harper's* claimed in early 1862 to sell 120,000 copies of each issue, which, suggested the editor, was "the *largest* circulation of any Journal in this country in which Advertisements are published." The previous year, the editor estimated that each issue was read by ten adults; see *Harper's Weekly*, January 4, 1862, 2, and June 15, 1861, 369. See also the February 6, 1864, issue, which featured a full-page tribute to Grant on the cover.

16. *New York Tribune*, June 7, 28, 1864. For earlier descriptions of Grant as "relentless" and "irresistible," see the *Tribune* on May 10, 14, and 28.

17. *Philadelphia Daily Evening Bulletin*, June 6, 1864; *Chicago Tribune*, June 15, 26, 29, 1864.

18. *New York Times*, June 7, 18, 1864.

19. *New York Herald*, June 3, 1, 4, 5, 14, 15; George Templeton Strong, *The Diary of George Templeton Strong*, ed. Allan Nevins and Milton Halsey Thomas, 4 vols. (New York: Macmillan, 1952), 3:453. For a description of the background of the mass meet-

ing, see the letter from twenty of its organizers to Abraham Lincoln, May 31, 1864, in Lincoln, *Collected Works*, 7:374 n. 1. The letter identified the organizers as "loyal citizens of New-York, without distinction of party" who sought "to reaffirm their devotion to the sacred cause of the Union, and to pledge their united energies to the support of the Government for the complete suppression of the Rebellion."

20. *New York Herald*, June 14, 17, 28, 1864.

21. William B. Styple, ed., *Writing and Fighting the Civil War: Soldier Correspondence to the New York Sunday Mercury*, 2nd rev. ed. (Kearny, N.J.: Belle Grove, 2004), 9–10, 264–65. On July 31, 1864, the *Sunday Mercury* boasted its circulation "in the Army exceeds that of all other papers published. The soldier would sooner go without his rations than his favorite paper" (274).

22. For examples of the widespread idea that the Democratic Party as a whole, or even a broader swath of the loyal citizenry, condemned Grant as a butcher, see James M. McPherson, *Battle Cry of Freedom: The Civil War Era* (New York: Oxford University Press, 1988), 742; Harry S. Stout, *Upon the Altar of the Nation: A Moral History of the Civil War* (New York: Viking, 2006), 338; and Orville Vernon Burton, *The Age of Lincoln* (New York: Hill and Wang, 2007), 185.

23. *Washington (Pa.) Reporter*, May 11, 1864; *San Francisco Daily Evening Bulletin*, May 17, 1864; *Ashland (Ohio) Union*, June 22, 1864 (quoted in *Sandusky [Ohio] Register*, July 6, 1864). All three newspapers accessed on July 6, 2014, on the "America's Historical Newspapers" database through the Alderman Library, University of Virginia, http://infoweb.newsbank.com.proxy.its.virginia.edu/iw-search/we/HistArchive?p_action=search.

24. *The Old Guard: A Monthly Journal Devoted to the Principles of 1776 and 1787* 2, no. 7 (July 1864): 165, and no. 8 (August 1864): 174, 189.

25. The number of men who chose not to reenlist is unclear. James M. McPherson and James K. Hogue, *Ordeal by Fire: The Civil War and Reconstruction*, 4th ed. (New York: McGraw-Hill, 2009), 460, gives the number as 18,000 but cites no source. John C. Ropes, "Grant's Campaign in Virginia in 1864," in Military Historical Society of Massachusetts, *The Wilderness Campaign, May–June 1864* (1905; reprint, Wilmington, N.C.: Broadfoot, 1989), 399, mentions "the expiration of the terms of service of many regiments, to the extent of about 6,000 men." Gordon C. Rhea's *Cold Harbor: Grant and Lee, May 26–June 3, 1864* (Baton Rouge: Louisiana State University Press, 2002), 420 n. 15, provides a range: "With 37 regiments leaving during May and June, Grant stood to loose [*sic*] between 5,000 and 9,000 veterans by expiration of terms of enlistment."

26. Charles S. Wainwright, *A Diary of Battle: The Personal Journals of Colonel Charles S. Wainwright, 1861–1865*, ed. Allan Nevins (1962; reprint, New York: Da Capo, 1998), 405–6, 425; Theodore Lyman, *Meade's Headquarters, 1863–1865: Letters of Colonel Theodore Lyman from the Wilderness to Appomattox*, ed. George R. Agassiz (Boston: Atlantic Monthly Press, 1922), 147; Theodore Lyman, *Meade's Army: The Private Notebooks of Lt. Col. Theodore Lyman*, ed. David W. Lowe (Kent, Ohio: Kent State University Press, 2007), 191.

27. Elisha Hunt Rhodes, *All for the Union: A History of the 2nd Rhode Island Volunteer Infantry in the War of the Great Rebellion, As told by the diary and letters of Elisha Hunt*

Rhodes, Who enlisted as a private in '61 and rose to command the regiment, ed. Robert Hunt Rhodes (Lincoln, R.I.: Andrew Morbray, 1985), 158–59; Robert McAllister, *The Civil War Letters of General Robert McAllister*, ed. James I. Robertson Jr. (New Brunswick, N.J.: Rutgers University Press, 1965), 435, 441.

28. Frank Wilkeson, *Recollections of a Private Soldier in the Army of the Potomac* (New York: Putnam's, 1887), 192, 196.

29. Lincoln to Frederick A. Conkling and others, June 3, "Speech at Great Central Sanitary Fair, Philadelphia, Pennsylvania," June 16, 1864, in Lincoln, *Collected Works*, 7:374, 395–96; John Hay, *Inside Lincoln's White House: The Complete Civil War Diary of John Hay*, ed. Michael Burlingame and John R. Turner (Carbondale: Southern Illinois University Press, 1997), 210; Earl Schenck Miers, ed. in chief, *Lincoln Day by Day: A Chronology, 1809–1865* (3 vols., 1960; reprint in 1 vol., Dayton, Ohio: Morningside, 1991), [3]:267; Gideon Welles, *Diary of Gideon Welles, Secretary of the Navy under Lincoln and Johnson*, ed. Howard K. Beale, 3 vols. (New York: Norton, 1960), 2:55, 58. Attorney General Edward Bates noted in his diary on June 25, 1864, that Lincoln was "encouraged by Grant's persistent confidence" but thought the chief executive "disappointed at the small measure of our success in that region" (Edward Bates, *The Diary of Edward Bates, 1859–1866*, ed. Howard K. Beale [1930; reprint, New York: Da Capo, 1971], 378).

30. Elizabeth Keckley, *Behind the Scenes; or, Thirty Years a Slave, and Four Years in the White House* (New York: G. W. Carlton, 1868), 133–34; Mary Todd Lincoln to Elizabeth Blair Lee, August 25, 1865, in Justin G. Turner and Linda Levitt Turner, *Mary Todd Lincoln: Her Life and Letters* (New York: Knopf, 1972), 268.

31. Dispatches 455, 550, from Lord Lyons to Lord John Russell, July 2, August 1, 1864, in James J. Barnes and Patience P. Barnes, eds., *The American Civil War through British Eyes: Dispatches from British Diplomats, February 1863–December 1865* (Kent, Ohio: Kent State University Press, 2005), 186, 202.

32. Dispatches 91, 93, from Alfred Paul to Foreign Minister Drouyn de Lhuys, June 25, July 8, 1864 (translations kindly made available by Dr. Donald E. Witt). For information on Paul, see Warren F. Spencer, "A French View of the Fall of Richmond: Alfred Paul's Report to Drouyn de Lhuys, April 11, 1865," in *Virginia Magazine of History and Biography* 73 (April 1965): 178–80.

33. For Grant's observations, see Ulysses S. Grant, *Memoirs and Selected Letters*, ed. Mary Drake McFeely and William S. McFeely (New York: Library of America, 1990), 598. Jason Phillips discusses the widespread belief in Lee's generalship during the Overland campaign in *Diehard Rebels: The Confederate Culture of Invincibility* (Athens: University of Georgia Press, 2007), 121–23. In explaining this belief, the book plays up the importance of rumor, which Phillips construes as "a parable for chivalrous warfare, reinforcing Rebel notions that such despicable enemies could never defeat gentlemen of the South led by Robert E. Lee." Yet Phillips also acknowledges that Grant's inability to capture Richmond and heavy Union casualties—each a fact and not a rumor—were crucial in persuading Confederates that Lee "appeared to be winning the war in the East."

34. On Holden and the North Carolina election, see William C. Harris, *William Woods Holden: Firebrand of North Carolina Politics* (Baton Rouge: Louisiana State University Press, 1987), 146–55. Holden charged that the soldier vote had been manipu-

lated, which likely was the case. "Even if the election had been fair," concludes Harris, "Vance still would have won a comfortable majority of the army vote" (152). The published edition of Holden's wartime papers does not contain a single reference to Lee; see William Woods Holden, *The Papers of William Woods Holden*, vol. 1, *1841–1868*, ed. Horace Raper and Thornton W. Mitchell (Raleigh: Division of Archives and History of the North Carolina Department of Cultural Resources, 2000). Casualties among North Carolina units at Chancellorsville and Gettysburg, which as a percentage were by far the highest in Lee's army, had spawned antiwar sentiment in that critical state during the summer and autumn of 1863. On this topic, see Glatthaar, *General Lee's Army*, 301–3.

35. Jefferson Davis to Joseph E. Davis, May 7, 1863, in Jefferson Davis, *Jefferson Davis: The Essential Writings*, ed. William J. Cooper (New York: Modern Library, 2003), 301–2. For more testimony regarding Lee as a rallying point, see Gary W. Gallagher, *The Confederate War* (Cambridge, Mass.: Harvard University Press, 1997), chaps. 2–3.

36. *Richmond Daily Dispatch*, June 1, 1864; *Confederate Union* (Milledgeville, Ga.), June 14, 1864; *Charleston Mercury*, June 6, 1864.

37. *Richmond Daily Dispatch*, June 13, 20, 1864; *Richmond Enquirer*, June 16, 7, 1864; *Confederate Union* (Milledgeville, Ga.), May 31, 1864.

38. Excerpts from Ross letters dated May 22, June 6, 14, 1864, in FitzGerald Ross, *Cities and Camps of the Confederate States*, ed. Richard Barksdale Harwell (1958; reprint, Urbana: University of Illinois Press, 1997), 220–21; Edmondston, *"Journal of a Secesh Lady,"* 576.

39. John B. Jones, *A Rebel War Clerk's Diary at the Confederate States Capital*, 2 vols. (1866; reprint, Alexandria, Va.: Time-Life Books, 1982), 2:231–32; George E. Butler to Emma Butler, June 9, 1864, in Elizabeth Paisley Huckaby and Ethel C. Simpson, eds., *Tulip Evermore: Emma Butler and William Paisley, Their Lives and Letters, 1857–1887* (Fayetteville: University of Arkansas Press, 1985), 43; Walter H. Taylor to Bettie Saunders, June 9, 1864, in Taylor, *Lee's Adjutant*, 167; Luther Rice Mills to John Mills, May 27, 1864, in George D. Harmon, ed., "Letters of Luther Rice Mills—A Confederate Soldier," *North Carolina Historical Review* 4 (July 1927): 299–300. On casualties, see also Robert Garlick Hill Kean, *Inside the Confederate Government: The Diary of Robert Garlick Hill Kean*, ed. Edward Younger (1957; reprint, Baton Rouge: Louisiana State University Press, 1993), 147–48 (entry for May 20, 1864), and Lycurgus Washington Caldwell to Susan Emiline Jeffords Caldwell, May 25, 1864, in John K. Gott and John E. Divine, eds., *"My Heart is So Rebellious": The Caldwell Letters, 1861–1865* (Warrenton, Va.: Fauquier National Bank, 199[?]), 225.

40. Lewis Warlick to Cornelia McGimsey, May 19, June 16, 1864, in Mike and Carolyn Lawing, eds., *My Dearest Friend: The Civil War Correspondence of Cornelia McGimsey and Lewis Warlick* (Durham, N.C.: Carolina Academic Press, 2000), 170, 164.

41. General John Gregg letter, folder titled "Materials before 1890," box 1, Harry F. Estill Collection, Sam Houston State University Archives, Sam Houston State University, Huntsville, Texas (typescript provided by Keith S. Bohannon and R. E. L. Krick); Thomas H. Carter to Susan Carter, May 24, 1864, in Thomas Henry Carter, *A Gunner in Lee's Army: The Civil War Letters of Thomas Henry Carter*, ed. Graham T. Dozier (Chapel

Hill: University of North Carolina Press, 2014), 246–47; Edgeworth Bird to Sallie Bird, June 1, 1864, in John Rozier, ed., *The Granite Farm Letters: The Civil War Correspondence of Edgeworth and Sallie Bird* (Athens: University of Georgia Press, 1988), 169.

42. Gabriel C. Wharton to Nannie Wharton, June 5, 6, July 5, 1864. I am indebted to Sue Bell for granting permission to quote from Wharton's letters, copies of which she also provided. The Wharton correspondence, which runs to hundreds of letters from both the general and his wife, is a major source of information on the last two years of the war.

43. Mary Greenhow Lee, *The Civil War Journal of Mary Greenhow Lee (Mrs. Hugh Holmes Lee) of Winchester, Virginia*, ed. Eloise C. Strader (Winchester, Va.: Winchester–Frederick County Historical Society, 2011), 371.

44. *New York Herald*, June 6, 12, 1864; *New York Times*, June 18, 1864; *Chicago Tribune*, June 8, 1864.

45. "General R. E. Lee, Commander-in-Chief of the Army of the Confederate Southern States," *Illustrated London News*, June 4, 1864, 534. The caption for the portrait got Lee's middle name incorrect—Edmund rather than Edward. The weekly had published another sketch of Lee in the field by its artist Frank Vizetelly on February 14, 1863; see W. Stanley Hoole, *Vizetelly Covers the Confederacy* (Tuscaloosa, Ala.: Confederate Publishing Company, 1957), 55. On readership, see Philip V. Allingham, "An Introduction to *The Illustrated London News*," an unpaginated essay accessed at http://www.victorianweb.org/periodicals/iln/intro.html on July 10, 2014. Allingham states that the illustrated newspaper's readership far exceeded that of all rivals: "For example, newspapers such as the *Daily News* only sold 6,000 copies at this time, and even the largest selling newspaper, *The Times*, sold only 70,000 copies."

46. *Le Temps*, May 25 (article by Ulysse Ladet), June 22 (L. Legault), July 14 (Ladet), August 30 (Edouard Hervé), 1864. Dr. Donald E. Witt provided the translations of *Le Temps*. For information on the newspaper, see George M. Blackburn, *French Newspaper Opinion on the American Civil War* (Westport, Conn.: Greenwood, 1997), 9, 68.

47. "Memorandum Concerning His Probable Failure of Re-election," in Lincoln, *Collected Works*, 7:514. Lincoln did not share the text of the memorandum with the cabinet when he passed it around on August 23 and asked the seven men to sign it; he did so on November 11, 1864, after the Republicans had won a resounding victory at the polls. See Hay, *Inside Lincoln's White House*, 247–48.

48. Winston Churchill, *The American Civil War* (New York: Dodd, Mead, 1961), 122–24. This volume, clearly designed to take advantage of the centennial of the conflict, was extracted from the third volume of Churchill's *History of the English Speaking Peoples* (4 vols., London: Cassell, 1956–58).

49. Benjamin Brown French, *Witness to the Young Republic: A Yankee's Journal, 1828–1870*, ed. Donald B. Cole and John J. McDonough (Hanover, N.H.: University Press of New England, 1989), 454–55.

50. William Ransom Johnson Pegram to Mary Evans Pegram Anderson, September 24, 1864, quoted in James I. Robertson Jr., ed., "'The Boy Artillerist': Letters of Colonel William Pegram, C.S.A.," *Virginia Magazine of History and Biography* 98 (April 1990): 246. See also Pegram to Mary Evans Pegram Anderson, July 21, 1864, quoted in

Keith Harris's essay below. Support for transferring at least some political authority to Lee grew during the rest of 1864. See Jones, *Rebel War Clerk's Diary*, 2:370–72 (entries for December 31, 1864, and January 1, 1865).

51. Russell P. Smith, ed., "'I should look forward to the future.' The Diary of Mary G. Caldwell," pt. 2, *Fredericksburg: History & Biography* 12 (2013): 40–44 (entries for July 25, 30, August 15, 1864).

52. George G. Meade, *The Life and Letters of George Gordon Meade, Major-General United States Army*, ed. George Gordon Meade, 2 vols. (New York: Scribner's, 1913), 2:201–2.

Repairing an Army
A Look at the New Troops in the Army of Northern Virginia in May and June 1864

⇥ ROBERT E. L. KRICK ⇤

When the veteran brigades of the Army of Northern Virginia pulled into their new positions below the North Anna River on May 22, 1864, they found a few thousand unfamiliar soldiers awaiting their arrival. Most of the new men had seen action elsewhere but had not served before with Gen. R. E. Lee's army. They represented the first in a long series of brigades, regiments, battalions, and even scattered companies sent from various corners of the Confederacy to central Virginia as reinforcements between mid-May and mid-June 1864. That infusion of fresh formations strengthened the army's position in at least two ways. In addition to replacing a portion of the losses suffered in preceding weeks at the battles of the Wilderness and Spotsylvania, the new arrivals buoyed the spirits of the remaining veterans. The men in the ranks still enjoyed high morale through the third and fourth weeks of active campaigning, yet they greeted the enhancement of their army as cause for renewed enthusiasm. Here was a tangible demonstration of the government's commitment to victory in the central Virginia theater.

Assessments of the spring campaign in Virginia routinely address the subject of reinforcements. The unprecedented losses accumulated by Lee and his antagonist Lt. Gen. Ulysses S. Grant between May 5 and 18 nearly defied repair. Both generals did what they could to replace casualties and keep their armies in fighting trim. Grant's efforts and successes are well known. Within days of launching his campaign, he began importing regiments to rebuild his army in the midst of the active operations. Most of them came from the defenses of Washington and Baltimore. Nearly all were units of heavy artillerists, raised for the purpose of manning the earthen fortifications that ringed those cities. Few ever had seen action. Grant extracted them from their relatively comfortable circumstances, pressed rifles into their hands, and converted them from heavy artillerists to frontline infantry in the space of a few days. Some of those regiments numbered more than 1,500 men. They rank among the very largest units ever fielded in the Civil War. Once they were attached to the Army of the Potomac, their actual role was as cannon fodder, prodded forward ahead of the veteran units in desperately violent assaults against entrenched Confederate positions.[1]

The work of R. E. Lee and his superiors in Richmond to emulate Grant's replacement program is less familiar. Few 1,500-man regiments languished in the South. Clearly the Confederates could not hope to match, in raw numbers, the new men supplied to the Federal army. But they did succeed in scraping together enough help from elsewhere so that by mid-June 1864, as the armies disengaged at Cold Harbor, Lee had approximately as many men in his army as had been with him when the campaign began at the Wilderness five weeks earlier. Each army had nearly replaced its staggering May losses.

The work of drawing new regiments to Lee's army from passive zones in the Confederacy began even before the spring campaign. It picked up pace in May and reached its conclusion around the first week of June 1864. Fully aware of what lay in store for the South when the action began, the authorities in Richmond determined their manpower priorities in advance of the crisis. Maj. Samuel W. Melton, an officer in the Adjutant and Inspector General's Office in Richmond, played a critical role in devising the complicated series of moves that reinforced Lee by borrowing men from other spheres or exchanging weak regiments for strong ones. Melton unveiled his plan on March 14, more than seven weeks before Grant crossed the Rapidan River. By the time the armies reached Cold Harbor, most of his recommendations had become reality.[2]

Melton neatly summarized the crux of the issue in a memorandum: "It is a question of the relative importance of the several armies of Generals Lee, Johnston, and Beauregard. . . . This point can only be determined by the War Department from a view of the whole field, and the War Department has determined it." In fact, President Jefferson Davis probably reached that decision himself and merely used the War Department as an instrument to implement that policy. Lee's army would receive reinforcements at the expense of the other commands.[3]

There are several ways to define what constituted "new troops" for the Army of Northern Virginia. Certainly it is appropriate to include the many new organizations brought in from outside Virginia in May and June. Other units had operated in Virginia before, but not in direct connection with the Army of Northern Virginia. The small army of Gen. P. G. T. Beauregard, in action just south of Richmond in May 1864, offers several other fuzzy examples. Beauregard's force included many veteran regiments from the Army of Northern Virginia, detached for the emergency, as well as some brigades—such as Brig. Gen. Alfred H. Colquitt's Georgians—that had served with Lee earlier in the war but had not been associated with the Army of Northern Virginia in recent months. Large portions of Beauregard's command joined Lee's army in time for Cold Harbor. This complicates the work of anyone attempting the chore of statistically measuring Lee's reinforcements during this period. It is much more useful to examine the organizations that were entirely new to the Army of Northern Virginia and to ask questions regarding their composition, their effectiveness, and how the veterans of the Confederacy's most successful army treated the newcomers.[4]

Heavy losses at the Wilderness and Spotsylvania, together with the unrelenting pace of operations, convinced Lee that he needed help immediately, regardless of the War Department's master plan. On the very day that fighting raged at the Bloody Angle near Spotsylvania Court House, he wrote President Davis on the subject. He had heard that most of the Union infantry in the Carolinas had transferred to southeastern Virginia. "Cannot we now draw more troops from those departments?" wondered Lee. The following day he began asking for a portion of Beauregard's army, and on May 14 he expressed hope that perhaps Maj. Gen. John C. Breckinridge's command in the Shenandoah Valley might be available. In fact, Breckinridge felt obliged to ask on that very same day for reinforcements to join him in the Valley. It is a telling fact that Lee cast a covetous eye toward a force as small as Breckinridge's, which numbered only 2,400 men, so early in the spring campaign.[5]

The president took Lee's pleas seriously, as he almost always did by 1864. He reassured Lee that he had "directed all organized infantry and cavalry to come forward from the Department of South Carolina, Georgia, and part of Florida." He also mentioned other schemes designed "to liberate the veteran troops" scattered around the South. Nearly all of the planning to help Lee, which dated back to March and continued into May, would produce a manpower surge for the Army of Northern Virginia, if only Lee could wait a few days more.[6]

As Grant gradually maneuvered the Confederate army southward, the railroads north of Richmond came into play. The Virginia Central Railroad and the Richmond, Fredericksburg, and Potomac Railroad intersected at

Maj. Gen. John Cabell Breckinridge. Library of Congress Prints and Photographs Division, LC-DIG-cwpb-07428.

Hanover Junction, some twenty-five miles north of the capital city. While Lee must have regretted how close the armies' operations had come to that vital point, he doubtless appreciated how much more convenient it had become to bring supplies and reinforcements to his command. The first evidence of the latter bonus awaited the army at the junction. The little division of General Breckinridge had arrived via the Virginia Central Railroad on May 20, in response to Lee's orders issued on the 17th. Breckinridge himself added ability and reputation to the Army of Northern Virginia's cadre of leaders. The men of his division enjoyed the credentials that came from their connection with the famous general.[7]

Every regiment and battalion in the two brigades that composed Breckinridge's division came from Virginia. Nearly all hailed from the southwestern part of the state, and most had spent virtually the entire war in that mountainous region. Several had sturdy records and good officers, but none of the units had fought with the big army before. The smaller scope and less regular style of warfare in Virginia's border counties did little to prepare Breckinridge's command for the reality of combat with the Army of the Potomac. Even entrenching, which the men of the 51st Virginia had to do every day between May 23 and May 26, was an unfamiliar task.[8]

Nonetheless, the force arrived at Hanover Junction riding a wave of success. Both brigades had participated in the triumph at New Market, in the Shenandoah Valley, the previous week. That victory over Maj. Gen.

Franz Sigel's invading force produced many far-reaching consequences, both strategically and operationally, and it abruptly freed Breckinridge to cross the mountains on the railroad to join Lee's army at Hanover Junction. The division commander's recent triumph enhanced his popularity. On May 23, while the Army of Northern Virginia suffered a pair of setbacks along the nearby North Anna River, a glee club from the army's Maryland battalion found time to serenade Breckinridge and earned "a little speech" from the ex-politician. The acclaim extended to his units as well. When the 22nd Virginia Infantry marched toward Cold Harbor the following week, veterans from Lee's army recognized it as one of the New Market regiments and cheered it.[9]

A pair of untested brigadier generals led Breckinridge's two brigades. The forty-one-year-old John Echols possessed a "towering figure," an engaging personality, and "a fine, hospitable, good natured face, not indicative of genius." His military lineage stretched back to the original Stonewall Brigade of Thomas J. Jackson. A lawyer by profession and a member of Virginia's secession convention, Echols had taken to army life with some success. He suffered a crippling injury at Kernstown in March 1862 while in command of the 27th Virginia Infantry, a bullet "entering near the shoulder, passing through the arm & shattering the bone." Ill health had plagued him ever since. Nonetheless, his appointment dated from April 16, 1862. Stonewall Jackson viewed Echols's elevation to brigade command as an unfortunate piece of politically driven tampering. "We are warm personal friends," Jackson wrote privately in 1862, but "the great interests of the country are being sacrificed by appointing incompetent officers." Echols finally reached the Army of Northern Virginia in May 1864. In contrast to Jackson, General Lee wrote that he considered Echols "a most excellent officer," an evaluation probably based more on hearsay and distant observation than on personal interaction.[10]

Brig. Gen. Gabriel C. Wharton commanded the other brigade in the division. Just sixteen months younger than Echols, he lacked the older general's battlefield experience but demonstrated greater war-long competence than his colleague. Wharton did not convert his antebellum education at the Virginia Military Institute into an army career. Instead he accumulated credentials as an engineer and miner. There is evidence that Lee thought well of Wharton, too, even before 1864, presumably basing his high regard primarily on recommendations from others.[11]

Events in the Shenandoah Valley limited Breckinridge's stay with the Army of Northern Virginia to just two weeks, but it was a fortnight packed

Repairing an Army

with action. During that period the division operated without connection to any of the veteran divisions or corps in the army. Breckinridge took orders directly from army headquarters. It is not known what plans, if any, Lee had for the long-term integration of the division into the Army of Northern Virginia's order of battle.

Other units began to trickle in, slowly enlarging the army's size. Scarcely a day passed between May 23 and June 3 without the addition of a new organization. Some had been summoned long before the crisis, such as the 4th, 5th, and 6th South Carolina Cavalry regiments. Others arrived after extended journeys across the South, sometimes in increments. Unreliable railroads and related transportation issues often converted necessarily long trips into agonizing ordeals. The officers in the War Department charged with coordinating this minuet must have endured extreme strain. The not-so-distant roar of battle and the welter of casualties clogging Richmond undoubtedly increased the logistical burdens associated with preparing new regiments for service in the Army of Northern Virginia.

The three South Carolina cavalry regiments new to the army belonged to a brigade created for veteran cavalier Brig. Gen. Matthew C. Butler. They represented one of the more substantial improvements planned for Lee's army. All three regiments possessed significant numbers. They had been summoned to Virginia in mid-March from soft duty in their home state. Two small veteran regiments from the Army of Northern Virginia exchanged places with the newcomers. The business of transporting General Butler's big command to Virginia, with all its accompanying horses and baggage, proved to be a difficult two-month saga. Most of the 5th South Carolina Cavalry arrived first, followed by the 4th and finally the 6th.[12]

The trio conformed to nearly all the stereotypes about new troops in any war. They arrived in Richmond groaning under the weight of personal possessions. Many of their number, officers and enlisted men alike, had servants who traveled with them, cooked their meals, and otherwise attended to their comforts. Oliver Middleton of the 4th South Carolina Cavalry wisely left his own servant in South Carolina, but even so he recognized the need to "curtail my baggage" within his first twenty-four hours around Richmond. Accustomed to a relatively easy life away from the front, Middleton immediately complained about the short rations issued to men in Virginia. "They say this is all that Lee's army gets," he told his mother, "so I suppose it is not *impossible* to subsist upon it, however *hard* it may be. We are, all of us, forever hungry and of course at first it goes rather hard with us."[13]

The 7th South Carolina Cavalry also joined the army's expanding corps of horsemen in May. It was a manufactured regiment created by combining five companies of the veteran Holcombe Legion Cavalry with five other miscellaneous companies then serving in South Carolina. Precedent existed for cutting and pasting to create a new regiment, though importing 50 percent of the unit from a different theater altogether seems odd, and ordering the regiment into action on the very day some of its components arrived, as was the case with the 7th, is stranger yet. In time the regiment comprised a portion of a new cavalry brigade led by Brig. Gen. Martin W. Gary.[14]

Georgian Pierce M. B. Young also stood in line to command some of the fresh cavalry troops. He already had a small brigade that served in Wade Hampton's old division. Brigadier General Young's original force consisted of one regiment—the Jeff Davis Legion—and two Georgia cavalry battalions: Cobb's Legion and Phillips's Legion. When the War Department projected how the army's order of battle might look after all of the summoned reinforcements arrived, it recognized that some of the new cavalry had no natural home. To solve that, the Adjutant and Inspector General's Office issued instructions on May 21 for Young to "take charge of the bodies of cavalry arriving here from the south[,] . . . prepare as rapidly as possible for active field service," and ultimately join them in the field as their commander.[15]

New cavalry companies poured into Richmond almost daily at the end of May, so Young must have operated under even more specific orders that helped him identify which of the various units belonged to him. He awaited the arrival of the 20th Georgia Cavalry Battalion, Love's Alabama Cavalry Battalion, and the large, newly formed 7th Georgia Cavalry. The three were part of a plan to create an almost-all-Georgia brigade for Young (with the exception of Love's Alabamians) by extracting the Georgians from his original brigade and combining them with the new units. The business of organizing that brigade even took precedence over field command. Young stayed in Richmond late in May and left the leadership of his small original brigade to its senior colonel, Gilbert J. Wright.[16]

Lt. Col. John M. Millen and his inexperienced 20th Georgia Cavalry Battalion arrived first. The six companies reached Richmond about May 20. Like some of the South Carolinians who had preceded them, the Georgians reached the war zone without their horses. When the animals arrived, the battalion hastened north toward Atlee's Station, where it joined Lee's army on the 27th. It marched without General Young. He elected to

Lt. Col. John MacPherson Millen (*right*), a previously unpublished antebellum view. Courtesy of Chris Ferguson.

remain in Richmond to await the appearance of the rest of his command. With every soldier needed at the front, someone decided Millen's battalion could be more useful operating independently in the field than sitting in Richmond. The battalion joined the army just in time to participate in one of the war's largest cavalry battles the next day.[17]

The organization called Love's Alabama Cavalry Battalion is the least known of all the troops that joined Lee during the North Anna/Cold Harbor period. The battalion does not appear in any order of battle associated with the campaign, nor is it mentioned in any of the standard accounts of that three-week period. Capt. Andrew P. Love organized his command, sometimes called the 4th Alabama Cavalry Battalion, in October 1863. At some point, probably in May 1864, he received orders to transfer his 160-man force to Virginia. The battalion reached the crowded Confederate capital in the last week of May and discovered, as one of the men wrote, that "the Whole world here is alive with soldiers."[18]

ROBERT E. L. KRICK

Two Georgia cavalry battalions united earlier in the spring to create the 7th Georgia Cavalry. As a full-sized regiment, it would become the backbone of Young's retooled brigade. Unlike Millen's and Love's battalions, the 7th did not reach Richmond by the end of May. Its journey from Savannah to Virginia offers more direct evidence of the immense pressure under which Confederate railroads operated during the critical spring campaigns. The 7th traveled by road rather than by rail; consequently the regiment took forty-five days to make the march. The men arrived in Richmond on June 2, and then they had to await the arrival of their weapons and saddles.[19]

In the meantime, a confusing and poorly documented series of events finally returned General Young to the army, but without either his new brigade or his old one. Brig. Gen. James B. Gordon, the longtime leader of a North Carolina cavalry brigade, had died of wounds earlier in May. A veteran colonel briefly succeeded him until the rookie 3rd North Carolina Cavalry joined the brigade on May 24. Col. John A. Baker of the 3rd then took control by virtue of seniority. That proved unsatisfactory, in all likelihood because of Baker's unfamiliarity with his men and with cavalry tactics in Virginia. In the search for a suitable replacement, someone thought of the capable Pierce Young. Although the various bits of paperwork that must have accompanied this shift do not survive, or at least have not been found, it is known that Young assumed command of the Tar Heel cavalry brigade sometime between May 29 and 31. While leading his men into action at Ashland on June 1, Young fell with a serious lung wound. Others would finish piecing together his new brigade without him.[20]

The unsuitable Colonel Baker and his 3rd North Carolina Cavalry had been in Virginia for much of the war, operating extensively along the Pamunkey and Blackwater rivers, but had not been with Lee's army before. The regiment saw some light duty under General Beauregard around Drewry's Bluff in mid-May before joining the North Carolina brigade of Lee's army on May 24.[21]

Among the infantry, Breckinridge's division attracted considerable attention because it greeted the army's veterans at the North Anna on May 22, and because it was a full division, albeit a small one. Other units destined to play important roles in the army's operations within the next two weeks reached the lines north of Richmond about the same time, but with less ado. They included a Georgia battalion, four battalions of Floridians, and an awkwardly sized regiment from South Carolina.

Lt. Col. Henry D. Capers led a unit called the 12th Georgia Artillery Bat-

Repairing an Army

Lt. Col. Henry Dickson Capers, a postwar photograph that betrays its subject's somewhat casual sartorial sense. Author's collection.

talion, although its men abandoned their cannon for small arms long before reaching Virginia. A battalion in the Confederate army generally had fewer companies than the typical ten seen in a full-strength regiment. But the precise number varied. Capers had six companies in his battalion, most of which had seen some action around Charleston before leaving South Carolina. They received their summons to reinforce Lee on May 17. Unlike their frustrated comrades in the South Carolina cavalry regiments, the men of the 12th Battalion encountered little difficulty in traveling to Virginia. The final leg of their route took them through the fresh carnage of the Second Drewry's Bluff battlefield below Richmond, where "an immens[e] quantity of blood" sobered everyone. Capers reported to army headquarters at Hanover Junction on either May 23 or May 24, after executing the long journey from Charleston in just one week. Lee instructed him to join Brig. Gen. Clement A. Evans's brigade in the army's Second Corps. The commanding general closely monitored these accessions to his army, even when they dribbled in a few hundred men at a time.[22]

Both the battalion and its leader proved to be welcome additions to Evans's depleted Georgia brigade. Lieutenant Colonel Capers represented a prominent South Carolina family. He attended both the South Carolina Military Academy and the Medical College of South Carolina in antebellum years. Before organizing the battalion in 1862, he had worked as chief clerk and disbursing officer for the Confederate States Treasury, earn-ing the admiration of that department's chief, Christopher G. Memminger. Writing after the war, one of the old hands in Evans's brigade claimed that Capers brought more than 1,000 men with his battalion to Virginia. In fact, the 12th numbered fewer than 500 men when it reached Lee's army. The disparity between the veteran's estimate and the true number probably is a typical case. The new units must have seemed larger than they really were when placed beside the sadly thinned remnants of the veteran regiments.[23]

The Florida battalions became scattered on their northward journey. They eventually joined the army over a period of several days late in May. Lee immediately sent all four of them to the one existing Florida command. That brigade—Brig. Gen. Edward A. Perry's—already enjoyed a good reputation as a reliable combat unit, but heavy losses and the difficulty of luring new recruits up from Florida had winnowed the brigade's strength down to an unacceptably low number. The three original Florida regiments in the brigade, understandably proud of their unique identity as the only organization from that state in Lee's army, harbored fears that their regiments might be consolidated or otherwise diluted. That did happen in other parts of the army—particularly in the brigades most affected by the disaster at Spotsylvania's Bloody Angle—but the arrival of the 1st, 2nd, 4th, and 6th Florida Battalions saved the Florida brigade by adding perhaps 1,500 men to its rolls and making it a legitimate organization once again.[24]

The veterans certainly rejoiced at the addition of their fellow Floridians, but the replenishment of the brigade triggered controversy as well. For most of the war General Perry led the three regiments, but a wound at the Wilderness knocked him out of action. For the next several weeks Col. David Lang of the 8th Florida Infantry, a highly regarded officer, supervised the brigade as its senior colonel. His men hoped and expected that he would be promoted to brigadier general and given permanent command. But the arrival of the battalions directly from Florida ruined that scheme, for they brought with them their own brigadier general, Joseph Finegan. His rank ensured that he would take command of the Florida brigade. "For a long time there was a deep grouch in the thinned ranks of the veteran brigade," one of its number recalled. "They never did get over Gen. Finnegan's taking rank over the gallant Lang and knocking him out of his well earned brigadier general's commission which was earnestly desired by the whole command." The new arrangement, he concluded, had "grievously wronged" the longtime members of the brigade.[25]

Finegan could not help the ill feeling produced by his arrival. He had

Brig. Gen. Joseph Finegan, photographed wearing the insignia of a colonel. A native of Ireland who settled in Florida, Finegan led Floridian units throughout the war. Library of Congress Prints and Photographs Division, LC-DIG-cwpb-06278.

held a brigadier general's rank since April 1862 but saw little action in the war's first three years, though he did win some acclaim as one of the Confederate heroes of the recent battle of Ocean Pond, or Olustee, in northern Florida. Finegan's subsequent career in Virginia proved that he had the personal charisma that could motivate men, particularly in times of crisis, but it was an asset largely neutralized by a lack of military ability. Barely a week after reaching Virginia, Finegan demonstrated both of those aspects of his generalship at Cold Harbor.[26]

The four battalions that accompanied Finegan from Florida appear in most literature of the Overland campaign as the 9th, 10th, and 11th Florida Infantry regiments. The order converting the 6th Florida Battalion and some other scattered companies into the 9th Florida Infantry had in fact existed since late April, three weeks before their journey to Virginia began. The miscellaneous companies apparently did join the 6th Battalion before leaving Florida, but the name change definitely did not take effect until the army reached Petersburg later in June.[27]

ROBERT E. L. KRICK

The directive creating the 10th and 11th Florida from the remaining three battalions dated from the second week of June, while they occupied the deadly entrenchments at Cold Harbor. Thus from North Anna through most of Cold Harbor, the men in the four battalions continued to call themselves by their original designations, and any order of battle for Finegan's brigade during that period should reflect that.[28]

There is little doubt that the new Florida soldiers were inadequately prepared for immediate service with the Army of Northern Virginia. None of them even carried cooking utensils to Virginia, making the simple business of eating that much more difficult. The various battalions came directly from the district commanded by Maj. Gen. J. Patton Anderson. On May 27, the very day that several of the battalions arrived in Richmond, Anderson penned a thoughtful assessment of their condition for the authorities. He enumerated three serious problems. His report referred only to the Florida battalions, but some of his analysis can be applied to many of the other reinforcements that arrived for Lee's army about the same time.

Anderson noted that "nearly every company in these Battalions was raised after the passage of the Conscript Act," which invited questions about their patriotism and fighting spirit. Moreover, a luxurious lifestyle in their home state had prevented them from training for service at the front. "As they are," remarked the general, "their inefficiency and want of instruction is lamentable." That point connected to the third of Anderson's concerns: a lack of qualified leaders. Of the many officers affiliated with the four battalions, only Lt. Col. Theodore W. Brevard of the 2nd Battalion impressed the commander. "He will make a fine colonel," Anderson predicted.[29]

The 20th South Carolina Infantry might be the best known of the many additions to the Army of Northern Virginia during the North Anna/Cold Harbor phase of the campaign. That notoriety originated with the regiment's poor performance at Cold Harbor and also with its unprecedented size. When the 20th reached Virginia from Charleston, it numbered somewhere between 1,100 and 1,600 men, making it far larger than any regiment then in the army, and possibly larger than any other regiment ever to serve in the field under Lee. It joined Maj. Gen. Joseph B. Kershaw's old brigade at the end of May. The veterans immediately dubbed it the "Twentieth Army Corps" and correctly noted that it outnumbered the rest of the brigade (six emaciated units) all by itself.[30]

The situation with the 20th South Carolina resembled the simultaneous controversy in the Florida brigade. Kershaw had moved on to command a

Col. Laurence Massillon Keitt, an ardent supporter of secession who served in the Provisional Confederate Congress before taking up military duty. Courtesy of Museum of the Confederacy.

division in the First Corps, leaving his old brigade in the hands of a series of senior colonels. When the 20th arrived and joined that brigade, its colonel outranked all the others. Thus Laurence M. Keitt (pronounced "Kitt"), the erudite commander of the 20th, assumed control of one of the army's best brigades. He had adequate field experience at Morris Island in his home state and impressed General Beauregard enough to garner an October 1863 recommendation for promotion to brigadier general. That commission never materialized, and despite his credentials, Keitt's unfamiliarity with battlefield procedures in Virginia would become painfully apparent in his debut as brigade commander at Cold Harbor.[31]

The most convincing proof of the War Department's determination to scrape together aid for Lee's army that spring comes from its willingness to accept help in even the smallest increments. The cobbling together of miscellaneous companies into the 7th South Carolina Cavalry is one instance. A better one comes from the obscure 28th Georgia Siege Artillery Battalion, which had converted from artillery into infantry earlier in 1864. The battalion operated primarily in Florida and never served in central Virginia as an intact formation at any time during the war. When Finegan's battalions moved north in May, the 28th probably had orders to accompany them. The Georgians' trip ended prematurely when the commander at Savannah grabbed the battalion for emergency duty defending that key city. Strangely, two companies of the 28th eluded that dragnet and continued on to Virginia anyway. The reasoning behind that fracture remains unclear. The pair of companies attached themselves to the 4th Florida Battalion and saw action at Cold Harbor. Their presence is almost completely undocumented, and they do not appear in standard orders of battle or even in sources generated by the Floridians. A poorly composed letter written just after Cold Harbor by one of the men in the two Georgia companies survives to summarize his views on his first weeks in Virginia: "If we cant whip them up her[e] I think we had beter quit I am mitey tiard of the War and am tiard of seing men shot down every day. . . . am in hopes that I may come out clear of the bulites I have had some mitey close shotes at me." Little else is known about the role of the orphaned Georgia companies.[32]

The authorities certainly had their best success in appropriating available commands from the remote fringes of the Confederacy, yet there is evidence that they considered extending their reach to include some mainstream units, too. The War Department actually ordered the 10th and 19th South Carolina Infantry, the 26th Alabama Infantry, and the 47th, 55th, and 56th Georgia Infantry to Richmond in mid-May. Those six regiments, most of which belonged to the Army of Tennessee, stayed farther south for one reason or another, significantly reducing the effect of the initiative to get more men into Virginia.[33]

The new regiments that did join the army in May and June received the sort of reception from the veterans that virtually all fresh soldiers have endured as long as there have been armies. The old Florida regiments chaffed the new ones, just as the seasoned fighters of the Army of the Potomac needled the men of the huge heavy artillery regiments across the lines. Most conversations revolved around two subjects: the physical appearance of the rookies and the fate that awaited them on Virginia's battlefields. Nearly every jibe reminded the new men that they had exchanged the soft life of some backwater post for the deadly realities of the battlefield. More often than not the barbs lay couched in some piece of wit or drollery that softened the sting and amused the speaker, if not the listener.

In addition to the remarks about the "Twentieth Army Corps," the 20th South Carolina's men endured "much good-humored badgering." Their fellow Carolinians in Butler's cavalry brigade heard plenty, too. Most of the

Repairing an Army

three mounted regiments wore a locally produced brown cloth uniform that looked "very unsoldierly in style" and set them apart from their gray-clad comrades. "The Army of Northern Virginia was largely composed of fellows who were sure to lay hold of everything that could be compelled to do duty as a joke," explained one cavalryman from the Atlantic coast, and the South Carolina troopers provided an irresistible topic.[34]

The harmless badinage may have reached new heights in the Florida brigade. H. M. Hamill, one of the new men, recalled "how the old soldiers made mock of our green and unsoldierly looks and ways, and dubbed us with nicknames that made us for a time the jest of the army." The men carried all manner of outdated weapons and wore unmatched uniform pieces. "Some of us had brought along our neckties and handkerchiefs," observed Hamill, "and dazzled the eyes of Lee's clay-colored veterans . . . with our nicely laundered white shirts." Another soldier confronted the problem of having too much to carry in the field. "I am at a loss to know what to throw away; I will have to quit my under shirt."[35]

David L. Geer of the 5th Florida failed to notice the shirts and instead remembered what "a hard-looking lot of soldiers" Finegan led. He thought the men in the new battalions had an unhealthy "smoked" appearance, and "being so far down south, they had not received many clothes—only what their mothers and wives had spun or woven for them . . . little homespun jackets and the most of them with bed quilts instead of blankets." When a curious woman asked one of Finegan's officers about the battalions' origins, he replied by saying that they were from "the Land of Flowers," whereupon she "threw both of her hands up and exclaimed: 'Oh! Don't they look like flowers!'" Finegan's men proved within days of the unflattering remark that their failure to look menacing mattered little on the field of battle.[36]

The heavy-handed banter welcomed the neophytes into the army while offering the veterans an opportunity to amuse themselves. It also accompanied an inevitable uneasiness on both ends of the situation. The ragged veterans of many campaigns had their brightly burnished reputation to prize and protect. They must have worried, at least briefly, whether the thousands of new men would meet the army's high standards for combat efficiency. A man in the 61st Georgia wrote later that his brigade harbored doubts about Capers's battalion of Georgians. "Some of our boys said that some of their officers looked too proud and dudeish for soldiers" and that they would not stand up to enemy fire. George Boatwright of the battalion confirmed that apprehension, writing on May 29, 1864, that the veterans "prophesied that we would all run."[37]

For their part, many of the new men noted the steady self-confidence of the Army of Northern Virginia's veterans. Starting their fourth week of continuous operations against Grant's army, Lee's men spoke optimistically to their new comrades about the campaign's outcome. James D. Brock of the 12th Georgia Battalion was one of many who recognized the high morale. He mentioned it in a poorly spelled letter to his wife, writing that "the trupes up hear appear to be confident of whiping this fite."[38]

Most of the reinforcements so welcome to the army arrived during a small window of relative quiet in the operations of the Overland campaign. After the initial encounters along the North Anna River on May 23, the Union army did nothing more than launch a few tepid probes against Lee's lines before marching away to the east. There were meaningful battlefield actions nearly every day, but no major fight again until May 28. That respite conveniently allowed many of the new regiments and battalions to join the army, where they began to get acquainted with their commanders and one another. Others continued to trickle in, but a large portion of the new troops had arrived by the time the armies reached Cold Harbor.

The soundest measurement of the rookie formations is their performance on the battlefields. It probably was nothing more than coincidence that nearly all of the rawest regiments found themselves in at least one combat crisis between May 28 and June 3, 1864. Most acquitted themselves well at the very first opportunity. For nearly all of the new cavalrymen, that chance arose on the 28th at the battle of Haw's Shop. Historians have long neglected that noteworthy encounter, perhaps because so much of it resembled an infantry fight, although all organized participants on both sides belonged to cavalry units. Few cavalry battles in the war's history equaled Haw's Shop for unblinking, stand-up action. The men of the 4th and 5th South Carolina Cavalry, together with the 20th Georgia Cavalry Battalion, filled key roles in the drama. Their ordeal bore only a superficial resemblance to earlier cavalry affairs in Virginia. Horses now galloped to the field of action, and their riders dismounted. Carbines replaced sabers and pistols as preferred weapons.

Maj. Gen. Fitzhugh Lee's division of Virginians established the dismounted Confederate battle line in the woods around Enon Church, just west of Haw's Shop, on the 28th. They resisted several Federal probes from the east but could not muster the power to sweep their foes from the field.

Both sides hurried more men into action. For the defenders, that included portions of the 4th and 5th South Carolina Cavalry, numbering slightly fewer than 1,000 men. Bad saddles had chafed the backs of many of the 4th's horses during the protracted journey to Virginia, temporarily disabling the animals and leaving that regiment with only 400 of its approximately 1,000 men mounted. Both units officially belonged to the brigade of Matthew C. Butler. Their general had not arrived, and the two regiments went into battle as a sort of miscellaneous command, nominally led by Col. Benjamin H. Rutledge of the 4th. Butler's absence also ruptured the chain of command; matters of seniority and authority vexed the primary officers and produced confusion at a critical point in the battle.[39]

The South Carolinians advanced on foot to the firing line, yelling all the way. If they later rued their poor luck in making their Virginia debut in so violent an affair, they should also have realized that their weapons gave them an advantage against their foe. The two regiments carried short-barreled, muzzle-loading Enfield rifles, ill suited for efficient use from a horse's back. But on foot, in a brushy environment, those same unwieldy cavalry weapons became assets. Both units immediately affected the course of the battle with their firepower and increased range. Pulling into position, the two regiments blasted away at the Union battle line a few yards ahead, "and there like stakes they stood" until the situation became so critical that the Carolinians had to leave in haste.[40]

Meanwhile the less conspicuous Georgia battalion had similar experiences. On the morning of the 28th, Lieutenant Colonel Millen somehow thought that the day's agenda included a review and inspection. He had "put on his newest uniform and sash and other things calculated to make him look well." Millen soon realized the true state of affairs as his men neared the front. Charles Hansell of the 20th later described his own bemused dismay when he saw "what looked like a large ball coming over the wood and straight toward us." The solid shot—"something I had never seen before"—killed a horse, wounded a man, and reminded the soldiers of the battalion that unpleasant duty lay ahead.

Hansell claimed that he had the time and poise to observe his comrades as they prepared to enter their first action. "Most of them stood it all right," he believed, "but some few were so badly rattled that they had no idea where they were going or what they were doing. In one or two instances no attention was paid to the calls, commands, or curses of their officers; but the men rode right into a pond that was at the bottom of the hill."[41]

The Georgians finally reached the front and stood under fire for an extended period. They operated independently of the South Carolinians, and apparently of nearly everyone else, too. It is difficult to gauge the effect the Georgia battalion had on the battle. The men fought hard enough to incur very substantial casualties, but when their field officers, Lieutenant Colonel Millen and Maj. William G. Thomson, dropped with mortal wounds, the battalion fell apart. The 20th failed to carry away its dead and even abandoned most of its wounded on the field, which helps to confirm that its first brush with battle in Virginia was a trying affair.[42]

Love's little battalion of cavalry also arrived at the battlefield in time to witness the conclusion of the fight, although the Alabamians never occupied a spot on the front line. Remarkably, their horses were not even trained for cavalry duty, so the dismounted action at Haw's Shop suited the battalion's capabilities. In 1862 that would have been a fatal flaw for a regiment or battalion of cavalry, but in 1864 units could better cope with using their horses exclusively for transportation. When they arrived on the scene at Haw's Shop, Love's men dismounted and formed a solid skirmish line to help cover the withdrawal of their weary comrades. Even that duty exposed them to fire. "The balls flew thick and fast at least I thought so," one trooper told his wife the next day.[43]

After the war the men of the 4th and 5th South Carolina Cavalry enjoyed reading the praise they saw from the pens of Union cavalrymen who had faced them at Haw's Shop. The tenacity of the inexperienced men combined with their firepower to make their defense a memorable one. Many of the accolades originated in 1864 rather than in rosy postwar memoirs, and they began at the very top of the Union cavalry command. Maj. Gen. Philip H. Sheridan noted in his battle report that "these Carolinians fought very gallantly in this their first fight." James H. Kidd served at Haw's Shop with the 6th Michigan Cavalry of George Custer's brigade. Six days after the battle, he described the engagement and singled out the new Confederate troopers, who "fought desperately but then had to give way. Many of them refused to surrender and were shot down." Dr. William S. R. Brockenbrough, who lived not far from the battlefield, spoke with a Federal horseman who specifically mentioned the Carolina cavalry. The enemy trooper offered the plausible theory that the 4th and 5th suffered excessive casualties because "they were then fresh troops full of enthusiasm but had not learned to take care of themselves like the older + more experienced troops."[44]

Two days after Haw's Shop, on May 30, more of the imported reinforcements saw action. The weak regiments and battalions in Breckinridge's infantry division occupied key ground on the southern side of Totopotomoy Creek. That creek carved a sizable gash through the countryside, which made it an attractive defensive position. Much of Lee's army entrenched behind the creek and succeeded in keeping the Federal army from finding any promising opening during the final days of the month. Yet in places along the creek—such as on Breckinridge's front—the Confederates learned that the terrain posed difficulties. Abrupt slopes bordered the approaches to the swampy creek on both sides. In the absence of the preferred gradual slopes, with their extended fields of fire, the Virginians had to occupy the forward shoulder on their side of the creek. That arrangement allowed them to see and cover the creek bottom. It also reduced the distance any attacking force would have to cover.

Those tactical considerations became important on May 30–31, when parts of the Union Second Corps launched aggressive probes across the creek. Breckinridge found himself outnumbered and incapable of holding his section of Totopotomoy Creek's southern slope. His two brigades eventually ceded permanent possession of that ground, a misfortune that contributed to a complete realignment of the left-center of Lee's defensive line.

Far to the east on that same Monday afternoon, the Confederate cavalry again exchanged blows with a few brigades of Union horsemen. The action occurred along Matadequin Creek, and the participants represented the eastern flanks of their respective armies. South Carolinians did most of the fighting for the Confederates. The 4th and 5th South Carolina Cavalry, marginally more seasoned than they had been forty-eight hours earlier, stood in the middle of the action. Unlike at Haw's Shop, the men had direct leadership. Matthew Butler had arrived after May 28, but before May 30, and handled his men as a cohesive brigade for the first time. Once again the new regiments held their positions with more determination than good sense. They narrowly escaped disaster at Haw's Shop when they inflexibly stayed in position too long. At Matadequin Creek a portion of the 4th South Carolina Cavalry stubbornly stuck to its position near the Liggan House, "refused to surrender + were consequently shot down."[45]

Most of the brand-new 7th South Carolina Cavalry also assembled in time to participate at Matadequin Creek as part of Martin W. Gary's nascent brigade. Some of the regiment's companies had seen duty as pickets and scouts near Drewry's Bluff during the third week of May before crossing the James River for official organization. No example offers a stronger illustration of the desperate haphazardness associated with the process of reinforcing the army with new formations. Lt. Col. Alexander C. Haskell took command of the 7th on that very morning. His orders to proceed toward Matadequin Creek came not from R. E. Lee but, rather, from Maj. Gen. Robert Ransom, commanding a vaguely defined department that included Richmond.[46]

Haskell had just six of the regiment's ten companies present. The others had not yet reported to the regiment from South Carolina, but two of the missing four arrived on the day of the battle, just in time for the fight. Diarist William G. Hinson served in one of those two and left precise evidence about the peculiar circumstances. "Met the six other companies at 2 o'clock under Col. Haskell," he reported, "who had just taken command a few moments before. Met the enemy at . . . 2:30 o'clock and engaged them." One can only wonder how this affected morale, leadership, discipline, and tactical cohesion—all delicate and interrelated subjects on a battlefield, even for well-trained regiments. Available evidence suggests that the 7th South Carolina Cavalry fought well, although once again in the moment of defeat the unit suffered what probably were unnecessary casualties because of poor tactics. Six of the eight company commanders fell killed or wounded, and well-aimed Federal bullets wounded both field officers.[47]

An episode occurred that same evening that stung the memories of the cavalry veterans after the war. It also received considerable attention at the time. While the men were maneuvering in the blackness of the night toward the Old Cold Harbor crossroads from the Matadequin Creek battlefield, something provoked a panic that swept up and down the column. Butler's South Carolinians employed pungent language in accusing the 20th Georgia Battalion of precipitating the affair. Some evidence suggests that the Carolinians deserved some or all of the blame. The origin of the terrifying event is less important than what happened.

It began in a deeply cut country road northeast of Old Cold Harbor. "Here we heard one or two shots and then the noise of many horses coming very rapidly," explained a Georgian. Packed into the dark road four abreast, the mounted men lost their poise. "Capt. Paine [Thomas S., then commanding the 20th Georgia Cavalry Battalion as its senior captain] was knocked off his horse before he could give a command, and the rest of us were going at nearly full speed in a few jumps of our horses, everyone feeling that his only safety lay in getting ahead of the crowd." Soon the horses "became perfectly frantic with terror." Fear rippled through the column, and the situation spiraled out of control. A well-disciplined company from the 4th South Carolina Cavalry tried to arrest the progress of the panic, "but they were ridden down to a man." Georgia trooper Charles P. Hansell "didn't go far before I heard a horse fall in front and then another over that one, and almost instantly my horse fell. It seemed to me that I was struck all over by the hoofs of running horses."

As the number of unmanageable animals increased, so did the momentum. Men in the road faced critical danger and the imperative need for a snap judgment. The uncertain roar approached rapidly from behind. Those in its path either dismounted in time to hurl themselves against a roadside fence, or they were trampled. Hansell eventually reached the safety of the fence and listened as hundreds of tons of horseflesh galloped past, crushing anything in the road. "The cries for help and groans, and the fearful shrieks of one broken-backed animal" haunted a memoirist even a quarter of a century later. At least one member of the Georgia battalion died in the episode, and "the whole camp was a sight to behold the next morning, bloody faces, dirty clothes, no hats."[48] A Georgian named Reynolds judged the nighttime chaos "a much worse affair" than even the fight at Haw's Shop two days earlier. "I am afraid my arm is broken," he concluded.[49]

It is likely that the 4th South Carolina Cavalry and the 20th Georgia Cavalry Battalion should share the blame for the unfortunate episode. Skittish horses, a lack of discipline among the rank and file, and inexperience in the officer corps probably produced the stampede. A highly placed staff officer in Fitzhugh Lee's division labeled the 4th as the culprit and scoffed in his diary about seeing "hatless dragoons" and a road "strewn with cavalry equipments." Similar things happened in other cavalry brigades during the Civil War, but this deadly event especially embarrassed everyone involved because it emphasized, in a spectacular fashion, the very point that the new men naturally had been attempting to overcome. Hard fighting could not entirely conceal it. They were indeed still awkward and inexperienced regiments.[50]

The next day Philip Sheridan's cavalry snatched the Old Cold Harbor intersection away from its Confederate defenders. R. E. Lee determined to retake it and marshaled available infantry for a strike on the morning of June 1. Joseph Kershaw's division led the First Corps as it angled toward the landmark crossroads from the northwest. Maj. Gen. Robert F. Hoke's division, some elements of which had not seen service with Lee's army before, failed to cooperate. In a badly mismanaged offensive, only Keitt's brigade from Kershaw's division attacked the entrenched enemy. The brigade predictably did not succeed, and its failure received unusual attention then and later because of the comprehensiveness of the defeat.

Keitt arrived in Richmond on May 29 and immediately paid a courtesy call on President Jefferson Davis. He asked Davis "to send me to Kershaw's [old] Brigade, and he gave me a note to Gen'l Lee, to carry out my wishes if possible." In fact, Lee needed someone to take the helm of that trusty brigade. On the very day that Keitt lobbied Davis, and in the midst of stressful military operations along Totopotomoy Creek, Lee sent a letter of enquiry to First Corps commander Richard H. Anderson on the subject. "I have heard . . . that Kershaw's old brigade is much in need of a good brigade commander," Lee wrote, "and . . . I desire you to consult General Kershaw at once, so that a good commander may be recommended . . . as soon as practicable." In addition to indicting the leadership qualities of the brigade's senior colonel and acting commander (John W. Henagan), Lee's note also implies that he did not know of Keitt's imminent arrival. Even a written suggestion from Davis would not have carried sufficient weight had Lee planned some other assignment for Keitt, so it is likely that the president's endorsement combined with the pressing crisis to create a natural solution for Lee. Keitt left Richmond for the front, where he assumed command of Kershaw's old brigade on the morning of the 31st. His own horse had not arrived, and the colonel had to borrow an animal from General Kershaw. On the morning of June 1 the division commander assigned his old brigade the task of retaking Old Cold Harbor. He may have done so because of the incredible size of Keitt's regiment, thinking that raw numbers could offset inexperience and provide a decisive edge.[51]

That line of reasoning failed to achieve the desired results. Colonel Keitt climbed atop the horse "like a knight of old" and led his brigade—nearly half of which had never seen him before and may not even have known his name—in an ill-conceived attack. Keitt apparently failed to take even the most fundamental precautions, such as advancing skirmishers to develop the enemy position. The Confederate attack never threatened the security of the Union perimeter at the crossroads. It is not clear why junior officers in the brigade did not help their inexperienced leader through his first day in command, as a matter of self-interest if nothing else. The conspicuous colonel fell wounded almost at once, "a martyr to the inexorable laws of the army rank," and died the next day, having commanded an Army of Northern Virginia brigade for approximately twenty-four hours.[52]

His old regiment, the 20th South Carolina, melted on the spot. If the

South Carolina cavalry regiments demonstrated too much tenacity at Haw's Shop and Matadequin Creek, the newly arrived infantrymen representing that state showed too little. Artillerist Robert A. Stiles watched
from nearby as the 20th "went to pieces in abject rout." "I have never seen any body of troops," he noted, "in such a condition of utter demoralization; they actually groveled upon the ground and attempted to burrow under each other in holes and depressions." Stiles claimed that he and one of Kershaw's staff officers "actually spurred our horses upon them and seemed to hear their very bones crack, but it did no good; if compelled to wriggle out of one hole they wriggled into another."[53]

That evening a veteran of the brigade nearly instigated a fistfight by telling a 20th South Carolina man that his regiment "had disgraced our brigade [and] run the first fight they got into." The 20th "was a splendid looking body of men," in the view of the brigade chaplain, but "its actions however have not been in keeping with its appearance." Details of the debacle circulated through the army and drew criticism from men who were not even on the scene. A Georgia soldier explained in a letter to a newspaper that June 1 "was the first fight" for the 20th, "and they could not stand the fiery test to which the men of their brigade (Kershaw's) have so often been subjected." Another Georgian in Kershaw's division, writing less than two weeks later, singled out the 20th by name and announced, "We don't want no such men in this army." A source friendly to the regiment later lamented the timing of the 20th's arrival, calling it "unfortunate for Colonel Keitt and his command. . . . The men were ill-prepared to meet the requirements" of service with the Army of Northern Virginia, although "they had all the courage of the veteran troops, but lacked the acclimation." If the 20th took its full complement of more than 1,000 men into the critical charge on June 1, which is likely, its approximate loss of only 77 men that morning offers unmistakable evidence of the regiment's performance.[54]

The infantry positions at Cold Harbor began to take shape by June 2. Both army commanders adjusted their lines by taking men from the Totopotomoy Creek area and marching them to the southern end of the front near the Chickahominy River. Those maneuvers often mandated extensive rearrangements. The movements associated with filling gaps and shortening fronts offered good offensive prospects for vigilant on-site commanders. One such episode on June 2 brought Capers's large battalion of Georgians into the public eye.

Lt. Gen. Jubal A. Early commanded Lee's Second Corps by then. He seized an opportunity to drive a wedge into a crease in the Union lines created by a phased withdrawal of Maj. Gen. Ambrose E. Burnside's Ninth Corps toward Bethesda Church. Early threw most of his corps forward in a wheeling arc, creating extensive havoc among certain elements of both the Fifth and Ninth Corps. The Georgia brigade of Clement Evans attacked in step with comrades from other divisions and found itself well placed to inflict maximum damage. Forcing their way in among Federalists from Griffin's division of the Fifth Corps, the Georgians exchanged small arms fire with the defenders and then exuberantly chased several regiments through two or three lines of breastworks.

The 12th Georgia Artillery Battalion, conspicuous for its size in the worn-down Second Corps, fought well in its first opportunity. Newspapers in Virginia and Georgia singled out the battalion for special attention. The Confederate attack occurred in the midst of "a violent storm" that provided a dramatic stage for the rookies. The battalion advanced to the charge with a color-bearer carrying a "fine silk flag" with inscribed battle honors from Fort Sumter and Battery Wagner to remind the men of their earlier achievements. Capers's men claimed to have taken 700 prisoners, which undoubtedly is an inflated number but one that helps to convey the degree of the Confederate victory. As the largest unit in the brigade, the 12th naturally suffered the heaviest loss—about fifty-five men—which must have been poor compensation for the extra publicity. The popular Capers fell, on his twenty-ninth birthday, with a severe hip wound that knocked him out of field duty for the balance of the war. James D. Brock, who one week earlier had told his wife of the army's confidence in ultimate victory, fell shot in the head while approaching the third consecutive line of Union earthworks.[55]

The veterans of Evans's brigade who worried about the "dudeish" appearance of the battalion's officers found, in this instance at least, that new troops were not always unreliable. "We never had any doubts about the fighting qualities of the officers and men of the Twelfth Georgia Battalion again," wrote G. W. Nichols. "They won the respect of the brigade at once." The battlefield success and the ensuing acclaim undoubtedly sat well with the battalion, but George Boatwright took care to note a further bonus from the victory: "Our boys equiped themselves with blankets, over clothes, and cantines."[56]

The final great test of the North Anna/Cold Harbor phase of the Overland campaign occurred on June 3. Grant planned his assault as an irresistible seven-mile wave. Today it is remembered for poor tactical coordination and a general sense of bloody futility. That thumbnail summary unfairly obscures the details of much competitive action, including the partially successful efforts of the Union Second Corps. While most of the Army of the Potomac either sat idle or went forward to defeat, one division of that corps smashed a hole in the Confederate line. John Echols's Virginia brigade defended the broken point in the Confederate line.

In fact, nearly all of the Confederates involved in that localized crisis were new to the army. The Federals breached the line held by Breckinridge's division of Virginians and then encountered Finegan's Florida brigade, which conveniently lay in reserve immediately behind the endangered point. The inexperience even spilled over into the leadership of one of the Virginia brigades. At some time between May 22 and June 1, John Echols became too sick to command. One of his friends identified the illness only as "an organic affection of the heart, which has been much aggravated by the exposure and fatigue which he has lately undergone." Senior colonel George S. Patton of the 22nd Virginia Infantry assumed control of the brigade just before its great crisis at Cold Harbor.[57]

A quirk in the terrain led to an awkward position for Breckinridge's two Virginia brigades. A knob of relatively high ground interfered with their defensive dispositions and produced an elevated salient in a portion of the line. The brigades of Wharton and Echols occupied entrenchments at the crest of that hillock and resigned themselves to all of the disadvantages associated with defending salients. Their weapons could not cover a significant piece of low ground in front, yet if they entrenched farther to the rear, that same unseen ground could permit Federal attackers to mass in security. C. W. Humphreys of the 26th Virginia Battalion in the Echols/Patton brigade later claimed that insufficient manpower compounded their problems that morning. He asserted that in his battalion, at least, each man bore responsibility for about three feet of the line—a poor equation for successful defense.

When the attacking tip of the best corps in the Federal army hit the badly arranged Virginia units, it broke through easily. Geography and manpower bore meaningful parts in that achievement, but it seems certain that weak—or at least inexperienced—leadership played some role, too. Breckinridge could not be found; Echols remained absent with his illness. New to this type of warfare and confronted with a higher-quality opponent, the Virginians folded. Some of the men in the Echols/Patton brigade resisted the onslaught and crossed bayonets with the 7th New

York Heavy Artillery for a few terrible moments, but a great many submitted to capture.[58]

The Federal breakthrough caromed off Gabriel Wharton's brigade, which stood to the right of the Echols/Patton group. Union brigades facing Wharton did not advance with the vigor demonstrated by their adjacent colleagues. The few available sources from the brigade suggest that Wharton's men had an easy time of it. The 51st Virginia, on the brigade's left, had some rifles that helped keep the Federals away from a direct assault on Wharton. Rufus Woolwine, a diarist in that regiment, wrote of the Union breakthrough in the adjacent brigade but did not mention any direct action for his own regiment. The 62nd Virginia stood a bit farther down the line from the breakthrough and may not even have fired a shot, despite being only three or four regiments away from the point of impact.[59]

Finegan's men literally awoke to the sound of the guns. Peering up the slope a few hundred yards to the east, they could see the contested earthworks silhouetted against the earliest pre-dawn light. The Floridians hurled themselves into the gap. They "came like the wind," admitted an admiring soldier in Patton's brigade. After a short melee that included most of the gruesome episodes common in hand-to-hand fighting, the southerners prevailed. The new Florida general did admirable work in confronting this first crisis. One of his soldiers retained "a very vivid memory" of how Finegan's "stumpy figure and fiery horse went flashing to and fro" as the general animated his brigade during its counterattack.[60]

The older troops of Finegan's brigade rejoiced at the conduct of the new battalions. Many saluted their performance, both in person and in writing. A cry of "Three cheers for Finnegan's brigade" drew shouts of appreciation. "I need not say that we felt good over it," admitted a Florida lad new to combat. Council Bryan of the 5th Florida offered an on-the-spot assessment. Writing home on June 3, he reported that "the new troops fought like 'tigers' and we feel proud of them."[61]

The Cold Harbor success of June 3 understandably elevated the spirits of Finegan's men. The Florida units, old and new alike, did not fail to notice that they had saved a portion of the line lost by Breckinridge's Virginians. David Geer later crowed about seeing the heroes of the Shenandoah Valley "running over us like a bunch of Texas steers."[62]

Whatever good feeling Finegan produced among the Florida brigade veterans on June 3 evaporated later that same day. Although the Confederates had retaken the balance of their original line in the morning, enemy skirmishers—and indeed the main body of the Union Second Corps—lay uncomfortably close. Finegan determined to drive the Federal picket line away from his front, which could only be accomplished by a direct assault. The general collected fragments of his brigade to make up the strike force. Nearly everyone greeted his orders with disbelief, scorn, and sadness. "Some of the men began remonstrating against it as an egregious folly coming from a greenhorn," wrote Alfred Scott. Men unfortunate enough to be among the attacking party made postmortem arrangements before setting off.[63]

The charge failed, as everyone except Finegan thought that it would. It cost the brigade several prominent and popular officers and "nearly every man [of the attacking party] . . . killed, wounded, or missing." The episode demonstrated Finegan's unsuitability for the tactical component of brigade command. He further alienated his men by ordering a second probe ("a rather foolish night charge" in the words of Lieutenant Colonel Brevard) of the same nature in the twilight of the same evening. Although it fared better than the first, that localized attack greatly enlarged the brigade's casualty list in return for what the men viewed as a dubious triumph.[64]

Also on June 3, the 7th Georgia Cavalry finally reached the Army of Northern Virginia. It represented the last of the many regiments, battalions, and miscellaneous companies to buttress Lee's army between May 21 and June 12. The 7th and several other units officially joined Young's old brigade on June 6. Col. Gilbert J. Wright still commanded the brigade because of Young's serious injury five days earlier.[65]

Literature on the Overland campaign often mentions the deleterious effect of almost continuous daily operations upon the soldiers of both armies, yet rarely is the subject given full weight. The difficulty of measuring effect, of calculating the full significance of mental and physical weariness, is an obstacle. A perusal of letters and diaries penned during that critical period will demonstrate to any thoughtful reader the breadth of the issue. The cavalry branches of the two sparring armies seem to have felt the cumulative effect most of all. The new troops, a great many of them freshly arrived from backwater posts, particularly cringed at the unrelenting pace.

Joseph B. Martin of the 20th Georgia Cavalry Battalion realized after only one week in Virginia that "it is something unusual to wake up in the morning without hearing the booming of cannons." "I think we are very near perpetual motion," mused a comrade. "There is no rest here in Virginia. Always going," agreed a South Carolina diarist. An Alabama trooper offered more details, noting that occasionally "we go two days without any thing to eat for Man or Horse except the grass which is very fine, for the latter. . . . I am learning how to do without eating or sleeping." Finegan's inexperienced Floridians, supposedly a sickly crowd when they arrived, suffered particularly. A man in the 6th Florida Battalion itemized his sufferings in a June 5 letter to his wife that detailed the collective ill health of his battalion. "I must say to you it is a hard life," he concluded, "and no telling when one may be killed but I cant say it was any worse than I expected."[66]

The particulars of entrenched warfare at Cold Harbor affected everyone, veteran and replacement alike. Daylight lasted for sixteen long hours. The men could barely stir before sunset. An officer in Breckinridge's division, in recounting his experiences between June 4 and 6, lamented the proliferation of mortars as an especially unpleasant aspect of that period. "There is perhaps nothing in modern warfare that can have a more demoralizing effect on troops in entrenchments," he suggested, "than a continuous fire from mortar batteries. . . . The sound of a bomb slowly, as it seems, rising in the air, has a most painful effect. By force of imagination every man expects the bomb to fall right on him, and the anxiety and suspense . . . is intense." There can be little doubt that Breckinridge's men welcomed the moment on June 7 when they left Lee's army forever and returned to the Shenandoah Valley.[67]

An appraisal of the military talents of the new general officers that joined the army in May and June offers nothing conclusive. Breckinridge, Wharton, and Echols all left so quickly that no fair assessment is possible. Joseph Finegan was the only other general to unite his command with the Army of Northern Virginia during this period. He stayed until March 1865, leaving just in time to avoid the collapse of the army. Thoughtful men in his brigade did not respect his ability, while the evidence from his superiors is slender and unclear. Brig. Gen. William Mahone commanded the division in which Finegan served for the duration of his stay in Virginia. With characteristic dishonesty, Mahone offered conflicting evaluations. He approved Finegan's resignation and wrote that he regretted "to part with this gallant and most efficient officer whose capacity and valuable service entitle him to a superior command." At nearly the same time, Mahone reported to R. E. Lee that "the condition of his Brigade in *tone*, discipline and organization demands vigorous attention and the services of the best man at its head to save it from utter disintegration. . . . The sooner the better."[68]

The new units generally performed well, with a few specific exceptions. The disastrous debut of the 20th South Carolina stands out as the greatest failure. The cavalry stampede on the night of May 30, while embarrassing enough for everyone involved, was not really a case of courage or even ability but, rather, one of inexperience. The collapse of the Echols/Patton brigade at Cold Harbor on June 3 certainly must be classed a failure, though the brigade's poor alignment and the numerical disparity between it and the attacking Federals mitigate the question.

It is likely that given a choice in May, R. E. Lee would have preferred a higher ratio of infantry to cavalry among his reinforcements. The grinding operations around Petersburg between mid-June 1864 and April 2, 1865, extracted a heavier toll on foot soldiers than on horsemen. Lee's inability to counter Union forces that mixed infantry and cavalry to provide both mobility and striking power eventually compromised the Confederate position west of Petersburg. But the large numbers of new cavalrymen had a useful role in the war's final months. They repeatedly assisted in blocking Federal raids. They guarded the army's vulnerable flanks at ever-increasing distances from Petersburg itself. Best of all, the new horsemen proved adept at fighting in the 1864–65 style. Their presence helped offset the tremendous late-war advances made by Union cavalry in the fields of manpower, weaponry, and horseflesh.

The sum of the many parts makes it clear that the Confederate authorities labored conscientiously to restore Lee's army to its pre-campaign strength. Their efforts brought in divisions, brigades, enormous regiments, and many battalions. They even secured individual companies and must have felt that the reward justified the effort. An evaluation of the reinforcement project must recognize the limitations on Confederate manpower and transportation by 1864. It also must remember the dire crisis in Richmond itself, provoked by the presence of two Federal armies simultaneously menacing the city from opposite directions. In that environment particularly, the men responsible for rebuilding the Army of Northern Virginia to the greatest possible extent must be judged successful.[69]

The new men—thousands of them—proved to be valuable ingredients in Lee's successful defense of Richmond through June 12. They adequately neutralized the reinforcements sent to Grant's army, so that by June 3, 1864, the competing armies stood in virtually the same relative balance as they had on May 4, 1864, prior to the Battle of the Wilderness. The final sizable surge of new troops had arrived in good time to lend substantial weight to the defense of Richmond; but, as Lee soon discovered, the 65,000 men he had under arms at Cold Harbor would have to last him for the duration of the war.

ROBERT E. L. KRICK

1. The most familiar examples of those heavy artillery units from the May–June 1864 period are the 1st Massachusetts Heavy Artillery, the 1st Maine Heavy Artillery, the 2nd Connecticut Heavy Artillery, and the 7th and 8th New York Heavy Artillery. Several others fought with the Army of the Potomac, too, but those five regiments earned the most acclaim, primarily because of their staggering combat losses.

2. U.S. War Department, *The War of the Rebellion: A Compilation of the Official Records of the Union and Confederate Armies*, 127 vols., index, and atlas (Washington: Government Printing Office, 1880–1901), ser. 1, 51(2):835–37, 36(2):488, 1,013 (hereafter cited as *OR*; all references are to ser. 1). The four Florida battalions that joined the army, as detailed below, received their summons only on May 16. That clearly is one instance of the authorities reacting to the crisis in central Virginia, rather than planning for it in advance.

3. *OR* 51(2):354, 35(2):372–74. The latter citation is to an apposite case where the secretary of war invoked Davis's name to help deflect an angry South Carolinian on the wrong end of the arithmetic.

4. Johnson Hagood, Thomas L. Clingman, and James G. "One Wing" Martin are examples of generals whose brigades joined the army at Cold Harbor but are not treated in this essay because of their service below Richmond with Beauregard between May 5 and 30, 1864. The 64th Georgia Infantry and a handful of other units new to Virginia stayed at Petersburg through the Overland campaign, not uniting with Lee's army until the middle of June. This essay will not look at artillery that joined the army during the May–June period. Alfred C. Young III, *Lee's Army during the Overland Campaign: A Numerical Study* (Baton Rouge: Louisiana State University Press, 2013), is a helpful volume for numbers and losses, although like all such works it should be used with caution. Young concluded (233–34) that about 25,500 reinforcements reached Lee's army during the campaign; but he adopted a broader definition, and that sum included Maj. Gen. George E. Pickett's division and other veteran commands merely returning to the army from detached duty.

5. Robert E. Lee, *The Wartime Papers of R. E. Lee*, ed. Clifford Dowdey and Louis H. Manarin (Boston: Little, Brown, 1961), 728–30, 734.

6. *OR* 51(2):933.

7. Augustus Forsberg memoir, Leyburn Library, Washington and Lee University, Lexington, Va. (repository hereafter cited as WL); Lee, *Wartime Papers*, 732–33; Rufus J. Woolwine diary, May 20, 1864, Virginia Historical Society, Richmond (repository hereafter cited as VHS). Woolwine's diary appeared in the *Virginia Magazine of History and Biography* 71 (October 1963). Some sources might accurately call Breckinridge's command a "demi-division."

8. Forsberg memoir, WL.

9. S. T. McCullough diary, May 23, 1864, Albert and Shirley Small Special Collections Library, University of Virginia, Charlottesville (repository hereafter cited as UVA); Terry Lowry, *22nd Virginia Infantry* (Lynchburg, Va.: H. E. Howard, 1988), 62.

10. *Address of Capt. Jas. Bumgardner, Jr. Before R. E. Lee Camp, Confederate Veterans, Friday, May 8, 1903, Presenting Portrait of General John Echols* (Staunton, Va.: Daily News Printing, 1903), 5, 9; Edward O. Guerrant, *Bluegrass Confederate: The Headquarters Diary*

of Edward O. Guerrant, ed. William C. Davis and Meredith L. Swentor (Baton Rouge: Louisiana State University Press, 1999), 597; Echols's official compiled service record (hereafter cited as CSR), M331, roll 83, National Archives, Washington, D.C. (repository hereafter cited as NA); William C. Davis, ed., *The Confederate General*, 6 vols. (Harrisburg, Pa.: National Historical Society, 1991), 2:92–93; Thomas J. Jackson to A. R. Boteler, May 6, 1862, Boteler Papers, William R. Perkins Library, Duke University, Durham, N.C. (repository hereafter cited as DU); Robert E. Lee, *Lee's Dispatches: Unpublished Letters of General Robert E. Lee, C.S.A.*, ed. Douglas Southall Freeman (New York: Putnam's, 1915), 216. In fairness to Echols, it should be mentioned that Jackson's grumbling applied equally to William B. Taliaferro, who was mentioned in the same sentence as Echols and certainly could not be counted among Stonewall's "warm personal friends." Jackson's accusation is partly proved by documents in Echols's CSR, which include a petition from prominent western Virginians asking that Echols receive advancement for the incredibly weak reason that "hitherto no promotion in the C. S. Army has been made of a person residing West of the Allegheny Mountains." This referred only to Virginians living in that region.

11. Davis, *Confederate General*, 6:120–21; R. E. Lee to R. S. Ewell, August 11, 1863, in *Autograph Album: A Magazine for Autograph Collectors* 1 (October 1933): 64. In the letter, Lee proposed giving Wharton a brigade in Maj. Gen. Edward Johnson's division, but Johnson disliked the idea. Wharton led the 51st Virginia Infantry for the first half of the war. His commission as brigadier general dated from July 8, 1863, and the brigade he commanded included the 51st.

12. The 5th arrived at Richmond on May 3, 1864, but the first of its horses did not reach the regiment until May 12. For much of the period between May 5 and May 19, the 5th operated as scouts—mounted and dismounted—for Beauregard's army below Richmond. See Ruth Barr McDaniel, comp., *Confederate War Correspondence of James Michael Barr and Rebecca Ann Dowling Barr* (Taylors, S.C.: Faith Printing Co., 1963), 241. The regiment then joined Lomax's brigade of Fitzhugh Lee's division north of Richmond on May 20 and participated in Lee's May 24 disaster at Kennon's Wharf on the James River. See Janet B. Hewett and others, eds., *Supplement to the Official Records of the Union and Confederate Armies*, 100 vols. (Wilmington, N.C.: Broadfoot, 1994–2001), 6:808 (hereafter cited as ORS). For extensive details on the obstacles encountered by the 4th South Carolina Cavalry, see W. Eric Emerson, *Sons of Privilege: The Charleston Light Dragoons in the Civil War* (Columbia: University of South Carolina Press, 2005), 65–66. The 4th Cavalry reached Richmond on May 24 and marched toward the army on the morning of the 26th, reaching it on the 27th; see Thomas L. Pinckney diary, May 27, 1864, Eleanor S. Brockenbrough Library, Museum of the Confederacy, Richmond, Va. (repository hereafter cited as MOC). Col. Hugh K. Aiken of the 6th South Carolina Cavalry preceded his men to Richmond, leaving Maj. Thomas B. Ferguson to lead the command to Virginia. A May 23 letter from Aiken reflects the urgency of the times. "We are much needed here—will go into service at once," he wrote Ferguson, and "We are very much censured for the delay." The grumpy authorities, in fact, required Ferguson to "prepare a report accounting for each day" of the trip (U. R. Brooks, *Butler and His Cavalry in the War of Secession* [Columbia, S.C.: The State

Company, 1909], 216). The removal of the South Carolina regiments from their home state produced controversy, some of which can be traced in *OR* 35(2):362, 364, 372–74.

13. Edward L. Wells, *A Sketch of the Charleston Light Dragoons* (Charleston: Lucas, Richardson & Co., 1888), 36; Oliver H. Middleton letter, May 24, 1864, Middleton Family Papers, South Carolina Historical Society, Charleston (repository hereafter cited as SCHS).

14. *Adjutant and Inspector-General's Office, Special Orders No. 65/30*, March 18, 1864, established the 7th as an entity, though it took ten weeks to pull the various companies together. C. Foster Smith, *Jeremiah Smith and the Confederate War* (Spartanburg, S.C.: The Reprint Company, 1993), 37–50, nicely explains the history of the regiment's birth and growth, particularly in May 1864. Also see *OR* 51(2):836. The details of the 7th's debut in combat appear later in this essay.

15. *OR* 36(3):808, 812–13.

16. *OR* 51(2):836.

17. Charles P. Hansell, "A History of the 20th Georgia Battalion," drawer 283, box 27 (microfilm), Georgia Department of Archives and History, Atlanta (hereafter cited as GDAH).

18. *ORS* 13:71–72; William H. Locke letters, May 28, 29, 1864, UVA; Compiled Service Records of Confederate Soldiers Who Served in Organizations From the State of Alabama, M311, roll 18, National Archives and Records Service, Washington, D.C. (hereafter cited as NARA). Even Alfred Young's thorough *Lee's Army* fails to account for Love's Battalion. Locke's May 28 letter says he reached Richmond on the 26th, although the battalion did not join the army until the 28th. A dispatch in *OR* 51(2):925 dated May 12 gives the battalion's mounted strength as 160; however, Captain Love signed a forage requisition on May 29 for 214 horses, suggesting that perhaps his force increased by the time it reached Virginia. A few letters by William H. Bray of the battalion offer a second source on this virtually unknown command. Bray's letters are in Gerald R. Mathis, *In the Land of the Living: Wartime Letters by Confederates from the Chattahoochee Valley . . .* (Troy, Ala.: Troy State University Press, 1981).

19. *ORS* 17:525; John W. Latty, *The Gallant Little 7th: A History of the 7th Georgia Cavalry Regiment* (Wilmington, N.C.: Broadfoot, 2004), 79, 82.

20. *ORS* 60:89; Lynwood Holland, *Pierce M. B. Young: The Warwick of the South* (Athens: University of Georgia Press, 1964), 83. Holland's biography ignores both the story of Young's enlarged brigade and his emergency assignment to the North Carolina brigade. Incredibly, it also misdates Young's wound by two days. A short note from Young, dated May 29, 1864, is in the Frederick M. Dearborn Collection at the Houghton Library, Harvard University. Young wrote it at Atlee's Station, which also was the location of army headquarters; therefore his shift into the field from Richmond probably dates from that day. His note does not mention the North Carolina brigade but instead asks a Richmond staff officer "to interest yourself for me in getting my other regiments on as soon as possible."

21. *ORS* 60:89; *OR* 51(2):950; Walter Clark, ed., *Histories of the Several Regiments and Battalions From North Carolina in the Great War, 1861–'65*, 5 vols. (Goldsboro, N.C.: Nash Brothers, 1901), 2:778–79.

22. *ORS* 17:714, 720, 723; George W. Boatwright letter, May 29, 1864, photocopy in bound volume no. 15, Richmond National Battlefield Park Library, Richmond, Va. (repository hereafter cited as RNBP); Lee, *Lee's Dispatches*, 206. Lee's personal involvement in these details is proved by a telegram to Richmond on May 30, in which he noted the arrival of Capers's men and took the opportunity to enquire about the status of another small battalion he awaited.

23. Robert K. Krick, *Lee's Colonels: A Biographical Register of the Field Officers of the Army of Northern Virginia*, rev. 5th ed. (Wilmington, N.C.: Broadfoot, 2009), 79; "Lieut. Col. Henry D. Capers, C.S.A.," *Confederate Veteran* 16 (June 1908): 278–79; George W. Nichols, *A Soldier's Story of His Regiment* (Jessup, Ga.: privately printed, 1898), 161. Capers wrote a biography of Memminger after the war, as well as a work of fiction, and lived until 1912. The May 1864 strength of the 12th Battalion is from *OR* 35(2):493, 36(3):808, 51(2):955.

24. *OR* 36(2):1013 gives the Florida contingent's strength at 1,100, but *OR* 35(2):494 offers a better estimate at 1,656. Young, *Lee's Army*, 166, postulates that the number was at least 1,250. For two examples of the battalions' random arrival, see Gary Loderhouse, *Far, Far from Home: The Ninth Florida Regiment in the Confederate Army* (Carmel, Ind.: Guild Press, 1999), 39, 43, and letter of "A.F.G.," June 7, 1864, P. K. Yonge Library of Florida History, University of Florida, Gainesville (repository hereafter cited as UF). Loderhouse says that the 6th Battalion arrived at army headquarters on May 26, the men not even having been told they were going to Virginia until they had left the state of Florida entirely. "A.F.G." wrote that the 2nd Battalion reached the Army of Northern Virginia about midday on the 28th after "severe marching" from the South. "A.F.G." was almost certainly A. F. Gould, 2nd Florida Battalion.

25. Alfred L. Scott memoir, VHS, 8. Scott misspelled Finegan's name, as shown in the quotation. Apparently all four battalions had joined Lee by May 28; the initial order (*OR* 36[3]:843) combining the two organizations into one brigade dates from then. The assignment must have been intended as a trial measure, because the official merger only became effective on November 25, 1864, per Army of Northern Virginia Special Orders No. 287/14, "Orders and Circulars Issued by the Army of the Potomac and the Army and Department of Northern Virginia C.S.A., 1861–1865," M921, roll 4, NA.

26. Joseph Finegan's CSR, M331, roll 93, NA (misfiled as Finnegan). G. H. Dorman, *Fifty Years Ago: Reminiscences of '61–'65* (Tallahassee, Fla.: T. J. Appleyard, State Printer, n.d.), 14, relates a typical story about Finegan from later in the summer of 1864. When the brigade captured a cannon, the general supposedly climbed atop it "and hollowed out, 'Promotion for me!'"

27. *Adjutant and Inspector-General's Office, Special Orders No. 99/3*, April 28, 1864; *OR* 35(2):343, 350, 496. J. Patton Anderson, in whose military district the Florida battalions served before going to Virginia, had been attempting to create two regiments out of the four battalions since at least March. The 6th Florida Battalion reportedly carried 425 men to Virginia, a number that fits nicely with the estimated sum of 1,500 to 1,600 for the four battalions together.

28. *Adjutant and Inspector-General's Office, Special Orders No. 133/17–18*, June 8, 1864, officially created both the 10th and 11th Florida Infantry. There are conflicting dates

for that order: one of the Florida officers cited it in an official document (*ORS* 17:369) as dating from June 9, but the original printed announcement issued by the Adjutant and Inspector-General's Office is from June 8 and must be considered accurate. Company B of what became the 11th Florida did not accompany the other companies to Virginia and was not present at Cold Harbor (*ORS* 17:389).

29. Thomas C. Elder letter, May 29, 1864, Elder Papers, VHS; J. Patton Anderson letter, May 27, 1864, original sold by Historical Collectible Auctions, Burlington, N.C., October 2001. The able Brevard likely was not present for the brigade's big moment at Cold Harbor on the morning of June 3, although he arrived on the field from Richmond later that day; see T. W. Brevard letter, June 7, 1864, George Fairbanks Papers, Florida Historical Society, Tampa (repository hereafter cited as FHS). Maj. Gen. Samuel Jones, in reviewing his peremptory orders to send the Floridians to Virginia in May, doubted "if one-half of the men ordered will leave Florida" and predicted that "my order will cause desertions and disorganization" (*OR* 36[2]:1013). That pessimism probably explains why nobody informed the men in the battalions where they were going until they were across the state line.

30. D. Augustus Dickert, *History of Kershaw's Brigade* (Newberry, S.C.: Elbert H. Aull, 1899), 365, 375; William R. Stillwell letter, June 14, 1864, United Daughters of the Confederacy typescripts, vol. 14, GDAH; James A. Milling, "Jim Milling and the War, 1862–1865," photocopy of a typescript memoir in author's possession; Wesley Nichols, *Autobiography and Civil War Recollections of . . .* (Leesville, S.C.: Twin-County News Print, 1915), 10; Laurence M. Keitt letter, May 31, 1864, Keitt Papers, DU; W. C. Hall diary, May 29, 31, 1864, typescript in bound vol. no. 47, RNBP. Dickert gives the regiment's size as 1,600, while Stillwell (of a different brigade in the same division) places the number at 1,120. Dickert is likely a more reliable source. Keitt merely wrote that the regiment was a "trifle larger" than the balance of the brigade. The 20th South Carolina left Charleston on May 25, arrived in Richmond four days later, and reached Lee's army on May 31.

31. Roswell S. Ripley's CSR, M331, roll 212, NA. Many sources spell Keitt's name phonetically, thus proving the "Kitt" pronunciation. See, for example, Nichols, *Autobiography*, 10. Keitt had served in the United States Congress before the war and was a "silver-tongued orator" of some repute. For a biographical sketch, see Dickert, *History of Kershaw's Brigade*, 374.

32. *ORS* 17:746, 752–54; *OR* 35(2):521–22; Oscar P. Smith letter, June 13, 1864, in the Ophelia Jane Smith Gordon Papers, drawer 199, microfilm box 58, GDAH; undated [June 1864] letter of Charles F. Terrill, typescript in possession of Keith S. Bohannon, Carrollton, Ga. Veteran Army of Northern Virginia general Lafayette McLaws commanded at Savannah and negotiated the redirection of the 28th Siege Artillery Battalion. Companies F and H were the two that continued on to Virginia. The latter company lost all its papers, including muster rolls, at Cold Harbor. That loss further impairs any effort to reconstruct the history of the two companies. They stayed with the Florida brigade through the remainder of the war, inexplicably separated from their parent organization and mixed with men from a different state altogether. The odd situation understandably left the two companies in Virginia "dissatisfied on account of their involuntary absence" from their Georgia comrades. A failed effort

by the battalion's commander to retrieve his missing companies in October 1864 is documented in Letters Received by the Confederate States Adjutant and Inspector General's Office, M474, B-3253-1864, NARA. Thanks to Keith Bohannon for extensive assistance in piecing together the details of this peculiar case.

33. *OR* 35(2):484, 486, 36(2):1011.

34. Dickert, *History of Kershaw's Brigade*, 365; Wells, *Charleston Light Dragoons*, 38.

35. H. M. Hamill, "A Boy's First Battle," *Confederate Veteran* 12 (November 1904): 540. Loderhouse, *Far, Far from Home*, 45, provides the quotation about the soldier abandoning his undershirt to save weight.

36. David L. Geer, "Memoir of the War," *Lake City (Fla.) Index*, February 2, 1906.

37. Nichols, *Soldier's Story of His Regiment*, 162; George W. Boatwright letter, May 29, 1864, RNBP.

38. James D. Brock letter, May 25, 1864, transcript in bound vol. no. 68, RNBP. Although the phrase "whipping this fight" sounds strange to modern ears, one routinely sees it in soldier letters from the Civil War, especially among southerners. It was an awkward way of describing victory.

39. Brooks, *Butler and His Cavalry*, 212; Wells, *Charleston Light Dragoons*, 35; Thomas L. Pinckney diary, May 26, 1864, MOC. Many horses remained unshod, making them unfit for service too. J. M. Barr of the 5th South Carolina missed the battle, together with about seventy-five comrades, because they were in Richmond having their horses shod; see McDaniel, *Confederate War Correspondence*, 241. Some literature, both old and new, incorrectly spells the name of this battle with an extra vowel: Hawe's Shop.

40. Letter of "Gills Creek," May 29, 1864, printed in *Lancaster (S.C.) Ledger*, June 14, 1864; Brooks, *Butler and His Cavalry*, 210. A great many Confederate horsemen carried Enfield rifles because of the unavailability of the preferred carbine. "Breech-loading carbines were procured only in limited quantities. . . . The deficiency was made up, generally, by Enfield rifles" (H. B. McClellan, *I Rode with Jeb Stuart: The Life and Campaigns of Major General J. E. B. Stuart* [1958; reprint, New York: Kraus, 1969], 260–61). Many sources make special mention of the Carolina regiments' Enfields. The sheer size of the units and their complete reliance on Enfields may explain that extra attention, as the weapon was not unfamiliar to the army. For recent examples of the emphasis on the Carolinians' armament, see Ernest B. Furgurson, *Not War but Murder: Cold Harbor, 1864* (New York: Knopf, 2000), 49, and Gordon C. Rhea, *Cold Harbor: Grant and Lee, May 26–June 3, 1864* (Baton Rouge: Louisiana State University Press, 2002), 67.

41. Hansell, "History of the 20th Georgia Battalion," GDAH.

42. Ibid.; J. M. Reynolds letter, June 1, 1864, Dickey Family Papers, drawer 49, microfilm box 78, GDAH; Arthur M. Martin, *The Flemington Martins* (Columbia, S.C.: State Printing Co., 1970), 17; Thomas G. Pond, "Casualties in Millen's Battalion," *Savannah Republican*, June 16, 1864. Reynolds recorded 67 casualties in the battalion; Pond listed 69 by name and further mentioned "that we did not have 225 men in the action." All sources agree on the subject of the battalion's unraveling after the fatal injuries to its officers. Martin even failed to retrieve the corpse of his slain brother. For the fullest biographical sketch of Millen, see Chris Ferguson, *Hollywood Cemetery: Her Forgotten Soldiers* (n.p.: privately printed, 2001), 77.

43. William H. Locke letter, May 29, 1864, UVA.

44. Brooks, *Butler and His Cavalry*, 211–12; *OR* 36(1):793; James H. Kidd, *One of Custer's Wolverines: The Civil War Letters of Brevet Brigadier General James H. Kidd, 6th Michigan Cavalry*, ed. Eric J. Wittenberg (Kent, Ohio: Kent State University Press, 2000), 88; William S. R. Brockenbrough letter, September 16, 1864, Middleton Family Papers, SCHS. Brooks smugly reproduced a varied collection of Union quotes that praise the Carolinians, some of them less than plausible. The Federal units probably were impressed in part by the unusual size of the South Carolina regiments.

45. William S. R. Brockenbrough letter, September 16, 1864, Middleton Family Papers, SCHS; William H. Locke letter, June 4, 1864, UVA; J. M. Reynolds letter, June 7, 1864, Dickey Family Papers, GDAH; unsigned letter in *Savannah Republican*, October 25, 1864. Love's Alabama Battalion also fought at Matadequin Creek but did not lose a man. It is not known whether the battalion served under Butler or operated independently on that occasion. The leaderless 20th Georgia Cavalry Battalion did operate with Butler's brigade from May 29 until June 6.

46. Louise Haskell Daly, *Alexander Cheves Haskell: The Portrait of a Man* (Norwood, Mass.: Plimpton Press, 1934), 127, 130–31.

47. Smith, *Jeremiah Smith and the Confederate War*, 49; "The Diary of William G. Hinson during the War of Secession," *South Carolina Historical Magazine* 75 (January 1974): 17–18. The 42nd Virginia Cavalry Battalion also belonged to Gary's brigade. The addition of extra companies a few weeks later converted the battalion into the 24th Virginia Cavalry. The core of the regiment served in central Virginia, under several different names, for most of the war. Although not indigenous to the Army of Northern Virginia, it was a local organization and does not fall under a strict interpretation of "new" troops joining the army in late May and early June 1864. See Darryl Holland, *24th Virginia Cavalry* (Lynchburg, Va.: H. E. Howard, 1997), for a full explanation.

48. Hansell, "History of the 20th Georgia Battalion," GDAH; Wells, *Charleston Light Dragoons*, 54–55. Wells says that this drama occurred between nine and ten o'clock.

49. J. M. Reynolds letter, June 1, 1864, Dickey Family Papers, GDAH.

50. *ORS* 6:812. For an elaborate postwar explanation regarding the South Carolinians' innocence, see Brooks, *Butler and His Cavalry*, 227–29. On the other hand, an unsigned letter from a member of the 20th Georgia Cavalry Battalion published in the *Savannah Republican*, October 25, 1864, maintained that General Butler "has taken occasion to exonerate our battalion from its share in the blame of this unfortunate occurrence."

51. Laurence M. Keitt letter, May 30, 1864, Keitt Papers, DU; *OR* 36(3):851; Milling, "Jim Milling and the War." Dickert, *History of Kershaw's Brigade*, 367, reports that the 20th South Carolina joined the brigade "about the 28th of May," which seems to be an error. Chapter 3 in Carol Reardon, *With a Sword in One Hand and Jomini in the Other: The Problem of Military Thought in the Civil War North* (Chapel Hill: University of North Carolina Press, 2012), offers a brief assessment of the troubles in the Union army caused by injecting new units into old formations during the Overland campaign. The Army of Northern Virginia confronted the same issue at the same time.

52. Dickert, *History of Kershaw's Brigade*, 369–70.

53. Robert A. Stiles, *Four Years under Marse Robert* (New York: Neale, 1910), 274.

54. Milling, "Jim Milling and the War"; William P. DuBose, *Faith, Valor, and Devotion* (Columbia: University of South Carolina Press, 2010), 276; letter of "Tivoli" in Atlanta *Southern Confederacy*, June 17, 1864; William R. Stillwell letter, June 14, 1864, GDAH; Dickert, *History of Kershaw's Brigade*, 368; W. C. Hall diary, June 1, 1864, typescript at RNBP. "Tivoli" was a member of the 8th Georgia Infantry.

55. George W. Boatwright letter, May 29, 1864, photocopy at RNBP; letter of "W.R." in Richmond *Whig*, June 4, 1864; Nichols, *Soldier's Story of His Regiment*, 162; unsigned "Letter from Virginia" and full casualty list in Augusta *Daily Constitutionalist*, June 10, 1864; Krick, *Lee's Colonels*, 79; Nicholas Tompkins to Mrs. J. D. Brock, June 3, 1864, transcript at RNBP. Two companies skirmished along the North Anna on May 26, but this was the first major action in which the battalion fought together. The complete absence of the battalion's Company C from the casualty list suggests it did not participate at Cold Harbor, leaving Capers with only five companies.

56. Nichols, *Soldier's Story of His Regiment*, 163; George W. Boatwright letter, June 4, 1864, photocopy at RNBP. Boatwright was fatally wounded at the battle of Monocacy the following month.

57. *OR* 51(2):981–82, 36(3):864. The latter source proves that Patton was in command by June 1. Echols had aggressive friends who represented his interests in political circles all during the war. His May–June illness prompted one of those supporters to suggest to R. E. Lee that Echols could best protect his health by receiving a promotion to command of the Department of Southwestern Virginia. In a typical response, the commanding general suggested that if Echols really was as gravely ill as reported, "then I do not think he will be able to take command" of that department. See Robert K. Krick, "The Confederate Pattons," in Gary W. Gallagher, ed., *The Shenandoah Valley Campaign of 1864* (Chapel Hill: University of North Carolina Press, 2006), 341–69, for a complete look at Colonel Patton's life.

58. C. W. Humphreys, "Another Account of Breckinridge's Brigade at the Cold Harbor Battle," *Atlanta Journal*, February 22, 1902. Humphreys offers a dramatic and partisan account from the perspective of the Virginians. He reported that 156 members of his small battalion became prisoners of war that morning.

59. Forsberg memoir, WL; Rufus J. Woolwine diary, June 3, 1864, VHS; Daniel K. Schreckhise letter, June 6, 1864, bound vol. no. 168, RNBP; inspection report for Wharton's division, September 30, 1864, M935, roll 10, NARA. The specific mention of rifles on the brigade's left implies that some of Wharton's men still carried smoothbore muskets, even in the fourth summer of the war. The earliest available inspection report for the division is dated nearly four months later, shortly after the Third Battle of Winchester, by which time everyone in both brigades carried rifles. However, there had been ample opportunity to improve the quality of their small arms during the summer campaign in the Shenandoah Valley, after Cold Harbor.

60. Humphreys, "Another Account of Breckinridge's Brigade"; Hamill, "Boy's First Battle," 540. A fine source for more details on the Floridians' experience on June 3 is Zack C. Waters, "'Tell Them I Died Like a Confederate Soldier': Finegan's Florida Brigade at Cold Harbor," *Florida Historical Quarterly* 69 (October 1990): 156–75. The 2nd Maryland Infantry Battalion also participated in the counterattack, mingled

among the Floridians, and did equally good work. The battalion was new to Lee's army under that name but in fact was a reconstituted and renamed descendant of the original Maryland regiment that fought so well with the army during its early years.

61. Hamill, "Boy's First Battle," 540; Council Bryan letter, June 3, 1864, Bryan Papers, Florida State Archives, Tallahassee. Hamill, in common with almost everyone else, misspelled General Finegan's name.

62. Geer, "Memoir of the War."

63. Alfred L. Scott memoir, VHS, p. 24.

64. T. W. Brevard letter, June 7, 1864, FHS; "A.F.G." letter, June 7, 1864, UF. One of these two attacks cost the life of Pickens Butler Bird, the thirty-one-year-old major of the 6th Florida Battalion. See a full biographical sketch of that promising officer in Ferguson, *Hollywood Cemetery*, 19.

65. Carolyn C. Swiggart, *Shades of Gray: The Clay and McAllister Families of Bryan County Georgia during the Plantation Years* (Darien, Conn.: Two Bytes Publishing Co., 1999), 70–71; Hansell, "History of the 20th Georgia Battalion," GDAH; J. M. Reynolds letter, June 7, 1864, Dickey Family Papers, GDAH; *ORS* 17:618; William H. Locke letters, June 8, 22, 30, 1864, UVA. The 20th Georgia Cavalry Battalion joined the Jeff Davis Legion Cavalry Battalion on June 6 and eventually dissolved altogether, with the six companies spreading out among the 8th Georgia Cavalry, the 10th Georgia Cavalry, and the Jeff Davis Legion Cavalry. Love's obscure Alabama battalion also joined Young's old brigade on June 6 and was subsumed into Phillips's Legion by June 24. Amazingly, trooper W. H. Locke of the Alabama battalion rode a mule into the fight near White House Landing on June 21, having lost his horse earlier in the week. For an unbelievably complicated document announcing the rearrangement of all the Georgia, Alabama, and Mississippi cavalry companies in the army in July 1864, see *OR* 40(3):763.

66. Martin, *Flemington Martins*, 17; J. M. Reynolds letter, June 7, 1864, Dickey Family Papers, GDAH; McDaniel, *Confederate War Correspondence*, 241; William H. Locke letter, June 4, 1864, UVA; letter of W. A. Hunter quoted in Loderhouse, *Far, Far from Home*, 48.

67. Forsberg memoir, WL.

68. William Mahone endorsement on March 4, 1865, letter of resignation by Joseph Finegan, in Finegan's CSR, M331, roll 93, NA; William Mahone to Walter H. Taylor, March 20, 1865, in CSR of T. W. Brevard, M331, roll 32, NA. General Butler's South Carolina brigade was new to the army, too, but Butler himself was an old veteran in Virginia.

69. Steven H. Newton, *Lost for the Cause: The Confederate Army in 1864* (Mason City, Iowa: Savas, 2000), is a significant book that did not receive the attention it warrants when first published. It is a carefully documented investigation of Confederate army strengths during the final year of the war. The incessant mathematics can demoralize the reader, but the basic arguments advanced by Newton are interesting. He contends that the Confederate authorities failed to fully support Lee's army in the spring of 1864, that they had adequate resources to better cope with Grant and Butler, and that they chose instead to disperse their strength in remote theaters. "Historians must

now deal with Confederate strategic choices," argues Newton, "rather than simply attributing the near-disasters during the first weeks of the campaign to the lack of manpower" (53). The question of the administration's commitment to Lee's army must be measured in degrees of relativity. This essay shows that the War Department went to considerable lengths to provide the Army of Northern Virginia with more soldiers. Because Newton's work covers a much broader geographical range, his conclusions are not necessarily discordant with mine.

I Told Him to Go On

Enduring Cold Harbor

⊰ KATHRYN SHIVELY MEIER ⊱

Two accounts are commonly used to describe soldier experience at the battle of Cold Harbor. The first comes from *Campaigning with Grant*, the 1897 memoir of Lt. Gen. Ulysses S. Grant's staff officer Col. Horace Porter. Wrote Porter of the eve of the June 3, 1864, assaults, "In passing along on foot among the troops at the extreme front . . . I noticed that many of the soldiers had taken off their coats" and were "calmly writing their names and home addresses on slips of paper, and pinning them upon the backs of their coats, so that their dead bodies might be recognized upon the field, and their fate made known to their families." Unsubstantiated by other eyewitness narratives, Porter's tale may in fact be apocryphal. The second account comes from Confederate brigadier general Evander M. Law's 1887 recollection of the Union attacks on his lines: "The assaulting column swept over the old works" to become "a mass of writhing humanity, upon which our artillery and musketry played with cruel effect. . . . I had seen the dreadful carnage in front of Marye's Hill at Fredericksburg, and on the 'old railroad cut' which Jackson's men held at the Second Manassas; but I had seen nothing to exceed this. It was not war; it was murder."[1] As lines selected from broader recollections, both these depictions problematically emphasize the battle of Cold Harbor as an exceptional instance of horror in a campaign and war filled with it, and this limited perception has influenced academics and popular audiences alike.[2]

A more thorough reading of Law's account, however, indicates how soldiers survived the Overland campaign's capstone battle, which, rather than a departure, was more of the continuous operations, field fortifications, and assaults endemic to the spring and summer of 1864.[3] Just prior to his famous lines about murder, Law remembered exhorting a panicked soldier of his brigade with a prodigiously bleeding but superficial facial wound: "I told him to go on; he was not hurt. . . . He broke into a broad laugh, and the tears still running down his cheeks, trotted off, the happiest man I saw that day."[4] As an army officer Law performed his duty, and this soldier's collapse was fleeting and resolved. Indeed, rather than depict the fighting at Cold Harbor as mere slaughter, someone using this same reminiscence could view the battle as an exercise in endurance and resourcefulness buttressed by military structures of officership and camaraderie. Stressful as the two-week battle of Cold Harbor proved, it featured a rhythm of pressure and relief, as did the campaign at large. Over its course, few men broke; most managed to take Law's advice and go on.[5]

Nonetheless, many recent studies of Civil War soldiers emphasize the small group of men who could not cope with military service and became dysfunctional during or after the war. Such scholarship seeks "a virtual epidemic of emotional and psychiatric trauma," often exclusively underscoring instances of stressful combat without considering the broader context of soldiering, including the men's active attempts to shape their wartime experiences, or how structural influences, such as supplies, factored in.[6] Soldiers undoubtedly suffered—perhaps more than the literature allows by narrowing the scope to just combat—but by focusing on the few soldiers who broke down, perhaps permanently, we overlook the majority of volunteers who proved remarkably durable despite periodic despair or fatigue.[7]

To understand how soldiers endured the battle of Cold Harbor, or indeed, the grinding shift toward continuous operations, we must first place their experience within its proper context. Civil War soldiers experienced a range of stresses in addition to combat, such as environmental exposure, food shortages, and persistent illness. Further, Cold Harbor was not so exceptional as the opening accounts would lead us to believe. Even the environs smacked of continuity with the soldiers' past, as those men who fought on the old grounds of the 1862 battles for Richmond remarked in mid-June 1864. "My own beloved," scribbled a South Carolinian private, "You will see . . . that we have again changed our position and are now near the old battle field of two years ago. In fact, our Regt. is camped on the identical field of 'Frazier's Farm,' and I can look around me now and see several human skulls and numerous bones of the human bodies which have been removed from their shallow graves. These are all the evidences of the bloody strife which made this place historic." Likewise did South Carolinian Capt. Joseph B. Lyle observe at Gaines' Mill "neglected oats growing over" the graves of fallen soldiers; "skulls lay scattered." And in a particularly evocative account, another Confederate soldier noted, "We constantly come in contact with the traces of the memorable struggles of two years ago—shot & shell scatters over the ground—piles of human bones—sculls bare & ghastly crunching under your horses feet or wagon wheels & many other memorials of the former invasion & defeat."[8] Rather than encountering Cold Harbor as a discrete event, soldiers experienced it as part of a continuum; many of them literally had been there before.

Second, we must give Cold Harbor participants credit for actively, and for the most part successfully, surviving the mental and physical strains associated with the battle.[9] They did so by the same means they had used throughout the war: employed their military training, which stressed leadership and elbow-to-elbow camaraderie; drew on cultural conventions intended to circumscribe and script suffering, from sentimentalist writings to religion to notions of masculinity and courage; and resorted to what I term self-care, attempts to overcome perceived obstacles to mental and physical health.[10] Self-care techniques addressed a wide variety of challenges. Soldiers dealt with environmental threats, for example, by eradicating insects or reducing exposure; supplied deficiencies by foraging for food or other things; and mitigated homesickness by corresponding with loved ones.[11] When the mounting hardships at Cold Harbor threatened to impede the usual coping mechanisms, soldiers improvised, made do, and perhaps most important, relied upon the reprieves from frontline service to recover.[12] In short, they continued to endure.

The battle of Cold Harbor came on the heels of a month's relentless maneuver and combat involving strains that accompanied the use of significant fieldworks—lying in trenches, dodging sharpshooters, and conducting deadly assaults. Operations by the end of the battle of North Anna, May 23–26, had yielded nearly 65,000 total casualties. The maneuvering toward Cold Harbor from May 26 to June 12 involved more of the same style of combat but also, lest we minimize the less glamorous but equally strenuous side of soldiering, a significant amount of marching coupled with sleepless nights of digging earthworks and repositioning. Soldiers on both sides admitted to dangerously high levels of fatigue. Pvt. Edgar W. Clark of the 3rd Michigan Infantry wearily confirmed, "Some nights we will advance and then build breastworks and fortify our positions and work all night." Historian Carol Reardon reminds us that "lack of sleep destroyed endurance and eroded morale," making it a serious impediment to mental and physical health.[13]

On the night of May 26, Grant began to withdraw the Army of the Potomac from the North Anna River to Totopotomoy Creek along a punishing, roundabout route that required crossing the Pamunkey River twice and, for some corps, thirty-five miles of marching. From privates to the

In this sketch from early June 1864, Edwin Forbes captured a new feature of campaigning during the summer of 1864—construction of bombproofs for protection against enemy fire. Library of Congress Prints and Photographs Division, LC-DIG-ppmsca-20705.

general in chief (who was suffering from a migraine so severe that on the 27th he took chloroform for relief), Federals reached the point of physical and mental exhaustion, compounded in many cases by the typical soldier illnesses, such as headache and diarrhea. As the U.S. medical department reported in this period, "The number of men who fell out of the ranks was very large. All the ambulances were filled to overflowing, and a few men unavoidably left behind."[14]

For the soldiers of Maj. Gen. Winfield Scott Hancock's Second Corps, who had to be rushed from Totopotomoy Creek to Cold Harbor for assaults that Grant initially planned for June 2, the movement "was the most exasperating, patience-trying, and exhausting march the Second Corps ever made. . . . The night was unusually dark. By some blunder, we got on the wrong road; we became entangled in the woods; the artillery and infantry got mixed up in unutterable confusion; the heat was oppressive; the sand, shoe-mouth deep; the air thick with choking dust." The corps did not reach the battlefield until "after the time the general assault was to have been made," by then suffering "a condition of almost utter physical exhaustion." Grant postponed the attack several times on June 2, not only because "Hancock's men were so tired with their night's march of nearly 12 miles from their previous position on our extreme right, and the heat and dust so oppressive," but also because of "a violent rain-storm."[15]

Demanding as the marches proved, most Union soldiers managed to remain in the ranks by their own considerable efforts. Sgt. James Snook of the 50th New York Engineers was "sore & stiff as an old Horse" after being continually on the move with a persistent case of diarrhea and without a "good nights rest" for eight days straight. He did what he could to sustain himself along the way, plucking strawberries, napping at every halt; finally on May 29, "I went to the River & washed my feet & legs & changed my shirt. and got Lewy Caits to wash 2 Shts. & 1 drawers for me at 10 cts. apies." At last he collapsed for a full night's sleep, which somewhat refreshed him. Still Snook's illness lingered, rendering him "tired most to death" for the battle of Cold Harbor; however, he never reported to sick call and carried on constructing earthworks.[16] Despite considerable obstacles, Snook modeled a meticulous self-care routine that kept him at his duties.

When Gen. Robert E. Lee, still debilitated from dysentery that had plagued him at the North Anna, shifted his army on May 28, his men also contended with sleeplessness and vexing marches, despite the fact that they enjoyed interior lines that made for slightly shorter passage to the Totopotomoy. As Richmonder Pvt. Creed T. Davis completed a twenty-five-mile march, he begged and received "a few hours leave of absence" to recover. As a result, "I stood the march finely," though when reveille sounded on May 28 at 3:00 A.M., he "arose from my blankets tired. Fortunately I had a cup of coffee, which refreshed me very much."[17] Little reprieves, such as a few hours outside of the ranks, and the small comfort of a cup of coffee revived this weary Confederate from his considerable exhaustion.

The final three days of May saw enough fierce fighting at Totopotomoy Creek to keep the men continually on the alert before the bulk of both armies began maneuvering toward Cold Harbor on the night of the 31st. There they would remain until June 12, constructing entrenchments, shifting their lines, and conducting assaults. When they reached Cold Harbor, the work of erecting fortifications began all over again. One Confederate Marylander lamented: "As usual, we took our picks and spades and went to work throwing up redoubts, which were finished but in a temporary manner, by midnight. Much fatigued we unrolled our wet blankets for the first time for two or three nights, to take a short rest the best we could in water and mud."[18] To some Confederates, all the digging and marching seemed the product of poor planning on the part of officers, a sign that morale was in peril.[19] "Placed in position yesterday long enough to throw up breastworks for some body else to fight behind," Private Davis explained on June 1. "We are ordered to another part of the lines. Marched all last night and found ourselves this morning only one mile from the place from which started last evening. This was occasioned by ignorance of the roads. Many of the boys during the halts fell asleep on the road sides and were left behind."[20]

Once in position, soldiers also found lying behind earthworks, in rifle pits, and in trenches mentally stressful. Capt. T. C. Morton of the 26th Virginia Infantry recalled picket duty in "the cramped position" of the "narrow, single rifle-pits," looking "anxiously for the appearance of the 'relief.'" Morton expanded: "Independently of the physical strain that the picket has to endure, the sense of responsibility, as he feels himself to be the eyes and ears of the army, is an intense mental tax, that no one but he who has experienced it can realize." To his recollection, such arduous waiting wore on his morale: "As I sat there thinking, as I had never thought before, for never had death seemed so near, for the enemy's line was within ear-shot." Even at night those in the first line of trenches had to remain at the ready. After a fatiguing day of entrenching with cumbersome wooden planks (because of a shortage of tools) and an unsuccessful assault, the 7th Virginia Infantry "did not sleep much as we were aroused up several times thinking the enemy were advancing. Finding it to be false we would go back to bed again." Intermingled anxiety and sleeplessness made for worn-down soldiers.[21]

In such cases, the men had little choice but to wait their turn to be called off the lines for mental relief. For one Georgian noncommissioned officer, "our Brigade was relieved from duty in the trenches last night for the first time after nine days at this place and nineteen days on the south side . . . hotly engaged four days, and skirmishing and under artillery fire the rest of the time. Thus, you will see that we are grateful for these days of rest which we have been promised." With reluctance he admitted, "Tomorrow night it will expire and then we expect to go to the front again."[22] Though enervated soldiers found it disappointing to contemplate a return to action, rest behind the lines enabled them to resume their duties.

As many of these accounts suggest, environmental factors such as weather, terrain, and insects compounded the stress brought on by marching, sleeplessness, and waiting in field fortifications.[23] Contemporary disease theory held that changeable weather and low, marshy terrain could trigger illness and even melancholy. Though this science is faulty by modern standards, behaviors such as avoiding intense heat or standing water could indeed help prevent sunstroke or contact with malarial mosquitoes and proved useful in staving off disease as well as mental fatigue.[24] Civil War soldiers therefore sought to mitigate the sources of environmental discomfort, which proved a challenging endeavor when they were confined to earthworks and engaged in heavy combat.

While the majority of men complained of intense heat and intermittent thunderstorms, many refused to helplessly suffer nature's whims.[25] One soldier from Richmond wrote home regarding a variety of ways soldiers sought to diminish the effects of blistering sun: "There is an ice house on the farm & in hand plenty of ice-water, which is very palatable in this extremely hot weather." Bathing provided acute relief—"I wish you would bring a piece of soap if you can get it," he instructed his local friend—as did good, old-fashioned shade: "Hot, hot, hot, we are just sweltering, laying around in any shady place we can find." Heat dried out the dirt, generating irksome clouds of dust. "The heat is intolerable, and the roads are covered with dust six or eight inches deep, which every gust of wind sweeps up, covering everything with a dirty, white coating," bemoaned Massachusetts surgeon John G. Perry on June 10. Although rain nearly flooded the trenches when it did come, some soldiers managed to see the benefits: "About sundown copious showers came up, accompanied with heavy thunder and sharp lightning. The rain was most welcome, because it cooled the air, laid the dust and filled the hollows with pure water, which we had sadly lacked for several days. It wet us all to the skin, but we did not care about that; in fact, we enjoyed it as the first 'bath' we had had for a fortnight."[26] As historian Earl Hess elucidates, reshaping one's environmental trials into a positive experience was a typical soldier coping mechanism.[27]

In addition to exposure to the weather, soldiers dreaded campaigning in wooded, marshy terrain and sought to counteract the perceived ill effects on their health. Popular conceptions of health posited that swamps were miasmatic, conducting fevers and diarrhea, and while bacteria and disease vectors were not yet understood, lowland forests clearly featured unpalatable water and teemed with irksome insects.[28] Col. Theodore Lyman, staff officer to Maj. Gen. George G. Meade, wrote of Hancock's aide-de-camp Maj. William G. Mitchell that "there were many wood-ticks eating him, but . . . he had not strength to fight them!" Additionally, the mosquitoes common to Virginia already had begun to congregate in late spring, and hordes of flies buzzed from dead bodies to latrines to one's meal.[29] An official Union medical report noted with concern that dead army horses were

I Told Him to Go On

scattered at "regular intervals of from 50 to 100 yards, and the infantry had the full benefit of the results of their putrefaction." Though soldiers missed the connection between the resulting flies and prevailing illnesses, such as typhoid and diarrhea, the fact that the dead bodies were damaging to health was not lost on them or their surgeons. They considered the rotting flesh itself to be miasmatic: "Owing to the heat and the stench from half-buried bodies of men and horses, numbers of soldiers became sick."[30]

As a defense against insects, soldiers often relied on smoke from their fires or frequent bathing; however, the most comprehensive self-care technique used to address exposure to pests, miasmas, and weather was the erection of elaborate shelters. In the midst of a rainstorm, soldiers huddled under their rubber blankets and piled boughs of cedar and pine to provide flooring and roofing for their trenches.[31] Others constructed beds of straw or stretched tarpaulins over the top of their rifle pits.[32] The earthworks were not merely designed to protect from enemy fire; the soldiers took great pride in constructing temporary homes that provided comfort under grating environmental conditions and activity amid the waiting. Sgt. Joseph K. Taylor of the 37th Massachusetts Infantry marveled to his father of the Cold Harbor battlefield: "It is amusing to see the tents or fortifications (fortified burrows they might be called) which the soldiers have built around this vicinity. Some have dug large holes in the ground, and covered them with logs and piled a bank of earth [on] top, leaving a space sufficient for a passage in and out of the subterranean abodes, while others . . . have thrown up a small rifle pit and pitched their tents behind it, but most all of these private residences are fortified in some manner." Even in the most exposed positions, the men made do and attained the coveted prize of sleep. "It was the first time I had ever been on the lines at night, and it was a strange and novel scene. About two-thirds of the men were asleep. Fast asleep! Lying in every conceivable position, propped up or leaning against the breastworks, or lying in the ditch, with a cartridge box or blanket for a pillow . . . every man, asleep or awake clasping his Enfield rifle."[33] Field experience and military training taught veterans the importance of shelter and sleep at the ready, enabling them to survive the twenty-four to forty-eight hours they inhabited the frontline trenches.

At the first opportunity of relief, soldiers fell back to positions where they could enjoy the shelter of trees or actual roofs over their heads, which noticeably alleviated the physical and mental fatigue engendered by exposure on the battlefield. On June 8, Pvt. Charles Wellington Reed, a light artillerist from Massachusetts, explained, "About noon we packed up and

changed camp to a fine pleasant situation in the edge of a pine grove."
Reed's repeated use of the word "pleasant," despite scorching weather, suggested a marked improvement in his spirits once behind the lines: "June 9 in the pines near Coal Harbor. Rather warm but deliciously cool and pleasant in the shady woods with its gentle breeze." The next day he welcomed another "delightful cool and pleasant day."[34]

Other soldiers explored and rested in nearby civilian homes, enjoying not only respite from exposure but also amusement and distraction. Pvt. John West Haley from Maine was particularly vocal about his exploits in civilian abodes whenever he was released from the earthworks. At one point, he visited (and ransacked) "the house of a minister who had vacated when we approached and left everything at our mercy. There was a piano, stuffed furniture.... We played on the piano, and took what we could of the other things." With evident satisfaction Haley quipped, "When the cat is away the mice will play." In a separate incident, while pilfering apples from a civilian's orchard and beans near "an old house," he found a man confined to a cage, "or what was once a man.... He was as wild as a beast and this was the only way that anything could be done with him. No clothing could be kept on him. His food was let down through a hole in the wall far above his head.... His finger nails were more than an inch long and his hair also was of tremendous length, and on the whole he was the most perfect wreck of a human being I ever saw." Odd as the incident was, it provided an absorbing diversion the day after the grim assaults of June 3 and following several days of lying in works Haley had dubbed "the filthiest place we have lodged in thus far."[35]

Besides exhaustion compounded by environmental factors, soldiers at Cold Harbor and throughout the Overland campaign dealt with unreliable access to food and water. These material necessities topped the list of soldier concerns with swift and profound implications for their commitment to the task at hand.[36] Because of the rapid and unremitting pace of the Overland campaign, supply trains had difficulty keeping up with the armies, particularly on the Union side.[37] A New York engineer erecting pontoons on the Pamunkey River complained on May 28 that he had gone "20 hours without eating" and by June 1 fell ill from weakness and exhaustion. A musician of the 2nd Vermont Infantry confirmed, "We have been very hard up for rations. I have seen soldiers that had not had a cracker to eat for two days and offered a dollar for two of them." Even those men who better managed their resources, as they often drew several days' rations at a time, were intensely relieved as the supply trains caught up on May 30 and

31. "Our supply train came up before noon and we drew two days rations. They were very acceptable as I had only 4 hardtack left and I had made up my mind to forage soon," confessed a Connecticut artillerist with considerable relief.[38] Foraging may well have meant falling out of the ranks and being construed a straggler.

The perpetually poorly fed Rebel soldiers likewise lived on the lean in late May. A Confederate Marylander described men on the North Anna as "suffering greatly from the want of bread + water, this being the second day since they have had anything to eat. They are drinking the muddy water in the trenches." By May 25, however, they "found rations, cold steel pone." As Lee's army drew closer to Richmond, some Confederate regiments celebrated a relative bonanza in supplies sufficient to make them magnanimous toward the starving civilians in Richmond. "Wee git plenty to eat Bacon corne bread cotte shugar peas and the poore people of Richmond has cauld on the soulders to give them one days of thare rations and wee have give them one days rations," explained Virginian Cpl. Archibald F. McGrady. Confirmed South Carolinian Frederick P. Leverrett, "The men have been better fed since being about Richmond. We have Bacon & Corn Meal & salt, occasionally flour; sometimes Coffee & Sugar [and once] Onions."[39] Waxing and waning of bare necessities understandably corresponded to peaks and valleys in soldier morale.

No matter the quantity and quality of one's rations, being confined to the breastworks made it difficult to cook, to receive prepared food from the company cooks, and to secure adequate water. Soldiers were able to achieve some limited cooking, such as boiling coffee, but they had to do so without breaching the top of their fortifications for fear of being picked off by the merciless sharpshooters.[40] For soldiers on the front lines, running out of food often meant simply waiting to be deployed to the rear. On June 9, Richard Robertson of the 8th Maine Infantry was feeling rather morose: "Our company is all out of rations nothing to eat." It was not until June 11 that he and his regiment "moved back a mile or so + have got our dinner."[41] Waiting on food was one thing; being deprived of water was quite another. Some soldiers dipped canteens into the trenches when it rained, an unsanitary enterprise considering the mud and the filth produced by soldiers who feared venturing aboveground to relieve themselves, while others braved the hailstorm of bullets to quench their thirst.[42] Nightfall facilitated the latter: "Darkness was always welcome when such days of proximity to the foe were the order. Welcome darkness gave you

"The Federal Army Intrenched before Petersburg—A Night Scene in the Trenches." Edwin Forbes, whose wartime sketches often appeared in *Frank Leslie's Illustrated Newspaper*, depicted Union soldiers in various poses of relaxation behind their breastworks. Paul F. Mottelay and T. Campbell-Copeland, eds., *The Soldier in Our Civil War*, 2 vols. (New York: Stanley Bradley Publishing Company, 1893), 2:290–91.

an opportunity to straighten up and move about, and go back and get canteens of water."[43]

In an incident at Totopotomoy Creek, Virginian Captain Morton recalled with some drollness the ordeal of having cooked food delivered to the trenches. A soldier detailed to prepare a meal from his company "was on his way back to the line with a camp-kettle full of corn-bread and beef on his arm when the cannonading commenced. He ran toward the breastworks for protection, while the hungry men in the trenches watched his race through the ploughing shot and shell, almost as solicitous for the safety of their breakfast, perhaps, as for that of their comrade." Regrettably, a round exploded right in front of their sprinting cook. "When the smoke cleared away the bloody fragments of the man and the scattered contents of the camp-kettle lay mingled together on the ground before our eyes." According to Morton the loss of the meal weighed more heavily on the soldiers than did the casualty. "Lor', boys," exclaimed one onlooker, "Just look. Joe Flint is all mixed up with our breakfast, and it aint fit for nothing!" For the moment hunger dominated their sympathies. With some chagrin Morton confessed, "Such want of sentiment . . . sounds strange and heartless to us now, but in those times of courage and every-day suffering, the hungry soldier's remark, finding an echo in the empty stomachs of his fellows, did not seem so much out of place."[44]

Morton could have tempered the tale in retrospect, but instead he provided insight into soldiers' priorities as well as their means of coping with carnage that might strike some as rather unsavory. As historian Earl Hess explains, "living with war" meant embracing the macabre, in which the men could still have fun, joke, and "laugh at the sight of a man who had been shot in an unusual way." Likewise does Frances Clarke note the cultural importance of sangfroid, the "breezy unconcern" that distinguished the model mid-nineteenth-century sufferer, enabling him to laugh and banter in the face of wounds and death.[45]

Subsisting too often on hardtack and cornbread compelled soldiers on both sides to seek variety in their diets, contributing to improved dispositions and physical health. Some of them bartered and exchanged rations with other regiments or even across enemy lines.[46] The connection between the dreaded scurvy, which caused weakness, pain, and a depression of spirit, and lack of fruits and vegetables was not lost on the men. Wrote one soldier from Massachusetts, "I was very near having the scurvy from being deprived of all acids. I craved acid and acrid substances, ate sorrel, green berries etc." Foraging or taking from local residents was the usual remedy for a paucity of vegetables. Michigander Private Clark remarked with palpable eagerness, "Green berries are getting good to eat. I went yesterday and got a lot of huckleberries and cooked them. I have had green peas and green apples." Some of the men proved willing to risk life and limb, so great was their longing for "something green." A private from Maine wanted green apples "bad enough . . . to cross an open field, where the bullets were flying thick and fast." He, too, was anxious about scurvy: "we had sorely felt the need of something sour for a long time the scurvy had broken out among us and fruit is the best remedy known for this disease."[47]

As the accounts thus far have made clear, both sides abided a dire lack of sanitation at Cold Harbor. Though contemporary science had not yet laid bare the world of the microbe, the hygiene reform movements of the antebellum era had raised awareness of the necessity of keeping one's body and clothing washed. Furthermore, soldiers considered bathing refreshing and restorative of their spirits.[48] The rapid rate of campaigning and constant lying about in defensive fortifications posed the main impediments to cleanliness in the Overland campaign, making it difficult to relieve oneself, change undergarments, wash out wool uniforms, and bathe. Surg. Daniel M. Holt called Cold Harbor "a stinking hole" for its trench conditions. A soldier from Maine trembled in his pit, "I want to piss but I dare not get up." He never explained the outcome of his dilemma, but one can venture a guess. A soldier of the 12th Virginia Infantry wrote his friend Stanley on June 10, 1864, with a touch of exasperation, "Yesterday I washed and changed my clothes *for the first time since the 18th of May*—part of the 'honor and glory' of soldiering, what do you think of that; does that accord with your preconceived notions of a soldier's life?"[49]

Not only could good hygiene prevent disease, but it also swiftly improved the countenance of sick and demoralized men. Vermonter Herbert George explained in his correspondence that every time he began to feel ill from the battle of North Anna through Cold Harbor, he bathed or changed clothes as a means of relief. On May 24, he recorded, "While we lay resting back near the North Anna river to day Charlie & I went swimming & washed our shirts which made us feel much better," and on the 28th, "I went swimming in the Pawmunkey to day had a nice time in the water." Though his headache subsequently grew almost unbearable, he was not able to bathe and launder his clothes again until early July. On July 4, he was detailed to "really dirty and dusty" railroad work but when he finally "changed [his] clothes," he felt "100 percent better." A week or so later found George still relying on hygiene to address his illness: "Head aches yet and dont feel very smart. Went and washed in the Appomattox and feel some better." Even for a regimental surgeon, washing was a thing of celebration worthy of writing home to one's wife about: "For the first time since the opening of the campaign *had my clothes washed*!"[50]

As the Union official medical records confirmed, the physical conditions at Cold Harbor caused a surge of illness among the troops, a reminder that misery at the battle extended beyond the booming of cannon and musketry.[51] The U.S. medical department noted that the number of sick in the Army of the Potomac "increased largely during the first half of June, and the severity of cases became greater," citing "malarial and typho-malarial fevers and diarrhea" as the "prevailing diseases." The report attributed the spike to the same problems dwelt upon by the soldiers: fatigue, or the "constant labor and watchfulness of the previous month"; the terrain, which was "low and marshy in character, the water derived almost entirely from surface drainage"; and "the condition of the men in the trenches," which was "very bad, in a sanitary point of view." Among trench conditions cited were a lack of vegetable rations for more than a month, beef "used . . . from cattle who were exhausted by the long march through the country but scantily provided with forage," and the soldiers' simplistic cooking, amplified by the fact that the "men had to lie close behind the breast-works to avoid the sharpshooters." Further, "dead horses and offal of various kinds were scattered over the country everywhere, and between the lines were many dead bodies of either party unburied and decomposing in the burning sun." Because of the enormous casualty toll exacted by the previous battles of the Overland campaign, a "large number of recruits joined the army at this place, and contributed greatly to swell the sick list," as was typical with an influx of men new to crowds and contagious diseases. The report found "no distinct cases of scurvy . . . at this time, but a scorbutic taint was undoubtedly affecting the army and depressing its health and spirits." In response June 6 saw a push to augment the fresh vegetable ration and to police the digging of sinks and burying of offal, while June 7 saw the famed truce between Grant and Lee, which enabled burial of the dead between the lines.[52]

In the ranks, soldiers coped with increasing illness in the usual ways despite limited mobility in the earthworks. Prevention was always the best policy, and the self-care techniques, such as bathing or foraging, that thwarted exposure and dietary deficiencies proved most helpful in staving off sickness. When disease did strike, straggling remained the most common means by which to secure rest, recuperation, and aid from locals. Wrote Richard Robertson of the 8th Maine Infantry at his weakest, "A good many of the boys fell out by the way[.] I thought I must fall out" too. He and his comrades scattered about the woods to recover in the thick shade. Those who did straggle in times of sickness faced potential scorn from senior officers, particularly surgeons, who accused them of feigning illness to avoid duty. Surg. J. Franklin Dyer contemptuously noted, "Loafers and malingerers gather about the hospital on the plea of sickness. . . . I have sent for a detachment of the provost guard to escort them to their regiments, for it is useless to send them except under guard. There are hundreds of men straggling in the woods—coffee boilers who drop out on the march when they get a chance. They steal whenever they can and never fight."[53] Robertson's preceding story should make one think twice before accepting Dyer's assessment uncritically; resting in the shade revived soldiers and enabled their return to the ranks.[54]

Because of class conceptions of manly duty, officers faced more pressure than the enlisted to remain in the ranks even when sick.[55] Surgeon Dyer once again critiqued, "Colonel Wass has not been with his regiment for some days." Though he did not deny the colonel's illness, he pressed that "it is a very unfortunate thing for an officer's reputation to be sick at such a time. He had better keep with his command as long as he can stand—do anything but go to the rear. I know officers and men now with their commands who are suffering from slight wounds, and sickness besides, who will not go to the rear, while others go on the slightest excuse if permission can be obtained."[56] According to the cultural conventions of the time, the middle to upper classes were cheerfully to bear affliction and to police the lower classes from falling victim to moral weakness.[57] Lest we be too quick to disparage Victorian policing of suffering, social shaming did serve to buttress the endurance of soldiers and keep them at task. Further, enlisted men sought to emulate the behavior of the elite, though as historian Frances Clarke notes, "in a more egalitarian context . . . indicating that they were good sports."[58]

Sometimes the pressures of illness, environmental strain, and exhaustion simply outweighed cultural anxiety. Pvt. George B. Battle eventually resigned himself to his fate: "We fought for three or four hours . . . in a drenching rain" then "lay there half the night, in the mud and water, behind our little mound of earth thrown up with our bayonets and hands" before marching back to his regiment's original breastworks six miles away, "reaching there about daybreak. Since then I have been troubled with a weakness in the back and a general exhaustion or over fatigue. I was not able to keep up and do duty with the Regiment, so I was sent off with a lot of wounded, as that was no place for a sick man."[59]

As Battle's evident dismay indicates, most soldiers hoped to avoid being sent to the hospital. Virginian Private Davis confirmed, "The long looked for relief came last night. But it will be a very short respite. . . . I am quite sick with the diarhoea this morning, but will try and keep up with the battery, rather than go to the Hospital."[60] Part of the fear of hospitals was being removed from familiar faces from home.[61] If a sick man could manage to remain in the ranks, comrades would nurse him and keep his anxious family apprised of his progress. "Gene is suffering . . . with stomach ache. . . . I shall see that he is well taken care of. He stands it finely on the whole," reassured Robert A. Stiles of the Richmond Howitzers. Going to

I Told Him to Go On

the hospital also potentially meant being exposed to a sicklier environment with overburdened staff. A steward recounted the turmoil of the Union hospital depot at White House Landing: "It was soon covered with tents, kitchens, and feeding-stations, and more than eight thousand men passed through our hands. . . . As one looks back upon that hospital encampment and all the suffering witnessed there, its distinctive features are lost in the confused recollection of agonizing sights and sounds, of sleepless nights, of days crowded full of effort to relive the victims of that fearful conflict."[62]

As many soldiers had learned by experience, lying in the hospital could exacerbate sickness rather than foster recovery because of the poor medical practices of the time. Lt. Samuel T. McCullough went into the hospital for a gunshot wound but ended up with a crippling illness. He noted that he had not been able to change his underclothes for four weeks. In some cases for Confederate soldiers in Richmond hospitals, food was even more difficult to procure in the city than it had been in the ranks because of exorbitant inflation. This lack of food only contributed to their weakened states. Explained one such Georgian, "I am mending and would soon be well again if I could only get something fit to eat which we do not have. . . . If you see any body coming here send me a box of something to eat and I will pay them for bringing it. Everything is so high here we can't afford to buy nothing."[63] In short, as mentally and physically taxing as remaining with one's regiment could be, the hospital often proved a worse venue for health.

Throughout the Overland campaign, soldiers on both sides learned that evacuation from the front lines was no easy feat, contributing to the stress of being sick or wounded at the battle. The challenge stemmed in large part from the nature of defensive warfare, with its no-man's-lands and profusion of sharpshooters. Additionally, though both sides had come a long way in improving medical structures from the beginning of the war, the vast number of casualties incurred during the Overland campaign burdened both medical departments to their breaking points. On the Confederate side, several of the Richmond hospitals had closed temporarily in early 1864, their patients sent to Chimborazo and Jackson to enable nurses to return to the field. The burden of sick and wounded in May and June forced all the hospitals to reopen, with patients spilling out onto their lawns in temporary bivouacs waiting for access to the coveted bed spaces. Additionally, by the end of the Overland campaign the Army of Northern Virginia still suffered from deficient ambulance evacuation, which all too often meant soldiers served double duty as stretcher bearers, who conveyed the wounded and sick to waiting trains.[64]

On the Union side the new ambulance corps, which generalized Army of the Potomac medical director Jonathan Letterman's evacuation system to the entire U.S. army in December 1863, had been steadily training throughout the spring of 1864. Ironically, the congressional bill that enabled the ambulance corps actually reduced the number of ambulances designated for the Army of the Potomac, because the new allotment depended on the size of regiments. Thus the men under Letterman's purview faced the Overland campaign with 400 fewer ambulances than they had possessed at Gettysburg. This shortage combined with the quick pace of the campaign and the unexpectedly large volume of casualties encumbered the system. Furthermore, until May 30 the main hospital depot for the Army of the Potomac was at Fredericksburg, a long journey that produced heartrending reports from drivers of the sick and wounded begging to be shot and divested of their misery. Relocating the depot to White House Landing in late May significantly shortened the lines, making the trek somewhat more endurable.[65]

Under these circumstances, both Confederates and Federals went to great lengths to remove wounded soldiers to safety and care of their own volition, a practice that illustrates the strength of esprit de corps and courage under fire. Vermonter Samuel E. Pingree provided a detailed account of these attempts. If a man got wounded, "we dig a sap to him & bring him in—this don't pay unless he is wounded in fore noon for it takes half a day to dig to them generally & if afternoon we let him lay till dark then get him." As with tending ill comrades, soldiers knew they would have to provide an account of the assistance they had offered to fallen soldiers' families, so they felt external pressure in addition to the expectations of military comradeship. One New York heavy artillerist wrote to his friend's parents informing them of their son's wounding: "I saw Alexander on the night after the battle as he was brought from the field, and assisted in carrying him into a house and laying him on a feather bed which was thrown on the floor. He was badly and I thought mortally wounded. . . . I gave him some water, bathed his head and made him as comfortable as possible under the circumstances," finally assisting him to an ambulance train he believed bound for Washington.[66] The loving, gentle care afforded the wounded soldier speaks to the intimacy of friendships fostered in the ranks.

This account as well as the letter of another New Yorker, Lt. James W.

Hildreth, further reveals that soldiers assisting the wounded might have well been construed as stragglers, as they were absent from the ranks for hours or even days at a time. "John Hatch of Pike was shot through the shoulder but not very bad," Hildreth related to his own parents. "I took him to the rear & stayed all night with him in the woods. Yesterday we went to the hospital. He was wounded by a sharp shooter." Thus did Hildreth miss at least a night and a day of service before reporting back to his battery. No doubt Hildreth's parents spread the news to Hatch's family, providing some modicum of comfort in their distress, yet Hildreth had exposed himself to possible disciplinary consequences in the process. Soldiers such as Hildreth faced a cultural dilemma when it came to upholding their reputations of moral courage: on one hand, Hildreth had risked his life to save his friend, but on the other, he faced potential ridicule as an undedicated straggler.[67]

For men shot too far from friendly lines to be recovered, occasionally civilians would rally to their assistance, easing the lonely and frightening experience of being wounded and separated from one's unit. Georgian Pvt. J. M. Reynolds wrote of being "wounded slightly in left temple by a Minnie ball," which broke his arm. "After the fall came my worse part—being out off from our lines I had a hard time getting back again—I went about six miles down the Yankee lines in the rear," sometimes crawling "within forty yards of their tents. I would never have reached our lines but for the kindness of an old man."[68] The old man saved Reynolds not only from capture but also from despair in some of the most trying hours of his life.

The rotting bodies and wailing wounded between the lines who could not be recovered, as well as the accumulating losses of friends, prompted moments of deep sorrow for those lying in the trenches. Some began to contemplate their own probability of being wounded or killed. Explained Private Davis, "I never think of death except when actually engaged in battle. Then indeed I am filled with fear." Sergeant Kilbourn, a soldier in the 2nd Connecticut Heavy Artillery, a unit that suffered tremendous losses in its first field combat, penned listlessly, "I am feeling week and have nothing to complain of though I cannot but feel sad at the loss of dear friends." Isolated in his rifle pit, Vermonter Captain Pratt ticked off a lengthy list of friends who had perished or been wounded so far at Cold Harbor, though one weighed most heavily on him. "Poor Mike was killed. Like losing a brother. Sharpshooters picking [men] off. . . . Number shot going after water." When he was finally relieved, he took the opportunity to bury his dear friend. "Oh how sorry I feel for Mike, can hardly realize he is dead. . . .

KATHRYN SHIVELY MEIER

Oh war, how horrible. Great god, When will the punishment of our nation cease." In many cases it fell to these men to deliver the sad news of their friends' departures to their families, as was the case for Georgian Nicholas Tompkins. "It is in sadness that I announce to you the Death of your Husband, J. D. Brock. . . . We tender to you our simpathies in this your great bereavement. We have lost a good sociable member out of our company + the confederacy a brave soldier. We hope and believe he is in a better world than this."[69] While these accounts exhibit clear distress and pain at the loss of friends, the active roles soldiers played in stewarding their departed friends' bodies and memories did offer some solace. As Tompkins's letter reminds us, religion also played a major role in fostering comfort.[70]

Despite periodic despondency in the trenches, many soldiers on the front lines of Cold Harbor alluded to a sense of mental relief when Grant and Lee finally agreed to a burial truce on June 7.[71] One recollection in the *Southern Historical Society Papers* explained the mental burden everyone in the vicinity had been suffering under: "The cries and groans and appeals for help appalled the sternest. And yet another day and night passed, and still a third, and the fallen lay where they had been stricken down. The cries of hundreds had ceased, as death had mercifully come to their relief." At the time, however, many of the men were more concerned with the nauseating stench than their sympathies: "The *very worst* day of the campaign! Discord and disorder on every hand. The woods full of dead, dying and wounded men. Literally *heaps* of dead men meet the eye on all sides. Stench like that of putrid carcasses, flavors your food, while the water is thick with all manner of impurities." As the bodies were finally cleared away, mental and physical relief palpably washed over the ranks. One Mississippian commented on fraternization across the lines: "Over the breastworks went Rebel and Yank, and met between the lines, and commenced laughing and talking, and you would have thought that old friends had met after a long separation. Some were talking earnestly together, some swapping coffee for tobacco, some were wrestling, some boxing, others trading knives." Meanwhile the grim task of the pioneer corps carried on "burying the dead, and hustling them into the ground as rapidly as possible, the dead were terribly swollen, and as black as an Ethiopian and it was really a horrible scene."[72] The contrast should serve to remind us that in the midst of the most terrible scenes of Cold Harbor, the men gratefully embraced even the smallest opportunities for relief.

Thus moments of discouragement were authentic but not necessarily crippling. Even the regiments new to carnage could recover from loss

I Told Him to Go On

during a reprieve from frontline service. The notebook of Confederate Pvt. Henry R. Berkeley is instructive on this process of healing. Prior to the battle of Cold Harbor he confessed, "My company has been very fortunate, not having yet had but one single man wounded." Yet on June 3 his trials began: "To-day we were ordered into position under a most tremendous artillery fire. . . . I am the only one of six-mess-mates left, who went in to the fight this morning, who has not been wounded. We had eight men killed on the field and some 40 wounded, and thirty-five horses killed. Yet notwithstanding this heavy loss, we held our position and are still ready to do good work." By the end of the day, he had also lost his "noble friend and bosom companion," Edmund: "I little thought, when we separated this morning, that it was for the last time on earth. Such is war." Berkeley's battery was relieved on June 4, and he "went by our field Hospital and saw Edmund Anderson's body. He looked perfectly natural. His friends in Richmond have been notified of his death and will come for his body to day." After several days of rest, Berkeley found the strength to regroup, even replacing his departed messmates on June 6: "Formed a mess to-day with John McCary and John McCausland; they are from Lynchburg. They are good-men." Messes provided true friends, who not only bolstered each other's spirits but also shared food and nursed fellow messmates in times of illness. They were essential to support and recovery. Further, Berkeley "bathed and put on some clean clothes [and was] very much refreshed by it."[73] Continued camaraderie and self-care rituals therefore provided means of persevering through the darkest hours of the Overland campaign.

Even long after the war, soldiers continued to employ the same means of coping with the carnage they had witnessed, or at least remained concerned with upholding their public record of manly forbearance and courage.[74] For instance, returning to General Law's opening account in more detail, one is struck by his lighthearted, almost playful tone. Allegedly, Law found the Alabamian from his brigade "running to the rear through the storm of bullets that swept the hill . . . crying like a big baby, and was the bloodiest man I ever saw." The man believed himself "'dead! I am killed! Look at this!' showing his wound," in which a minié ball had barreled through his cheek and the flesh of his neck. "Finding it was only a flesh-wound, I told him to go on; he was not hurt. He looked at me doubtfully for a second as if questioning my veracity or my surgical knowledge. . . . Then as if satisfied with my diagnosis, he broke into a broad laugh" and "trotted off, the happiest man I saw that day."[75]

KATHRYN SHIVELY MEIER

In a similar vein, Captain Morton recalled an incident involving John Ford, a member of his company. A shell landed just a few feet from Ford with "the fuse still smoking and spitting and an explosion momentarily imminent. John took in the situation at a glance" and, deciding "that the safest thing for him to do was to get down into the ground, commenced at once to work down into the sand with hands, legs, and head." The men encouraged him: "'scratch John! scratch! she's a going off!' . . . The sand all around him was in commotion, and in the few seconds that the fizzing fuse gave him, he burrowed like a great gopher till nothing but the top of his hump could be seen as the loose sand settled around it." Morton and his men held their breath "expecting the next second to see the poor fellow blown to atoms. Then the explosion came with a tremendous jar that shook the ground and sent a hundred pieces of iron singing through the air." As the dust lifted, "the first sight that came to view was the head of Ford, happily, still on his shoulders." Ford called out, "'Who-eeh,' as cheerily as if he had treed a coon instead of been face to face with death a second before. An answering cheer and a laugh went up from the boys on the line, and the incident was the next minute forgotten."[76] While both reminiscences were written by officers who had a special stake in maintaining public reputations, historian Frances Clarke notes that enlisted men sought to emulate their superiors with such displays of "breezy" forbearance.[77]

Civil War surgeons, an officer class singled out by some scholars as more prone to psychological breakdown because of their intimate interactions with battle wounds, were, in fact, governed by the same cultural and military conventions as their military peers.[78] Like all soldiers, they experienced a waxing and waning of their responsibilities that enabled respite and recovery. Though Ohio surgeon Almon Clarke remembered his field service as exceptionally taxing, in part because he was subject to orders rather than his sympathies, the rhythms of his service are also apparent. When he was removing a bullet from a wounded man's shoulder in his field hospital "among the trees in the yard of the old Cold Harbor Tavern," suddenly a riding crop lashed across his cheeks wielded by none other than the medical director of the Sixth Corps. "In a loud and irritating manner he demanded to know what I was there for, and denied that I had been ordered there by any one, saying that my place was a nearer the troops." Clarke's superior violated his personal honor as well as his sense of duty to his men. Clarke was then ordered "a quarter mile nearer the front. As soon as I could recover voice I urged the immediate need of my service where so many of my own men were hurt and some of them dying, but to no purpose; so,

I Told Him to Go On

controlling myself the best I could I started with my orderly for the place indicated, and did not dress another wound that day, as the injured were all back at the tavern." Though "we remained there several days, shells bursting over us and bullets hitting the trees," he found very little work to do, transitioning from a period of high stress to prolonged inactivity.[79]

As Clarke's memoir confirms and medical historian George W. Adams writes, work for surgeons alternated between frenzied periods and dry spells with just the single hour of sick call. Even Surgeon Dyer, who was so critical of those military officers who strayed from their regiments when sick, spent a great deal of the battle of Cold Harbor loafing. On June 1 he arranged for the wounded to be sent to White House Landing and then "went up to division headquarters at Washington Jones's house and slept. There was a constant skirmish fire all night, and a good many orders received and sent out. But I got a number of the *Atlantic Monthly* from General Tyler and read an article on doing housework, a very quiet sort of reading for such times, continually interrupted by sharp firing, or the whistle of a stray bullet." The next morning while Hancock's troops labored toward the front lines for their famed assault, Dyer and Brig. Gen. John Gibbon breakfasted together and read the newspaper in a jolly mood. "I was enjoying the fragrance of a bouquet of roses; the band of the Eighth New York was playing. The Negroes ... were gaping and listening to the music, while three hundred yards in front there was pieces of artillery firing and farther in front a sharp skirmish going on, every moment someone being hit—orderlies coming and going—business going on as usual—boys washing dishes and blacking boots, everybody minding his own business."[80] For Dyer the battle of Cold Harbor appeared more akin to leave than to some of the most desperate combat of the war.

Whether a surgeon or otherwise, one of the most important ways that Civil War soldiers actively bolstered faltering spirits was by writing and receiving letters from home. Correspondence connected soldiers to their loved ones, refocusing their minds away from the battlefield on pleasanter thoughts. One soldier wrote from a rifle pit to his sweetheart in Mechanicsville, "I send you a relic of Rebellion which will put you in mind of orange blossom. I took it from Hanover Courthouse while we were skirmishing with the rebs."[81] Wright drew comfort from the knowledge that the blossom served as a physical link between his correspondent and himself.[82] Likewise did Armistead Blanton seek "to hear something from those whose minds are not distracted by the 'din of battle' and the 'crash of arms.'" He explained, "After more than two months of marching, fighting, laying in trenches and campaigning generally, in which I have been almost secluded from the outer world I feel some anxiety to know how things are going on in the quiet and sequestered shades of private life." Writing home also gave soldiers the opportunity to beg supplies they sorely lacked. Richmonder William B. Myers entreated, "I hate to trouble you with repeated requests but if you could send me out a couple more bottles of whiskey it would greatly assist us. We are all much fagged by the campaign which is . . . the most harassing of the war."[83] Whiskey was widely used as a panacea for pain relief. Letters provided both mental and material support.

Late May through early June saw several interruptions in the mail service, resulting in sporadic dips in morale that rebounded when letters reappeared. One embittered Alabamian wrote home on June 4, "Dear Elise I am not in good spirits today and you must excuse this letter. Why don't you write no letter for five days." The swift and biting response should remind us that nineteenth-century Americans interpreted homesickness as a far more serious mental ailment than holds sway in the modern consciousness, even characterizing so-called nostalgia as potentially fatal. Connecting with loved ones through correspondence thus took on a deeper significance, its absence felt most acutely.[84]

There were several reasons for spotty mail service on both sides. As South Carolinian Leverrett explained to his sister on June 8, "Since I've begun writing, all at home have ceased sending me letters in return. This may be due, however, to derangement in the mail. Nearly all the clerks in the Post Office in Richmond have been sent out to various military Companies. It is said that the ladies have offered to take their places in the P.O. but the Post Master General thinks they do not or cannot understand the work & according keeps the Country deprived in great measure of the Mail." Additionally the pace of the campaign impeded some soldiers' abilities to write home or receive their letters in a timely manner. A cavalryman from Cobb's Legion explained: "Dear Martha, Your last letter was received and read yesterday on the battlefield. Your first was received ten or fifteen days ago, but, like this, under circumstances very inconvenient to be answered." The campaign had simply transpired at too breathless a pace: "I have not had time to write—only at the dark, dim hour of night, when, soul and body both exhausted, the soldiers lay in silent groups with their bridles in their hands, have I had time to write. The coming of tomorrow has always found us in the saddle, or engaging the enemy."[85]

On the Union side, just as the supply trains struggled to keep up with the Army of the Potomac, so also did the mail. "We have had a mail to-

I Told Him to Go On

day for the first time since May 16th. . . . How pleasant to hear from home again!" rejoiced one soldier from Connecticut on June 4. On May 31, a Vermont musician told his sister that the "mail has only gone out three times since we left Brandy Station." Some unlucky men were simply "out of paper now. . . . I have to borrow all" of it. Cpl. George H. Bates from the 2nd Connecticut Heavy Artillery was grateful under the circumstances for the Christian and Sanitary Commissions and hoped "the people will keep up these good institutions. If it hadn't been for the Sanitary Commission a good many of these letters which the friends at home receiving from the soldiers would have had to have gone without for they distribute paper and the like of that."[86]

Finally, just as the sharpshooters impeded every other basic activity in the trenches, so also they prevented many a soldier from sitting down to write home, such as Captain Morton. "Just before the shelling commenced, I was sitting on the ground among some low bushes with pencil and paper, writing upon my knee what I thought might be my last letter to my wife." Presently, "two or three minies dropped in the bushes near, and as each one seemed to cut a little closer, I thought a sharpshooter with a telescopic rifle . . . had perhaps been attracted by my white paper and it would be safest to move." After he settled in against another oak tree, "the next minute I thought the earth had opened and that I and the tree were falling into it. As soon as I could shake myself together and rub some burnt powder out of my eyes, I realized that a shell had burst against the tree right behind me." He passed a hand over his limbs to make sure they were still intact, and his lieutenant "ran up and congratulated me on being alive, saying that as he knew where I had been sitting a minute before and hearing the shell explode at the spot, he had come expecting 'to pick up what was left of me.'"[87]

Aside from letters home, soldiers indulged in other forms of written comfort to recover their spirits, such as poetry and religious texts. As one soldier lamented on June 4, "My health is pretty good but my heart is sick of the suffering I have seen." In a subsequent letter he confirmed, "Frank, I don't feel like writing anything keen, as we have been up so much nights. I feel dozy most of the time. . . . My friend Shirley was killed in the charge the 1st, June. I miss him very much." But he appeared to rally by quoting from "a verse I found; I know it true: The memory of a clasping hand / The pressure of a kiss / And all the trifles sweet and frail / That make up love's first bliss / If with a firm unchanging faith / And Holy trust and high / Those hands have closed, those lips have met / These things shall never die." He

KATHRYN SHIVELY MEIER

affirmed, "That is my faith and my fix." Noting that some of the boys have "little hymn books and are making quite a Camp meeting," complete with singing and praying, he appeared relatively heartened by the end of the letter.[88] Virginian Private Davis lamented his lack of a Bible: "I am not the possessor of a Testament, and I believe every other man in the company has one," for it offered comfort in the face of potentially imminent death. One Richmonder, whose father was a minister, requested letters, supplies, and spiritual tracts to bolster his mental and physical health. "Please try to write me daily, or arrange for some friend to do so. . . . Please send me by Mr. Gibson or otherwise the washing soap, & some [new] tracts. I have just the testaments, psalms, & c."[89]

Unpredictable mail delivery also meant many soldiers did not receive newspapers in the manner to which they had grown accustomed; thus an important link with home that helped to situate soldiers' fragmented personal experiences within the larger context of the campaign and political events was compromised.[90] Indeed a recurring theme among letters written during the battle of Cold Harbor is that soldiers had little sense of where their individual roles fit into the larger picture. "I know very little about our campaign as a whole. . . . We have no communication with the infantry, and hence or inability to keep posted with their movements," explained a Georgian cavalryman. A 2nd Vermonter whose enlistment was up on June 20 made vague allusions to the carnage his regiment had suffered and appeared to have little interest in pondering the larger picture. "We have seen the hardest times. . . . Our Brigade you know is awfully cut," he wrote; "it never saw hard fighting until it commenced on this campaign. It is useless for me to try to describe any of our operations. You of course have read all about it, we have lost a large amount of men, and have also been reinforced, so I think our army is as large as it was when we left camp. . . . I am waiting anxiously for the 20th of next month to come around, and then good bye army." Another man from the same unit wrote to his cousin, "You have read & heard how busy this army have been since we crossed the Rapidan . . . and on that account you will probably have charity to overlook my long reticence towards you. . . . I should take great pride & pleasure in writing you a truthful history of the operations of this & the rebel army since the opening of the [campaign]. . . . But as I have attended religiously to my own duties and passed camp rumors lightly by, I can speak knowingly of but a limited portion of these great devellopements."[91] The lack of perspective may have actually helped the soldiers to cope with the mental strain of the Overland campaign, as they knew little

I Told Him to Go On

more than where they belonged in the midst of the battle, and even that posed a particular challenge.[92]

The larger context of Overland casualties was staggering and disheartening indeed. As Gary W. Gallagher notes in his essay in this collection, precise numbers are elusive, and much depends on how one frames the chronological limits of the operations. Yet Gallagher estimates that casualties for the United States between May 5 and June 18 reached 65,000, or 40 percent of the Army of the Potomac, while the Confederates lost 34,500, or 36 percent of the Army of Northern Virginia.[93] It did the soldiers little good to dwell upon this tremendous toll; if they had survived, they were the lucky ones.

The reminiscence of 2nd Lt. William S. Long, a veteran of the 44th North Carolina Infantry color guard, is an apt summary of soldier experience at Cold Harbor. Writing in 1903 to his son, Long adopted a dramatic tone regarding the assaults on June 1: "As we reached within two hundred yards of the [enemy] battery and works, our line stopped short for a moment as one does for a deep breath." Long shook out the folds of his "old tattered flag," and the "hot flash" of smoke singed his cheeks, while "the earth shook, the dirt flew" as "grape, shell, canister crashed, tore, whistled, shrieked and plunged through flesh and earth." The Confederates gathered themselves, and "mad with thirst, hunger, crazed with the blood, wild with anger, excitement and suffering, with fear and trembling, with emotion, we surged on." Meanwhile, the enemy artillery, "hellish monsters[,] vomited fire, sulphur, smoke, lead iron, and death. . . . Dante's Inferno was a Sunday school picnic to what I saw that day."[94]

At first glance, Long's remembrance seems to fit well with the current spate of Civil War veteran studies that emphasize the near-impossibility of mental forbearance in such fearsome battle. "Can man stand such things?" asked Long rhetorically. "No. We were transformed into beasts. We were maniacs. We danced, we raged, we cursed, we ran, we stumbled, we fell, we rose, we yelled, we rushed."[95] But despite Long's postwar doubts, these bursts of emotion, adrenaline, and shouting, and a touch of the elbow with comrades, actually sustained men in the midst of tremendous stress. What might appear to be the men breaking down was, in fact, part of a ritual of endurance in battle. Indeed, even Long's embellished prose was a sign of coping using the cultural capital available to him.[96]

Upon closer reading, the less thrilling but no less important aspect of Long's account made up the bulk of soldier experience at Cold Harbor. For not two hundred yards from enemy lines and scrambling toward uncertain death, Long recalled with equal clarity, "I want to tell you that I was so thirsty by that time that the bare memory of it makes me dry." As his fellow North Carolinians "came to the open" and "stopped for a breath," someone exclaimed, "Come on boys, there is water over there," while "another said, 'For those that get there.' Many did not get water." Indeed, according to Long, when the men checked their equipment before the charge, "each man felt for his ammunition" and his "canteen."[97] Soldiers in both armies had been lying in their fortifications for hours that would drag into days, but they were too chastened by sharpshooters to venture out for the barest necessities of water, food, and even the chance to relieve themselves. Thus when we consider what tested soldiers' bodies and minds, we should not divorce combat from the larger soldier experience—that is, the exhaustion, deprivation, and exposure that settled as a gloom over Cold Harbor. From there we can move forward to understand how, startling as it may appear in hindsight, Private Long and soldiers on both sides relied upon a large reserve of cultural and military resources to sustain themselves.

Notes

The author would like to thank Robert E. L. Krick for generous access to the impressive collection of manuscripts he has accumulated at Chimborazo in Richmond, Va., the staff of the Virginia Historical Society in Richmond, and Peter C. Luebke, Caroline E. Janney, and Gary W. Gallagher.

1. Horace Porter, *Campaigning with Grant* (1897; New York: Century, 1906), 174; Evander M. Law, "From the Wilderness to Cold Harbor," *Century*, June 1887, 297–99. As memory accounts, both serve the authors' purposes in supporting (Law) or refuting (Porter) the Lost Cause idea that Grant was a butcher for ordering assaults against Lee's entrenched lines on June 3, 1864. Moreover, Porter was combating the contemporary interpretation that characterized Union soldiers as so chastened by assaulting Confederate earthworks as to be cowardly. In contrast, Porter presents the assaulting Federals as "gallant and subordinate as any forces in the history of modern warfare" (174). For contemporary portrayals of Grant the butcher in the midst of the Overland campaign, see Joan Waugh, *U. S. Grant: American Hero, American Myth* (Chapel Hill: University of North Carolina Press, 2009), 83–87; for Grant's positioning in Lost Cause lore, see Gary W. Gallagher, *Lee and His Generals in War and Memory* (Baton Rouge: Louisiana State University Press, 1998), 199.

2. Both Porter's and Law's accounts were contemporarily popular; Law's was reprinted in the renowned *Battles and Leaders of the Civil War*, ed. Robert Underwood Johnson and Clarence Clough Buel, 4 vols. (New York: Century, 1887), 4:139–41. For an example of modern scholarly emphasis on Law's phrase, see Ernest B. Furgurson, *Not War but Murder: Cold Harbor, 1864* (New York: Knopf, 2000), xi and title. The modern popularity of all three accounts is evident in Ken Burns, *The Civil War*, episode 6, "The Valley of the Shadow of Death." Burns's documentary, which has held

I Told Him to Go On

considerable sway over the current generation of Americans, uses the three fragments in rapid succession as a stand-in for the entire two-week battle.

3. One reason for the emphasis on Cold Harbor as the battle that broke U.S. soldiers is that some contemporary accounts attributed Union failure to take Petersburg before a costly siege to the "Cold Harbor Syndrome," claiming that after the futile attempt to break Lee's line on June 1–3, U.S. soldiers saw it as useless to attack entrenched Confederates. As Gordon C. Rhea explains, soldiers learned to dread attacking earthworks because of experience accumulated throughout the Overland campaign—this "syndrome" was not solely a product of the June 3 assaults at Cold Harbor. See Rhea, *Cold Harbor: Grant and Lee, May 26–June 3, 1864* (Baton Rouge: Louisiana State University Press, 2002), 268. Several contemporary accounts corroborate Rhea's assertion. For example, see John S. Jones, "From North Anna to Cold Harbor," in W. H. Chamberlin, ed., *Sketches of War History, 1861–1865: Papers Prepared for the Ohio Commandery of the Military Order of the Loyal Legion of the United States, 1890–1896* (Cincinnati: Robert Clarke Co., 1896), 4:156, and Francis A. Walker, *History of the Second Army Corps in the Army of the Potomac* (New York: Scribner's, 1886), 522–23.

4. Law, "From the Wilderness to Cold Harbor," 298–99.

5. How does one determine if a soldier broke? Some scholars use suicides as evidence for a concept that is very difficult to define, although linking a suicide to the effects of a particular battle is problematical. Diane M. Sommerville summarizes this problem: "Suicidal soldiers rarely left behind evidence explaining the motives for their decisions to end their lives, so many important details about individual soldier suicides elude us" (Diane M. Sommerville, "'A Burden Too Heavy to Bear': War Trauma, Suicide, and Confederate Soldiers," *Civil War History* 59 [December 2013]: 461). See also Eric T. Dean Jr., *Shook over Hell: Post-Traumatic Stress, Vietnam, and the Civil War* (Cambridge, Mass.: Harvard University Press, 1997), 5. In many cases, stress was cumulative and proximity to arms simply made it easier to fulfill a whim. In other cases, soldiers who took their own lives had displayed symptoms of mental distress before they were engaged in battle, suggesting they had preexisting conditions. On this point, see Earl J. Hess, *The Union Soldier in Battle: Enduring the Ordeal of Combat* (Lawrence: University Press of Kansas, 1997), 90–91, and Kathryn Shively Meier, *Nature's Civil War: Common Soldiers and the Environment in 1862 Virginia* (Chapel Hill: University of North Carolina Press, 2013), 63. The Union's official medical records indicate that just two U.S. soldiers committed suicide in May 1864 and one in June 1864. If we are to explain the effects of Cold Harbor on these three Union casualties, we should begin by comparing these numbers with the suicide rate among the general populace. See U.S. War Department, *The Medical and Surgical History of the War of the Rebellion, 1861–65*, 6 vols., index, and illustrations, 2nd issue (Washington, D.C.: Government Printing Office, 1870–88), 1:329.

6. Sommerville, "'Burden Too Heavy to Bear,'" 454. The literature in this vein begun by Eric T. Dean's *Shook over Hell* tends to privilege combat trauma as an explanation for soldier breakdown without examining the full picture of mental stress as described by soldiers, which included such concepts as homesickness and environmental strain, and without taking into account structural problems or solutions. (For an explication of the contemporary conception of potentially fatal homesickness,

or nostalgia, see Frances Clarke, "So Lonesome I Could Die: Nostalgia and Debates over Emotional Control in the Civil War North," *Journal of Social History* 41 [Winter 2007]: 253–82.) To elucidate the problem of failing to consider the structural, Sommerville writes, "Most curious are cases of new Confederate recruits who committed suicide before ever seeing battle," and whose self-inflicted deaths are attributed to "'fear reactions' to the prospect of being sent to the war zone," patterned after Richard Gabriel's study of World War II psychiatry and war (461). More likely the men's problems predated military service and had been overlooked during initial inspection of recruits. After all, the U.S. Sanitary Commission noted in October 1861 that 53 percent of soldiers in the Army of the Potomac had to be discharged "on account of disabilities that existed at or before their enlistment, and which any intelligent surgeon ought to have discovered on their inspection as recruits" (U.S. Sanitary Commission, *Documents of the U.S. Sanitary Commission*, 3 vols. [New York: n.p., 1866], 1:4). Both sides struggled with securing surgeons of good quality who could effectively examine recruits; moreover, diagnosis of mental disorders was extremely rudimentary at the time. It is therefore doubtful the deficiencies surgeons neglected to identify remained confined to the physical.

7. Other scholars have suggested that Civil War soldiers were by and large equipped to handle the manifold strains of soldiering; indeed, one of the purposes of this essay is to collect and integrate the arguments of modern scholars who have discussed soldier agency. See Meier, *Nature's Civil War*; Hess, *Union Soldier in Battle*; Frances M. Clarke, *War Stories: Suffering and Sacrifice in the Civil War North* (Chicago: University of Chicago Press, 2011); Carol Reardon, "A Hard Road to Travel: The Impact of Continuous Operations on the Army of the Potomac and the Army of Northern Virginia in May 1864," in Gary W. Gallagher, ed., *The Spotsylvania Campaign* (Chapel Hill: University of North Carolina Press, 1998); and James M. McPherson, *For Cause and Comrades: Why Men Fought in the Civil War* (New York: Oxford University Press, 1997). For those scholars who focus on men who could not cope with wartime experiences, see Dean, *Shook over Hell*; Michael C. C. Adams, *Living Hell: The Dark Side of the Civil War* (Baltimore: Johns Hopkins University Press, 2014); Drew Gilpin Faust, *This Republic of Suffering: Death and the American Civil War* (New York: Knopf, 2008); and essays contained in *Civil War History* 59 (December 2013).

8. Col. William D. Rutherford (3rd South Carolina Infantry) to "my own beloved," June 14, 1864, William Rutherford Letters, bound vol. no. 133, Richmond National Battlefield Park (Chimborazo site), Richmond, Va. (repository hereafter cited as RNBP); Joseph Banks Lyle diary (5th South Carolina Infantry), June 8 or 9[?], 1864, Mss1L9881a1111, Virginia Historical Society, Richmond (repository hereafter cited as VHS); Robert A. Stiles (Richmond Howitzers Virginia Artillery) to sister, June 15, 1864, Robert Augustus Stiles Papers, Mss1St535a1-56, VHS. See also Letter of "Bibb" from Colquitt's Brigade to Mr. Clisby, June 4, 1864, in *Macon Daily Telegraph*, June 14, 1864, bound vol. no. 68, RNBP. Please note that all original spelling in soldier accounts is preserved without the use of [*sic*].

9. I am not suggesting that the battle, or rather the cumulative strains of the Overland campaign, did not push some men to the breaking point, although it remains very difficult to identify the exact origins of a given soldier's collapse. One of the

more famous accounts of the Overland campaign, by New York artillerist Pvt. Frank Wilkeson, portrayed a teenager new to combat at the start of the campaign who grew "heartsick and weary of the fighting." Early in the siege of Petersburg, he "claimed his discharge, which had been ordered by Secretary of War Stanton while we were fighting in front of Cold Harbor" to accept a commission in the 4th U.S. artillery (Frank Wilkeson, *Turned Inside Out: Recollections of a Private Soldier in the Army of the Potomac* [1887; reprint, Lincoln: University of Nebraska Press, 1997], 178).

10. For incisive discussions of the military training and cultural resources soldiers used to cope with their wartime experiences, see Hess, *Union Soldier in Battle*, and Clarke, *War Stories*.

11. For more on self-care, see Meier, *Nature's Civil War*, which deals with 1862 and focuses primarily on lulls in campaigns. This essay provides the opportunity to show that soldiers avidly practiced self-care at this late point in the war and on the front lines of battle.

12. As Carol Reardon notes at the end of her essay assessing the impact of continuous operations on soldier morale at Spotsylvania Court House, even a brief respite from the trenches and an influx of supplies and mail could significantly repair a damaged regiment's fighting spirit. It could also restore faltering physical health. See Reardon, "Hard Road to Travel," 195. Vermonter Samuel E. Pingree explained this rhythm of campaigning succinctly: "Each Reg't. holds the front line for 24 hours & the line next the front (the 2d line being of equal danger & importance) also 24 hours— then is relieved for 48 hours and goes about half a mile to the rear to straighten up, wash up, sleep up & clean up arms" (Samuel E. Pingree [2nd Vermont Infantry] to Cousin Hunton, June 10, 1864, bound vol. no. 90, RNBP).

13. Pvt. Edgar W. Clark (3rd Michigan Infantry) to "My Dear Wife," May 26, 1864, bound vol. no. 74, RNBP; Reardon, "Hard Road to Travel," 179.

14. Rhea, *Cold Harbor*, 59; U.S. War Department, *The War of the Rebellion: A Compilation of the Official Records of the Union and Confederate Armies*, 127 vols., index, and atlas (Washington, D.C.: Government Printing Office, 1880–1901), ser. 1, 36(1):242 (hereafter cited as *OR*; all references are to ser. 1).

15. Jones, "From North Anna to Cold Harbor," 153–54; *OR* 36(1):87.

16. Sgt. James M. Snook (50th New York Engineers) diary, May 25–June 7, 1864, bound vol. no. 7, RNBP.

17. Pvt. Creed T. Davis (Richmond Howitzers, Virginia Artillery) diary, May 27–28, 1864, Mss5:1D2914:1, VHS.

18. Pvt. John W. F. Hatton (1st Maryland Artillery), June 1864 memoir, 580, bound vol. no. 118, RNBP.

19. Reardon discusses complaints about leadership as a sign of eroding morale; see Reardon, "Hard Road to Travel," 188.

20. Creed T. Davis diary, June 1, 1864, VHS.

21. T. C. Morton, "Incidents of the Skirmish at Totopotomoy Creek, Hanover County, Virginia, May 30, 1864," in J. William Jones and others, eds., *Southern Historical Society Papers*, 52 vols. (Richmond, Va.: Southern Historical Society, 1876–1959), 16:50–51 (hereafter cited as *SHSP*); Sgt. George P. Clark (7th Virginia Infantry) diary, June 1, 1864, accession #11025, Albert and Shirley Small Special Collections Library,

University of Virginia, Charlottesville, accessed online, Virginia Center for Digital History, http://www2.vcdh.virginia.edu/fellows/chdoc8.html (accessed July 16, 2014).

22. Sgt. Ezekiel Dunagan Graham (6th Georgia Infantry) letter, June 9, 1864, bound vol. no. 15, RNBP.

23. As Carol Reardon writes, "Consciously or not, a soldier's physical environment rules much of his conduct, and neither private nor general could control many of these intangibles" (Reardon, "Hard Road to Travel," 177).

24. Conevery Bolton Valencius, *The Health of the Country: How American Settlers Understood Themselves and Their Land* (New York: Basic Books, 2002), 165–71; Meier, *Nature's Civil War*, 45–58.

25. See, for example, 2nd Lt. Samuel T. McCullough (2nd Maryland Infantry) diary, May 1864, bound vol. no. 118, RNBP.

26. William H. Tatum, to "Dear T.," June 8, 1864, folder 8, William Henry Tatum Papers, 1838–1903, VHS; John G. Perry, *Letters from a Surgeon of the Civil War*, comp. and ed. Martha Derby Perry (Boston: Little, Brown, 1906), 188; Augustus Buell (Battery B, 4th United States), *The Cannoneer: Recollections of Service in the Army of the Potomac by A Detached Volunteer in the Regular Artillery* (Washington, D.C.: National Tribune, 1890), 218.

27. Hess, *Union Soldier in Battle*, 130–31.

28. For an account that connects the swampy terrain and poor-quality water to health problems, see Frank B. Fay, *War Papers of Frank B. Fay: With Reminiscences of Service in the Camps and Hospitals of the Army of the Potomac, 1861–1865*, ed. William Howell Reed (Boston: privately printed, 1911), 117–57.

29. Pvt. Robert P. Bryarly (1st Virginia Cavalry) diary, June 7, 1864, bound vol. no. 92, RNBP; Theodore Lyman, *Meade's Headquarters, 1863–1865: Letters of Colonel Theodore Lyman from the Wilderness to Appomattox*, ed. George R. Agassiz (Boston: Atlantic Monthly Press, 1922), 134. Rhea, *Cold Harbor*, 117, discusses the insects.

30. *OR* 36(1):242; Almon Clarke, "In the Immediate Rear: Experience and Observations of a Field Surgeon," in *War Papers being Read before the Commandery of the State of Wisconsin: Military Order of the Loyal Legion of the United States* (Milwaukee: Burdick, Armitage and Allen, 1896), 98.

31. Rhea, *Cold Harbor*, 28; James M. Snook diary, May 24, 25, 1864, bound vol. no. 7, RNBP.

32. Daniel M. Holt, *A Surgeon's Civil War: The Letters and Diary of Daniel M. Holt, M.D.*, ed. James M. Greiner, Janet L. Coryell, and James R. Smither (Kent, Ohio: Kent State University Press, 1994), 192–93; Creed T. Davis diary, May 26, 1864, VHS; Sgt. Dwight C. Kilbourn (2nd Connecticut Volunteer Heavy Artillery) diary, May 30, 1864, bound vol. no. 67, RNBP.

33. Sgt. Joseph K. Taylor (37th Massachusetts Infantry) to his father, June 11, 1864, in Joseph K. Taylor, *The Civil War Letters of Joseph K. Taylor*, ed. Kevin C. Murphy (Lewiston, N.Y.: Edwin Mellen, 1998), 195; Asst. Surg. Legrand Wilson (42nd Mississippi Infantry) memoir, 162, bound vol. no. 119, RNBP.

34. Charles W. Reed, *A Grand Terrible Drama: From Gettysburg to Petersburg: The Civil War Letters of Charles Wellington Reed*, ed. Eric A. Campbell (New York: Fordham University Press, 2000), 225–26.

35. Pvt. John West Haley (30th or 31st Maine Infantry) diary, May 24, June 4, 1864, Mss5:1H1374:1, VHS.

36. As Rhea notes, on May 30 and at many other points in these two weeks, "Water was foul and rations nonexistent," with food shortages particularly on the Union side. "When Meade, Hancock, and their staffs rode out [to the lines of the Union Second Corps] a crowd of filthy blue-clad soldiers greeted them chanting, 'Hardtack! Hardtack!'" (Rhea, *Cold Harbor*, 117–18; see also, for other examples, 90, 93, 102, 105, 152).

37. Ibid., 93, 102; Reardon, "Hard Road to Travel," 181–82.

38. Cpl. Octave Bruso (50th New York Engineers) diary, May 28, 1864, bound vol. no. 202, RNBP; Musician Frederick W. Simonds (2nd Vermont Infantry) to "sister Jane," May 31, 1864, bound vol. no. 90, RNBP; Dwight C. Kilbourn diary, May 30, 1864, bound vol. no. 67, RNBP.

39. McCullough diary, May 24, 25, 1864, bound vol. no. 118, RNBP; Cpl. Archibald F. McGrady (29th Virginia Infantry) to "Dear Friend," June 12, 1864, bound vol. no. 195, RNBP; Frederick P. Leverett, *The Leverett Letters: Correspondence of a South Carolina Family*, ed. Frances Wallace Taylor, Catherine Taylor Matthews, and J. Tracy Power (Columbia: University of South Carolina Press, 2000), 316.

40. See Franklin L. Stuart (23rd North Carolina Infantry) to sister, June 2, 1864 [from Lewis Leigh Collection], bound vol. no. 10, RNBP.

41. Richard Robertson Jr. (8th Maine Infantry) diary, June 9, 11, 1864, bound vol. no. 138, RNBP.

42. See, for example, "Bibb" from Colquitt's Brigade to Mr. Clisby, June 4, 1864, in *Macon Daily Telegraph*, June 14, 1864, copy in bound vol. no. 68, RNBP.

43. Edgar S. Roberts (2nd Connecticut Heavy Artillery), "War Reminiscences" (concerning May, 31, 1864), *Connecticut Western News*, August 17, 1911[?], bound vol. no. 67, RNBP.

44. Morton, "Incidents at Totopotomoy Creek," 48–49.

45. Hess, *Union Soldier in Battle*, 146–47; Clarke, *War Stories*, 72.

46. See Lt. Thomas Tileston Greene (61st Alabama Infantry) to Elise, May 25, 1864, bound vol. no. 152, RNBP.

47. See Taylor to his father, June 11, 1864, in Taylor, *Civil War Letters*, 195; Pvt. Clark to "My Dear Wife," June 20, 1864, bound vol. no. 74, RNBP; and John West Haley diary, June 7, 1864, VHS. See also James M. Snook diary, May 26, 1864, bound vol. no. 7, RNBP; William Henry Tatum to sister, June 2, 1864, folder 8, William Henry Tatum Papers, 1838–1903, VHS; and James G. Davis, ed., *"Bully for the Band!": The Civil War Letters and Diary of Four Brothers in the 10th Vermont Infantry Band* (Jefferson, N.C.: McFarland, 2012), 152.

48. See Meier, *Nature's Civil War*, for antebellum sanitation movements (32) and cleanliness as self-care (100–104).

49. Holt, *Surgeon's Civil War*, 203; Richard Robertson (8th Maine Infantry) diary, May 31, 1864, bound vol. no. 138, RNBP; H. Randolph (12th Virginia Infantry) to Stanley, June 10, 1864, section 3, Bird Family Papers, 1825–1980, VHS.

50. Davis, *"Bully for the Band!"* 152–62. See also Capt. Robert Pratt (5th Vermont Infantry) diary, [June 9, 1864], bound vol. no. 90, RNBP, and Holt, *Surgeon's Civil War*, 199.

51. Because the official Confederate medical records burned in Richmond in 1865, the Union medical records are far more reliable at providing a full account of sickness during a given campaign.

52. *OR* 36(1):246–48.

53. Richard Robertson diary, May 31, 1864, bound vol. no. 138, RNBP. See also James M. Snook diary, May 23, 1864, bound vol. no. 7, RNBP, and J. Franklin Dyer, *The Journal of a Civil War Surgeon*, ed. Michael B. Chesson (Lincoln: University of Nebraska Press, 2003), 164.

54. It has long been a trend in Civil War literature to accept officers' assessments of stragglers as malingerers and cowards, even conflating them with deserters. Only recently has the literature begun to treat stragglers as distinct from deserters, citing supply problems and self-care as legitimate and often restorative reasons to straggle. For examples of the latter trend, see Joseph L. Harsh, *Taken at the Flood: Robert E. Lee and Confederate Strategy in the Maryland Campaign of 1862* (Kent, Ohio: Kent State University Press, 1999); Keith S. Bohannon, "Dirty, Ragged, and Ill-Provided For: Confederate Logistical Problems in the 1862 Maryland Campaign and Their Solutions," in Gary W. Gallagher, ed., *The Antietam Campaign* (Chapel Hill: University of North Carolina Press, 1999), 101–42; and Meier, *Nature's Civil War*. For examples of the former, see Ella Lonn, *Desertion during the Civil War* (1928; reprint, Lincoln: University of Nebraska Press, 1998); Mark A. Weitz, *A Higher Duty: Desertion among Georgian Troops during the War* (Lincoln: University of Nebraska Press, 2000); Weitz, *More Damning than Slaughter: Desertion in the Confederate Army* (Lincoln: University of Nebraska Press, 2005); Mark V. Wetherington, *Plain Folk's Fight: The Civil War and Reconstruction in Piney Woods Georgia* (Chapel Hill: University of North Carolina Press, 2005); John F. Reiger, "Deprivation, Disaffection, and Desertion in Confederate Georgia," *Florida Historical Quarterly* 48 (January 1970): 279–98; and Kevin C. Ruffner, "Civil War Desertion from a Black Belt Regiment," in Edward L. Ayers, ed., *The Edge of the South: Life in Nineteenth-Century Virginia* (Charlottesville: University Press of Virginia, 1991), 79–108.

55. For class conceptions of manliness, see Clarke, *War Stories*; Lorien Foote, *The Gentlemen and the Roughs: Violence, Honor, and Manhood in the Union Army* (New York: New York University Press, 2010); Kanisorn Wongsrichanalai, "Leadership Class: College-Educated New Englanders in the Civil War," *Massachusetts Historical Review* 13 (2011): 67–95; Mary Ryan, *Cradle of the Middle Class: The Family in Oneida County, New York, 1790–1865* (New York: Cambridge University Press, 1983); and Stephen W. Berry, *All That Makes a Man: Love and Ambition in the Civil War South* (New York: Oxford University Press, 2003).

56. Dyer, *Journal of a Civil War Surgeon*, 166.

57. Gerald F. Linderman, *Embattled Courage: The Experience of Combat in the American Civil War* (New York: Free Press, 1989), 29–31.

58. Clarke, *War Stories*, 72.

59. Pvt. George B. Battle (4th North Carolina Infantry) to mother, May 25, 1864, bound vol. no. 83, RNBP.

60. Creed Thomas Davis diary, June 6, 1864, VHS.

61. As Charles George explained to his "darling" Ellie on June 8, 1864, "I enjoy

I Told Him to Go On

myself more here—I mean in the band—than anywhere in the army. The band is my home and I get homesick for it when away from it" (Davis, *"Bully for the Band!"* 153). Though soldiers were generally reticent about expressing too much discouragement, when Massachusetts soldier George H. Dodge became too sick in the hospital to write home, a Christian Commission worker did so for him: "Geo. says he feels most discouraged sometimes—he has had so much bad luck" (Milo Hildreth to Dr. David N. Dodge on behalf of George H. Dodge [27th Massachusetts Infantry], June 5, 1864, Dodge Family Papers, 1864 January 18–June 7, VHS).

62. Robert A. Stiles to Rosa Ann Stiles, June 15, 1864, folder 1, Robert Augustus Stiles Papers, 1836–1905, VHS; Fay, *War Papers of Frank B. Fay*, 122.

63. Samuel T. McCullough diary, June 5, 6, 8, 11, 1864, bound vol. no. 118, RNBP; Pvt. John Wood (53rd Georgia Infantry) to his wife, June 2, 1864, bound vol. 68, RNBP.

64. General Hospital No. 1, Winder Hospital, and Howard's Grove all closed in Richmond in the spring of 1864. See H. H. Cunningham, *Doctors in Gray: The Confederate Medical Service* (1958; reprint, Baton Rouge: Louisiana State University Press, 1993), 63–65, 119, 122, 157.

65. George Worthington Adams, *Doctors in Blue: The Medical History of the Union Army in the Civil War* (1952; reprint, Baton Rouge: Louisiana State University Press, 1996), 95, 98–100.

66. Samuel E. Pingree (2nd Vermont Infantry) to Cousin Hunton, June 10, 1864, bound vol. no. 90, RNBP; Pvt. J. H. Baker (8th New York Heavy Artillery) to Alexander Mabon, bound vol. no. 141, RNBP.

67. Lt. James W. Hildreth (4th New York Heavy Artillery) to mother and father, June 7, 1864, bound vol. no. 7, RNBP. Earl J. Hess speaks to the cultural importance of maintaining an image of moral courage generated by one's essential character, rather than fleeting "physical" courage in the heat of battle; see Hess, *Union Soldier in Battle*, 75. See also Linderman, *Embattled Courage*, 7.

68. Pvt. J. M. Reynolds (10th Battalion Georgia Infantry) to William J. Dickey, June 1, 1864, bound vol. no. 68, RNBP.

69. Creed Thomas Davis diary, June 5, 1864, VHS; Dwight C. Kilbourn diary, June 5, 1864, bound vol. no. 67, RNBP; Robert Pratt diary, June 6, 1864, bound vol. no. 90, RNBP; Nicholas Tompkins to Mrs. J. D. Brock, June 3, 1864, with notification of the death of James D. Brock (12th Georgia Artillery), bound vol. no. 68, RNBP.

70. Clarke, *War Stories*, 70.

71. Grant had previously prohibited flags of truce to collect the dead and wounded caught between the lines; see Reardon, "Hard Road to Travel," 191. As Ernest B. Furgurson explains, sending out a white flag was an admission of defeat, and both Grant and Lee were reluctant to agree to a truce in order to bury their dead at Cold Harbor. The negotiation of terms took several days. See Furgurson, *Not War but Murder*, 205. For the official correspondence between Grant and Lee on the truce, see *OR* 36(1):600–609, 638–39, 666–67.

72. "A Sight Dreadful Even to Veterans," June 3, 1864, in *SHSP* 29:285; Holt, *Surgeon's Civil War*, 196; Legrand Wilson memoir, p. 163, bound vol. no. 119, RNBP. See also Dwight C. Kilbourn diary, June 7, 1864, bound vol. no. 67, RNBP; Pvt. Edgar Clark to cousin, June 10, 1864, bound vol. no. 74, RNBP; Pvt. Matthew A. Wood (Grimes

Battery, Portsmouth Light Artillery) diary, June 7, 1864, VHS; Pvt. Orrin S. Allen (112th New York Infantry) to Frank, June 8, 1864, "Dear Frank: the War Years, 1862–1865: the Civil War Letters of Orrin S. Allen to his Wife Francis [*sic*] E. Wade Allen and family," transcribed by William L. Rockwell, 2001, VHS.

73. Pvt. Henry R. Berkeley (Kirkpatrick's Battery, Nelson's Battalion) diary, June 3–6, 1864, Notebook of Henry R. Berkeley, 1861–65, VHS. Berkeley transcribed this notebook from his diaries after the war, and it is unclear if he made any changes.

74. See Clarke, *War Stories*, 72, and Hess, *Union Soldier in Battle*, 75, 96, 146–47. See also Foote, *Gentlemen and the Roughs*, chaps. 1–2.

75. Law, "From the Wilderness to Cold Harbor," 298.

76. Morton, "Incidents at Totopotomoy Creek," 49–50.

77. Clarke, *War Stories*, 72.

78. Eric Dean suggests that Civil War surgeons and hospitals workers would have been severely affected by stress because of their jobs; see Dean, *Shook over Hell*, 79–80.

79. Clarke, "In the Immediate Rear," 96–97.

80. Adams, *Doctors in Blue*, 65; Dyer, *Journal of a Civil War Surgeon*, 164.

81. Letter written "in the rifle pits before Richmond," discovered in clerk's office, *Hanover County Historical Society Bulletin* 67 (Fall 2002): 1–2, Anne Geddy Cross Collection, VHS.

82. Karen Lystra discusses the cultural significance of nineteenth-century American letters in *Searching the Heart: Women, Men, and Romantic Love in Nineteenth-Century America* (New York: Oxford University Press, 1989), 4.

83. Alexander W. Wallace (30th Virginia Infantry) to Henry, July 17, 1864, section 16, Armistead, Blanton, and Wallace Family Papers, 1790–1911, VHS; William Barksdale Myers to Gustavus Adolphus Myers, June 2, 1864, section 2, Gustavus Adolphus Myers Papers, 1801–1869, VHS. For letters as self-care, see Meier, *Nature's Civil War*, 120–21.

84. Lt. Thomas Tileston Greene (61st Alabama Infantry) to Elise, June 4, 1864, bound vol. no. 152, RNBP. By contemporary definition, nostalgia, or acute homesickness, involved mental and physical symptoms, including fluctuations in appetite, sleeplessness, heart palpitations, and sadness; see Clarke, "So Lonesome I Could Die," 253.

85. Leverett, *Leverett Letters*, 316; Henry F. Jones (Cobb's Legion Cavalry) to Martha, June 1, 1864, bound vol. no. 68, RNBP.

86. Dwight C. Kilbourn diary, June 4, 1864, bound vol. no. 67, RNBP; Frederick W. Simonds to Sister Jane, May 31, 1864, bound vol. no. 90, RNBP; Jim A. to Helen, June 11, 1864, Jim A. Letters, 1864, written to Helen, VHS; Cpl. George H. Bates (2nd Connecticut Heavy Artillery) to Parents, June 7, 1864, bound vol. no. 67, RNBP.

87. Morton, "Incidents at Totopotomoy Creek," 50.

88. Pvt. Orrin S. Allen (112th New York Infantry) to Francis Allen, June 4, 1864, Orrin Sweet Allen Papers, 1826–1902, VHS. For more poetry, see Sgt. Reuben L. Whitehurst (16th Virginia Infantry) diary, June 11–12, 1864, Reuben Lovett Whitehurst Papers, VHS.

89. Creed Thomas Davis diary, June 5, 1864, VHS; Robert A. Stiles to Joseph Clay Stiles, June 7, 1864, section 1, Robert Augustus Stiles Papers, 1836–1905, VHS.

90. See Robert Pratt diary, June 10, 1864, bound vol. no. 90, RNBP.

91. Jones to Martha, June 1, 1864, bound vol. no. 68, RNBP; Frederick W. Simonds to "sister Jane," May 31, 1864, bound vol. no. 90, RNBP; Samuel E. Pingree to Cousin Hunton, June 10, 1864, bound vol. no. 90, RNBP.

92. Even keeping with one's own regiment amid disorienting combat could pose a challenge. Men who became separated from their units looked for recognizable faces and corps badges for guidance to the familiar. Pvt. John W. Haley explained: "At night went on picket, and such climbing and dodging around I have seldom been called to do, we did not know which way to look for the enemy, bullets came from every way except one. After dark were relieved and ordered to report to our Regt.," but it was too dark to see. The men slept under a tree; they had long since learned to wait for daylight to identify their corps and division using patches. "Each Corps has a patch of a certain form, and each Div of a Corps. Three in number, are represented by the national colours. Thus the 3rd corps had a diamond patch, the 1st div of that corps would have red patches on their caps," and so on. "So it will be seen that we had only to look at a man's cap and we knew in an instant where we belonged" (John West Haley diary, June 4, 1864, VHS).

93. See Gary W. Gallagher, "The Two Generals Who Resist Each Other: Perceptions of Grant and Lee in the Summer of 1864," in this book.

94. 2nd Lt. William S. Long (44th North Carolina Infantry) to "My Dear Boy," March 3, 1903, bound vol. no. 84, RNBP.

95. Ibid.

96. Hess, *Union Soldier in Battle*, 133–37.

97. Long to son, March 3, 1903, bound vol. no. 84, RNBP.

Breastworks Are Good Things to Have on Battlefields

Confederate Engineering Operations and Field Fortifications in the Overland Campaign

⊰ KEITH S. BOHANNON ⊱

While the 1864 Overland campaign was the first time that Confederate soldiers in the Army of Northern Virginia engaged in sustained fighting behind earthen and log defenses, many men already had experience in constructing earthworks. During the Mine Run campaign in late November 1863, Gen. Robert E. Lee's assistant adjutant general, Lt. Col. Walter H. Taylor, claimed that the men had constructed a strong line of works in "an incredibly short time." Lee personally supervised some of the work, Taylor noting that the commanding general "gave his attention to the whole line, directing important changes here and there." The Army of the Potomac never tested the strength of these earthworks because its commander chose instead to withdraw across the Rapidan River and send his army into winter quarters. When active campaigning resumed the following spring in the Wilderness, Lee envisioned the Mine Run entrenchments as a fall-back position for his army.[1]

As Earl J. Hess notes in *Trench Warfare under Grant and Lee*, continuous confrontation with an aggressive general like Ulysses S. Grant led Lee's Confederates to accept "the need for fieldworks on a continuing basis from Spotsylvania on to the end of the war." This belief in the necessity for field fortifications stood in contrast to the disdain many Rebel soldiers exhibited for breastworks in the campaigns of 1862 and early 1863. The reluctance to order the construction of fieldworks, relates Wayne Hsieh in *West Pointers and the Civil War*, likely related to a long-standing fear among officers who had served in the antebellum U.S. Army that extensive use of entrenchments would enervate troops. John Bell Hood, one of the Army of Northern Virginia's most aggressive generals in 1862 and 1863, claimed that Lee "well knew that the constant use of breastworks would teach his soldiers to look and depend upon such protection as an indispensable source of strength; would imperil that spirit of devil-me-care independence and self-reliance which was one of their secret sources of power, and would, finally, impair the morale of the army."[2]

Hood overstated Lee's reluctance to utilize earthworks, given the Virginian's early war nickname the "King of Spades." Just days after assuming command of the army defending Richmond in the first week of June 1862, Lee ordered the preparation of a line of entrenchments east of the city. He did not, however, plan a static defense of the Confederate capital. Instead he intended to hold the fortifications with a small portion of his army while using the balance of his troops in an offensive movement. This example points to Lee's willingness, particularly by 1864, to use entrenchments to defend a position while also sending troops to attack the enemy elsewhere. Lee utilized such tactics on numerous occasions during the 1864 Overland campaign, although each time the assaults failed to achieve more than localized success or to halt the Union army's advance southward.[3]

Lee's army was ill prepared in some ways for operations in the spring of 1864 that would involve the constant construction of field fortifications. The soldiers had few entrenching tools throughout the Overland campaign, as evinced by numerous accounts of men having to dig earthworks with bayonets, canteen halves, and their bare hands. The army's engineer regiment, which Lee opposed creating in 1863, organized and began training not long before the start of the Overland campaign. Until the second week of June, these engineer companies did relatively little work building or improving defensive lines. Lastly, there was a shortage of engineer officers in the army, despite Lee's efforts to increase their number. Some of the engineers with the army likely spent as much, if not more, time on the critical job of making maps (one of their main responsibilities) as they did supervising the construction of earthworks.

On April 12, 1864, less than a month before the opening of Lt. Gen. Ulysses S. Grant's spring offensive, Robert E. Lee informed Confederate secretary of war James A. Seddon that conflicting intelligence made it difficult to ascertain the goals of the enemy. One possibility for which the southern army must be prepared, Lee stated, was an investment of Richmond. In such a situation, Lee knew that engineers on his staff and those assigned to corps and division commanders would direct the critical tasks of choosing lines of defense. This small group of engineers, Lee had noted at the end of March 1864, "have done well, but their numbers were inadequate to the duties" assigned them. The general recommended reorganizing the engineer corps and increasing its size "commensurate with the wants of the service."[4]

KEITH S. BOHANNON

Maj. Gen. Martin Luther
Smith, a native New
Yorker whose remarkably
varied service in the
Confederacy included
a stint with Lee's army
in 1864. Library of
Congress Prints and
Photographs Division,
LC-DIG-cwpb-05324.

Lee particularly worried about finding a chief engineer for his army. He wrote his son, Brig. Gen. George Washington Custis Lee, on March 29, 1864, that the enemy would likely soon make another attempt on Richmond. In order to meet this offensive, Robert E. Lee believed that "the Corps of Engrs attached to this army should be reorganized and strengthened" with a "proper" chief engineer assigned. If Custis did not take a position commanding troops around Richmond, the elder Lee offered to put his son's name forward for the chief engineer position. The younger Lee had served in the antebellum army's engineer corps, and his father thought the position of chief engineer likely would be agreeable to the son.[5]

The day after writing Custis, General Lee listed his choices for chief engineer in a letter to Col. Alfred L. Rives, acting head of the Confederate Engineering Bureau. The chief engineer should have the rank of brigadier general, Lee explained, and "exercise authority over the troops engaged in engineer constructions on which the whole army is at times employed." Lee knew only three suitable and available officers who could fill the post: Maj. Gen. Martin L. Smith, Col. Walter H. Stevens, and Custis Lee. Lee's letter to Rives exuded a sense of urgency, stating that if these men were unavailable, any "good officer, bold, energetic, and intelligent" would be acceptable.[6]

Secretary of War Seddon recommended and Jefferson Davis accepted the appointment of Martin L. Smith as Lee's chief engineer. On April 6, Smith received orders from the Confederate Adjutant and Inspector General's Office to "proceed without delay" to the headquarters of the Army of Northern Virginia. Lee knew about Smith's orders by April 9, informing Custis of them that day. Smith remained in Richmond, where he had been staying with Gen. and Mrs. Alexander R. Lawton, until the morning of April 15, when he departed to join Lee. General Orders No. 30, dated April 16, 1864, announced to the army that Smith was chief engineer.[7]

Martin L. Smith, an 1842 West Point graduate and topographical engineer in the antebellum army, had served earlier in the Civil War as chief engineer in charge of the defenses of New Orleans and later as a division commander and chief engineer in the 1862 and 1863 campaigns against Vicksburg. Officers who served with Smith during the Overland campaign spoke favorably of him. Brig. Gen. Edward Porter Alexander characterized Smith as "a fine tactician" and "a skillful field engineer," sentiments Lt. Gen. James Longstreet echoed in his memoirs. When Smith transferred to the Army of Tennessee in July 1864, Lee offered his "high appreciation of the zealous and efficient manner" in which Smith had performed all of his duties.[8]

Smith outlined his expectations of division and corps engineer officers in Lee's army in a circular distributed on May 3, 1864, two days prior to the opening of the Overland campaign. (The circular conforms closely to engineer duties as outlined in General Orders No. 90, C.S. Adjutant and Inspector General's Office, June 26, 1863.) Engineer officers were to remain with the advance of their commands. If their units moved into an unfamiliar region, engineers were to make sketches showing prominent terrain features, streams, roads and bridges in need of repair, possible campsites, and all defensible positions. When in close proximity to the enemy, engineer officers were to reconnoiter Union positions. If the Confederate army formed a line of battle, the corps and division engineers were to move rapidly along the front, noting whether the lines were continuous "or if any portion be too far in advance or too much withdrawn."[9]

Smith's May 3 circular mentions nothing about engineer officers assisting with the construction of breastworks. The actions of Lee's corps commanders on the first day of the battle of the Wilderness, May 5, 1864, suggests that decisions about whether to fortify lines had not been mandated through army-level general orders. As numerous historians writing about the Wilderness have noted, Lt. Gen. Richard S. Ewell's Second Corps troops fighting on the Orange Turnpike constructed hasty entrenchments of logs and dirt on May 5. Most of the men in Lt. Gen. Ambrose P. Hill's two Third Corps divisions, exhausted on the evening of the 5th after a day of fierce fighting, did not erect works or straighten their lines, expecting that Longstreet's divisions would relieve them before dawn the next day. Hill deserves some of the blame for the vulnerability of his divisions when the Federals attacked on the morning of May 6, but Lee has also rightfully drawn criticism for not ordering that the Third Corps lines be straightened and fortified. Martin Smith's presence on Ewell's front on the evening of May 5, helping supervise the construction of fieldworks and abatis, deprived the Confederate high command on the Plank Road of an officer who might have supported the arguments of Hill's division commanders to retire their lines and build earthworks.[10]

The construction of the Mule Shoe salient during the Spotsylvania Court House phase of the Overland campaign illustrates some of the difficulties in laying out a line of entrenchments. Capt. William W. Old of Maj. Gen. Edward Johnson's staff wrote after the war of positioning troops on the night of May 8, 1864, along a ridge line that apparently overlooked the enemy. Old, who had been in the saddle almost continuously since the morning of May 5, was ignorant of the topography and had no assistance from engineer officers. Ewell, Johnson's corps commander, and Martin Smith both justified on May 9 holding the ridge to prevent the enemy from placing batteries on it to command the Confederate position.[11]

Despite a limited supply of entrenching tools, Johnson's men strengthened and improved their portion of the Mule Shoe salient between May 9 and the morning of May 12. They also discovered that stretches of this line were subject to enfilade fire. The southerners reacted by digging traverses—short works extending back from the main line at a ninety-degree angle—while engineer officers assisted in the placement of artillery in the salient. When a column of assaulting Federals temporarily breached the southern lines along the western face of the salient in the late afternoon of May 10, Lee responded by ordering Ewell to "rectify his line and improve its defenses," adding a ditch and abatis in front of the trenches where they had been broken. Despite the temporary breakthrough and the protests of at least one artillery officer about the weakness of the salient, Lee, Smith, Ewell, and Ewell's division commanders, Johnson and Maj. Gen. Robert E.

Breastworks Are Good Things to Have on Battlefields

Rodes, remained convinced on May 11 that the Mule Shoe could be held as long as artillery batteries remained along the lines.[12]

Lee's decision on the night of May 11 to withdraw artillery from the Mule Shoe to facilitate the movement of the army weakened the Confederate position substantially, allowing a massive Federal assault to break through the salient on the morning of May 12. Although Lee's troops retook much of the salient and ultimately fashioned another, stronger line along the base of the Mule Shoe, the fighting on May 12 was costly to the Army of Northern Virginia. Less than two weeks later, Second Corps artillerist Col. Thomas H. Carter wrote his wife that Lee had taken "the whole blame on himself" for what happened at the Mule Shoe, "saying it was one of his blunders."[13]

While Lee certainly made a mistake in ordering southern batteries out of the Mule Shoe on the night of May 11–12, the salient was also a "wretchedly defective line," in the words of Colonel Carter. Many years after the war, Brig. Gen. James A. Walker, who had commanded the Stonewall Brigade in the Mule Shoe, wrote that he frequently had heard Confederate engineers censured for allowing the construction of the salient, but Walker claimed they had nothing to do with the disaster on May 12. Lt. Col. Isaac Hardeman, captured in the Union breakthrough on May 10, believed that the southern earthworks were imperfect "owing to the lack of an engineer" competent enough "to make a correct alignment." The recollections of Lt. McHenry Howard of Brig. Gen. George H. Steuart's staff seem to contradict those of Walker and Hardeman, pointing out how engineer officers on May 9 ordered the men of Steuart's brigade to destroy the works they had built initially and construct a new line that ended up forming the northernmost part of the salient.[14]

Lee might have blamed himself for ordering the withdrawal of artillery from the Mule Shoe, but Confederate mapmaker Jedediah Hotchkiss suggests that the commanding general also found fault with one of his engineers for allowing the construction of the large salient. Hotchkiss claimed that Lee had been "very much out with Col. [Walter H.] Stevens . . . for the disposition that had been made of the troops at Spottsylvania C.H." Although Stevens was the chief engineer for the Department of Richmond, he accompanied the Army of Northern Virginia through at least the Wilderness and Spotsylvania phases of the Overland campaign. While the specific activities of Stevens at Spotsylvania are unknown, he might have been one of the engineer officers overseeing the construction of earthworks by Johnson's men.[15]

KEITH S. BOHANNON

If Lee had been upset with his engineers because of the Mule Shoe disaster, the recommendations of Martin Smith and others to Lee along the North Anna River on the evening of May 23, 1864, likely lessened any displeasure. After reconnoitering, Smith proposed construction of a defensive line often described as an inverted V, the left flank anchored on the Little River, the apex at Ox Ford on the North Anna River, and the right running behind a swamp near Hanover Junction. Grant's failure to attack Lee along the North Anna led Martin Smith to believe that "the Yankees have lost all the boldness and dash which characterized their first movements and are now proceeding with caution." The placement of the North Anna line was a major achievement for Smith, although the presence at Lee's May 23 conference of other engineer officers, including Maj. Samuel R. Johnston and Col. William P. Smith, suggests it was a collaborative effort. Smith was undoubtedly correct when he wrote to his wife on May 29, 1864, that he seemed "to have acquired the confidence of Genl Lee to the extent of his being willing to place his troops on the lines of my selection and stake the issue of a battle; more than this is hardly to be expected."[16]

When Smith became Lee's chief engineer, he ordered that all engineer officers submit weekly reports of their operations along with longer reports of battles and campaigns. Although these reports appear not to have survived, personal diaries exist for at least two individuals covering the Overland campaign. The published journal of Second Corps mapmaker Jedediah Hotchkiss illuminates the activities of the Confederate army's most famous topographical engineer. At Spotsylvania, Hotchkiss sketched and copied maps, reconnoitered portions of the Union line at the request of General Lee, and copied and collected information to create maps. After the Union assaults at Cold Harbor, Hotchkiss ventured away from the Second Corps and sketched the Confederate line of battle at the request of Lee. The mapmaker also went to the far southern end of the army's line with chief engineer Smith, to make sketches for forts.[17]

The diary of Capt. Oscar Hinrichs, an engineer assigned to Edward Johnson's division, reveals an officer whose status was in question following the near-destruction of his command on May 12 at Spotsylvania. On May 27, Hinrichs joined the staff of Maj. Gen. John B. Gordon, for whom he prepared a map on June 2. A lame horse kept Hinrichs away from the front during much of the army's time at Cold Harbor, but by June 9 he had orders to prepare another map for Gordon.[18]

If Hotchkiss and Hinrichs are typical of the small number of engineers assigned to Lee's army, such officers probably spent as much time prepar-

Breastworks Are Good Things to Have on Battlefields

ing maps and reconnoitering as they did supervising the placement and construction of earthworks. As a result, the Confederate high command regularly relied on experienced officers outside the engineer corps to assist in establishing new lines. The personal correspondence of Gen. Edward Porter Alexander, First Corps artillery officer, indicates that chief engineer Smith relied on Alexander's expertise in locating artillery positions along the lines at Spotsylvania and the North Anna River. In many instances, multiple field officers assisted the engineers in surveying lines. On May 18 at Spotsylvania, for example, chief of artillery Brig. Gen. William N. Pendleton noted that a section of line on the Confederate right flank had been examined and arranged by himself, Smith, Brig. Gen. Armistead L. Long (Second Corps chief of artillery), and Col. Reuben L. Walker (Third Corps chief of artillery). Nonetheless, the officers also wished Porter Alexander to inspect the line and exercise his judgment on its strength.[19]

Smith and his engineer officers also received limited assistance with the construction of field fortifications from the army's pioneer companies and the 1st Confederate Engineer Regiment, although these organizations spent most of their time performing other duties. Every infantry division had a pioneer company commanded by an engineering officer that assisted the foot soldiers in creating or repairing roads and bridges. Each pioneer company during the Overland campaign had one four-horse wagon at its disposal, which it shared with the division provost guard.[20]

Col. Thomas M. R. Talcott commanded the 1st Confederate Engineer Regiment, which the C.S. Adjutant and Inspector General's Office ordered to join Lee's army on April 12, 1864. R. E. Lee considered Talcott, an antebellum civil engineer who had served on the commanding general's staff for eight months, an officer "marked by ability, zeal[,] devotion & integrity." Most of the field and company-grade officers in the 1st Regiment also had prewar experience as civil engineers.[21]

Lee had opposed the creation of this engineer regiment in the summer of 1863, worried that it would consist primarily of pioneer companies taken from their assigned divisions. He also did not believe, based on experience in past campaigns, "that the duties specially assigned to such troops would authorize the withdrawal of so large a body of the best men from the ranks of the army at this time." Secretary of War Seddon insisted on the creation of the regiment, claiming that many of the men in it would be recent conscripts or recruits and thus not deplete the ranks of Lee's army.[22]

Colonel Talcott's engineer troops received little specialized training prior to the advent of the Overland campaign. Several companies spent February 7 through March 10, 1864, guarding prisoners in Richmond before Talcott argued that he needed to train his regiment. When the regiment finally joined Lee's army, the men spent several weeks performing infantry drills and drilling with pontoons.[23]

During most of the Overland campaign, the companies of the 1st Engineer Regiment handled pontoon trains and built, repaired, or improved bridges in the army's rear over the South Anna and Chickahominy rivers. Their regiment spent little time prior to Cold Harbor locating or creating earthworks, one exception being the construction of rifle pits in the army's rear at Guinea Station and Stanard's Mill on the Po River in mid-May. According to Lt. Henry Harris of the 1st, his regiment joined the main army on the lines at Cold Harbor on June 10.[24]

Infantrymen built the great majority of earthworks during the Overland campaign. At Spotsylvania, Theodore Lyman of Union major general George G. Meade's staff noted the speed with which the Rebels dug rifle pits: "Within one hour there is a shelter against bullets, high enough to cover a man kneeling, and extending often for a mile or two. When our line advances, there is the line of the enemy, nothing showing but the bayonets, and the battle-flags stuck on top of the work." Lyman took it as "a rule that, when the Rebels halt, the first day gives them a good rifle-pit; the second, a regular infantry parapet with artillery in position; and the third a parapet with an abattis in front and entrenched batteries behind. Sometimes they put this three days' work into the first twenty-four hours."[25]

Entrenching tools such as shovels, picks, and axes were often unavailable to Lee's men during the Overland campaign. Porter Alexander claimed the supply was not one fourth what it should have been. C.S. Engineer Bureau officials desperately attempted to furnish tools throughout May and June 1864, but records suggest that the supply never met the demand. Col. Alfred L. Rives noted on June 3 the receipt of a request "to have two thousand shovels kept in hand for the use of Genl Lee's Army." Rives sent to Lee's headquarters the next day, at the request of Major General Smith, 300 shovels, 60 picks, and 120 axes.[26]

On June 7, Rives told Adjutant General Cooper to remind line officers of "the great importance of practicing economy in the use, and care in the preservation of the entrenching tools &c furnished by this Bureau." "The supply on hand is extremely limited," noted Rives, "and in the present scarcity of labor & material, great difficulty is experienced in responding"

Breastworks Are Good Things to Have on Battlefields

to requisitions. Rives claimed that many officers and men "exhibited a de-gree of carelessness & extravagance" with tools, "which threatens serious result."[27]

Entrenching tools remained in constant use in the final days of May 1864, as Lee's army fell back from the North Anna River to a line on Toto-potomoy Creek. When Lee received signs that Grant might be trying to move around the Confederate right flank on the Totopotomoy line, the Confederate commander sent Maj. Gen. Fitzhugh Lee's cavalry to defend an important crossroads at Old Cold Harbor. To support the cavalrymen, Lee ordered Maj. Gen. Robert F. Hoke's infantry division to move from Richmond to Cold Harbor.

On the evening of May 31, Union cavalry drove Fitzhugh Lee's horse-men and one of Hoke's brigades westward from the Old Cold Harbor crossroads, with Hoke's division subsequently entrenching astride the Cold Harbor Road. The following morning, Federal cavalrymen repulsed a poorly planned advance toward Beulah Church by two brigades of Maj. Gen. Joseph B. Kershaw's division. The southerners standing in column behind Kershaw's attacking brigades came under fire from random bullets, wrote Porter Alexander, and "without any general instructions . . . began to dig dirt with their bayonets and pile it with their tin cups to get a little cover. Others followed suit, and gradually the whole column was at work intrenching the line." In time, added Alexander, "it became known that the enemy were accumulating in our front, and then, as the country was generally flat, orders were given to close up the column and adopt its line as the line of battle, distributing our guns upon it at suitable points. Our intrenchments were scarcely more than . . . a line of knee-deep trench with the earth thrown in front. It was entirely without abattis or obstruction in front, except at a point on our picket line where a small entanglement had been left by our cavalry." Kershaw's trenches extended north of Hoke's, the slightly elevated position of the two divisions ultimately forming the backbone of the entire Confederate line at Cold Harbor.[28]

Unlike the Confederate positions at the North Anna River and Toto-potomoy Creek, which engineer officers wholly or partially planned, no one supervised in advance the southern lines at Cold Harbor. Kershaw's works illustrate a point made in the memoirs of one of his brigade com-manders, Brig. Gen. Benjamin G. Humphreys. During the Overland cam-paign, Humphreys wrote, "the officers['] greatest difficulty was in keeping [the men] from digging until the line was established by our engineers." Three years of experience fighting in the open field, Humphreys claimed, had changed the men's notions of the art of war and convinced them that "breastworks are good things to have on a battlefield."[29]

The unplanned nature of Kershaw's and Hoke's lines likely accounts in part for their main weakness, a 75-yard gap between the earthworks of the two divisions in the vicinity of a thickly wooded and swampy ravine. Hoke initially filled the gap by positioning Brig. Gen. Johnson Hagood's brigade about 150 yards in front of the ravine. Unfortunately for the Confederates, Hoke later on June 1 sent Hagood's men south of the Cold Harbor Road to extend the division's southern flank in response to an advance of the Union Sixth Corps. This move left the swampy ravine unprotected. Hoke apparently failed to notify the generals commanding troops on either side of the gap, including Kershaw, of Hagood's departure.[30]

Around 6:00 P.M. on June 1, the Union Sixth and Eighteenth Corps advanced westward against Hoke and Kershaw. The distance between Union and Confederate lines was approximately 1,400 yards, with southern pickets dug in 300 yards in front of their main line. Hoke's men had been laboring on their works since the previous night while Kershaw's troops had been entrenching and clearing fields of fire for several hours. Hoke's soldiers north of the Cold Harbor Road had erected abatis across much of their front, leaving only two paths through the entanglements. When advancing Union soldiers funneled into these openings, the Confederates concentrated their fire on these avenues in successful efforts to repulse the attacks.[31]

A Union advance into the ravine between Hoke and Kershaw proved disastrous for the Confederates. Federals seized the works abandoned by Hagood and outflanked the Confederate lines to the north and south, capturing hundreds of prisoners in the process. Brig. Gen. Thomas L. Clingman, whose North Carolina brigade was immediately south of the ravine, claimed that the Federals approached to within a few yards of his position due to the dense woods and smoke. Confederate reinforcements counterattacked and eventually restored most of the southern position.[32]

That night an artillerist from the 1st Richmond Howitzers watched the entrenching activities of his battery's infantry support, the 20th South Carolina Infantry. This regiment had just joined Lee's army and suffered heavily in Kershaw's attack on the morning of June 1. Having served mainly as garrison troops on the South Carolina coast, the men of the 20th constructed enormous earthworks at Cold Harbor, "in many places eight feet high and six to seven feet thick." When the veteran artillerists began ridiculing the South Carolinians, pointing out the impossibility of fighting

Breastworks Are Good Things to Have on Battlefields

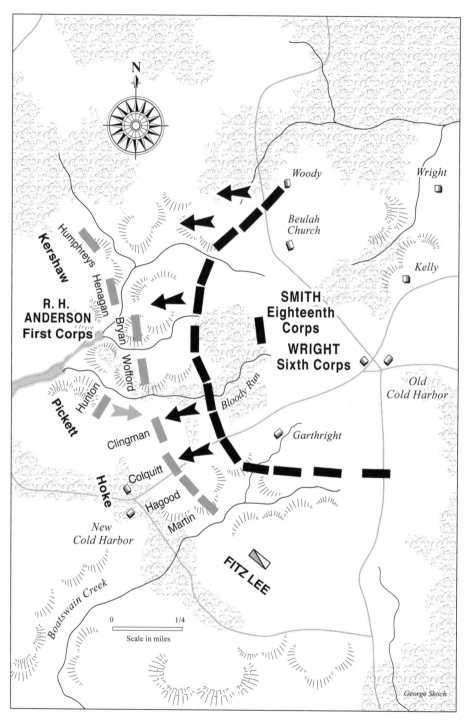

Battle of Cold Harbor, June 1, 1864

Edwin Forbes's study of Brig. Gen. James B. Ricketts's attack on the evening of June 1, 1864, shows Union troops approaching two lines of Confederate works—shallow rifle pits in front and the principal line of logs and dirt running behind the woods and off to the viewer's left. Library of Congress Prints and Photographs Division, LC-DIG-ppmsca-20708.

from behind such a massive embankment, the green soldiers "began to shovel down the top, a little." Capt. Edward S. McCarthy of the Richmond Howitzers informed Kershaw of the impractical works, and the division commander ordered them taken down to a proper height. Some South Carolinians built firing steps inside the works to solve the problem, while others got boxes and logs to stand on so as to be able to fire over the top.[33]

During the night of June 2, Lt. Gen. Richard H. Anderson ordered the construction of a new and stronger line linking Kershaw's and Hoke's positions in the vicinity of the previous evening's Federal breakthrough. Four brigades from Maj. Gen. Charles W. Field's and Maj. Gen. George E. Pickett's divisions worked throughout the night constructing the line. Brig. Gen. Evander M. Law took credit after the war for laying out these additional works, although he had been under orders and supervision from his division commander, Charles Field. Law claimed that the works he replaced on the right of Kershaw's division had been built the previous evening after repulsing the Federal breakthrough. They were "ill-adapted to resist an attack," Law opined, especially assaults as heavy as those launched by the Federals at Spotsylvania.[34]

Law and two staff officers went out on the night of the 2nd and drove stakes into the ground to locate the new position before bringing up men to construct the earthworks. The new line placed a ravine in front, Law claimed, and gave the Confederates "a clear sweep across [the ravines] from the slope on the other side." One of Law's men remembered working all night on the new trenches, completing them "by the first streaks of day." A member of Brig. Gen. Montgomery D. Corse's Virginia brigade arrived in the same vicinity at 10:00 P.M. on June 2, when he and his comrades began "entrenching ourselves with our bayonets [and] by day [were] very well fortified."[35]

By dawn on June 3, an enlisted man in Law's 4th Alabama Infantry noted that the new works had a five-foot-high parapet "with a ditch four feet deep in front and a wide shallow ditch on the inside, and a banquette for the men to stand on while firing." The Confederates also brought up additional cannon and placed them in lunettes. Just prior to sunrise, Georgians of Brig. Gen. Goode Bryan's and Brig. Gen. William T. Wofford's brigades leveled the earthworks that they had constructed the previous day.[36]

South of Kershaw's division, Hoke's men posted along the Cold Harbor Road dug reserve trenches and erected abatis in front of their main position on June 2. The frontline trench of Brig. Gen. James G. Martin's brigade of Hoke's Division, constructed using bayonets and shingles, was six feet across its top. South of Hoke's position, Maj. Gen. John C. Breckinridge's division had reached Turkey Hill between 3:00 and 4:00 P.M. on the 2nd, relieving Fitzhugh Lee's cavalrymen then skirmishing with the enemy. Breckinridge's men, who had only joined Lee's army along the North Anna line and had little experience constructing earthworks, immediately began strengthening the works thrown up by Fitz Lee's cavalrymen, all the time under the fire of enemy sharpshooters. When Robert E. Lee heard that the men of Brig. Gen. Gabriel C. Wharton's and Col. George S. Patton's brigades of Breckinridge's division had constructed breastworks that were too high, he ordered that the works be either lowered or improved with firing steps.[37]

Unfortunately for Breckinridge's soldiers, poor placement of the line initially dug by Fitzhugh Lee's cavalrymen had resulted in a salient with sides about 200 yards long. The ground dropped off a short distance in front of the salient, affording defilade that would allow advancing enemy troops to get within 40 to 80 yards of the southern works. Breckinridge stationed approximately 450 infantrymen under Col. George M. Edgar of Patton's brigade in the salient, along with two or three cannon. The Virginians could not change the layout of works, since they were already under fire from enemy skirmishers in their front. Edgar also could not get reinforcements but strengthened the works by having his men labor on them nearly all night in the drizzling rain on June 2.[38]

The salient occupied by Edgar's Virginians, the gap on June 1 between Hoke's and Kershaw's lines, the poorly placed works on Kershaw's right replaced on the night of June 2–3, and the oversized earthworks of the 20th South Carolina and Breckinridge's men all suggest that Confederates often constructed earthworks without supervision from engineer officers. (Engineer officers were not infallible, but their oversight might have resulted in fewer such flaws in the lines.) Given the short roster of engineer officers in Lee's army, the great difficulty in moving through narrow and crowded trenches, and the eagerness of soldiers to entrench as quickly as possible for protection when they halted, it is hardly surprising that mistakes occurred along an entrenched line that ultimately stretched for seven miles.

Despite the flaws in the Confederate lines at Cold Harbor, the overall position was one of considerable strength. Anderson's corps and a portion of Hoke's division manned the central portion of Lee's position on June 3. The men in these commands had been building and strengthening their works for more than two days. The southern end of the line, held by part of Hoke's division with Brig. Gen. William Mahone's brigade entrenched in his rear in reserve, Breckinridge's division, and Maj. Gen. Cadmus M. Wilcox's division, had been in place for more than twelve hours. The men in the Second Corps and Maj. Gen. Henry Heth's division, holding the northern end of Lee's line, had also had at least twelve hours to entrench. Although the final Confederate line attempted to exploit the terrain, the southerners faced disaster if their lines collapsed because only a couple of bridges spanned the Chickahominy River in their rear.[39]

On the morning of June 3, attacking Union troops from Brig. Gen. Francis Channing Barlow's division of the Second Corps reached the hollow in front of Breckinridge's salient. The Federals then seized the salient, despite being slowed by a line of abatis in front of the parapet. Fortunately for the Confederates, reserves located a few hundred yards in the rear promptly counterattacked and drove Barlow's unorganized men out of the works. Fire from Confederate Third Corps batteries located to the south on the same ridge as Breckinridge's line assisted in the repulse of Barlow.

After the Confederates retook Edgar's Salient, they constructed their

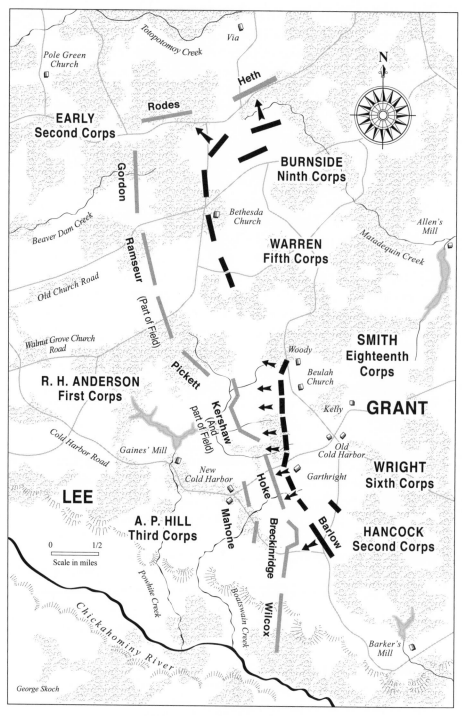

Battle of Cold Harbor, June 3, 1864

main line, probably on the night of June 4. Some sources suggest that the Confederates either completely or partially leveled the salient in Breckinridge's line, while others hint that the southerners continued occupying it with sharpshooters. The Federals remained in close proximity, however, due to what *New York Times* correspondent William Swinton claimed was "a fault of engineering of which the rebels are not often guilty." The Confederate lines had "been drawn on the *rearward* slope of the crest and thrown too far back," Swinton claimed, so that after falling back only a short distance, the Federals were under cover and could construct improvised parapets.[40]

When Federal attackers advanced against the Confederate center and left on the morning of June 3, they encountered a maelstrom of fire. A large reentrant angle in the Confederate center allowed southern artillerists to pour a flanking fire down the length of Union lines advancing across open terrain. North of the Cold Harbor Road, Federals from the Eighteenth Corps charged into open ground in front of a smaller reentrant angle occupied by brigades from Field's and Kershaw's divisions. The Confederate infantry line here included men in the bottom of the trenches passing loaded muskets to others firing over the parapets. North of the Eighteenth Corps's advance, Porter Alexander positioned southern cannon in front of the Confederate breastworks to fire into the right flank of the advancing Federals. The Eighteenth Corps troops, facing devastating fire from three directions, suffered some of the heaviest casualties in the Union army on June 3.[41]

Given Grant's tenacity up to this point in the campaign, General Lee had good reason to believe that the Federals might try to breach his lines again after June 3. That afternoon, Lee ordered his subordinates to "thoroughly examine their lines . . . and cause them to be strengthened as far as practicable with abattis & otherwise."[42]

No Union assaults took place at Cold Harbor after June 3, as the Federals instead commenced several days of siege operations. This was particularly the case along the fronts of the Union Second and Sixth Corps, where the opposing lines were very close. Maj. Gen. Winfield Scott Hancock reported how the Second Corps advanced its line "by regular approaches," while commencing to dig a mine. Col. J. Warren Keifer spoke of advancing zigzag lines to advance toward the enemy works. Some Confederates compared these operations to those during the 1863 siege of Vicksburg, although Lee's men believed their army superior to that commanded by Lt. Gen. John C. Pemberton.[43]

Breastworks Are Good Things to Have on Battlefields

Martin L. Smith noted the developments along Hancock's Second Corps line in his diary on June 6, commenting that the "enemy [are] approaching our line at McGehee & Stewarts houses." That same day, Colonel Talcott of the 1st Confederate Engineers prepared the construction of a countermine to blow up a Federal sap roller being advanced by Barlow's men toward the southern lines. Talcott's men never started the mine, as the Federals abandoned the siege activities shortly thereafter.[44]

While the opposing lines on the southern end of the Cold Harbor battlefield were often close, this was not the case everywhere. Earl Hess's statement that most of the Army of Potomac by the evening of June 3 was "only forty yards from the enemy" is an exaggeration. North of the trenches held by Hoke's and Kershaw's divisions, which are preserved within the Cold Harbor unit of the Richmond National Battlefield Park, Union and Confederate lines were a considerable distance apart. Surviving trench fragments constructed by George Pickett's division are between a quarter- and a half-mile away from the closest Federal lines. In such places, trench systems were probably less complex than those where the opposing trenches were closer. Nonetheless, an 1867 battlefield map drawn from surveys directed by Union engineer Maj. Nathaniel Michler suggests that even where the lines were separated by hundreds of yards, Confederates worried about enfilading enemy artillery fire and built closely spaced traverses to protect against it.[45]

Lt. Gen. Jubal A. Early's position north of Pickett's division was quite some distance from opposing Union lines. Early, Lee's most aggressive corps commander by the time of Cold Harbor, had attacked the Federals several times prior to Grant's main assault on June 3. On May 30, Lee told Early to attack the flank of the Union Fifth Corps near Bethesda Church. Although Early's men overran one Federal division, Union artillery repulsed a further southern advance, costing the Second Corps an estimated 450 casualties. Three days later, Lee ordered Early to attack the retiring troops of the Union Ninth Corps. "Endeavor to get upon the enemy's right flank," instructed Lee, "and drive [him] down in front of our line." Two divisions of Early's corps, along with Heth's division on the far northern end of the Confederate line, achieved some local successes, capturing several hundred prisoners, but did not roll up the Union army's right flank.[46]

On the morning of June 6, Early's troops again advanced when they discovered that the enemy had withdrawn from their front and much of that of Anderson's First Corps to the south. Lee reacted by again ordering Early to attack the Union right flank and rear. Early's skirmishers pressed south against the Union Ninth Corps, encountering a "labyrinth of fortifications" and an impassable swamp Early claimed "could be crossed only by a narrow causeway defended by an entrenched line with artillery." Early further insisted that a division from Anderson that was supposed to support him did not get into position until night. Because Early's position was "too much exposed," he retired his men.[47]

The next day, Early received orders from Lee to move south in front of Anderson's eastward facing line. The Confederate Second Corps pushed south, accompanied by a portion of Lt. Col. Robert A. Hardaway's artillery battalion. Hardaway's guns opened on the Federals, "so as to favor a movement from Anderson's front," wrote Early. Early once again criticized Lee's First Corps commander, claiming that Anderson did not advance as he had been ordered to do. Anderson's report on the Overland campaign is silent on this matter, although the official diary of the First Corps claims that skirmishers from Pickett supported and cooperated with Early.[48]

Porter Alexander wrote after the Civil War that Lee had been "anxious to take the offensive" with Early's corps on June 6 and 7. Unfortunately for the Confederates, the adverse terrain and strong, complex lines of Union entrenchments prevented any chance for success. Although surviving sources do not mention it, Early's men were also likely at risk of coming under friendly fire as they advanced south against the Ninth Corps position, which endured a considerable bombardment from Confederate artillery positioned along Pickett's and Kershaw's lines roughly three-quarters of a mile to the west.[49]

Some of the southern artillery fire against the Union Ninth Corps on June 7 came from cannon being used as mortars along Kershaw's lines. This practice started after June 3 in part as a reaction to the Federal use of mortars against the Confederate trenches. At various points along the southern lines, artillerists sank into the ground the trails of twelve- and twenty-four-pounder howitzers and some Parrott rifles, using them as improvised mortars. (Lee's army did not utilize actual mortars until the siege of Petersburg.) Confederate chief of artillery William N. Pendleton noted that this use of howitzers protected the gun crews from incessant sharpshooting.

Pendleton also proposed to the army's chief of ordnance on June 10 that the howitzers start firing "stink shells," projectiles he had read about in a "recent paper." This undoubtedly referred to an account originally published in the May 16, 1864, *New York World* of a "Yankee revelator" who somehow attended a demonstration behind Confederate lines at a location ten miles from Richmond in mid-April 1864. There a small party of civilians and southern army officers, including Brig. Gen. John H. Winder, witnessed an iron shell designed for use in a mortar emit a stench that "was among the most fetid and villainous that ever assaulted the olfactories of men."

The shells Pendleton proposed would likewise explode and have a "suffocating effect of certain offensive gases." If this was not feasible, Pendleton wondered whether such gases could be created by "a continuously burning composition." Pendleton's proposition did not address the possibility of wind blowing noxious gasses over Confederate lines. Lt. Colonel W. LeRoy Broun of the Richmond Arsenal responded to Pendleton's proposal by noting that he had no "stink-balls on hand, don't keep them; will make if ordered."[50]

On the same evening that Pendleton penned his proposal about stink shells, Jed Hotchkiss "went with Col. Talcott and his Eng. Regt. to the road near Cold Harbor and showed him the outlines of the fort he had to construct." Capt. Henry H. Harris, commanding Company C of the 1st Engineer Regiment, elaborated in his diary on the work his men did on this fort. After sundown on the tenth, Harris's men drew picks and shovels from two accompanying wagons and marched to the front line, where they "laid off the plan of a strong redoubt just in rear of the line of battle." After the moon went down, the engineers commenced digging, trying to keep silent since the enemy was only 120 yards away.

On the night of June 11, clouds obscured the moon, allowing the engineers to work without disturbance, "although many men had to be exposed in bold relief while working on the parapet." The following evening, the men worked undisturbed in the ditches but avoided working on the parapet until after 1:00 A.M., when the moon went down. Harris notes that they completed some parts of the ditch and began "the inner excavations." Such assignments to work on complex redoubts and fortifications were typical by this stage of the Overland campaign for pioneer detachments in both armies.[51]

The operations at Cold Harbor following June 3 resulted in trench systems and defenses more elaborate than any previously constructed in the Eastern Theater. Pvt. John C. Plowden of the 25th South Carolina Infantry noted on June 12 that "the works in front of our Bregad is so blocked up with sharp sticks and Brush that it is almost impossible to get through them." The ground behind the southern lines, noted Lt. Mellish M. Lindsay of General Cadmus Wilcox's staff on June 11, "is perfectly honeycombed with holes in which the men ensconce themselves. . . . Besides these there

KEITH S. BOHANNON

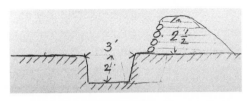

Brig. Gen. Edward Porter Alexander paid careful attention to Confederate
entrenchments in his memoir written in the 1890s. The former artillerist included this
sketch depicting a cross section of the Rebel works at Cold Harbor. Gary W. Gallagher,
ed., *Fighting for the Confederacy: The Personal Recollections of General Edward Porter
Alexander* (Chapel Hill: University of North Carolina Press, 1989), 409.

are numberless trenches leading from one rifle pit to another, and back
towards the rear. It is a queer looking arrangement but certainly a most
comfortable one, for though the two lines of battles are so near each other
and firing is quite constant, very few of our men are hit."[52]

Several enlisted men in Wilcox's division gave far more credit to the
skill of Yankee sharpshooters than did Lieutenant Lindsay. A member of
the 8th Alabama Infantry said that the Federals were "within 75 yards of
our first line and are picking off everybody that exposes himself." The Alabamians noted that since they had no zigzag trenches leading to the rear,
going for water, ammunition, or any other necessary article was extremely
dangerous.[53]

Porter Alexander, who walked long stretches of line while placing cannon, also recognized the hardships of trench life. "Our average ditches
would not exceed 3 feet wide and 2 feet deep, with the parapet two & a
half feet high. They would answer fairly well for men to kneel on the berm
& load & fire from. But when two ranks of men had to occupy them day &
night, in rain & shine, for days at a time it is hard to exaggerate the weary
discomfort of it." The situation was even worse for pickets stationed in
small "gopher holes" holding one or two men located very close to Union
sharpshooters.[54]

Soldiers became increasingly skilled at placing and constructing earthworks, largely because they threw up multiple lines in a short time. A
North Carolina lieutenant claimed that between May 5 and June 2 his regiment dug thirteen lines of works. An Alabama officer remembered that by
the time his men left Spotsylvania, they "were becoming as expert as the
Yankees" at entrenching and "were proud of our efforts and skill."[55]

Despite the soldiers' increasing skill at constructing earthworks, flaws
in hastily constructed entrenched lines nearly resulted in disaster for Lee's

Breastworks Are Good Things to Have on Battlefields

army on several occasions. The placement of lines at night in close proximity to the enemy, directed by staff officers with no formal engineering training, led to positions with serious weaknesses. At other times, terrain factors such as the swampy ravine between Kershaw's and Hoke's divisions at Cold Harbor resulted in gaps or weakened sections of the line. Throughout the campaign, Lee's army received desperately needed reinforcements, but often these troops had little experience constructing field fortifications, resulting in flawed lines such as the one at Edgar's Salient at Cold Harbor that the Federals were able to exploit.

Union siege operations at Cold Harbor after June 3 contributed to Lee's uncertainty about Grant's intentions. As early as June 4, Lee predicted that Grant would try once again to go around the Confederates, this time crossing the Chickahominy River. At the same time, Lee paid attention to his front, informing Secretary of War Seddon on June 9 that the "enemy has been quiet today, apparently engaged in strengthening his entrenchments." Two days later, Lee wrote to Jefferson Davis, "I see no indications of his [Grant's] attacking me in his present position. Think he is strengthening his defenses to withdraw a portion of his force, and with the other move to the James River. To attack him here I must assault a very strong line of intrenchments and run great risk to the safety of the army."[56]

On June 12, Martin L. Smith went reconnoitering in the country "for Entrenched Camp. With Chickahominy for our side." Earl Hess interprets this frustratingly vague passage to suggest that Lee might have been considering the preparation of "a small, well-fortified position to his rear in case he might need to disengage from the Cold Harbor lines." An equally plausible interpretation would be that Lee wanted an entrenched camp south of the Chickahominy to avoid having to fall back farther west into the fixed defenses of Richmond. Whether to construct such an entrenched camp became moot on June 13 when Lee discovered the Federals were gone from Cold Harbor. The Confederate commander reacted by sending the First and Third Corps south of the Chickahominy while ordering Early to take the Second Corps to Lynchburg to counter a Union threat to the Shenandoah Valley.[57]

Robert E. Lee had hoped that the spring campaign of 1864 would allow him to maneuver to advantage against his opponent and defeat the Army of the Potomac on the battlefield. His efforts to reorganize and increase the engineers in the army were made in part to facilitate such operations, given the important role that engineers played in constructing bridges, improving roads, and maintaining the army's pontoons. Although the heavy

KEITH S. BOHANNON

casualties at the Wilderness and Spotsylvania forced the Army of Northern Virginia to fight primarily on the defensive behind earthworks, Lee still sought opportunities to send a portion of his command outside of fortifications to attack the enemy, as displayed on numerous occasions at the Wilderness, Spotsylvania, and North Anna, and at Cold Harbor with the multiple forays of Jubal Early's divisions.

While Martin Smith claimed in a May 29, 1864, letter to his wife that "as we near our base, our situation really becomes stronger," Lee believed otherwise, dreading the prospect of being immobilized behind earthworks. Instead, the Confederate commander constantly sought ways to wrest the strategic initiative from his opponent in an open field contest. "The time has arrived," wrote Lee to A. P. Hill in June 1864, "when something more is necessary than adhering to lines and defensive positions. We shall be obliged to go out and prevent the enemy from selecting such positions as he chooses. If he is allowed to continue that course we shall at last be obliged to take refuge behind the works of Richmond." Such a situation, Lee said presciently to Hill and others, would result in a siege, which "would be but a work of time" before it forced a surrender of the Army of Northern Virginia.[58]

Notes

The author extends his thanks to the following for their assistance with this essay: Gary W. Gallagher, John Hennessy, Caroline E. Janney, Robert E. L. Krick, Robert K. Krick, Kathryn Meier, Eric Mink, and Richard Williams.

1. Walter H. Taylor, *Lee's Adjutant: The Wartime Letters of Colonel Walter H. Taylor, 1862–1865,* ed. R. Lockwood Tower (Columbia: University of South Carolina Press, 1995), 94; G. Campbell Brown, *Campbell Brown's Civil War: With Ewell and the Army of Northern Virginia* (Baton Rouge: Louisiana State University Press, 2001), 247.

2. Earl J. Hess, *Trench Warfare under Grant and Lee: Field Fortifications in the Overland Campaign* (Chapel Hill: University of North Carolina Press, 2007), 42–43; J. Tracy Power, *Lee's Miserables: Life in the Army of Northern Virginia from the Wilderness to Appomattox* (Chapel Hill: University of North Carolina Press, 1998), 63; Wayne Wei-siang Hsieh, *West Pointers and the Civil War: The Old Army in War and Peace* (Chapel Hill: University of North Carolina Press, 2009), 165; John B. Hood, *Advance and Retreat* (1880; reprint, New York: Da Capo, 1993), 131.

3. Hsieh, *West Pointers and the Civil War,* 172.

4. Robert E. Lee, *The Wartime Papers of R. E. Lee,* ed. Clifford Dowdey and Louis H. Manarin (Boston: Little, Brown, 1961), 696; U.S. War Department, *The War of the Rebellion: A Compilation of the Official Records of the Union and Confederate Armies,* 127 vols., index, and atlas (Washington, D.C.: Government Printing Office, 1880–1901), ser. 1, 33:1245 (hereafter cited as *OR;* all references, unless otherwise noted, are to ser. 1).

5. *OR* 33:1245; Lee, *Wartime Papers*, 686.

6. *OR* 33:1245–46.

7. Ibid., 1265, 1287; Lee, *Wartime Papers*, 695; Sarah A. Lawton to Hattie, April 15, 1864, Alexander-Hillhouse Papers, Southern Historical Collection, University of North Carolina, Chapel Hill (repository hereafter cited as SHC).

8. William C. Davis., ed. *The Confederate General*, 6 vols. (Harrisburg, Pa.: National Historical Society, 1991) 5:179; Edward Porter Alexander, *Military Memoirs of a Confederate: A Critical Narrative* (1907; reprint, Dayton, Ohio: Morningside, 1977), 505; James Longstreet, *From Manassas to Appomattox: A Memoir of the Civil War in America* (1896; reprint, New York: Barnes and Noble, 2004), 482; *OR* 40(3):788–89; Hess, *Trench Warfare*, 13. Hess describes Smith as a "superb field engineer, tireless in his work and possessing a good eye for terrain."

9. T. M. R. Talcott, "Reminiscences of the Confederate Engineer Service," in Francis Trevelyan Miller, ed., *The Photographic History of the Civil War*, 10 vols. (New York: Review of Reviews, 1911) 5:270; Albert H. Campbell, "The Lost War Maps of the Confederacy," *Century*, January 1888, 481; National Archives and Records Service, *Preliminary Inventories No. 101 War Department Collection of Confederate Records* (Washington, D.C.: National Archives and Records Service, 1957), 40; *OR* 36(2):944; *OR*, ser. 4, 2:609. Assessing Confederate engineering activities is difficult due to the scarcity of surviving records. T. M. R. Talcott wrote that "the records of the engineer bureau are said to have been removed when Richmond was evacuated" but may have been destroyed at Charlotte, N.C., and Fort Mill, S.C., during the flight of the Confederate government. Albert H. Campbell, topographical engineer, wrote of placing several boxes of original maps and other archives from his office on a train leaving Richmond on April 2, 1865, and later hearing that they likely had been destroyed. A small body of C.S. Engineer Bureau letters and telegrams sent and registers of letters is in the U.S. National Archives.

10. Gordon C. Rhea, *The Battle of the Wilderness, May 4–5, 1864* (Baton Rouge: Louisiana State University Press, 1994), 443–45; William S. Dunlop, *Lee's Sharpshooters; or, the Forefront of Battle* (1899; reprint, Dayton, Ohio: Morningside, 1982), 391. On the controversies in the Confederate high command on May 5, see Peter S. Carmichael, "Escaping the Shadow of Gettysburg: Richard S. Ewell and Ambrose Powell Hill at the Wilderness," in Gary W. Gallagher, ed., *The Wilderness Campaign* (Chapel Hill: University of North Carolina Press, 1997), 136–59

11. William W. Old, "Trees Whittled Down at Horseshoe," in J. William Jones and others, eds., *Southern Historical Society Papers*, 52 vols. (Richmond, Va.: Southern Historical Society, 1876–1959), 33:20–21, 23 (hereafter cited as *SHSP*); *OR* 36(1):1071; William J. Seymour, *The Civil War Memoirs of Captain William J. Seymour: Reminiscences of a Louisiana Tiger*, ed. Terry L. Jones (Baton Rouge: Louisiana State University Press, 1991), 120; A. L. Hull, "Maj. Gen. Martin L. Smith," *Confederate Veteran* 6 (1898): 530. An 1898 obituary of Martin L. Smith offers a different interpretation, claiming that he and Robert E. Lee had wanted to abandon the Mule Shoe for a stronger position in the rear. An unnamed "officer in command of that point" supposedly opposed the change, and Lee yielded.

KEITH S. BOHANNON

12. Seymour, *Civil War Memoirs*, 119; *OR* 36(2):983; Thomas H. Carter to My Precious Wife, May 16, 1864, Thomas H. Carter Papers, Virginia Historical Society, Richmond (repository hereafter cited as VHS).

13. Thomas H. Carter to My Precious Wife, May 24, 1864, Thomas H. Carter Papers, VHS.

14. James A. Walker, "The Bloody Angle," *SHSP*, 21:232–33; Isaac Hardeman, Reminiscences, drawer 283, box 27 (microfilm), Georgia Department of Archives and History, Morrow (repository hereafter cited as GDAH); McHenry Howard, *Recollections of a Maryland Confederate Soldier and Staff Officer under Johnston, Jackson and Lee* (1914; reprint, Dayton, Ohio: Morningside, 1975), 286.

15. Undated [but ca. 1890] mss. by Jedediah Hotchkiss, Jedediah Hotchkiss Papers, roll 49, frames 455–67, Library of Congress, Washington, D.C. On Stevens accompanying J. E. B. Stuart on May 7, 1864, see Theodore S. Garnett, *Riding with Stuart: Reminiscences of an Aide-De-Camp*, ed. Robert J. Trout (Shippensburg, Pa.: White Mane, 1994), 56; Compiled Service Record of Walter H. Stevens in M331, U.S. National Archives, Washington, D.C. (repository hereafter cited as NA); and *OR* 36(3):848. Stevens, who had returned to the defenses of Richmond at Drewry's Bluff by May 29, 1864, succeeded Martin L. Smith as chief engineer of the Army of Northern Virginia. Stevens received Lee's endorsement for promotion to brigadier general on August 22, 1864, with Lee writing that Stevens's duties had been "arduous & dangerous."

16. Gordon C. Rhea, *To The North Anna River: Grant and Lee, May 13–25, 1864* (Baton Rouge: Louisiana State University Press, 2000), 321–23; Edward Porter Alexander, *Fighting for the Confederacy: The Personal Recollections of General Edward Porter Alexander*, ed. Gary W. Gallagher (Chapel Hill: University of North Carolina Press, 1989), 389; Martin L. Smith to "My dear Sarah," May 29, 1864, James S. Schoff Collection, University of Michigan, Ann Arbor (repository hereafter cited as UM). For evidence of Lee's reliance on Smith, see *OR* 36(3):832, 855, and Martin L. Smith diary, May 24, 25, 1864, Charles E. Phelps Collection, Mss. 1860, Maryland Historical Society, Baltimore (repository hereafter cited as MHS).

17. Jedediah Hotchkiss, *Make Me a Map of the Valley: The Civil War Journal of Stonewall Jackson's Topographer*, ed. Archie P. McDonald (Dallas, Tex.: Southern Methodist University Press, 1973), 202–10.

18. Oscar Hinrichs, *Stonewall's Prussian Mapmaker: The Journals of Captain Oscar Hinrichs*, ed. Richard B. Williams (Chapel Hill: University of North Carolina Press, 2014), 120–35.

19. E. P. Alexander to father, May 29, 1864, E. P. Alexander Papers, box 2, SHC; *OR* 36(2):1020; Alexander, *Fighting for the Confederacy*, 389. Although no examples were found from the Overland campaign of engineer and general officers disagreeing on where to place fortified lines, it seems likely that such occasions arose. For an example of this from 1862 involving the chief engineer of the Second Corps, James K. Boswell, and Generals Robert E. Rodes and Daniel Harvey Hill, see Thomas F. Skinker, *Samuel Skinker and His Descendants* (St. Louis: privately printed by author, 1923), 257, 266.

20. Hess, *Trench Warfare*, 16; General Order 27, April 5, 1864, Orders and Circulars Issued by the Army and Department of Northern Virginia, C.S.A., M 912, NA; Robert

Stiles, *Four Years under Marse Robert* (New York: Neale, 1903), 301. Stiles remembered that his division's pioneer corps spent much time at Cold Harbor creating and keeping roads clear to get ammunition up to the lines.

21. *OR* 33:1278; R. E. Lee affidavit on Talcott dated "November 24, 1865, Lexington, Va.," T. M. R. Talcott Papers, reel C551, VHS.

22. *OR* 27(3):1017, 1038–39.

23. Harry L. Jackson, *First Regiment Engineer Troops P.A.C.S.* (Louisa, Va.: R.A.E. Design and Publishing, 1998), 26–34; *OR* 33:1190; David Joyce letter, April 18, 1864, item 147, HCA Auction Catalog, February 25, 2010. Lee and J. E. B. Stuart watched the engineers construct and break down a pontoon bridge in the second week of April 1864; an engineer private boasted in a letter that "we taken it up in eleven minutes and put it down in seventeen.... It is one hundred and twenty feet long" (Joyce letter).

24. Henry H. Harris diary, entries for May 4–June 13, 1864, research files of Robert K. Krick, Fredericksburg, Va.; Jackson, *First Regiment Engineer Troops*, 35–50. For a detailed account of the engineers assisting in the location of lines at Cold Harbor, probably on or after June 10, see William W. Blackford, *War Years with Jeb Stuart* (New York: Scribner's, 1945), 257–58.

25. Theodore Lyman, *Meade's Headquarters, 1863–1865: Letters of Colonel Theodore Lyman from the Wilderness to Appomattox*, ed. George R. Agassiz (Boston: Atlantic Monthly Press, 1922), 99–100.

26. Alfred L. Rives to Capt. T. T. L. Snead, June 3, 1864, and Alfred L. Rives to General M. L. Smith, June 4, 1864, Letters and Telegrams Sent by the Engineer Bureau of the Confederate War Department, M 628, RG 109, NA; Alexander, *Fighting for the Confederacy*, 370.

27. Alfred L. Rives to Samuel Cooper, June 7, 1864, Letters and Telegrams Sent by the Engineer Bureau of the Confederate War Department, M 628, RG 109, NA. For efforts to procure axes just prior to the Overland campaign, see George P. McMurdo to Engineer Department, April 1, 1864, Register of Letters Received, 1862–1864, Confederate Engineer Department, M 628, RG 109, NA.

28. Gordon C. Rhea, *Cold Harbor: Grant and Lee, May 26–June 3, 1864* (Baton Rouge: Louisiana State University Press, 2002), 202–3; Alexander, *Military Memoirs*, 536.

29. Benjamin G. Humphreys memoir, unpaginated typescript, Mississippi Department of Archives and History, Jackson.

30. Rhea, *Cold Harbor*, 202, 203; Hess, *Trench Warfare*, 146; Joseph B. Kershaw to E. P. Alexander, July 9, 1868, Alexander Papers, SHC.

31. Alexander, *Military Memoirs*, 537; Rhea, *Cold Harbor*, 202, 242.

32. Rhea, *Cold Harbor*, 244; Thomas L. Clingman to Editors, *Richmond Daily Whig*, June 5, 1864.

33. William Meade Dame, *From the Rapidan to Richmond, and the Spotsylvania Campaign* (1920; reprint, Richmond, Va.: Owens, 1987), 199–201. Dame claims that Robert E. Lee took the 20th out of line on the night of June 2 and made the regiment into a sapping and mining corps.

34. Rhea, *Cold Harbor*, 264; Joseph B. Kershaw map accompanying July 9, 1868, letter to E. P. Alexander, Alexander Papers, SHC; Charles W. Field, "Campaign of 1864 and 1865," *SHSP*, 14:549; Evander M. Law, "From the Wilderness to Cold Harbor," in

Robert Underwood Johnson and Clarence Clough Buel, eds., *Battles and Leaders of the Civil War*, 4 vols. (1887; reprint, New York: Thomas Yoseloff, 1956), 4:138–39.

35. Law, "From the Wilderness to Cold Harbor," 138–39; William McClendon, *Recollections of War Times* (Montgomery, Ala.: Paragon Press, 1909), 211; Janet B. Hewett and others, eds., *Supplement to the Official Records of the Union and Confederate Armies*, 100 vols. (Wilmington, N.C.: Broadfoot, 1994–2001), 14:545 (hereafter cited as *ORS*).

36. Jeffrey D. Stocker, ed., *From Huntsville to Appomattox: R. T. Coles's History of the 4th Regiment, Alabama Volunteer Infantry C.S.A.* (Knoxville: University of Tennessee Press, 1996), 173; Thomas A. Nicoll to editor, June 3, 1864, *Selma (Ala.) Daily Reporter*, June 20, 1864; *OR* 36(1):1049.

37. Washington L. Dunn diary, June 1, 1864, U.D.C. Bound Typescripts, GDAH; Rhea, *Cold Harbor*, 292; Hess, *Trench Warfare*, 156; *OR* 36(3):870.

38. C. W. Humphreys, "Another Account of Breckinridge's Brigade at the Cold Harbor Battle," *Atlanta Journal*, February 22, 1902; Terry Lowry, *26th Battalion Virginia Infantry* (Lynchburg, Va.: H. E. Howard, 1991), 45–46. One account claims that the field officers in Patton's brigade sent a lieutenant to Breckinridge to report on the weakness of the line, but he was unable to find the general in the rainy darkness.

39. Rhea, *Cold Harbor*, 307.

40. Ibid., 328; Hess, *Trench Warfare*, 158; H. W. Long, "Reminiscences of the Battle of Cold Harbor," Richmond National Battlefield Park Library, Richmond, Va. (repository hereafter cited as RNBP); C. O. Bailey to mother, June 7, 1864, Bailey Family Papers, SHC; William Swinton, "The Grand Campaign," *New York Times*, June 7, 1864.

41. Rhea, *Cold Harbor*, 329–57; Alexander, *Military Memoirs*, 541.

42. Circular signed by R. E. Lee dated "Headquarters, ANVa. June 3, 1864," Minor-Venable Collection, Albert and Shirley Small Special Collections Library, University of Virginia, Charlottesville (repository hereafter cited as UVA).

43. *OR* 36(1):346, 735; Hess, *Trench Warfare*, 175, 200, 206; James B. Daniel to wife, June 7, 1864, RNBP. The opposing lines within the Cold Harbor unit of the Richmond National Battlefield Park are approximately 275 yards apart, while south of the Cold Harbor Road the lines were sometimes no more than 100 yards apart.

44. Martin L. Smith diary, June 6, 1864, Phelps Collection, MHS; Hess, *Trench Warfare*, 172; Jackson, *First Regiment Engineer Troops*, 45–46. For evidence of Confederates at Cold Harbor using sap rollers made from barrels of sand, see Robert H. Stafford to family, June 12, 1864, Stafford Family Papers, Ms #2618, Gilder-Lehrman Collection, New-York Historical Society, New York.

45. Hess, *Trench Warfare*, 164; map titled "Operations at Cold Harbor in the Middle Section of the Battlefield June 2–12, 1864," in *Hanover County, Virginia: A Survey of Civil War Sites in Hanover County, Virginia* (Hanover Court House, Va.: n.p., 2002); plate 92, no. 2, in George B. Davis, Leslie J. Perry, and Joseph W. Kirkley, *The Official Military Atlas of the Civil War* (Washington, D.C.: Government Printing Office, 1891–1895); Robert E. L. Krick to author, May 13, 2008. The Michler map shows regularly placed traverses along a roughly one-mile stretch of Confederate trench line north of the current National Park Service unit and also along an equally long stretch of trenches south of Edgar's Salient.

46. *OR* 36(3):867, 51(1):245; Rhea, *Cold Harbor*, 124–25, 156, 305–6. Lee might have

delivered the June 2 orders to attack in person, inasmuch as Early notes that he met the army commander on June 2 at Mr. Hunter's house along the Mechanicsville Turnpike.

47. *OR* 51(1):245–48; Robert E. Lee, *Lee's Dispatches: Unpublished Letters of General Robert E. Lee, C.S.A, to Jefferson Davis and the War Department of the Confederate States of America, 1862–65*, ed. Douglas Southall Freeman (1915; reprint, with additional dispatches and foreword by Grady McWhiney, Baton Rouge: Louisiana State University Press, 1994), 220; Jubal A. Early, *Lieutenant General Jubal Anderson Early, C.S.A.: Autobiographical Sketch and Narrative of the War Between the States* (Philadelphia: Lippincott, 1912), 364.

48. Early, *Autobiographical Sketch*, 364; *OR* 36(1):1059, 1090.

49. Alexander, *Fighting for the Confederacy*, 413; *OR* 51(1):247–48.

50. *ORS* 36:666, 782; *OR* 36(1):888–89, 1050–51; "The Last Invention Out," *Mobile Advertiser and Register*, July 6, 1864; Alexander, *Military Memoirs*, 542; David G. McIntosh, "A Description of Col. David G. McIntosh's Visit in August 1911 to Some of the Battlefields Around the City of Richmond," David G. McIntosh Papers, U.S. Army Military History Institute, Carlisle, Pa. It is unknown whether Broun or the Richmond Arsenal ever produced stink shells, but it seems unlikely.

51. Hotchkiss, *Make Me a Map of the Valley*, 210; W. Harrison Daniel, ed., "H. H. Harris' Civil War Diary (1863–1865)," pt. 2, *Virginia Baptist Register* 36 (1997): 1846. Robert E. L. Krick, historian at the Richmond National Battlefield Park, believes the works described by Harris stood a short distance south of the Cold Harbor Road along a section of line occupied by Colquitt's brigade. Farmers destroyed the redoubt in the mid-twentieth century. See Robert E. L. Krick email to author, October 19, 2006.

52. John Covert Plowden, *The Letters of Private John Covert Plowden*, ed. Henry B. Rollins (Sumter, S.C.: Wilder and Ward, 1970), 126; Mellish M. Lindsay to "My dear friend," "Hd Qtrs. Wilcox's Div. June 11th, 1864," acc. no. 4093, box 3, UVA.

53. "FCFR" [member of 8th Alabama Infantry], "Letter from Virginia," *Mobile Advertiser and Register*, June 17, 1864; "R-R" [member of 8th Alabama Infantry], "In the Trenches Near Gaines' Mill," *Mobile Advertiser and Register*, June 21, 1864; Alexander, *Fighting for the Confederacy*, 409. Alexander claimed that the absence of zigzag-covered approaches behind the southern lines was due to labor shortages.

54. Alexander, *Fighting for the Confederacy*, 409.

55. J. E. Green quoted in Power, *Lee's Miserables*, 63; Stocker, *From Huntsville to Appomattox*, 171.

56. *ORS* 6:814; Lee, *Wartime Papers*, 770–71.

57. Martin L. Smith diary, June 12, 1864, Phelps Collections, MHS; Earl J. Hess, *In The Trenches at Petersburg: Field Fortifications and Confederate Defeat* (Chapel Hill: University of North Carolina Press, 2009), 14–15. Smith also noted on June 12 that four engineer officers, Col. Walter H. Stevens, Lt. Col. John A. Williams, Capt. William D. Stewart, and Lt. E. O. Mason, reported to him for duty. These officers had previously been assigned to the defenses of Richmond.

58. Martin L. Smith to "My dear Sarah," May 29, 1864, Schoff Collection, UM; Lee, *Wartime Papers*, 759–60; *OR* 40(2):702–3. For another example of Lee's telling

a subordinate that the army could not stand a siege, see J. William Jones, *Personal Reminiscences, Anecdotes and Letters of Gen. Robert E. Lee* (New York: Appleton, 1876), 40. Clifford Dowdey and Louis H. Manarin provide only a month and year, June 1864, for the Robert E. Lee letter quoted here but place it after a document dated May 31 and before one dated June 1. The editors of the *Official Records* placed it in the middle of some June 30, 1864, correspondence.

Francis Channing Barlow's Civil War

⊰ JOAN WAUGH ⊱

Winslow Homer's painting *Prisoners from the Front* conspicuously featured his friend and distant cousin Union brigadier general Francis Channing Barlow (1834–96). Barlow's figure symbolized the imminent U.S. victory over the rebellious Confederacy represented in human form by the three captives. The painting, not completed until after the war, was inspired by a series of sketches Homer made while observing the movements of the Federal army during the Virginia campaigns from April to August 1864. Some experts believe the sketches were made in mid-to-late May after the battle of Spotsylvania, where Barlow's unit captured 3,000 Rebels. One contemporary critic described the Yankee officer as "the hard, firm faced New England man, without bluster, and with the dignity of life animated by principle." When it debuted in April 1866 at New York City's National Academy of Design, most northern viewers easily identified the baby-faced Barlow, one of the best-known "boy generals" of the Army of the Potomac, as the "moral center" of the picture.[1] Strikingly self-confident, General Barlow gazes at the three Rebels—the defiant youthful cavalier, the worn-down older man, and the humble yeoman farmer's son—perhaps imagining how such a war-torn country would turn this trio of present enemies into reconstructed loyal citizens.

What combination of fate, character, and circumstance brought the young, New York–born, Massachusetts-bred, Harvard-educated lawyer and aspiring Republican politician to the Civil War battlefields and eventually to the killing fields of Cold Harbor and Petersburg? This essay will answer that question, providing ballast, background, context, and critical commentary fleshing out the idealized Barlow immortalized by Homer's masterful work. After examining his family origins, education, and early war career, it will turn the spotlight on Barlow's lowest point—from Cold Harbor in June through August of 1864 in Petersburg, Virginia. One thing should be made clear. The facts support a praiseworthy if controversial record. Barlow, a volunteer who rose from private in 1861 to major general in May 1865, and the troops he commanded distinguished themselves in

Prisoners from the Front (1866). Winslow Homer's celebrated painting, which shows Francis Channing Barlow and three Confederate prisoners at Petersburg in June 1864, garnered warm praise when first exhibited a year after Appomattox. A writer for the *New York Evening Post* thought Homer's Barlow represented a "hard, firm-faced New England man, without bluster, and with the dignity of a life animated by principle." Metropolitan Museum of Art, New York, New York.

the battles of Fair Oaks, Antietam, Chancellorsville, Gettysburg, Spotsylvania, and Cold Harbor. But by the time of the battles of the Petersburg campaign, the quality of Barlow's generalship and the fighting skills of his men had declined markedly. Controversy and personal instability stalked Barlow in those summer months. His published letters as well as testimony from both admirers and critics suggest a desperate man caught up by the torments of war that eventually rendered him incapable of leading troops. Indeed, Barlow's alarming manifestations of physical and mental fatigue may well be categorized in modern terms as "combat trauma," forcing him to take a nine-month leave of absence before returning to active duty only in the last month of the war.[2]

Background

His family enjoyed status but not wealth. The middle of three sons, Francis Channing Barlow was born on October 19, 1834, in Brooklyn, New York, to the Reverend David Hatch Barlow, a Harvard-educated Unitarian minister, and Almira Penniman of Brookline, Massachusetts. The youngster's lineage included free thinkers, transcendentalists, composers, poets, abolitionists, and philosophers. When Francis was two, the family moved to Brookline, where his parents were members of the Boston-Concord literary circle that included Ralph Waldo Emerson, who later became the boy's hero and the student's inspiration. The Barlows were fairly comfortable financially until disaster struck when David Barlow, beginning a lifelong descent into alcoholism, abandoned his wife and three young sons. Almira returned briefly to her parents' house but soon moved with her children in 1841 to Brook Farm, a utopian community established in nearby Roxbury, Massachusetts. The unconventional Almira was admired for her beauty, pluck, and intelligence. She wanted her three sons—Edward, Francis, and Richard—to be educated in Brook Farm's highly regarded primary school. A few years later she moved again, this time to Concord, where Francis lived and breathed the antislavery sentiment common among many New England reformers. He received excellent preparation for entrance at age seventeen into Harvard, where he graduated first in his class in 1855.[3]

In college, Frank Barlow developed several of the character traits that would appear in compelling relief during the Civil War. He was very smart, supremely self-possessed, exhibited a strong temper, and did not suffer fools lightly. Those traits in their early stages led some students at Brook Farm to label him affectionately "Crazy Barlow." Edwin H. Abbott (Harvard '55) penned a perceptive obituary in which he observed of his late friend, "He always perceived existing facts and relations with singular precision and quickness. He prided himself in college upon having no illusions, and was resolved to see things as they really were. He then, and ever afterwards, spoke his thoughts without restraint, and with a singular and almost contemptuous disregard of consequences. He indulged throughout his life in a very unusual freedom, not to say license, of speech." Barlow's sole biographer, Richard F. Welch, observed that the recent college graduate "was already noted for his highly polished ego and strongly opinionated personality, characteristics which led him to freely express his disdain for people, behavior and ideas he considered ignorant or inferior."[4] Confirmation of both observations is found in letters Barlow sent to his brother and mother early in the war. He found little comradeship among fellow officers and looked down on the common soldiers. "I have not the desire to make the damned scoundrels like me," he wrote of the men, "+ do not think they do especially." Even worse, he complained to his mother, "I have not seen one person in Washington who was above the rank of commonplace + should like to get into the society of intelligent people."[5] Barlow's attitudes reflected his class and rank; his bold assertion of a preference for such narrow exclusivity proved a liability as a soldier in a largely amateur army of citizen-soldiers.

A true understanding of Francis Barlow's military career must begin with his education at Harvard, the nation's premier college then as now. Several scholars argue that Harvard-educated officers shared a unique attitude that combined martial courage with the idea that *they* in particular had a "calling" and a duty to lead, to educate, to control, and to enlighten the untutored masses. Naturally, this attitude sprang from place and privilege as well. Civil War specialist David W. Lowe asserted, "For members of Boston's highly stratified antebellum society, pedigree determined the course of life. Those born into wealth and position exacted daily deference from their social inferiors. If it came to war, few questioned the assumption that the upper classes would furnish officers, and the lower classes, the rank and file."[6] Biographer Welch described his subject's capacious ego as springing from an "assumption of place and prerogative." Welch and others contend that the idea of a special calling and the personality traits that it fostered were embedded in a character-driven upbringing stressing public service and philanthropy. Harvard's classrooms cultivated and strengthened the ideals of duty to society and country.[7]

Born into a generation in which sectional tensions over the expansion of slavery were a constant drumbeat, Harvard's best young men with names like Abbott, Adams, Dwight, Higginson, Holmes, Lowell, Lyman, Paine, Putnam, Sanborn, Sturgis, Shaw, and Weld eagerly joined a conflict that provided an opportunity to test their capacities as leaders in saving the imperiled Union. Barlow lost many college friends and acquaintances during the war, including two of his closest ones, Col. Robert Gould Shaw and Col. Charles Russell Lowell. Christian Samito, editor of Barlow's wartime letters, observed that Barlow had "wielded both his sword and his mind in support of the principles he risked his life to uphold."[8] This described well a man who throughout the conflict was by turns ambitious, prideful, sarcastic, and doubtful of northern will and occasionally of ultimate Union victory. Yet at the end, Maj. Gen. Francis C. Barlow achieved the distinction of being the highest-ranking officer among all the Harvard volunteers who fought for the United States.

After Harvard, Barlow moved to New York City. He gained admittance to the bar in 1858, and by 1861 he was a partner in a prosperous law firm with connections to the city's leading figures among Republicans and Democrats. Planning a career in both law and politics, he counted Democrat Charles Patrick Daly, one of New York's most influential judges, as a mentor.[9] He also dabbled in the newspaper business, writing the occasional editorial for the Republican-leaning *New York Tribune*. Slight of build and standing one inch less than six feet, the gray-eyed Barlow possessed a dynamic and energetic temperament that rarely failed to impress. The twenty-five-year-old lawyer became a soldier after Fort Sumter, when he enlisted as a private on April 21, 1861, in Col. Daniel A. Butterfield's 12th New York Militia Regiment. The day before he volunteered, Barlow married Arabella Wharton Griffith of Somerville, New Jersey. "Barlow married Miss Arabella Griffith at St. Paul's Chapel Saturday evening, left her at the church door, and went to Washington yesterday," recorded prominent New York diarist George Templeton Strong. Impressed that Barlow would take up his duties so quickly, Strong added, "We are *not* utterly corrupt and mercenary."[10]

Arabella was more than a decade her husband's senior, and her age combined with Frank's unusually youthful countenance invited more than a few nasty comments. A friend of the couple, acid-tongued New York diarist Maria Lydig Daly (the wife of Democratic judge Charles P. Daly), described Barlow as "Arabella's boy-husband" and recalled witnessing an embarrassing introduction of Frank as her son.[11] Despite the gossip their age gap provoked, they appeared to be devoted to each other. Strong later described Arabella as "a sensible, practical, earnest, warm-hearted woman, without a phrase of hyperflutination."[12] Mrs. Barlow worked as a nurse with the U.S. Sanitary Commission during the war, frequently under dangerous conditions at the big hospitals in Washington, D.C., and Petersburg, and earned reverent respect for her service. A doctor remembered Arabella's "sparkling wit, her brilliant intellect, her unfailing good humor . . . [and] her warm and loving nature." The marriage was cut tragically short by her untimely death from typhus in the summer of 1864, contributing mightily to Barlow's crisis during the Petersburg campaign.[13]

The Civil War: November 1861–December 1863

Barlow's initial enlistment proved disappointedly uneventful. After a few weeks protecting Washington's defenses, he mustered out of the short-term unit in August 1861, leaving as a first lieutenant. That November he returned to duty, commissioned as lieutenant colonel of the 61st New York Volunteer Infantry.[14] The unit attained prominence as a hard-fighting regiment in the Second Corps of the Army of the Potomac. Lt. Col. William F.

Fox singled out the 61st's leadership for warm praise in his study of Civil War regiments: "The Sixty-first had the good fortune and honor to be commanded by men who proved to be among the ablest soldiers of the war. They made brilliant records as colonels of this regiment, and, being promoted, achieved a national reputation as division generals." Fox continued, "The Sixty-first saw an unusual amount of active service and hard fighting. It served through the war in the First Brigade, First Division, Second Corps . . . commanded successively by Generals Richardson (killed at Antietam), Hancock, Caldwell, Barlow and Miles." [15]

Promoted to colonel in early 1862, Barlow prepared his unit for participation in Maj. Gen. George B. McClellan's Peninsula campaign. He admired his commander's strict disciplinary practices when he saw the visible improvement in the soldierly bearing of the men. The observant, newly minted colonel cultivated his own inclinations on how to make green volunteers combat-ready. He mastered tactical skills by reading military textbooks and emulating the examples of the professional officers with whom he came into close contact, working strenuously to apply lessons learned. Barlow became well known for imposing a harsh regimen, occasionally blurring the line between legitimate discipline and illegal coercion.[16]

In camp with the 61st, Barlow enforced a sturdy and steady discipline stressing obedience to authority and efficiency in training, and he applied business methods to organizing the distribution of food, clothes, and other supplies. His detailed written directives were distributed and put into practice under his watchful eye. Barlow disliked the casual anti-authoritarian approach to discipline common in the volunteer Union army. From the training camp near Alexandria, Virginia, he wrote, "Whoever comes under me will have to submit to severe discipline for I keep them all right in my hand." With each successive command, Barlow created "classrooms" that schooled both his commissioned and noncommissioned officers in drill, in camp discipline, and in tactics. "What takes up my time," Barlow claimed, "is the making rules + regulations + following them up throughout the Regt from highest to lowest."[17] Corp. Charles A. Fuller of the 61st provided a glimpse into the effect of Barlow's earliest efforts: "Discipline became stricter: the duties of the soldier were better explained, and the men sensibly improved." Fuller expounded, "At first, from his exacting requirements and severity he was quite disliked, if not well hated; but, as time went on, and it was seen that he knew more than any other man, or set of men, in the regiment—that he knew how to work his men to the best advantage, and would see that they had what the regulations prescribed, and, that, when danger was at hand, he was at the head *leading* them, this animosity was turned into confidence and admiration."[18]

Barlow and the 61st saw significant action during the 1862 Richmond campaign. The colonel's first combat experience occurred on June 1 during the second day of the battle of Fair Oaks. The 61st New York was attached to Brig. Gen. Oliver Otis Howard's brigade of Maj. Gen. Edwin Vose Sumner's Second Corps. In this engagement, Barlow and his men displayed admirable valor, with casualties totaling 110 killed and wounded. Although Fair Oaks proved a tactical standoff, Barlow was pleased with the outcome for his unit and provided detailed information to his family in several letters written right after the battle. "My men behaved really admirably," he affirmed proudly on June 2. "We were the only Regt. of the Brigade which did not break + run at some time or another."[19] Howard praised his subordinate, reporting, "I desire especially to notice the coolness and good conduct of Colonel Barlow of the 61st New York."[20]

Barlow also performed heroically on June 30 at the battle of Glendale, where he led his troops in a charge with the shout, "Up and at them, men!" Under severe fire at both Fair Oaks and Glendale, the 61st experienced heavy casualties, and Barlow's horse, "Billy," was killed. After participating in the battle of Malvern Hill on July 1, Barlow retreated with the army to Harrison's Landing. McClellan's failure to crush the Confederate army and take Richmond dashed hopes for an early end to the increasingly bloody conflict. Instead, the rise to prominence during the Richmond campaign of Confederate commander Robert E. Lee and his Army of Northern Virginia would prolong the war far beyond what most had expected at its inception.[21]

Barlow assessed the Union's war effort at the end of the summer of 1862 and found it pathetic. This fit a pattern of his rendering gloomy judgments about the course of the conflict. While he remained a loyal supporter of the Republican Party, Barlow repeatedly expressed doubt in its leadership's ability to win the war and in the loyal civilian population's will to endure hard times. Five quotations written between January 1862 and July 1864 illuminate Barlow's "chronic disgust" (arguably accurate) and pessimism. "I hardly think this disgusting country is worth fighting for," he wrote early in 1862. "If we are beaten," he predicted a few months later about he Army of the Potomac's prospects, "the North will give up." August of the same year brought forth an admonition against military service. "I would not enlist if I could help it," he declared of those not in uniform. "We shall have to acknowledge the S. Confederacy in the end." A letter written a week before Antietam warned that "The affairs of the Country look melancholy enough. . . . I think there is no prospect or hope of success in this war. . . . I am in a state of chronic disgust." After Lt. Gen. Jubal A. Early's raid on Washington, D.C., in the summer of 1864, Barlow's anger overflowed. "I am utterly disgusted with the craven spirit of our people," he fumed. "I wish the enemy had burned Baltimore + Washington + hope they will yet."[22]

Overall, Barlow's published letters do not explicitly engage with or analyze politics at great length, nor do they linger much on the ideals animating the Union cause.[23] Nonetheless, he showed himself to be a savvy observer of the national scene. Though the letters lack the literary quality one might expect from such an outstanding scholar, they are well written and interesting. Political views emerge inferentially in alternatively chatty, plaintive, affectionate, and angry missives. Details of camp and combat are described clearly, revealing a strong practical, rather than idealistic or religiously based, approach to life. Boston lawyer and Harvard classmate Edwin H. Abbott mused on Barlow's bent much later: "His total lack of reverence and apparent inability to be afraid . . . impaired his capacity to form high ideals." Decades after the war, the man who was forged in the fires of abolition and transcendental passions compared Lincoln favorably with George Washington as vital to preserving a Union worthy of its ideals. During the conflict, however, he was unsure as to whether or not that Union would be preserved by incapable leaders and a weak-minded people.[24]

Barlow did not limit his disdain to the northern people and their elected leaders. Along with other junior officers in McClellan's army, he expressed dismay at its defeat in the Peninsula campaign. Cautioning his brother Edward, "*all this is strictly private*," he proceeded to launch a blistering attack on the top generals of the Army of the Potomac: "I am thoroughly disgusted with our Generals. . . . You have no idea of the imbecility of management both in action + out if it." Referring to the inexplicably favorable press coverage of McClellan's latest gambit, he continued, "We are surprised to hear from the New York papers that we gained a great victory. We thought here that we had made a disastrous retreat leaving all our dead + wounded + prisoners + material + munitions of war in the hands of the enemy."[25]

From 1862 to 1865, Barlow's criticism of the top Union generals, from McClellan to Grant, remained consistent. He charged that higher officers, because they failed to develop and implement a clear strategy, wasted too many men and materials "without concert or system."[26] Yet, while Bar-

Francis Channing Barlow's Civil War

low's letters and recorded comments are notably absent of flowery patriotic sentiments and unleavened with much cheerfulness or optimism, his words and actions left no doubt about his devotion to the Union and determination to defeat the Confederacy. While expressing admiration for the courage of Rebel soldiers, Barlow believed that slavery deserved to die and should be replaced by free labor and the North's values, principles, and lifestyle in the restored Union.[27]

Barlow missed the Union debacle at Second Bull Run but moved into western Maryland in pursuit of the Army of Northern Virginia with General McClellan and the Army of the Potomac in early September 1862. He was placed in charge of the greatly diminished 61st as well as the 64th New York Infantry, both assigned to Brig. Gen. John C. Caldwell's Second Brigade in the Second Division of Sumner's Second Corps. On September 17, near Sharpsburg, his two small regiments participated in Sumner's midmorning attack, during which Barlow burnished his record as an adept and aggressive officer. By late morning he received orders to attack the enemy in a sunken road (later called Bloody Lane by soldiers in both armies), where two Confederate brigades anchored the center of Lee's line. His unit captured more than 300 prisoners and three colors in the effort. First Lt. Ezra Ripley of the 29th Massachusetts Infantry (Harvard '46), witnessing Barlow's actions, described the scene in a letter as the young colonel, accoutered in a new uniform, hurried on foot and "rushed up the hill at the head of his little regiment, looking so handsome, facing his men to cheer them, moving with such grace and elasticity, that it seemed as if he were dancing with delight." Ripley continued his admiring account, "I have seen brave men and brave officers; I saw that day colonels coolly and bravely lead their regiments; but I never saw such a sight as Barlow's advance, and never expect to again. It was a picture,—it was poetry."[28]

Barlow and his men proceeded to a cornfield "beyond the deep road," where they engaged in more heavy action. The Federals came under fire from Rebel artillery in a nearby orchard, and Barlow suffered a severe wound. His official report from a field hospital in Keedysville, Maryland, on September 22 described the scene: "After thus forming our line on the right of the Fifty-seventh New York Volunteers of Colonel Brooke's brigade, I was wounded in the groin by a ball from a spherical-case shot. . . . My own regiment, the 61st New York Volunteers, behaved with the same fortitude and heroism, and showed the same perfect discipline and obedience to orders under trying circumstances, for which I have before commended them, and which causes me to think of them with the deepest affection and admiration."[29]

Doctors treated Barlow's injury with water dressings only, thinking that he would not survive. Surprising them, he lived, but his painful wound did not heal quickly. A serious case of malaria further impaired his health, which a medical expert assessed several weeks later. The wound, with an open abscess, continued to bother Barlow into the middle of November. Further troubled with numbness in his left leg and loss of weight, he missed the battle of Fredericksburg in early December.[30] The expert ministrations of Arabella probably saved Barlow's life during a seven-month recuperation in New York City. During this time his promotion to brigadier general foundered, and a group of supporters led by Ralph Waldo Emerson sent a letter dated February 28, 1863, urging Maj. Gen. Ethan Allen Hitchcock to correct the omission. Emerson, who wrote the document, described Barlow as "a man of great national ability,—from a boy, first among his mates; at Harvard College, first in his class; and in the army. . . . We have looked on him as one of those valuable officers which the war was creating."[31]

His promotion came through, and Barlow was eager to return to duty. He sought reassignment to the Second Corps but instead was ordered to brigade command with Maj. Gen. Oliver Otis Howard's Eleventh Corps. New to the Army of the Potomac, the Eleventh already suffered from a poor fighting reputation, partly due to controversies surrounding its large German American contingent composing just fewer than half of its 11,000 soldiers. Barlow's appointment was expected to improve the morale and fighting readiness of demonstrably subpar troops.[32]

In April 1863, Barlow met with his new staff officers and immediately implemented his training and educational methods. His style of leadership had worked well with the men of his previous regiments—once they saw the benefits of organization and efficiency in camp, on the march, and on the battlefield. Officer Samuel S. Parmalee of the 1st Connecticut Cavalry watched Barlow with his soldiers and provided a report in a letter. "His old regt. hated him as they hated anything," noted Parmalee, "but he was the man after all they wanted to go into a fight with."[33] Barlow's new regiments could not yet appreciate the future benefits suggested by Parmalee. Civil War privates detested officers perceived as exceeding their authority or acting as if they were better than men in the ranks.[34] Barlow consistently did both. Whether in command of Yankee or German (typically called

"Dutch" during the Civil War) or Irish troops, he cultivated a deliberate aloofness from his men, believing it the best way for making real soldiers out of undisciplined volunteers. He also meted out the harshest possible punishments under the Civil War military justice system. Charles Fuller chronicled a disturbing incident he witnessed during the battle of Malvern Hill. When an exhausted soldier asked to be relieved of duty, Barlow "cursed and swore at him and called him a variety of unpleasant and detestable things and then he began to punch him with his fist wherever he could hit," ending the scene by kicking him on the backside with the parting jab, "Damn you, get away from here! You're not fit to be with my brave men." Afterward, Fuller remarked humorously, soldiers of the 61st "preferred to meet the rebels rather than the vocal scorn and denunciation of Barlow."[35]

Barlow's primary concern then and later was not with winning a popularity contest but, rather, with establishing a reputation as a commander of disciplined, well-trained, battle-ready units with good morale and confidence. A firm believer in the benefits of a highly disciplined life, he made instituting and promoting those characteristics and qualities a hallmark of his leadership. Information about his methods circulated in New York City, prompting Maria Lydig Daly to comment after hearing rumors of his hard methods, "Barlow, they say, is very cruel to his men. He may, however, be only a stern disciplinarian."[36] Much later, Barlow explained his reasoning: "War is a savage business, and it is idle to try to introduce tenderness into it, except so far as relates to the care of soldiers and the treatment of the sick and wounded. If, after every action each regiment should condemn to death every man who had fallen out without urgent reasons . . . it would establish a discipline and a spirit that would have saved thousands of lives." Criticizing Lincoln's lenient policy, Barlow concluded, "Harsh as this may seem, it would in the end be the greatest humanity, for when cowards and stragglers are pardoned and honored, it is at the expense of brave and faithful soldiers."[37]

That he could be kind as well as cruel is also well documented. The best kindness was making sure his men were well fed, clothed, and cared for medically, which he did to the best of his ability. Barlow never evoked the love and loyalty other soldiers manifested toward more likeable commanders, but his troops reluctantly appreciated his ability to instill battle readiness in them. This was no small feat with the undisciplined Civil War troops. Consistent praise was also forthcoming for Barlow's courage in battle. His officers remembered their commander's favorite exhortation before a fight: "Make your peace with God and mount, gentlemen. I have a hot place picked out for some of you to-day."[38] Indeed, Frank Barlow sought out those hot places. Arabella was quoted as saying that her husband "loves fighting for the sake of fighting, and is really bloodthirsty." Edward Barry Dalton, a family friend who served as a Civil War surgeon, wrote home, "I am . . . very much afraid for Barlow, for as we know, he is not only brave, but reckless. I think I never knew anyone so perfectly without fear of physical injury."[39]

The Eleventh Corps accompanied President Abraham Lincoln's latest commander of the Army of the Potomac, Maj. Gen. Joseph Hooker, as he moved toward a confrontation with Lee's army along the Rappahannock River line in late April 1863. Just before the battle of Chancellorsville, Barlow's brigade was detached from General Howard to assist Maj. Gen. Daniel E. Sickles's Third Corps. Thus Barlow was absent when Lt. Gen. Thomas J. "Stonewall" Jackson made his famous flank attack on May 2, sending much of the Eleventh Corps into a panicked retreat that contributed to another Union loss. Capt. Stephen Minot Weld (Harvard '60) of the 18th Massachusetts Infantry captured the prevailing tone among many officers when he stated a few weeks later, "The Corps has such a bad reputation that any good soldier feels himself disgraced to be in it."[40] The northern press reveled in portraying the whole Eleventh Corps as cowards, ignoring the fact that Barlow's brigade fought courageously. Angered that newspapers made no distinction between his troops and the rest of the corps, he fumed, "You can imagine my indignation + disgust at the miserable behavior of the 11th Corps." Former Harvard classmate and lawyer Robert Treat Paine received a letter with the simple declaration, "These Dutch won't fight. Their officers say so + they say so themselves + they ruin all with whom they come in contact." To be fair, Barlow cast *his* blame more widely when he admitted, "Some of the Yankee Regts behaved just as badly."[41]

Barlow's open contempt for the men who would fight under him at his next battle, in early July at Gettysburg, reveals a weakness as a military leader. His attitude may have undermined the morale of soldiers even if their training was first rate. This type of denigrating remark for immigrant troops was widespread among Barlow's Harvard cohort, who often viewed the men they led as almost impossible to make into good soldiers.[42]

Barlow assumed command of the First Division of the Eleventh Corps in late May 1863. Part of the advance forces of the newly appointed commander of the Army of the Potomac, Maj. Gen. George G. Meade, Barlow and the division marched toward Gettysburg early on the morning of July

1. Upon arrival, Barlow learned that General Howard was in command of both the First and Eleventh Corps. Maj. Gen. Carl Schurz, acting commander of the Eleventh, ordered Barlow to hurry through Gettysburg and take a position just north of the town. The goal was to prevent Confederate forces from seizing the high ground south of Gettysburg, which offered a superb defensive position for the Federals. Barlow eventually deployed his men on a rise known as Blocher's Knoll, forming a defensive salient that caused him to lose contact with the next division. Despite the gap in the line, Barlow believed that taking the high ground would offer him a better fighting position. As he explained the situation to Almira: "We ought to have held the place easily, for I had my entire force at the very point where the attack was made. But the enemies skirmishers had hardly attacked us before my men began to run. No fight at all was made. Finding that they were going I started to get ahead of them to try to rally them + [form] another line in the rear."[43] Although the eminent Gettysburg battle historian Harry W. Pfanz, among others, has condemned as rash the movement to what is now known as Barlow's Knoll, others concluded that nothing could have been done to prevent the disaster that struck Barlow's right flank as the Confederates slammed into him.[44]

Amid confusion and chaos on the afternoon of July 1, Barlow tried desperately to rally his troops and was again severely injured, shot through the body by a minié ball that barely missed his spine and left him paralyzed. Fleeing Federals passed by him, assuming he was dead, as they fell back to Cemetery Hill, leaving him the only Union general captured on the battle's first day. According to some accounts, Confederate brigadier general John B. Gordon was responsible for saving the stricken Barlow's life by giving him water and arranging his transport to a Confederate hospital. Barlow later described exactly what happened: "They put me on a bed + about dark 3 Confederate surgeons came. They gave me chloroform + probed my wound. When I woke up they told me that a Minie ball had passed downward from where it entered, + through the peritoneum + lodged in the cavity of the pelvis + that there was very little chance for my life."[45]

Late that evening, Arabella appeared on the battlefield and was given permission to go to her husband. Captain Weld observed her arrival: "On my way back I saw a lady riding in, through all those bullets, on a horse with a side-saddle, who turned out to be Mrs. General Barlow. She had heard of her husband's dreadful wounds and came in to nurse him. She came in safely . . . and undoubtedly saved her husband's life."[46] Paralyzed in his arms and legs, with his spine feared seriously compromised, Barlow was once again rescued by the expert and devoted ministrations of his wife. After a miraculous survival and ten months in the hospital, Barlow could have honorably retired from further service.[47] Apparently, that option was not even considered.

The Civil War: January–August 1864

During his convalescence, Barlow sent out feelers asking for another position outside the Eleventh Corps, something he had sought since Chancellorsville. His first choice was the Second Corps, under the command of the man he most admired in the Army of the Potomac, Maj. Gen. Winfield Scott Hancock. The feeling was mutual, according to Hancock's biographer David M. Jordan. "Hancock had spotted Barlow earlier as the kind of subordinate he would like to have," Jordan writes; "after Chancellorsville, he told Barlow that he would be delighted to have him, and he later wrote to Meade's chief of staff asking for Barlow as a division commander."[48] The request took some time to be approved. In the meantime, Barlow inquired into the possibility of leading a brigade of black troops or perhaps heading up the yet-to-be-formed Freedmen's Bureau, a job that later when to O. O. Howard. Events soon ensured his return to the Second Corps, when the Eleventh Corps transferred to the Western Theater and Hancock's appeal for Barlow's service was granted. Special Orders No. 40 from the adjutant general's office in Washington, dated January 26, 1864, announced Barlow's new assignment and instructed him to join General Hancock at Harrisburg, Pennsylvania, "for recruiting duty" for the Second Corps. On March 25, General Orders No. 11 from Hancock's headquarters made formal Barlow's assumption of command of the First Division in the corps.[49]

Barlow joined a newly reorganized Army of the Potomac under Meade and, exercising overall authority, Lt. Gen. Ulysses S. Grant. Reduced from the seven corps that had fought at Gettysburg to just three larger ones, the army lay in camps near Culpeper Court House. Grant planned a spring campaign, and northern hopes were pinned on the new general in chief's ability to strike a final blow against Lee, capture Richmond, and win the war. On April 1, Barlow officially assumed charge of the First Division of the Second Corps. The Second's fighting record was highly regarded, and Hancock's subordinate command was at that time arguably the best in the army. Historian Gordon C. Rhea asserts, "Hancock's was Meade's largest corps, as a consequence of its commander's recognized ability, and three of Hancock's four division commanders—Brig. Gens. Francis C. Barlow and

The top officers in the Army of the Potomac's Second Corps at Peters-
burg, including (*left to right*) Barlow, Maj. Gen. Winfield Scott Hancock, Brig.
Gen. David Bell Birney, and Brig. Gen. John Gibbon. Library of Congress
Prints and Photographs Division, LC-DIG-cwpb-01701.

John Gibbon and Maj. Gen. David B. Birney—were unquestionably among
the army's best." Barlow's brigade commanders were Col. Nelson A. Miles
(First Brigade, including the 61st New York), Col. Thomas A. Smyth (Second or "Irish Brigade"), Col. Paul Frank (Third Brigade), and Col. John R.
Brooke (Fourth Brigade). Barlow's favorites were Brooke and Miles, and
he often selected them to be in the vanguard of his assaults, which ensured
them both glory and huge casualties.[50]

Barlow commenced hard training for Grant's Overland campaign, during which the Second Corps and his division would play a vital part. His
methods drew the usual grumbles from his men. He was especially tough
on the newest recruits, many of whom were bounty volunteers or draftees.
Some of his comrades considered Barlow overly obsessive about prepara-

tion, but Samuel Parmalee said of the troops that "everything snaps in the Div[ision]." Barlow provided his own enthusiastic assessment in a letter written on April 9, 1864. "I am very well satisfied with what has been accomplished since I came here," he informed his mother. "I think I have been successful in making a good impression. I have not lost my temper or spoken or acted hastily to anyone + though I am thought strict I think I am well liked!" If nothing else, the slender, youthful twenty-nine-year-old Barlow certainly cut a striking figure, always carrying a cavalry saber into battle and dressing in a checked shirt, looking like, in the words of a bemused Theodore Lyman, "a highly independent mounted newsboy."[51]

When the Union army crossed the Rapidan River in early May, the Second Corps was in the vanguard. General Lee sought to block the Union's advance on May 5, and a battle ensued in the tangled woods known as the Wilderness of Spotsylvania. On May 5–6, Barlow, assigned to guard artillery at the extreme left of the Union line, played an inconsequential role in the first bloody engagement of the Overland campaign. As Grant shifted his forces leftward toward Spotsylvania Court House, hoping to flank Lee, the Second Corps covered the rear of the army. On May 9, the outline of the next series of clashes was forming. Confederate troops built a line of formidable entrenchments that produced a salient the soldiers quickly dubbed the "Mule Shoe." Union lines faced the Rebels' position with both sides fortified.

Hancock sent Barlow across the Po River on the 9th with orders to strike enemy supply trains and test Confederate strength. The next day, Barlow found himself in a precarious situation when Lee counterattacked. His position untenable, Barlow conducted a textbook fighting retreat, deploying his men in a skirmish line formation. Lt. Col. Francis A. Walker, assistant adjutant general of the Second Corps, praised the expertly done maneuver by Barlow's division. "Most regiments in the service had as little idea of skirmishing as an elephant," Walker explained. "But to Barlow's brigades the very life of military service was in a widely extended formation, flexible yet firm, where the soldiers were thrown largely on their individual resources, but remained in a high degree under the control of the resolute, sagacious, keen-eyed officers, who urged them forward, or drew them back, as the exigency of the case required." In these circumstances, added Walker with a flourish, "manhood rose to its maximum" and "almost anything seemed possible to vigilance, audacity, and cool self-possession."[52]

Barlow's troops rested after the action on the afternoon of May 10, while Col. Emory Upton orchestrated a nearly successful assault against Confederate lines on the west face of the Mule Shoe. Upton's effort convinced Grant to try again, applying greater force. He turned to Hancock's dependable Second Corps to make this massed attack, with the goal of smashing through the Mule Shoe and splitting the Army of Northern Virginia. On the evening of May 11, Barlow, Gibbon, and Birney received the news that they were selected to mount a dawn assault on the Confederate salient. Much later, Barlow recalled his frustration with the vague directions provided: "No information whatever, so far as I can remember, was given us as to the position or strength of the enemy, or as to the troops to be engaged in the movement (except that the 2nd corps was to take part in it), or as to the plan of attack, or why any attack was to be made at that time or place." Francis A. Walker related, with an eye toward Barlow's sarcastic and pessimistic sides, that before the battle, "General Barlow made anxious inquires about the nature of the ground over which he was to move, and not getting any satisfactory information desired, at length, to be told whether there was a ravine a thousand feet deep between him and the enemy. When he could not be assured even on this point, he seemed to think that he was called upon to lead a forlorn hope, and placed his valuables in the hands of a friend."[53]

Nevertheless, Barlow readied his division to assail the Mule Shoe from the left center. The ferocity of the ensuing surprise strike carried the massed Federal attackers across Confederate works at the apex of the Rebel salient. At the head of the First Division, the dismounted "Boy General" shouted out, "Forward! Double-Quick! Charge!" Disoriented Rebels stationed in a long stretch of works fell back into the center of the Mule Shoe or simply surrendered. Barlow's division captured more than 3,000 prisoners—including Maj. Gen. Edward Johnson and Brig. Gen. George H. Steuart—along with thirty colors and twenty guns.[54]

The Federal attack on May 12 blasted a hole in the Rebel line that was not exploited, as victorious Union soldiers, clogging the northern part of the salient, soon lost momentum. Confederates quickly regrouped, and fierce fighting on both sides brought a stalemate on the battlefield. Although disappointed not to score a decisive victory at a place henceforth known as "The Bloody Angle," Barlow expressed pride with his performance. "He related many anecdotes of the 'Salient,'" wrote Theodore Lyman after a lunch the two shared at Meade's headquarters.[55] Hancock's official report praised Barlow's "valor, ability, and promptness" at Spotsylvania, describing the attack on May 12 by Barlow's and Birney's divisions "as unsurpassed for its daring, courage, and brilliant success." Barlow was recommended for promotion to brevet major general "particularly for gal[lantry] and good con[duct] while leading his div[ision] in the assault on the enemy's works at Spotsylvania."[56]

A letter written to a friend on May 24 provided a troubling insight into Barlow's frame of mind after Spotsylvania evidently not apparent to Lieutenant Colonel Lyman at their meal. "I am not much delighted," Barlow stated, "with the performances here, though this is in the strictest confidence."[57] Grant and Meade went unmentioned but were clearly the objects of his remarks. Barlow complained that he and the other division commanders were expected to go into a fight with little or no reconnaissance of the area. They also suffered from a lack of communication not only between Grant and Meade but also between Meade and the corps commanders. It all made for a dreary mess.[58] Yet undeniably, the battle of Spotsylvania brought Barlow's military career to a high point, and he personally was singled out and celebrated by superiors and peers for delivering a stunning blow to the enemy.[59] At least Barlow's action at Spotsylvania helped send a clear message to the Confederacy—Grant's advance would not be stopped, even though the butcher's bill was rising every day.

Barlow and the battered Second Corps enjoyed little rest as the relentless Federal push brought them near a tiny crossroads northeast of Richmond called Cold Harbor. General Grant decided to go on the offensive again, and Union forces attacked Rebel fortifications in the area on May 31 and June 1. The Union commander next sought to use three Union corps, including Hancock's, to mount a coordinated attack against Confederate forces on June 2. On the evening of June 1–2, Barlow's division was ordered to march into position to the left of the line for a 5:00 P.M. assault, but a late arrival on the 2nd forced Grant to shelve the plan until early the next morning. The extra time gave the battle-weary men some respite but also provided Lee with the opportunity to bolster his defense with additional troops, strengthen existing breastworks and build new ones, and post artillery that would produce a converging field of fire. Collectively, these actions made the success of a mass assault unlikely, although Federal officers seemed utterly unaware of the enemy's newly formidable earthworks.[60]

By the night of June 2, approximately 60,000 well-entrenched Rebels faced 100,000 Federals across a seven-mile front reaching from north of Bethesda Church to the Chickahominy River. The Second Corps anchored the Federal left flank near Turkey Hill. Barlow's division was positioned at the extreme left, with Gibbon on his right and Birney's division held in reserve. Once again Barlow was destined to play a huge part in a massive attack, and once again, going into battle he lacked the necessary intelligence as to both the disposition of the enemy troops and the type of terrain over which he and his men would be fighting. At 4:30 A.M. on June 3, Union forces launched their assault. Almost instantly, a withering fire erupted from the Rebel fortifications, halting the Federals' forward movement and inflicting heavy casualties. Providing the only breakthrough of the day, the aggressive Barlow achieved success by forming his men in two lines and rushing through Maj. Gen. John C. Breckinridge's pickets to strike hard at the Rebel division's front line clustered along a sunken road. A period of intense fighting followed, with Federals driving the enemy from their works. Barlow and his men secured their breakthrough by claiming a portion of the Confederate entrenchments and capturing 300 prisoners and several pieces of artillery.[61]

The triumph proved fleeting. One of Barlow's best brigade commanders, John R. Brooke, was struck down in the fighting, as was his replacement, leading to confusion and disorganization. Gibbon's division, the other engaged Second Corps unit, encountered an unexpected (and thus unprepared-for) swamp and lost all direction. The final blow in the steps to a disastrous reversal occurred when the Federals failed to bring forward the second line of support. Confederate artillery fired on Barlow's line, turning the captured works into a vicious trap for his men. The enemy's counterattack prevailed by 8:00 A.M., and shortly after noon Grant officially called off the assault. The United States suffered more than 4,500 casualties on June 3 (3,500 of them in the principal, and most famous, attack that included Barlow's effort), while the Confederates lost fewer than 1,000. In sharp contrast to the Overland campaign's previous battles, all of which seemed inconclusive to most people in both the United States and the Confederacy, Cold Harbor was a clear victory for Lee and the Army of Northern Virginia.[62]

During the period June 2–12 at Cold Harbor, Hancock's Second Corps suffered the loss of more than 3,500 men, including 160 commissioned officers. The majority fell in the ill-fated assault on June 3. A few days later, Barlow advised Hancock's assistant adjutant general against further frontal assaults against the entrenched enemy. The "attrition suffered as a result of the army's recent campaigning," he stated, had damaged, perhaps irrevocably, the army's will to fight. Casualties in the First Division had left some "regiments in command of lieutenants, and brigades in command of inexperienced officers." Predicting the grim impact on his troops in the next phase of the campaign, Barlow described "a great horror and dread of

"General Grant's Great Campaign—General Barlow Charging the Enemy at
Cold Harbor, June 1, 1864." Combat artist Alfred R. Waud's sketch featured
what the editors called "one of the grandest charges of the war."
Harper's Weekly, June 25, 1864, 408–9, 410.

attacking earth-works again." He concluded with an ominous postscript:
"I think the men are so wearied and worn out by the harassing labors of
the past week that they are wanting in the spirit and dash necessary for
successful assaults."[63]

Barlow's prescient analysis indicated that the campaign had become an
unforgiving experience of almost constant combat. In past operations, the
armies usually rested after major battles, but the conflict's two top generals had engaged in fighting almost every day for more than a month. Both
armies lost almost half their original number, with Grant's casualties totaling approximately 55,000–60,000 and Lee's 32,000. The Second Corps,
the Army of the Potomac's proudest fighting force, was now dangerously
depleted. The Overland campaign thus brought something very different
to an already long and bloody conflict. Simply put, neither the Army of
the Potomac nor the Army of Northern Virginia was ever the same after
the battles of May 5–June 12. Yet while Lee bested Grant at Cold Har-

bor, the latter's overall strategy was succeeding and thus carrying an ominous portent for the Confederacy. Despite shocking losses, U.S. forces had moved to the outskirts of Richmond.[64]

After June 5, Grant maintained the initiative by switching his strategy from confronting and defeating Lee's army to crossing the James River to take Petersburg, the second-largest city in Virginia and a vital supply artery for the Confederacy. Petersburg's fall would open a straight avenue to nearby Richmond. With General Lee caught unaware, on the evening of June 12 the Union army began moving out of camps around Cold Harbor toward the James. By June 14, Federals were closing in on Petersburg. Speed was of the essence. Grant intended to attack the heavily fortified— but lightly defended in terms of Rebel soldiers—city using Maj. Gen. William F. "Baldy" Smith's Eighteenth Corps from the Army of the James and selected divisions from the Second Corps (including the First Division) and the Ninth Corps before Lee could send reinforcements. Frank Barlow moved a bit too quickly toward the target, and General Meade, worried that the First Division would lose contact with trailing units, sent his aide Theodore Lyman with orders to slow down. With the message delivered, Lyman captured for posterity a strange new quirk of his good friend: "Found Barlow in a cherry tree, by the roadside, and in a woman's garden. He invited me in his quaint style, to partake of the fruit also, remarking he knew it would not be long before Meade's staff got there!" It appeared that Barlow was occasionally found sitting in trees, whether or not there was fruit to be picked. Other incidents of his odd behavior reflected his growing mental strain and physical fatigue.[65]

Although a favorite of Hancock's, Barlow drew unfavorable notice from his commander in the movement toward Petersburg. James A. Beaver, colonel of the 148th Pennsylvania Infantry and later a brigade commander in the First Division, chronicled a period of tense relations between the corps chief and Barlow. Shortly after Barlow crossed the James, Hancock went looking for him, only to be told the division commander was asleep and could not be disturbed. Although many officers were exhausted and dealing with various ailments, illnesses, and injuries sustained in the preceding weeks of the campaign, Hancock clearly believed Barlow had exhibited unprofessional behavior.

According to Beaver, Hancock's displeasure did not end with that one incident. The first attack at Petersburg was scheduled for June 15, with General Smith of the Eighteenth Corps in overall command of the evening assault. In preparation, Hancock directed Barlow to bring up his division in the morning for positioning. Barlow did not appear when expected because of "the ignorance or treachery of a guide employed by division headquarters." Hancock fumed while Barlow, on the wrong road, went toward City Point. Too late, he realized his error and retraced his steps, arriving at headquarters in the late afternoon. Barlow sent his aide to ask Hancock what position he should take. Hancock angrily asked the officer, "Where's General Barlow?" The aide reported he had "stopped a little distance back to bathe his feet." Hancock replied, "That's it; that's it, always asleep or washing his feet." Some within hearing of the exchange "couldn't refrain from a hearty laugh" and thought Hancock "himself quietly joined" them.[66] But Barlow clearly believed he was being blamed for the failure to mount the assaults on time and struck back with a spirited defense. "I respectfully request that if any blame is attributed to me for delay in the march on the 15th," he wrote Hancock on June 26, "that I may be informed in order that the facts may be made known." His reputation suffered and his pride had been bruised, but worse blows to both were looming on the horizon.[67]

From June 15 through June 18, Union forces mounted a series of attacks on the lightly defended Petersburg fortifications.[68] Smith's initial assault on June 15 began around 6:00 P.M. Barlow and his troops faltered badly from beginning to end. Barlow and Birney were ordered to storm across an open field near the Shand House, where they came under intense fire. Barlow led the charge from the front, wearing his checkered shirt and waving his hat in the air. "Come on boys!" he shouted, but alas, his boys would not follow as they had on so many previous battlefields. Barlow fell back, only to order two more attacks, both equally unsuccessful. Sgt. Maj. Fred Lockley recorded his impression of the attacks in a letter. "Our division commander—Genl. Barlow—a very young man, appears to me to be rash; the way in which he uses up his men is fearful."[69] The next day demonstrated no improvement of Union coordination, and assaults conducted in a piecemeal fashion failed to bring success. As at Cold Harbor, every hour of delay provided the enemy with time to rush more men to the defense and further strengthen the works protecting Petersburg.[70]

June 17 featured three separate assaults carried out from before dawn through the evening. Barlow's performance was notably subpar all day, with the last movement particularly disastrous. A gap in the Confederate lines opened near the Shand house, and two units from the Ninth Corps looked for needed support from Barlow's division. As he did earlier, Barlow personally led his men into battle, but they faltered badly under withering fire, suffering many casualties. Numerous Federal soldiers surrendered

Harper's Weekly ran this portrait of Barlow five weeks after Cold Harbor, describing him as "conspicuous among the noble band of united heroes, officers and men, in the very active front of battle." *Harper's Weekly*, July 9, 1864, 437, 445.

rather than press the attacks. Stephen Minot Weld articulated the thoughts of many who served in the Army of the Potomac: "The feeling here in the army is that we have been absolutely butchered, that our lives have been periled to no purpose, and wasted. In the Second Corps the feeling is so strong that the men say they will not charge any more works."[71] Gen. P. G. T. Beauregard spoiled the Union plan on June 18 when he withdrew to a new defensive line closer to Petersburg, causing confusion in the Federal ranks. On June 19, General Grant inaugurated what would become a nine-month siege of Petersburg.

John F. Kennedy's quip that "victory has a hundred fathers, but defeat is an orphan" undoubtedly applies to most situations, but the fault for the Union failure to take Petersburg may be the exception that proves the rule. Due to a combination of long-standing command problems within the Army of the Potomac, confused and contradictory communications between Hancock and Smith, and the extreme battle fatigue of the men after many weeks of heavy fighting, Union assaults failed to capture works that most agreed should have been easily secured. General Lee arrived to take charge of the defense of Petersburg, but his appearance did not deter Grant's forces from pinning down the Confederates for the foreseeable future. That fact was scant consolation at the time to the men who wore the blue uniform. In four days of fighting outside Petersburg, the Union suffered 10,000–11,000 casualties to the Confederacy's 4,000. Francis Channing Barlow was one of many who sank into deep depression after the failed assaults.[72]

Indeed, Barlow must be counted among the soldiers at every rank whose previously strong coping mechanisms—whether courage, cause, family, friends, comrades, God, or some combination of all of them—approached the breaking point between the end of May and July 1864. Examples already cited attest to Barlow's distress, but others pointed to more serious problems than odd behavior or misdirected marches. Always a strict disciplinarian, he became ever more obsessed about disciplining his men, many of whom were new to the army and resistant to order. Barlow detested stragglers, shirkers, and deserters, believing that they prolonged the war for everyone else, endangering the prospect of victory for the United States. In late May, as Lieutenant Colonel Lyman's testimony below indicates, Barlow ordered shirkers tied up and thrashed, but harsher measures did not always produce the desired results. For the first time, Barlow recorded that despite a higher level of punishment for more soldiers, straggling was increasing rather than the opposite.

Complaints against Barlow also increased mightily. This only accentuated a pattern Col. James Wood of the 136th New York Infantry, an Eleventh Corps unit, recalled in a postwar letter: "Gen. Barlow had the *happy faculty* of making himself disagreeable to every officer and private of the brigade." He elaborated: "Even to his staff he was rude and overbearing, frequently and needlessly risking their lives in the execution of many useless commissions." To be fair, there was a history between Barlow and Wood. In April 1863, Barlow wrote that "Wood is disposed to be a little touchy + I shall have to take him down I fear."[73]

The letters and journals of Lieutenant Colonel Lyman, a keen observer of the Overland campaign and the battles around Petersburg, contain telling information regarding Barlow's state of mind. On May 26, Lyman rode with General Meade to Hancock's headquarters. "In their leisure," Lyman wrote in his journal that day, ". . . the 2d Corps commanders had turned their attention to the prosecution of stragglers! Barlow, in particular, tied them up in strings and thrashed them, to the great benefit of the service!" Nearly three weeks later, Lyman remarked in a letter that Barlow's division marched efficiently, which he attributed "partly to the terror in which stragglers stand of Barlow. His provost guard is a study. They follow the column with their bayonets fixed, and drive up the loiterers, with small ceremony."[74]

Barlow was feeling disconsolate, believing that his men not only might have given up the will to fight but also had lost faith in their commanders. No amount of discipline or drill exerted or ordered by him or others would make much difference now. In a letter to his brothers dated July 12, 1862, Barlow had predicted that without "a radical change in the leaders, the enemy will whip us again and again."[75] In June 1864, his loss of faith seemed centered at least as much on the men in the ranks. The almost daily combat, the loss of leadership, the unfamiliar and difficult terrain combined with the smoke and chaos of battle made it increasingly difficult for all of the officers in the army to exert authority over their exhausted and dispirited men. Battle-fatigued soldiers who believed their environment was out of control often, and understandably, developed severe morale problems. Men exposed to extreme levels of trauma often displayed a variety of behavior that indicated their ability to cope with war was breaking down. This breakdown might take different forms—disturbing nightmares, uncharacteristic cowardice, or extreme physical symptoms such as shaking, screaming, or curling up in the fetal position. At one time or another during the spring and summer of 1864, Barlow exhibited at least some of these symptoms but managed to carry on with his duties until physically unable to do so.[76]

These problems played out during the beginning of what became the longest military operation of the Civil War. Grant's siege at Petersburg sought to cut Lee's supply lines by capturing and destroying major railroad connections, all the while forcing the Rebels to extend their lines. On June 21, Grant ordered an attack on the Weldon Railroad by portions of Maj. Gen. Horatio G. Wright's Sixth Corps and three divisions from the Second Corps. An ailing Hancock (soon to be replaced by General Birney) moved south along the Union line to the railroad, crossing at Jerusalem Plank Road. Commanding a First Division numbering 5,570, Barlow was positioned behind entrenchments on the far left flank of Brig. Gen. Gershom Mott. Lee sent two divisions from the Third Corps of the Army of Northern Virginia out from behind Confederate fortifications to defend the railroad.[77]

On the morning of June 22, Barlow received orders to "move to the right and front to connect with and prolong the line of General Mott's division." This maneuver, he claimed in his report, "necessarily severed my connection with the Sixth Corps." Unprotected and unsupported, Barlow rallied his men to meet Confederate troops just emerging from nearby woods, ably led by Brig. Gen. William Mahone and raising the piercing Rebel yell. The southern attackers struck with a fury, sending a sizable number of Barlow's men to flight. Others refused to fight and were taken as prisoners. "I attribute the loss of prisoners," Barlow explained, "to the position in which we were placed by swinging forward." But he also blamed his men, stating they "did not meet the attack with the vigor and determination which they would have shown in an earlier period of the campaign." It is true Barlow lost several of his best officers in the fighting, but even his own soldiers began calling the debacle "Barlow's Skedaddle." Later, Francis Walker asserted that this event represented "perhaps the most humiliating episode in the experience of the Second Corps down to this time."[78] The Second Corps lost 2,400 men on June 22, 1,700 of them prisoners. In the fighting before Petersburg from June 15 through June 26, Barlow's division suffered 2,276 casualties, the highest number in any of Hancock's divisions.[79]

The Second Corps, already blamed by some of the northern press for failing to take Petersburg by assault, was cast anew as the villain of yet another humiliating defeat, with Barlow's First Division singled out for heavy criticism at what became known as the battle of the Jerusalem Plank Road, or the first battle of the Weldon Railroad. "You will have seen an account in the papers telegraphed from Boston putting the whole blame of the disaster of the 22nd on this Div.," Barlow complained to his brother. "It is an unmitigated lie + I have written to contradict it." Gibbon, insisted Barlow, "was attacked in his own front independently of us + must bear his own burdens."[80] No explanation could disguise one fact about Second Corps casualties that suggested a serious breakdown in morale and discipline—more than 70 percent of the losses on June 22 were prisoners. In the end, the battle's results were mixed. The Confederates held the Weldon Railroad until August 21, but the Federal army extended its lines farther to the west.

Barlow's reputation continued its downward plunge after Jerusalem Plank Road. Comments from two soldiers in the Second Corps reflect a wider disrespect, or at least concern, regarding his generalship. "It is an open secret," declared a private in the 17th Maine Infantry of Birney's division, "that Barlow isn't just right in his head, and his performance lends strength to this insinuation." This soldier also accused an overconfident Barlow of advancing far to the front of his command, then having to flee "to the uttermost parts of the field, the Rebels at his heels." Another man groused in a letter to a member of Nelson Miles's staff that "Barlow's stock is below par and the most bitter feelings exist toward him by every officer and man throughout the Div." (The second witness included praise of Miles in his letter as well.)[81]

The First Division continued to fare poorly on July 26–27 at the battle of Deep Bottom, where even Barlow's best soldiers refused to assault. The general's performance also was subpar during the battle of Second Deep Bottom on August 14. There it became painfully clear he could not summon the energy to organize and direct an assault—and if he could, his men could not make it. Even given the overall poor condition of the army at this point, Barlow noticeably and notably underperformed, made inexplicable mistakes, and behaved with caution instead of aggression. His unusual passivity sprang from a combination of chronic ill health, depression, and the belief that his men no longer possessed the fighting spirit. Suffering from diarrhea on August 17, he went to a corps hospital at City Point and the next day gave up command of the First Division. Francis A. Walker explained that Barlow "had fought against disease and the effects of his ghastly wounds, received at Antietam and Gettysburg, no less bravely then he had fought against the public enemy. During several days preceding [relinquishing command] he had been more like a dead than a living man."[82]

The intellectual arrogance and moral rectitude that drove Barlow's rigorous training methods and aggressive battlefield demeanor undoubtedly encouraged enemies to attack him for perceived flaws during the difficult summer of 1864. The Irish soldiers of his Second Brigade particularly loathed him. After the war, William O'Meagher, a surgeon with the 69th New York Infantry, termed Barlow a "malignant" man of "narrow intellect." Commenting for the record, O'Meagher remarked that the "general, though commonly counted a brave, fearless soldier, as his previous career would certainly indicate, was exceedingly unpopular, not only with the [Irish] Brigade, to which he rarely omitted an opportunity of showing his dislike . . . but with the whole division, by his reckless management of a splendid command." This harsh and somewhat unfair statement nonetheless represented an accurate depiction of how many of Barlow's men even beyond the Irish Brigade viewed him by August 1864.[83] They, like their commander, were worn out by the daily experience of the war—the fighting, the dying, and the surviving. Every day had become a challenge, and every day brought a new horror to absorb.

A personal matter commanded Barlow's attention and contributed to what was clearly his ongoing breakdown. Arabella Barlow, while serving as a Sanitary Commission nurse at the First Division Field hospital near City Point, fell very ill in mid-June. Barely recovered, she returned to work, and the couple visited each other a few times during the summer. Frank remained deeply concerned, but on July 15 he penned a reassuring note to his mother saying that Arabella "has been seriously ill, but the fever is broken +

in time she will be well again." He was shocked to receive news that she died of typhus on July 27 in a Washington, D.C., hospital without any of her family or friends in attendance. A heartbroken Barlow was granted a fifteen-day leave of absence to attend her funeral and burial in Somerville, New Jersey. Lyman recorded on the day after her death, "Barlow's wife has died at Washington of malignant typhus. As he was in presence of the enemy Meade could not, at first, grant him a leave; but did grant it hearing she had died without friends about her. The soft-hearted General glad of the excuse! Anyway, Barlow was entirely incapacitated by this sudden grief."[84]

At the same time that Arabella's health was failing, Barlow's also was deteriorating. The diarrhea that sent him to the hospital at City Point on August 17 was later pronounced "chronic." An attempt to resume division command shorty after going to City Point resulted in Barlow's being "carried, on a stretcher, from the field at Reams' Station, shortly before the opening of that battle" on August 25. Barlow's doctors initially ordered him to take a twenty-day medical leave, later extending it to deal with the persistent diarrhea. His official absence from the army was from November 5, 1864, until April 1, 1865.[85]

The End of the Civil War

For all practical purposes, Barlow's war was over. His devastating experiences in the Overland and Petersburg campaigns led to what contemporaries called an extreme "battle fatigue" and what later might have been described as "battle shock" or even "post-traumatic stress disorder." Combined with poor health, the psychological shock of his wife's death likely produced his inability to lead his men as he did in past battles. Barlow faced unrelenting violence on the battlefield, endured the loss of his close friends and comrades, incurred two serious wounds, and with each injury became more physically and mentally weakened.

Due to the grave nature of his various ailments, Barlow was accorded the rare option of taking an extended leave but chafed at being out of the action. One of his confidants, Col. Charles Russell Lowell, consoled him in a letter written on September 10, 1864. "Take care of yourself, old fellow," advised Lowell. "Unless you give yourself some time now, you will never half complete your career. What the devil difference does it make where a man passes the next six months, if the war is to last six years? If it is to be ended in one year, you have done and suffered your share in it." Colonel Lowell, destined to die in the battle of Cedar Creek less than six

Barlow just after Appomattox wearing the two stars of a major general. His youthful appearance masks the fact that he had suffered two serious wounds and great emotional strain during the conflict. Library of Congress Prints and Photographs Division, LC-DIG-cwpb-05951.

weeks later, ended with affectionate counsel: "There are better things to be done in the Country, Barlow, than fighting, and you must save yourself for *them* too."[86] The grieving widower surely took that advice to heart, demonstrated by his fierce determination in the postwar years to resume a full and productive life in public service and law.

After spending time with his mother in Concord, and with other family and friends, Barlow finished eight months of convalescence with a European trip. Before he left, he was notified of his brevet to major general. On April 6, 1865, he assumed command of the Second Division of the Second Corps and rejoined the fray in the final part of the last campaign of the Army of the Potomac. Held in reserve at Sailor's Creek, on April 6 near Farmville, he took possession of a key bridge needed by desperate Confederates to stop the onrushing Federal advance, helping to quicken Lee's surrender on April 9. Barlow was rewarded for his action with promotion to the rank of major general of volunteers on May 25, 1865.[87]

Frank Barlow soon resigned his commission and returned to civilian life, where he prospered as a lawyer, a Republican politician, and a reformer. Elected New York's secretary of state in November 1865, he reestablished his New York City law firm the next year and soon after helped to found the New York (later American) Bar Association. In 1867, Frank wed Ellen Shaw of Staten Island, the sister of his close friend the late Col. Robert Gould Shaw of the 54th Massachusetts Colored Infantry. They had two sons and a daughter. In 1869 President Ulysses S. Grant appointed Barlow United States marshal for the Southern District of New York, where his work earned him high plaudits. A firm believer in civil service reform, the independent-minded and characteristically blunt Barlow instituted a number of improvements that made him highly unpopular with Republican politicians resisting changes to lucrative corrupt practices. Barlow went on to hold a number of public offices in the Empire State, serving two terms as secretary of state and one as attorney general. In the latter capacity, he used the power of his office to initiate the prosecution of the Tammany Hall political machine, the infamous "Tweed Ring." Barlow's final act on the political scene came when Grant selected him to assist with the investigation into the irregularities surrounding the Hayes-Tilden presidential election of 1876. After he retired from public life in 1877, Barlow tended to his law practice and various business and banking enterprises. He maintained an active interest in veterans' affairs as well as keeping up on the publications on the Civil War until his death on January 11, 1896.[88]

Conclusion

Winslow Homer's *Prisoners from the Front* was prominently displayed in a recent exhibition titled "The Civil War and American Art." Thousands of visitors and tourists flocking to the 2012 showing at the Smithsonian in Washington, D.C., and to the 2013 exhibition at the Metropolitan Museum of Art in New York City could read the accompanying materials that identified the handsome United States officer and learn of Francis Channing Barlow's stellar war record.[89]

That record earned plaudits from Barlow's contemporaries, who knew him as one of the best division commanders in the storied Second Corps of the Army of the Potomac. Theodore Lyman commented that "Barlow was so brave that he made a joke of danger." At Petersburg, Capt. Charles Francis Adams Jr. penned this tribute after engaging in lengthy conversation with his fellow Harvard graduate: "I am more disposed to regard Barlow as a military genius than any man I have yet seen. . . . Should the war last and he survive, I feel very confident that he will make as great a name as any that have arisen in this war." To many during the conflict, Barlow represented the purest ideal of the United States volunteer soldier—valorous, dashing, and patriotic. In 1864, *Harper's Weekly* described him as "one of the most conspicuous soldiers of the war—one of its most heroic and romantic figures," adding, "During the present campaign no name has been more illustrious for valor and victory." Nelson A. Miles, who led a brigade in Barlow's division and later served as the last general in chief of the United States Army, remembered, "He was descended from an ancestry representing the highest type of American civilization, a man of superior intelligence, culture, and true patriotism. . . . He was a just and strict disciplinarian and intensely devoted to all the requirements of the military service. In battle he scorned all danger. I never knew him to give an order to retreat. His orders were constantly, forward, advance, attack and charge. His skill and fortitude on many of the hardest fought fields were crowned with success."[90]

Modern experts on Civil War soldiers argue that "courage was at the core" motivating nineteenth-century men to enlist, to fight, and to stay in the ranks. Initially connected with duty, honor, godliness, and manliness, courage was redefined for many men as the war went on to mean simply doing one's duty and little more. But that was not the case for officers such as Barlow who aspired to the classic definition of courage as "action taken without regard to fear." Long after Appomattox, former Union soldier Frank Wilkeson commented, "It is true the . . . volunteers [typified] by Major-General Francis C. Barlow of the Second Corps, commanded the universal respect of the enlisted men. We knew the fighting generals and we respected them, and we knew the cowards and despised them." Intelligent, audacious, and cool under pressure, Barlow inspired another appreciative observer to write, "The secret of Barlow's success in military life lay in his clear perception of the actual situation, and his fearless readiness to realize that perception in action."[91] Barlow was a practical man with a hard edge who reveled in his self-appointed role as a teller of unpleasant truths who rarely flinched from the consequences of his words or actions. Relentlessly unsentimental and practical, he emerged from the war as an acclaimed warrior. Despite the wounds inflicted and the losses suffered, Francis Channing Barlow survived and flourished, achieving a happy private life and a distinguished career as a public citizen of the reunited nation he fought so unsparingly hard to preserve.

Notes

I thank Gary W. Gallagher and Caroline E. Janney for their assistance with this essay. In addition, I thank Robert E. L. Krick for bringing my attention to several helpful sources.

1. Nicolai Cikovsky Jr., "Winslow Homer's 'Prisoners from the Front,'" *Metropolitan Museum Journal* 12 (1977): 155–72. See also Marc Simpson, *Winslow Homer Paintings of*

the Civil War (San Francisco: Fine Arts Museum of San Francisco and Bedford Arts, 1988), 246–59.

2. Two fairly recent publications provide the best sources for Barlow's life and career, one a biography and one a set of published letters: Richard F. Welch, *The Boy General: The Life and Career of Francis Channing Barlow* (Madison, N.J.: Fairleigh Dickinson University Press, 2003); Francis C. Barlow, *"Fear Was Not in Him": The Civil War Letters of Major General Francis C. Barlow, U.S.A.*, ed. Christian G. Samito (New York: Fordham University Press, 2004). See also Thomas B. Buell, *The Combat Generals* (New York: Crown, 1997).

3. Welch, *Boy General*, 19–26; Barlow, *Letters*, xiv–xviii.

4. Edwin H. Abbot, "Francis Channing Barlow," in New York Monuments Commission, *In Memoriam: Francis Channing Barlow, 1834–1896* (1923; reprint, Wolcott, N.Y.: Benedum Books, 2003), 131; Welch, *Boy General*, 27.

5. Francis Channing Barlow (hereafter FCB) to Edward Barlow, June 19, and FCB to Almira Penniman Barlow, July 5, 1861, in Barlow, *Letters*, 5, 7.

6. Theodore Lyman, *Meade's Army: The Private Notebooks of Lt. Col. Theodore Lyman*, ed. David W. Lowe (Kent, Ohio: Kent State University Press, 2007), 7. Two standard studies of Boston elites are George M. Fredrickson, *The Inner Civil War: Modern Intellectuals and the Crisis of the Union* (New York: Harper and Row, 1965), and Lawrence Lader, *The Bold Brahmins: New England's War against Slavery, 1821–1863* (Westport, Conn.: Greenwood, 1973). Two recent books highlight Harvard's influence in the Civil War: Carol Bundy, *The Nature of Sacrifice: A Biography of Charles Russell Lowell, Jr., 1835–64* (New York: Farrar, Straus and Giroux, 2005), and Richard F. Miller, *Harvard's Civil War: A History of the Twentieth Massachusetts Volunteer Infantry* (Hanover, N.H.: University Press of New England, 2005).

7. Welch, *Boy General*, 26.

8. Barlow, *Letters*, 230.

9. Daly and his wife, diarist Maria Lydig Daly, played a prominent role in New York City's society during the era and were friends of Frank and Arabella Barlow.

10. George Templeton Strong, *The Diary of George Templeton Strong*, ed. Allan Nevins and Milton Halsey Thomas, 4 vols. (New York: Macmillan, 1952), 3:132. Strong was a close friend of George Bliss Jr., a prominent Republican and Barlow's law partner.

11. Maria Lydig Daly, *Diary of a Union Lady, 1861–1865*, ed. Harold Earl Hamond (1962; reprint, Lincoln: University of Nebraska Press, 2000), 46, 80.

12. Strong, *Diary*, 3:261.

13. W. W. Potter, "Reminiscences of Field-Hospital Service with the Army of the Potomac," *Buffalo Medical and Surgical Journal*, October and November 1889, 23. See also "Death of Mrs. General Barlow," *Harper's Weekly*, August 13, 1864, 515.

14. Welch, *Boy General*, 37; Barlow, *Letters*, 20. Like so many officers, Barlow regularly counted on his supporters (such as Massachusetts senator Charles Sumner, John M. Forbes, Charles Russell Lowell, and Ralph W. Emerson) to push forward promotions. See Barlow, *Letters*, 121–23.

15. William F. Fox, *Regimental Losses in the American Civil War* (New York: Albany Publishing Co., 1889), 201.

16. On discipline, see Lorien Foote, "Rich Man's War, Rich Man's Fight: Class,

Ideology, and Discipline in the Union Army," *Civil War History* 51 (September 2005): 269–87; Foote, *The Gentlemen and the Roughs: Violence, Honor, and Manhood in the Union Army* (New York: New York University Press, 2010), 124–25; and Stephen J. Ramold, *Baring the Iron Hand: Discipline in the Union Army* (DeKalb: Northern Illinois University Press, 2010), 43–78. Barlow's friend Robert Gould Shaw often commented on how discipline was needed in the army from top to bottom. In a letter defending Barlow's methods, Shaw noted, "The discipline which the papers talk of could all be put in a very small package" (Robert Gould Shaw, *Blue-Eyed Child of Fortune: The Civil War Letters of Colonel Robert Gould Shaw*, ed. Russell Duncan [Athens: University of Georgia Press, 1992], 192).

17. FCB to his mother and brother Edward, December 14, 1861, in Barlow, *Letters*, 28–29.

18. Charles A. Fuller, *Personal Recollections of the War of 1861, as Private, Sergeant and Lieutenant in the Sixty-First Regiment, New York Volunteer Infantry* (Sherburne, N.Y.: News Job Printing House, 1906), 10.

19. Fox, *Regimental Losses*, 201; Barlow, *Letters*, 73.

20. Howard's report is in U.S. War Department, *The War of the Rebellion: A Compilation of the Official Records of the Union and Confederate Armies*, 127 vols., index, and atlas (Washington, D.C.: Government Printing Office, 1880–1901), ser. 1, 11(1):769 (hereafter cited as *OR*; all references are to ser. 1).

21. Barlow, *Letters*, 85–95; Welch, *Boy General*, 58–66.

22. FCB letters January 18 (to his mother), May 17 (to his mother and Richard Barlow), August 9 (to his mother and Edward Barlow), September 16 (to his mother and brothers), 1862, July 15, 1864 (to his mother), in Barlow, *Letters*, 39, 64, 104, 110, 209.

23. The index of *Letters* includes only a few entries for "political views," one for "Lincoln," and none for "emancipation." Barlow did write several letters indicating his interest in leading a black regiment.

24. Abbot, "Francis Channing Barlow," 131; FCB to E. L. Godkin, *New York Evening Post*, August 9, 1890, 7. In the letter published in the *Post*, Barlow ranged over a number of issues but kept his primary focus on opposing veterans' pensions.

25. FCB to Edward Barlow, July 8, 1862, in Barlow, *Letters*, 96–97. Neither Edward nor Richard Barlow fought in the war, although they were frequent visitors in Barlow's various camps. Edward Emerson Barlow spent a brief time as an assistant adjutant general. See Welch, *Boy General*, 174–75. Harsh assessments of General McClellan in the Peninsula campaign (and the Seven Days' battles) are in James M. McPherson, *Battle Cry of Freedom: The Civil War Era* (New York: Oxford University Press, 1988), 424–27, 464–71, 499–500, and Russell F. Weigley, *A Great Civil War: A Military and Political History, 1861–1865* (Bloomington: Indiana University Press, 2000), 129–34.

26. Barlow quotation in Strong, *Diary*, 4:57.

27. Welch, *Boy General*, 41; Barlow, *Letters*, 220. Three of Barlow's close friends— Charles Russell Lowell, Stephen Minot Weld, and Robert Gould Shaw—frequently expressed similar up-and-down assessments about the war and its leadership. See Edward W. Emerson, *Life and Letters of Charles Russell Lowell* (Boston: Houghton Mifflin, 1907); Stephen Minot Weld, *War Diary and Letters of Stephen Minot Weld, 1861–1865*

(1912; reprint, Boston: Massachusetts Historical Society, 1979); and Shaw, *Blue-Eyed Child of Fortune.*

28. *OR* 19(1):289–90 (FCB's official report of the battle); Ripley's letter, dated September 21, 1862, in Thomas Wentworth Higginson, comp., *Harvard Memorial Biographies,* 2 vols. (Cambridge, Mass.: Sever and Francis, 1866), 1:111–12. Ripley later died of injuries received at Vicksburg.

29. *OR* 19(1):289–90. A good general history of the battle is Stephen W. Sears, *Landscape Turned Red: The Battle of Antietam* (New York: Ticknor and Fields, 1983).

30. Jack D. Welsh, "Francis Channing Barlow," in *Medical Histories of Union Generals* (Kent, Ohio: Kent State University Press, 1996), 15–16.

31. Barlow, *Letters,* 121–23. Emerson's letter was signed by a number of members of the famous Boston literary group the Saturday Club. The list included Nathaniel Hawthorne, Oliver Wendell Holmes, James Russell Lowell, and Dr. Samuel Gridley Howe.

32. Ibid., 132; Welch, *Boy General,* 75–76. For a good overview of the Eleventh Corps, see A. Wilson Greene, "From Chancellorsville to Cemetery Hill: O. O. Howard and Eleventh Corps Leadership," in Gary W. Gallagher, ed., *The First Day at Gettysburg: Essays on Confederate and Union Leadership* (Kent, Ohio: Kent State University Press, 1992), 57–91. On the Germans in the Eleventh Corps, see Christian B. Keller, *Chancellorsville and the Germans: Nativism, Ethnicity, and Civil War Memory* (New York: Fordham University Press, 2007).

33. As quoted in Welch, *Boy General,* 38–39.

34. A number of books explore the tension between officers and enlisted men in armies of citizen-soldiers. See, for example, Bell Irvin Wiley, *The Life of Billy Yank: The Common Soldier of the Union* (Indianapolis: Bobbs-Merrill, 1943); Reid Mitchell, *Civil War Soldiers: Their Expectations and Their Experiences* (New York: Viking, 1988); James M. McPherson, *For Cause and Comrades: Why Men Fought in the Civil War* (New York: Oxford University Press, 1997); Steven E. Woodworth, ed., *The Loyal, True and Brave: America's Civil War Soldiers* (Wilmington, Del.: Scholarly Resources, 2002); and Aaron Sheehan-Dean, ed., *The View from the Ground: Experiences of Civil War Soldiers* (Lexington: University Press of Kentucky, 2007).

35. Fuller, *Personal Recollections,* 39–40.

36. Daly, *Diary of a Union Lady,* 173 (entry for September 13, 1862).

37. FCB to E. L. Godkin, *New York Evening Post,* August 9, 1890, 7.

38. John D. Black, "Reminiscences of the Bloody Angle," in *Glimpses of the Nation's Struggle. Fourth Series. Papers Read Before the Minnesota Commandery of the Military Order of the Loyal Legion of the United States, 1892–1897* (Saint Paul: H. L. Collins, 1898), 420–36 (quotation 424).

39. Daly, *Diary of a Union Lady,* 228 (entry for April 9, 1863); Welch, *Boy General,* 27.

40. Weld, *War Diary and Letters,* 252 (entry for July 30, 1863).

41. FCB to his mother and brothers, May 8, and FCB to Robert Treat Paine, August 12, 1863, in Barlow, *Letters,* 130, 168.

42. Welch, *Boy General,* 75; Foote, *Gentlemen and the Roughs,* 145–70.

43. FCB to his mother, July 7, 1863, in Barlow, *Letters,* 162.

44. Harry W. Pfanz, *Gettysburg—The First Day* (Chapel Hill: University of North Carolina Press, 2001), 246–49; Greene, "From Chancellorsville to Cemetery Hill," 88–89; Edwin B. Coddington, *The Gettysburg Campaign: A Study in Command* (1968; reprint, New York: Touchstone, 1997), 304–5. Coddington takes a measured view of the situation, noting that both the prejudice of native-born Americans and the defensiveness of the Germans played a role in making life difficult for the Eleventh Corps. He wrote, "General Schurz implied that General Barlow had acted without orders when he stretched his division to the Knoll, but there is evidence to indicate that he did so with Howard's approval" (301). For an overview of historians' treatment of Barlow, see Welch, *Boy General*, 248–59.

45. FCB to his mother, July 7, 1863, in Barlow, *Letters*, 162–63. The peritoneum is a membrane that forms the lining surrounding the stomach. See also Welsh, *Medical Histories of Union Generals*, 15.

46. Weld, *War Diary and Letters*, 233. See also E. F. Conklin, *Women at Gettysburg, 1863* (Gettysburg, Pa.: Thomas, 1993), 17–23.

47. The details of Barlow's Gettysburg salvation have long been subject to debate. See John B. Gordon, *Reminiscences of the Civil War* (New York: Scribner's, 1903), 151–52; William F. Hanna, "A Gettysburg Myth Exploded: The Barlow-Gordon Incident," *Civil War Times Illustrated* 24 (May 1985): 42–47; John J. Pullen, "The Gordon Barlow Story, with Sequel," *Gettysburg Magazine* 8 (January 1993): 5–8; and Welch, *Boy General*, 248–50.

48. David M. Jordan, *Winfield Scott Hancock: A Soldier's Life* (Bloomington: Indiana University Press, 1988), 105.

49. Barlow, *Letters*, 164–73; Welch, *Boy General*, 75–90; OR 33:427, 735.

50. Barlow, *Letters*, 174–75; Gordon C. Rhea, *The Battle of the Wilderness, May 5–6, 1864* (Baton Rouge: Louisiana State University Press, 1994), 38, 456.

51. Welch, *Boy General*, 94; FCB to his mother, April 9, 1864, in Barlow, *Letters*, 176; Theodore Lyman, *With Grant and Meade: From the Wilderness to Appomattox*, ed. George R. Agassiz (1922; reprint, Lincoln: University of Nebraska Press, 1994), 107.

52. Francis A. Walker, *History of the Second Army Corps in the Army of the Potomac* (New York: Scribner's, 1886), 450–51. The best overall analysis of the fighting at Spotsylvania on May 8–10 is Gordon C. Rhea, *The Battles for Spotsylvania Court House and the Road to Yellow Tavern, May 7–12, 1864* (Baton Rouge: Louisiana State University Press, 1997).

53. Francis C. Barlow, "Capture of the Salient, May 12, 1864," in *Papers of the Military Historical Society of Massachusetts*, 14 vols. (Boston: Historical Society of Massachusetts, 1881–1918), 4:245–62 (quotation 246); Walker, *Second Army Corps*, 469.

54. For details about the action on May 12, see Barlow, *Letters*, 191–96; OR 36(1):335–36; Welch, *Boy General*, 115–19; Rhea, *Battles for Spotsylvania Court House*, 221–23, 232–46; and Jordan, *Winfield Scott Hancock*, 128–31.

55. Barlow, "Capture of the Salient," 250–56; Lyman, *Meade's Army*, 160.

56. OR 36(1):337–39; Francis B. Heitman, *Historical Register and Dictionary of the United States Army, from Its Organization, September 29, 1789, to March 2, 1903*, 2 vols. (1903; reprint, Urbana: University of Illinois Press, 1965), 1:190. The brevet promotion came through on August 1, 1864.

57. FCB to Charles Dalton, May 24, 1864, in Barlow, *Letters*, 199. Barlow surely would have agreed with Frank Wilkeson's assessment of the top leaders of the Army of the Potomac in the campaigns of 1864 (although Wilkeson largely exempted Grant from his biting criticism). In his memoirs, Wilkeson called on surviving common soldiers "to leave behind them as their contributions, what they actually saw and did, and what their commanders refused, or neglected or failed to do" (Frank Wilkeson, *Recollections of a Private Soldier in the Army of the Potomac* [New York: Putnam's, 1887], vii).

58. Barlow's dissatisfaction with the leadership of the Army of the Potomac was widely evident in the army by the end of May. See Barlow, *Letters*, 194–95, 199–200, and Rhea, *Battles for Spotsylvania Court House*, 308–27. Barlow's "Capture of the Salient" provided a list of grievances against what he thought were a number of ill-advised and uninformed orders issued by headquarters before and during the battle.

59. Apart from his actions on May 12, Barlow's activities on May 9–10 gained very favorable notice. See, for example, Hancock's report in *OR* 36(1):331–32, and Cyrus B. Comstock's *The Dairy of Cyrus B. Comstock*, ed. Merlin E. Sumner (Dayton, Ohio: Morningside, 1987), 266 (entry for May 11, 1864). A member of Grant's staff, Comstock praised Barlow for "handsomely repulsing" Confederate attacks along the Po River on May 10.

60. Noah Andre Trudeau, *Bloody Roads South: The Wilderness to Cold Harbor, May–June 1864* (Boston: Little, Brown, 1989), 275–77; Gordon C. Rhea, *Cold Harbor: Grant and Lee, May 26–June 3, 1864* (Baton Rouge: Louisiana State University Press, 2002), 279–81; Ernest B. Furgurson, *Not War but Murder: Cold Harbor, 1864* (New York: Knopf, 2000), 142–48.

61. Rhea, *Cold Harbor*, 309 (map), 319–29; Walker, *Second Army Corps*, 510–13; Barlow, *Letters*, 200–201.

62. Rhea, *Cold Harbor*, 320–62 (reckoning of casualties on 362). Rhea's careful estimate of casualties revises downward, considerably, the earlier accepted figures. For the earlier numbers, see McPherson, *Battle Cry of Freedom*, 734–35.

63. Walker, *Second Army Corps*, 520–22; FCB to Lt. Col. Francis A. Walker, June 6, 1864, in *OR* 36(3):646–47.

64. For a convenient summary of the impact of the Overland campaign, see Gordon C. Rhea, *The Battle of Cold Harbor* (n.p.: Eastern National, 2001), 59–60.

65. Lyman, *Meade's Army*, 202. On the change of base, see Gordon C. Rhea's essay in this collection.

66. James A. Beaver, "The Colonel's Story," in J. W. Muffly, ed., *The Story of Our Regiment: A History of the 148th Pennsylvania Vols.* (1904; reprint, Baltimore: Butternut and Blue, 1994), 132–34.

67. Barlow's communication is in *OR* 40(2)437–39. See also Walker, *Second Army Corps*, 526–30, and Welch, *Boy General*, 158–61. Hancock soon regained his high regard for Barlow.

68. These attacks have been described as both the final scene in the Overland campaign and the opening of the siege of Petersburg.

69. Welch, *Boy General*, 150–52; J. E. Pomfret, ed., "Letters of Fred Lockley, Union Soldier of 1864–65," *Huntington Library Quarterly* 16 (1952–53): 81.

70. The best account of the fighting on June 15–18 is Thomas J. Howe, *The Petersburg Campaign: Wasted Valor, June 15–18, 1864* (Lynchburg, Va.: H. E. Howard, 1988); for Barlow's part, see esp. 30, 46, 49, 69–70, 103, 116, 121. See also Noah Andre Trudeau, *The Last Citadel: Petersburg, Virginia, June 1864–April 1865* (Boston: Little, Brown, 1991), chap. 3.

71. Welch, *Boy General*, 152–53; Weld, *War Diary and Letters*, 318.

72. John F. Kennedy, Presidential News Conference, April 21, 1961, http://www.jfk library.org/Research/Research-Aids/Ready-Reference/JFK-Quotations.aspx; Howe, *Wasted Valor*, 136–38; Jeffry D. Wert, *The Sword of Lincoln: The Army of the Potomac* (New York: Simon and Schuster, 2005), 371–75.

73. Wood to Augustus Hamlin, June 3, 1891, quoted in Welch, *Boy General*, 75; FCB to My dear Mother, April 24, 1863, in Barlow, *Letters*, 128.

74. Lyman, *Meade's Army*, 176; Lyman, *With Grant and Meade*, 157–58.

75. Barlow, *Letters*, 98.

76. Two books have been particularly influential in my understanding of the psychological stresses of warfare: Earl J. Hess, *The Union Soldier in Battle: Enduring the Ordeal of Combat* (Lawrence: University Press of Kansas, 1997), and Eric T. Dean Jr., *Shook over Hell: Post-Traumatic Stress, Vietnam, and the Civil War* (Cambridge, Mass.: Harvard University Press, 1997).

77. Trudeau, *Last Citadel*, 63–68; *OR* 40(1):328–29.

78. *OR* 40(1):328–31; Welch, *Boy General*, 165–67; Walker, *Second Army Corps*, 544; Wert, *Sword of Lincoln*, 376–77.

79. Wert, *Sword of Lincoln*, 376; *OR* 40(1):307.

80. FCB to Edward Barlow, July 2, 1864, in Barlow, *Letters*, 206.

81. John W. Haley, *The Rebel Yell and the Yankee Hurrah: The Civil War Journal of a Maine Volunteer*, ed. Ruth L. Silliker (Camden, Me.: Down East Books, 1985), 175; Welch, *Boy General*, 167.

82. Welsh, *Medical Histories of Union Generals*, 15; Walker, *Second Army Corps*, 578.

83. D. P. Conyngham, *The Irish Brigade and Its Campaigns* (New York: William McSorley and Co., 1867), 473–74 (O'Meagher contributed to Conyngham's book). For more on the Irish Brigade and Barlow, see Welch, *Boy General*, 192–94.

84. FCB to his mother, July 15, 1864, in Barlow, *Letters*, 211; Lyman, *Meade's Army*, 239. Arabella's obituary was published in *Harper's Weekly*, August 13, 1864, 515, where she was described as "amiable, accomplished, admired, beloved[;] Mrs. Barlow from the first has been among the most eminent of the many heroines in this war whose names are not loudly mentioned, but whose memory will be forever fresh in the grateful heart of their friends and country."

85. Walker, *Second Army Corps*, 578; Welsh, *Medical Histories of Union Generals*, 15. For details of Barlow's medical problems and leaves, see Barlow, *Letters*, 214–17.

86. Emerson, *Life and Letters of Charles Russell Lowell*, 343–44.

87. New York Monuments Commission, *In Memoriam*, 60; Welch, *Boy General*, 196–208; Barlow, *Letters*, 219–20.

88. Barlow's postwar career is outside the charge of this essay, but a good summary can be found in Welch, *Boy General*, 209–59, and Barlow, *Letters*, 219–30. See also

Barlow's obituary, *New York Times*, January 12, 1896, 17, and New York Monuments Commission, *In Memoriam*.

89. On the artworks in the exhibit, see Eleanor Jones Harvey, *The Civil War and American Art* (New Haven: Yale University Press and Smithsonian American Art Museum, 2012). *Prisoners from the Front* is on p. 170. See also Holland Carter, "American Eden, after the Fall: 'The Civil War and American Art,'" *New York Times*, January 10, 2013.

90. Edwin H. Abbott, "Francis Channing Barlow," *Harvard Graduates' Magazine* 4 (June 1896): 526–42 (quotation 530); Charles Francis Adams to Henry Adams, July 22, 1864, in Worthington C. Ford, ed., *A Cycle of Adams Letters*, 2 vols. (Boston: Houghton Mifflin, 1920), 2:167; *Harper's Weekly*, July 9, 1864, 445; New York Monuments Commission, *In Memoriam*, 44.

91. Wilkeson, *Recollections of a Private Soldier*, 185; New York Monuments Commission, *In Memoriam*, 131.

Grant's Disengagement from Cold Harbor
June 12–13, 1864
⊰ GORDON C. RHEA ⊱

The sun rose over Cold Harbor on June 4, 1864, illuminating a landscape of suffering and death. "Troops yet clung tenaciously to the ground nearest the Confederate works, wherever so much as half-cover could be obtained," a Union officer recalled. "In some cases our men lay within thirty yards of the enemy," he added; "at other places, according to the configuration of the ground, the line ran away to fifty, seventy, a hundred, or more." Blue-clad soldiers hunkered low in depressions and stacked corpses for shelter against the deadly fire. One man likened the sandy soil to a "boiling cauldron, from the incessant pattering and plowing of shot, which raised the dirt in geysers and spitting sands." Wounded soldiers cried out for water. "Under the rays of the hot June sun, the bodies of the fast decomposing dead sent over into our trenches a most sickening and nauseating stench," a Rebel recalled, "while the helpless and fly-infested wounded were left to die a most horrible death."[1]

A month earlier, Lt. Gen. Ulysses S. Grant had initiated a campaign to defeat Gen. Robert E. Lee's Army of Northern Virginia and bring the American Civil War to a close. Predicating his campaign on maneuver, Grant attempted to flank Lee out of his defensive position on the Rapidan River; when that failed, he ventured turning movements to break deadlocks at the Wilderness, Spotsylvania Court House, and the North Anna River. By early June, the military center of gravity had shifted to the nondescript crossroads at Old Cold Harbor, ten miles northeast of Richmond. With Lee's army backed against the Confederate capital and seemingly on its last legs, Grant ordered a massive frontal assault. On June 3, for the fourth time in as many weeks, the Confederates fought the Union juggernaut to a standstill. Sheltered behind an impregnable wall of earthworks, its flanks anchored on marshy streams, the Rebel force barred the way to Richmond.

Remaining at Cold Harbor was unacceptable to the Federal high command. The low-lying country was notorious for causing fevers, and a prolonged stalemate could only sour the Union army's spirit and the nation's morale. Bludgeoning was also not the way to go. The June 3 offensive had confirmed that the Army of Northern Virginia's earthworks could not be successfully breached and that the political price of another costly reverse might well be catastrophic. The Rebels had to eat, however, and their provisions arrived by way of a transportation network that converged in Richmond. By cutting the supply routes to the Confederate capital, Grant might compel Lee to abandon his Cold Harbor bastion and have a chance to engage him on open ground. Another major turning movement was in order, this time geared to disrupt Lee's source of supplies.

Richmond's arteries included the Virginia Central Railroad, the James River and Kanawha Canal, and most important, the Richmond and Petersburg Railroad. In the operation's first phase, Grant planned to hold Maj. Gen. George G. Meade's Army of the Potomac at Cold Harbor while Maj. Gen. Philip H. Sheridan's Union cavalry, in concert with Maj. Gen. David Hunter's Federal army in the Shenandoah Valley, wrecked the Virginia Central Railroad and the canal. Once that mission was accomplished, the Potomac army would steal from Cold Harbor, cross the James River, advance on Petersburg, and amputate Lee's remaining supply lines from the south.

Grant's proposed movement faced formidable obstacles. The hostile armies stood closely entwined at Cold Harbor, diminishing the Union force's prospects of stealing away without alerting Lee. And once under way, the Federals would have to cross the Chickahominy River under the enemy's very nose: if the Virginian learned of the disengagement in time, he might catch the Army of the Potomac astride the boggy stream and inflict serious injury. Grant also worried about the safety of Maj. Gen. Benjamin F. Butler's Army of the James, entrenched between the James and Appomattox rivers at Bermuda Hundred. The Potomac army's departure from Cold Harbor might free Lee to assail Butler and overrun the smaller Union force before Grant could intervene.

An attractive option was to slice southwest below Lee's army to a point near Malvern Hill, cross the James River to Bermuda Hundred, and join forces with Butler. The combined Union force could then easily overwhelm the thin Confederate line protecting the Richmond and Petersburg Railroad, cut off Lee's supplies, and take Petersburg at its leisure. But such a move, Union planners feared, risked opening the Army of the Potomac to an attack by Lee as it rounded the Confederate army's southern flank. A safer course, Grant decided, would be to cross the James farther downriver, where Union cavalry and infantry could screen the movement and prevent an attack during the crossing. Charles City Court House offered an ideal staging area—several crossing points were nearby, and Union-held Fort Powhatan controlled the southern shore.[2]

Transporting the Union force with its guns and wagons across the James near Charles City Court House, however, raised daunting logistical challenges. The river was nearly half a mile wide and eighty feet deep, and it rose and fell four feet with the tide. Constructing a pontoon bridge would be an engineering nightmare. Ferries might be used, but whether they could carry enough men and supplies to evacuate the Union force before Lee could strike was an open question. Despite these obstacles, Maj. Gen. Andrew A. Humphreys, Meade's chief of staff, considered Charles City Court House and nearby Wilcox's Landing the army's best crossing points. "The vicinity of Malvern Hill would have afforded better bridging places of the James than at Wilcox's Landing, and the routes to Butler's intrenchments, and to Petersburg, would have been ten or fifteen miles shorter than those by way of Wilcox's Landing," Humphreys later noted; "but the crossing near Malvern, as well as the preparations for it, would have been under the observation of the enemy, and exposed to interruption."[3]

Over the next two weeks, Grant, Meade, and their staffs set the wheels of the impending maneuver in motion. On June 6, Grant sent two aides to confirm the best point for the crossing, "taking into consideration the necessity of choosing a place which will give the Army of the Potomac as short a line of march as practicable, and which will at the same time be far enough down-stream to allow for a sufficient distance between it and the present position of Lee's army to prevent the chances of our being attacked successfully while in the act of crossing," he instructed. The next morning, Sheridan left Cold Harbor with two cavalry divisions on a raid against the Virginia Central Railroad. "Everything is progressing favorably but slowly," Grant wrote his friend and mentor Congressman Elihu B. Washburn on June 9. "All the fight, except defensive and behind breast works, is taken out of Lee's army," he promised, echoing a refrain that had guided his actions since leaving the North Anna. "Unless my next move brings on a battle," he predicted, "the balance of the campaign will settle down to a siege."[4]

Logistics remained a major concern. As the Union army maneuvered across central Virginia, ships had ferried food, fodder, and ammunition from warehouses in Alexandria down the Potomac River to Chesapeake

Bay, steamed inland along tidal rivers, and unloaded at temporary depots. For the movement across the James, Grant ordered the "flying depot" at White House Landing on the Pamunkey River dismantled and a new supply station constructed at City Point. On June 9, workers began taking down the enormous tent city at White House Landing and tearing up the Richmond and York River Railroad to render it useless to the Rebels.[5]

Moving the Union army's 110,000 soldiers across the James, along with their artillery, horses, and supplies trains, called for a vast assemblage of pontoons and bridging material. Brig. Gen. Henry W. Benham, heading the Potomac army's engineer brigade from his headquarters at Fort Monroe, reported 1,500 feet of bridging at Bermuda Hundred, 460 more feet of material at the Port Royal and White House sites, and fifteen canvas pontoon boats at Fort Monroe. Another 1,200 feet of bridging was on its way from New York. To bring order into this chaotic situation, Grant directed Benham to centralize the bridging material at Fort Monroe. And in response to Grant's query about transports, Brig. Gen. Montgomery C. Meigs, the quartermaster general in Washington, promised to forward all the ferryboats he could find.[6]

By June 11, Grant had firmed his plans. The Army of the Potomac would execute a forced march to Charles City Court House, cross the James on ferries and a pontoon bridge, and advance in force on Petersburg. The Eighteenth Corps, borrowed from Butler for the Cold Harbor offensive, would simultaneously travel by ship from White House Landing to Bermuda Hundred, rejoin Butler, and play a major role in the assault. Speed was important, as the safety of Butler's main force at Bermuda Hundred depended on the Potomac army crossing the James and advancing within supporting distance before Lee had an opportunity to attack. For Grant's gambit to succeed, Union planners had to anticipate every contingency, and the Army of the Potomac had to move with clocklike efficiency, a feat that it had seldom achieved.

UNION HEADQUARTERS promulgated orders late on June 11 spelling out details of the disengagement. The army was to withdraw from its entrenchments in secrecy during the night of June 12–13 and head by various routes to Charles City Court House. The trick was to move quickly behind an impenetrable cavalry and infantry screen before Lee could react. The Federal army had executed disengagements of comparable difficulty after impasses at the Wilderness, Spotsylvania Court House, and the North Anna River.

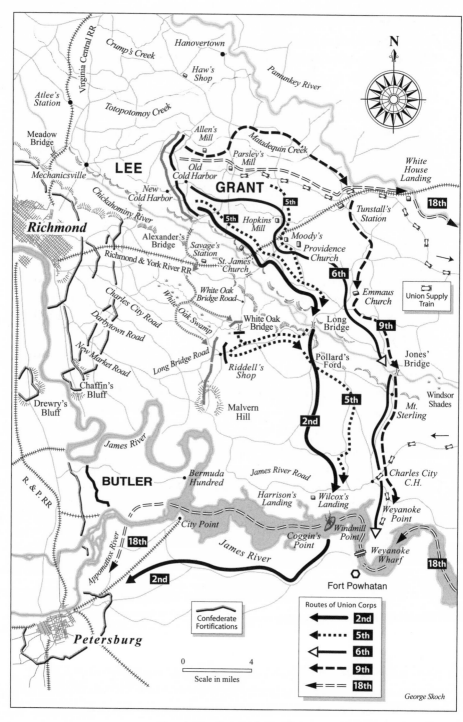

N

Crump's Creek

Hanovertown

Haw's Shop

Pamunkey River

Virginia Central RR

Atlee's Station

Totopotomoy Creek

Meadow Bridge

Allen's Mill

Matadequin Creek

White House Landing

Mechanicsville

LEE

Old Cold Harbor

Parsley's Mill

Chickahominy River

New Cold Harbor

GRANT

Hopkins' Mill

Tunstall's Station

18th

5th

5th

Moody's

Providence Church

Richmond

Alexander's Bridge

Savage's Station

St. James Church

6th

Emmaus Church

Union Supply Train

Richmond & York River RR

White Oak Bridge Road

Long Bridge

9th

Charles City Road

White Oak Bridge

White Oak Swamp

Jones' Bridge

Darbytown Road

Pollard's Ford

Windsor Shades

New Market Road

Long Bridge Road

Riddell's Shop

5th

Mt. Sterling

Chaffin's Bluff

Malvern Hill

2nd

Drewry's Bluff

James River

Charles City C.H.

BUTLER

Bermuda Hundred

James River Road

Weyanoke Point

R. & P. RR

Harrison's Landing

Wilcox's Landing

City Point

Coggin's Point

Windmill Point

Weyanoke Wharf

18th

Appomattox River

18th

2nd

James River

Fort Powhatan

Confederate Fortifications

Routes of Union Corps

2nd
5th
6th
9th
18th

0   4

Scale in miles

Petersburg

George Skoch

Grant's March to the James River

This time, however, Lee was alert for precisely the exercise that Grant had in mind, and Confederate cavalry posted along the Chickahominy stood ready to sound the alarm the moment the enemy started south.

Meade's talented chief of staff Humphreys drafted the operational details. A glance at a map suggests the complexity of his task. The Union force occupied a four-mile front from the Chickahominy River on the south to Matadequin Creek on the north. Pressed directly against the Rebel entrenchments along the formation's main north-south axis was Maj. Gen. Winfield S. Hancock's Second Corps, on the left; Maj. Gen. Horatio G. Wright's Sixth Corps, in the center; and Maj. Gen. William F. "Baldy" Smith's Eighteenth Corps, on the right. Maj. Gen. Ambrose E. Burnside's Ninth Corps completed the Union line's northern terminus, which angled eastward along the Matadequin. Two divisions from Maj. Gen. Gouverneur K. Warren's Fifth Corps guarded the left end of the Union line, extending east from Hancock's southern flank downstream along the Chickahominy. Warren's other two divisions formed a reserve behind the Union center near Old Cold Harbor, and cavalrymen from Brig. Gen. James H. Wilson's mounted division patrolled the countryside beyond each end of the Union formation, Col. John B. McIntosh's brigade to the north and Col. George H. Chapman's brigade to the south.

In broad outline, Humphreys proposed that the Army of the Potomac evacuate Cold Harbor in four coordinated columns. The movement was to begin with Warren's and Hancock's troops crossing the Chickahominy at Long Bridge. Once across, Hancock was to continue south while Warren turned west, screening Hancock's advance from the Rebels and creating the impression that Grant intended to launch an offensive toward Richmond north of the James. Simultaneously, Wright's and Burnside's corps were to follow separate routes to Jones' Bridge on the Chickahominy, downriver from Long Bridge, cross, and continue to the James River on roads east of Warren and Hancock. A third column, made up of the army's trains and accompanied by Brig. Gen. Edward Ferrero's division of United States Colored Troops, was to cross the Chickahominy east of Jones' Bridge at Windsor Shades and pursue a more remote road network to the James. While the first three columns funneled toward Charles City Court House, Smith's corps, comprising a fourth column, was to slice across Burnside's line of march on a beeline for White House Landing on the Pamunkey. There it was to board transports and retrace the route it had taken two weeks earlier from Bermuda Hundred, traveling down the Pamunkey and York rivers to Fort Monroe and steaming up the James for

Grant's Disengagement from Cold Harbor

a junction with Butler. If all went according to plan, two days of maneuver should see Smith arriving at Bermuda Hundred and the Army of the Potomac crossing the James on a combination of boats and pontoon bridges and marching on Petersburg unopposed.[7]

That, at least, was the idea. The challenge lay in the details. Of obvious concern were the risks entailed in disengaging the frontline troops. The movement was scheduled for night, and while the main body moved out, a skeleton force was to remain in the earthworks to create the illusion that the Union army was still entrenched. Headquarters also directed the preparation of a second line a short distance behind the main works. On June 9, Meade's chief engineer Maj. Nathaniel Michler completed plans for earthworks running south from Burnside's flank at Allen's Mill Pond, passing in front of Old Cold Harbor, and anchoring on the northern end of Elder Swamp, above Barker's Mill and behind Hancock. The fortifications, Michler wrote, were "to enable the troops to retire from the immediate front of the enemy without being molested, and to cover the movement off toward the east and along the east bank of the Chickahominy." Digging feverishly, Second and Sixth Corps details completed the new line on June 11.[8]

The big move began with some preliminary jockeying to better position the army. Warren's corps, slated to lead the advance across Long Bridge, was still divided, with Brig. Gens. Charles Griffin's and Lysander Cutler's divisions patrolling the Chickahominy near Hancock, and Brig. Gens. Romeyn B. Ayres's and Samuel W. Crawford's divisions encamped several miles away at the Leary farm, east of Old Cold Harbor. Headquarters directed Warren to march Ayres and Crawford several miles south to Mr. Moody's property, bringing those divisions closer to the other Fifth Corps divisions and within an easy marching distance from Long Bridge. To avoid detection, they were to take a roundabout path from Leary's farm southeast through Parsley's Mill, Ayres leading, followed by Crawford and the Fifth Corps reserve artillery, pontoon trains, and ambulances.[9]

Warren initiated this preliminary move at 4:00 A.M. on June 11, and by midafternoon, Fifth Corps camps sprawled across Mr. Moody's yard to nearby Providence Church. "No unnecessary fires will be allowed," Warren directed, "and great care must be taken to keep the woods from taking fire, and to extinguish it if it does break out."[10]

The next day—June 12—Warren issued orders for the march. At six o'clock that evening, Ayres and Crawford were to start south from Moody's, followed by the Fifth Corps reserve artillery under Col. Charles S. Wainwright. Simultaneously, a few miles away on the Chickahominy, Griffin and Cutler were to set off as well, taking Dispatch Station Road and subsidiary routes past Saint James' Church, Ratcliff's Old Tavern, Ruckle's, and White Hall and on to Long Bridge. Warren reminded Griffin to move "as promptly as you can, keeping well closed up," as Hancock would be coming close behind him. If all went according to plan, the two Fifth Corps columns, one from the north and the other from the west, would unite at Long Bridge before midnight.[11]

Warren also had to coordinate his advance with Hancock, whose Second Corps comprised the other component of the army's first column. In anticipation of the evacuation, Hancock slid his line somewhat south during the night of June 10–11, as did Wright, whose troops replaced the stretch of works adjacent to Cold Harbor Road vacated by Hancock's northern elements. Engineers also laid out a four-mile road "practicable for a column" running from Livesay's house near the southern end of Elder Swamp eastward to the Wicker farm, where it struck a major road that fed into Dispatch Station Road near Mr. Higgins's place. This new trail, Hancock reasoned, would speed his evacuation by affording his corps a second route to the rear.[12]

The assignment of cutting the new road fell to the engineer Maj. Wesley Brainerd, who began work early on June 12. "Arriving with axes," Brainerd recalled, "my men struck into the woods, felling trees as we advanced." By nightfall, they had completed a track wide enough for artillery. Passing over to Dispatch Station Road, Brainerd met Hancock's chief of staff Lt. Col. Charles H. Morgan, who informed him that Hancock was "much pleased with the road we had made," Brainerd reported.[13]

Midmorning on June 12, Hancock reviewed with his subordinates the withdrawal scheduled for that evening. At 8:30 P.M., Brig. Gen. John Gibbon's division, holding the northern end of Hancock's battle line, was to retire to the new set of reserve works between Old Cold Harbor and Elder Swamp; Brig. Gen. Francis C. Barlow's division in the Second Corps center was to drop back to Livesay's house and the road freshly cut by Brainerd; and Maj. Gen. David B. Birney's division, on the southern end of the Second Corps line, was to slide its northernmost brigades to the rear and left. "The picket line will be strengthened," Hancock directed, "and a few reliable regiments left in the advanced rifle pits until the greater part of the division is withdrawn."[14]

Once Barlow had completed his concentration at the Livesay farm, the evacuation's next stage would begin. Barlow was to set off first, follow

Brainerd's trail through the woods to the Wicker farm, turn south to Dispatch Station Road at the Higgins place, and head west behind Ayres's and Cutler's Fifth Corps divisions. Gibbon meanwhile was to leave the reserve line near Elder Swamp and follow in Barlow's wake, and Birney was to start east along Dispatch Station Road, bringing up the Second Corps tail. The pickets, supervised by Lt. Col. John S. Hammell of the 66th New York Infantry, were to assemble behind Birney and comprise the column's rearguard, gathering up the Fifth Corps pickets while marching east along Dispatch Station Road. "Division commanders are requested to adopt measures to prevent the men from falling in rear of the column and into the hands of the enemy, as happened in the last night march," Hancock's assistant adjutant general Col. Francis A. Walker cautioned.[15]

While Hancock marched to join them, Warren's two prongs were to merge at Long Bridge, cross the Chickahominy, and extend feelers west to screen the army's advance to the James. "It was expected that such a movement by General Warren would deceive Lee," chief of staff Humphreys later stressed, "and give him the impression that the Army of the Potomac was advancing upon Richmond, or, if intending to cross the James, that it would do so near Malvern Hill, at City Point, or above."[16]

Wright's and Burnside's troops were slated to combine into a second Union column. When the Sixth Corps disengaged after dark on June 12, it was to shift into the reserve line and continue on to Old Cold Harbor. From there, Wright's men were to march east to the Parsley home and arch southerly, pass by Hopkins' Mill, and come out at Mr. Moody's place, which Warren ought to have vacated several hours earlier. From Moody's, Wright's soldiers were to follow a looping march through Emmaus Church to Jones' Bridge and a junction with the Ninth Corps.[17]

Sandwiched into a short battle line between Hancock and Smith, Wright had the tricky task of coordinating his withdrawal with that of two adjoining corps while he rendezvoused with a third. His situation was complicated by Hancock's request that Sixth Corps troops relieve the northern portion of his line, where Gibbon's division was posted. The evening of June 10, Hancock, Wright, and Gibbon met at Grant's headquarters and agreed on a plan. At dark, Brig. Gen. Thomas H. Neill's division, in the center of the Sixth Corps line, was to forward enough troops northward to hold the adjacent segment of line occupied by Brig. Gen. James B. Ricketts's division, freeing Ricketts to slip behind Neill's and Brig. Gen. David A. Russell's divisions and occupy "as much of Gibbons' line as he can, forming double lines of battle." Ricketts, Wright warned, must "exercise great caution in relieving the Second Corps, waiting probably till after the moon has set." At 2:00 A.M. on the 11th, Ricketts withdrew according to plan and marched south behind the Sixth Corps line. The sun was up by the time he reached Gibbon, so he camped until nightfall, then replaced the northern portion of Gibbon's formation and posted his troops in two lines of battle.[18]

Meade's order assigning routes gave Burnside's Ninth Corps the longest trek. Like his fellow corps heads, Burnside was to withdraw as soon after dark on June 12 "as practicable." He would not, however, have a direct route to the Chickahominy. Instead, he was to angle northeast past Allen's Mill, skim along Matadequin Creek's southern branch, and detour widely through Clopton's and on to Tunstall's Station on the Richmond and York River Railroad, Brig. Gen. James H. Ledlie's division leading, followed by the divisions of Brig. Gens. Robert B. Potter and Orlando B. Willcox. If Smith's Eighteenth Corps—the third column of advance, moving on a direct route to White House—happened to be at Tunstall's Station, Burnside was to yield until Smith had passed and then continue on to Jones' Bridge by way of Baltimore Cross-Roads and Emmaus Church, "taking care not to interfere with routes of other corps." After uniting with Wright, this column was to press south through Vandom's, Clopton's, and Tyler's to emerge east of Charles City Court House.[19]

The army's wagon train—another column of advance, consisting of thousands of supply and baggage wagons, ambulances, and a herd of cattle—folded another complication into the mix. Ferrero, whose two brigades of United States Colored Troops had spent the campaign on rearguard duty, were to proceed from Old Church to Tunstall's Station and accompany the trains. To help minimize congestion and protect the slow-moving wagons, Humphreys sent the train on a route well east of the infantry, at first designating Windsor Shades as the crossing point on the Chickahominy but later changing the route farther downstream to Coles' Ferry out of concern that Windsor Shades was too marshy for the cumbersome wagons.[20]

Such was the plan. Whether the Army of the Potomac could execute a maneuver of such complexity remained to be seen.

AT TWO O'CLOCK on the morning of June 12, Grant's staffers returned from their reconnaissance and confirmed—much to the general's relief—that the area around Fort Powhatan, ten miles downriver from City Point, fully satisfied Grant's requirements for a crossing point. The army could access

Grant's Disengagement from Cold Harbor

the northern bank by several good roads from Charles City Court House, and roads on the southern bank ran to City Point and Petersburg. Nearby Coggins' Point offered excellent grazing land for horses and cattle. Most important, the river narrowed somewhat between Wilcox's Landing on the north bank and Windmill Point on the south.[21]

Communications flew between headquarters and the departments responsible for logistics. Mindful that bridges and transports had to be in place by the time the army reached the James, Grant dispatched Col. Frederick T. Dent of his staff to communicate the necessary orders to Benham and Butler. At 9:00 A.M., Assistant Secretary of War Charles A. Dana recorded that Grant had directed Butler "to throw a bridge and corduroy the marsh at [the James River opposite Fort Powhatan]." From White House, Brig. Gen. John J. Abercrombie predicted that the hospital could be ready to close by noon; the repair depot could pack up in five hours; the water transport services needed twenty-four hours' notice; the ordnance officer could be ready in two hours; and the commissary required eight hours. Notice went out to Quartermaster General Meigs that ships for 16,000 troops—Smith's corps—had to be at White House the next morning. "The movement is very important," headquarters stressed, "and it is necessary that all vessels suitable for transporting troops, which have been sent from this place to Washington and Alexandria, be returned at once, together with such vessels as can be spared."[22]

In response to Grant's request, Butler's chief engineer Brig. Gen. Godfrey Weitzel dispatched Lt. Peter S. Michie to examine the river near Fort Powhatan and determine the best site for a pontoon bridge. By day's end, Michie had identified three potential crossing points, and Weitzel notified Grant's staff that preparing the bridge approaches would take thirty-six hours. The time frame for the movement was now confirmed. If the engineers performed as Weitzel promised, the James River crossings would be ready the morning of June 14, just as the army's main body would be tramping through Charles City Court House.[23]

Late on the afternoon of June 12, Grant, Meade, and their staffs rode into Warren's headquarters at the Moody place. "Moody's is a little house, as it were on skids, like a corn barn," the aide Lt. Col. Theodore Lyman wrote, "and with several pleasant catalpas round it." The weather had turned unseasonably chilly, prompting the aides to build a campfire and pull on their greatcoats. "Boxes and boards are made into seats, or rubber blankets are thrown upon the ground to lie on, and all gather close to the crackling rail fire," a newsman observed. Assistant War Secretary

Dana strode nervously in front of the fire; Congressman Washburn, visiting from Washington, fell asleep with his feet to the flames; Brig. Gen. Henry J. Hunt, in charge of the artillery reserve, discussed guns with the engineer Brig. Gen. John G. Barnard; and quartermaster general Rufus Ingalls fretted about headquarters' supply train, which had lost a few wagons while crossing a narrow dam. Dana cursed the delay, which had postponed his dinner, as "a piece of damn folly." Stepping toward the fire, Grant put the incident into perspective. "If we have nothing worse than this—," he began, stopping mid-sentence to let his listeners contemplate the risks inherent in their undertaking. After stoking the fire, the commander in chief stretched out on a board, slid a bag under his head, and fell fast asleep.[24]

That evening, the two wings of Warren's corps—one concentrated at Mr. Moody's place, the other extending along the Chickahominy from Hancock's flank—started toward Long Bridge, where they were scheduled to converge. Workers had repaired the road from Moody's, and Warren, who accompanied the troops, seemed "in a good humor today," according to Colonel Wainwright. The artillerist remarked on the "great charm in moving on such a beautiful clear night through the quiet country, and on good roads."[25]

Warren and his entourage reached Long Bridge soon after dark. Brigadier General Wilson was already there with a mounted brigade under Colonel Chapman, whose five regiments—the 3rd Indiana, the 8th New York, the 1st Vermont, and the newly arrived 22nd New York and 1st New Hampshire Cavalry—were preparing to force their way across the Chickahominy. Ayres's and Crawford's troops settled beside the road to rest while the cavalrymen cleared the way. A few miles west, the other half of Warren's corps—Griffin's and Cutler's divisions—evacuated their posts along the Chickahominy, filtered back to Dispatch Station Road, and headed southeast toward Long Bridge.[26]

The Chickahominy at Long Bridge was a sluggish stream bordered by a broad floodplain. "Fancy a wide ditch, partly choked with rotten logs, and full of brown, tepid sickly-looking water, whose slow current would scarcely carry a straw along," Meade's aide Lyman noted. "From the banks of dark mould rises a black and luxuriant vegetation; cypress of immense size, willow oaks, and swamp magnolias, remind you that you are within the limits of a sub-tropical climate, and so does the unhealthy and peculiar smell of decaying leaves and stagnant water." A drawing of Long Bridge, Lyman thought, "might pass as the incarnation of malaria and swamp fever."[27]

Grant's Disengagement from Cold Harbor

The approaches to Long Bridge were in good condition, but the span no longer existed. Maj. George W. Ford's engineers were on hand to build a pontoon bridge, but Brig. Gen. Rufus Barringer's dismounted Confederate cavalry, assigned by Lee to watch the Chickahominy crossings, occupied rifle pits on the far bank. As Union engineers manhandled the pontoons into position, Barringer's Tar Heels put up "brisk" resistance, and Wilson's cavalrymen seemed incapable of driving them away. Warren cursed one of Wilson's staffers and instructed him to tell his boss "if he can't lay that bridge to get out of the way with his damned cavalry and I'll lay it."[28]

Spurred to action, Chapman sent his 8th New York Cavalry two miles downriver to Pollard's Ford. Barringer, it developed, was picketing there as well, and his Confederates shot at the New Yorkers when they came into sight. Led by Maj. Edmund M. Pope, the Union troopers crossed the stream on fallen trees. "It was rather amusing to see officers and men astride of the logs, hitching themselves across as fast as possible, at the same time endeavoring to keep their feet and firearms out of the water," a New Yorker later reminisced. "I could not help thinking, with something of a sportsman's instinct, what a beautiful raking shot could have been had upon us, when twenty or thirty of us would be crossing on the same log." Gaining the far bank, Pope's men drove off the Rebels and painstakingly worked upstream toward Long Bridge.[29]

Under mounting pressure to clear the way at Long Bridge, Chapman directed the 22nd New York Cavalry to try crossing nearer the bridge site. The troopers gamely started across fifty yards upstream, some wading, some swimming, and some clambering over "by the means of fallen trees and overhanging limbs," according to a witness. While the 22nd New York splashed through the swampy bottomland to the bridgehead, the engineer Ford and a squad from the 3rd Indiana Cavalry rowed across in a pontoon boat under "sharp fire." Together, the New Yorkers and the Hoosiers—reinforced by another pontoon load of cavalrymen—secured a hold on the Chickahominy's southern bank. Union casualties amounted to one engineer killed.[30]

Protected by Chapman's troopers, Major Ford's engineers began constructing the pontoon bridge. The stream's main course was 100 feet wide, separated by an island from a 60-foot-wide channel to the south. "Extensive swamps bordered the approaches," Ford later reported; "the river was filled with sunken piles and timber, the available passage was very narrow, the debris of the old bridge had to be cleared away, and the abutments cut down." At 11:15 P.M., Wilson informed Humphreys that his work would not

Union cavalrymen at Long Bridge on the Chickahominy River as Grant's movement toward the James River commenced. Edwin Forbes dated this sketch June 12, 1864, but it probably should be June 13 (unless the artist sought to show movement by moonlight). Library of Congress Prints and Photographs Division, LC-DIG-ppmsca-20711.

be finished until midnight. In fact, not until one clock on the morning of the 13th, after two and a half hours of labor, was the bridge ready for use.[31]

The rest of Chapman's troopers came across, accompanied by Lt. Charles L. Fitzhugh's Batteries C and E, 4th United States. Reaching the southern shore, they headed west on Long Bridge Road, sparring sporadically with Barringer's retreating horsemen. It was almost daylight on the 13th before the Fifth Corps infantry tramped over the bridge and fanned into the broad bottomland south of the Chickahominy. Crawford's division bivouacked on high ground overlooking the river, near the home of a Mrs. Maddox, about a mile and a half west of Long Bridge, where they could support Chapman. Warren established his headquarters nearby, and his staff lounged under locust trees in Mrs. Maddox's garden. Ayres's, Cutler's, and Griffin's troops camped on the floodplain near the bridge. "All felt glad that they were leaving the hated peninsula," a surgeon reflected as he gazed into the Chickahominy's fetid waters.[32]

DURING THE AFTERNOON of June 12, while Warren's soldiers prepared for the march to Long Bridge, the rest of Meade's army began vacating the entrenchments that had been their home for almost two weeks. By 3:00

P.M., workers had dismantled field hospitals and tucked sick and wounded men into wagons for the eighteen-mile ride to White House Landing. As darkness fell, frontline soldiers slipped to the rear. Silence was the watchword. "Every man had his tin cup tied fast and his tin plate, if he was rich enough to have one, safely stowed in his haversack, so when the movement was begun there was not a rattle or a jingle to be heard," a Federal related. In places, troops stole away on their hands and knees. Pickets maintained a slow patter of musketry well into the night, and regimental bands played, following a routine established days earlier. So far as the Confederates could tell, the Yankees were settling down for another night in their trenches.[33]

Hancock's Second Corps, on the southern end of the Federal position, left in stages as planned. Gibbon's division retired into the newly constructed reserve line, occupying the entrenchments from Old Cold Harbor to Elder Swamp; Birney's men filtered back to the Livesay grounds; and Barlow's soldiers prepared to press east along Dispatch Station Road, following behind Griffin's and Cutler's Fifth Corps troops. Artillery battalions traveled with their divisions, and caissons and reserve batteries gathered on the Livesay farm under the charge of Major John G. Hazard. "The night was clear and calm," an officer in the 8th New Jersey remembered. "To drown the noise of the tramp of men, and as a means to counteract any suspicion of the movement, the band played while the brigade was executing the movement, and followed out in rear of it."[34]

By 11:00 P.M., the entire Second Corps was in motion. "The moon was full; it was a beautiful night, but very cold, and the roads were dry and dirty," a man in the 26th Michigan Infantry wrote home. "We took byroads, across fields and through tangled and dark woods along the famous Chickahominy River." Another soldier recalled the "thrill of pleasure" that rippled through the ranks as the troops realized they were finally leaving Cold Harbor. When they judged they were too far away for the enemy to hear, they broke into song, "swinging along hour after hour, forgetting the fatigue and hardship," a soldier recounted.[35]

North of Hancock, Wright's soldiers retired into the newly constructed entrenchments and remained there until midnight, when they headed east toward Prospect Church. Wright's rearmost soldiers—Col. Emory Upton's brigade of Russell's division—guarded the Sixth Corps artillery trains until two in the morning, when the Corps pickets also left. During the evacuation, Wright's troops became entangled with some of Gibbon's men who had taken the wrong road and inadvertently stumbled into the Sixth Corps route. The traffic jam took a while to sort out, but by 2:00 A.M., Wright's column was off again. "We hailed, almost with acclamations, the announcement of our withdrawal from this awful place," a New Jersey soldier remembered. "No words can adequately describe the horrors of the twelve days we had spent there, and the sufferings we had endured."[36]

The Eighteenth Corps, adjoining Wright, disengaged without a hitch. Smith had sent a few brigades rearward during the afternoon, but most of his troops did not leave until after dark. A rumor circulated that the Eighteenth Corps was slated to remain until everyone else had gotten safely away, leading suspicious souls to speculate that they were "to be sacrificed for the salvation of the Army of the Potomac." The concern proved unfounded, much to the relief of Smith's men, who moved out in tandem with the Sixth Corps.[37]

The Ninth Corps, holding the northernmost end of the Union line, also crept from its works soon after dark. Campfires burned to conceal its disappearance. "So well was this accomplished that the enemy did not know for an hour after the departure of the corps that our pickets had been withdrawn," a soldier recollected, "and during this time they kept up their firing, by both artillery and musketry." Writing Burnside the next morning, a division commander reported that unsuspecting Confederates were still shooting briskly into the empty Union entrenchments.[38]

IMMEDIATELY SOUTH of the Chickahominy, Long Bridge Road ran west for a mile and a half across a floodplain, climbed a small rise by Mrs. Maddox's property, and angled southwest below a boggy stream named White Oak Swamp. Five miles out, White Oak Bridge Road struck off to the north, crossed the swamp, and continued on to the Chickahominy. Chapman's horsemen were directed to plug this road and press a mile west along Long Bridge Road to the intersection at Riddell's Shop, where Charles City Road and Willis Church Road merged with Long Bridge Road. These were the routes that Lee would likely use if he decided to assail the Union army as it marched south, and Chapman's and Warren's assignment was to close them to the Rebels.[39]

Opposition from Barringer's Confederates mounted as Chapman's troopers pressed west along Long Bridge Road. "We would march a short distance," a man in the 1st Vermont Cavalry remembered, "run into some rebels, and while the advance was getting ready to drive them away, we would come into line, dismount, and just as we would get to dozing in good shape, would mount up and move forward again." At 6:00 A.M., Wilson, who accompanied Chapman, informed headquarters that Confederates had delayed him "considerably" by barricading the road at several points.[40]

An hour of sparring brought Chapmen's troopers to White Oak Bridge Road, where they turned north toward White Oak Swamp. Falling back across the creek, Barringer's horsemen retired to an earthen fortification constructed during the Peninsula campaign in 1862 and dominating White Oak Bridge. As the northerners came into view, Capt. William M. McGregor's horse artillery opened fire from the fort, and Barringer's men charged. Fighting on foot, the 3rd Indiana spread out in skirmish formation and drove the Rebels back to the northern side of the creek. Major Pope then threw his 3rd Battalion into the fray, stabilizing Chapman's front while Fitzhugh's Battery E provided a counterweight to the Confederate ordnance. "A lively artillery duel ensued," Chapman related, in which Fitzhugh lost heavily in men and horses.[41]

As combat heated around White Oak Bridge, Warren dispatched Crawford's division to support Chapman. First to arrive was Col. James L. Bates's brigade, containing regiments from Massachusetts, New York, and Pennsylvania, and two batteries—Capt. Almont Barnes's 1st New York Light, Battery C, and Capt. Patrick Hart's New York Light, 15th Battery. Charging up White Oak Bridge Road, Bates's 94th New York and 12th Massachusetts spread out in skirmish formation, came under "severe shell fire," and entrenched, sealing the way across the swamp. "We lay close to a little ravine that held some of the largest black snakes I ever saw," a New Englander remembered. "We killed four of five of these old residents, and we saw crossing the path that ran from the road to the swamp, a dozen more." Despite persistent Rebel gunnery, Union losses amounted to only a handful of deaths and less than twenty men wounded. The chief casualty was Capt. George B. Rhodes, commanding the 88th Pennsylvania, sliced nearly in half by a solid shot. At 8:30 A.M., Wilson informed headquarters that Chapman had "driven the enemy's cavalry across White Oak Swamp and hold[s] the ridge commanding the crossing." A single Union corps, he added, would suffice to protect the position "against almost any force."[42]

Leaving the job of plugging White Oak Bridge Road to Bates's infantrymen, Chapman pulled back to Long Bridge Road and continued west toward Riddell's Shop. Elements of Barringer's brigade contested his advance but retired under superior Union numbers.

Camped a few miles south near Malvern Hill was Brig. Gen. Martin W. Gary's Confederate cavalry brigade, consisting of the 7th South Carolina, the Hampton Legion, and the 24th Virginia regiments. Rushing to Barringer's assistance, Gary's troopers deployed in a belt of woods east of Riddell's Shop, blocking the way "with obstinacy," Chapman later conceded. Directing the 1st Vermont, 3rd Indiana, and 8th New York to fight on foot, Chapman rushed his troopers forward. "The dismounted men advanced in front of the enemy," a Vermonter recalled of the charge, "while the 8th New York flanked them and the battery shelled them." After a "rattling fight," Gary's horsemen retreated at the "double quick," according to a Federal, or more deliberately, according to southern accounts.[43]

It was now 11:00 A.M. Under orders to hold Riddell's Shop, Chapman arranged his veteran 1st Vermont, 3rd Indiana, and 8th New York into a line, the left end resting on Willis Church Road and the right wing well across the Charles City Road. Fitzhugh's artillery and the relatively inexperienced 1st New Hampshire and 22nd New York cavalry formed a second line in the rear. To better defend the intersection, the Union troopers piled fence rails and dirt into makeshift breastworks. Supporting them was another of Crawford's brigades, this one under Col. James Carle and consisting of the 190th and 191st Pennsylvania, newly formed from the former Pennsylvania Reserves. Part of the 190th joined Chapman's horseman, the rest of the regiment waited in reserve in a shallow depression, and the 191st deployed out of sight on the left. Writing headquarters, Wilson reported that Chapman was still advancing and that Crawford occupied the Riddell's Shop crossroads and the road through White Oak Swamp.[44]

All afternoon, Chapman skirmished with Gary's and Barringer's Confederate horsemen. "It was a period of extraordinary anxiety and hard work, during which much ammunition was expended and much noise made" recalled Wilson, who supervised the operation. A Hoosier remembered the day-long running battle as "the hardest fight we have had for a long time." Little did he suspect that veteran Confederate infantry was on the way, and that the day's combat would soon resume in earnest.[45]

PROTECTED BY Chapman's and Crawford's screening action, the rest of the Union army marched unimpeded along its assigned routes. Near sunrise on June 13, Hancock's lead elements strode into St. James Church, a mile short of Dispatch Station on the Richmond and York River Railroad. Soldiers packed the tiny wooden structure and covered its walls with graffiti. "May he be hung, drawn, and quartered," one man wrote of Grant, then went on to explain what he meant: "Hung with the laurels of victory, drawn in the chariot of peace, and quartered in the White House at Washington." After

Grant's Disengagement from Cold Harbor

resting at the church grounds for two hours, the Second Corps resumed its march. Still leading, Barlow reached Long Bridge at 9:30 A.M. Gibbon's troops arrived about eleven o'clock and halted to boil coffee while Birney's division tramped over the pontoon bridge.[46]

Shortly after noon, the Second Corps passed through Warren's bivouacs on the bottomland below the Chickahominy. Birney now led, followed by Barlow and Gibbon. By 3:00 P.M., Colonel McIntosh's cavalry brigade, bringing up the Union rear, had crossed the Chickahominy, and Major Ford's engineers had dismantled the pontoon bridge. The day warmed, and dust filled the air. A sergeant remembered men "all prostrate in the boiling sun—faces begrimed and features pinched, clothes stained with sweat and dust, and feet swollen and blistered." Another Yankee gazed back from a hilltop transfixed by the "vibrating movements of that living column," he later wrote. "It resembled the rippling waters of the restless ocean, or the undulated appearance of endless grain fields, ripe in the head, in the gentle breezes of summer."[47]

After leaving Cold Harbor, Wright's corps had advanced east through Prospect Church and on to Hopkins' Mill, where marshy bottomland rendered the road impassable for wagons and guns. Separating from Wright's infantry, the Sixth Corps wagons retraced their route to Prospect Church and cut over on another path to Dispatch Station Road. Wright's infantry continued on to Summit Station, halted ten minutes for breakfast, passed through the empty Fifth Corps camps around Moody's, and headed for Emmaus Church and Jones' Bridge. The going was "very tiresome," a New Yorker entered in his diary, "as we not only have to hold our load but we are also troubled to keep awake." No rain had fallen for a week, and the parched, sandy roads resembled "beds of ashes." "The men, deprived of their coffee, chocked with dust, and burned with heat, marched wearily toward night," a soldier recalled.[48]

Burnside's troops also made good progress, reaching Tunstall's Station near daybreak. Wagon trains packed the roads around the station, and after waiting impatiently several hours for the way to clear, Burnside sent an irate note to headquarters. "The delay would not have been so great had these trains traveled all night as our troops did, but instead of that they hauled out by side of the road and took a good night's rest," he complained. The Ninth Corps was off again around 11:00 A.M. and "struggled onward," an officer recalled, "between and around the long lines of white-topped wagons which crowded the roads."[49]

The engineer Maj. Edmund O. Beers joined the Sixth Corps at Emmaus

Church with bridging material for the last leg of the jaunt to the Chicka-hominy. It was 3:30 P.M. when Wright reached Jones' Bridge—or Forge Bridge, as the crossing was sometimes called. "Have just heard that head of General Burnside's column was at Olivet Church, five miles from here, I think, at 2:20 PM," Wright informed headquarters. "My men are much exhausted, as the march has been a long one," he added, "much longer than I had supposed from the maps." Rather than forging ahead, Wright pro-posed resting for the night and resuming the march to Charles City Court House early the next morning.[50]

The Chickahominy at Jones' Bridge was deep, sluggish, and narrow, "lined with deep swamps thickly covered with underbrush and emitting a miasm more disagreeable if possible than that of the Yazoo," a soldier claimed. After clearing away flood wood and shards from the old bridge, Beers's engineers constructed two pontoon bridges, one of canvas and the other of wood. Wright's soldiers started over at 5:00 P.M. and bivouacked a mile south at Mount Sterling, near the Jordan family home. They were "completely tired out and foot-sore," a marcher noted. "Never felt any worse," another man agreed. "Those last miles were doled out in suffer-ing by inches," a Vermonter concurred. "If a man wants to know what it is to have every bone in his body ache with fatigue, every muscle sore and exhausted, and his whole body ready to sink to the ground, let him diet on a common soldier's fare till he has only the strength that imparts, and then let him shoulder his knapsack, haversack, gun, and equipments, and make one of our forced marches." Burnside's troops neared the bridge just as Wright's rearmost elements were disappearing south and settled into fields by the Chickahominy for the night.[51]

The Sixth Corps had covered twenty-two miles since leaving Cold Har-bor, and the Ninth Corps about twenty-five. A guideboard at a nearby crossroads read, "To New Kent C.H., 10 miles. To Charles City C.H., 6 miles." Wright informed Burnside that he expected to start at four the next morning and advised the Ninth Corps commander that "as you take the same road as myself, you can decide when to start so as not to be delayed by me. Three hours is not too much time to allow me for drawing out on the road."[52]

Of the Union army's columns, Smith's Eighteenth Corps had the short-est, but not necessarily the easiest, distance to cover. The troops left Cold Harbor through fields littered with bloated horse carcasses and at Tun-stall Station wove around "a hundred acres of wagons," a soldier estimated. The morning's high point was a boy selling lemons by the roadside that men "purchased, distributed, and [ate] down like apples, peel and all," a marcher recalled. At the end of the eighteen-mile trek, clusters of exhausted soldiers dotted the fields around White House Landing. "Some crawled on their hands and knees to the river bank, two or three rods away, and drank like so many animals," a New Englander reported. A newsman noted that the sutlers, "with an unbroken confidence in Grant, still kept open house and largely increased their personal property by supplying the ravenously hungry command of Baldy Smith." Sanitary Commission workers provoked bitter criticism when they offered canned goods to officers but not to enlisted men. "This creates much ill-feeling," a soldier complained, "and threats of mobbing the concern are freely indulged in."[53]

Midmorning, the Eighteenth Corps began boarding transports for the hundred-odd-mile journey by water to Bermuda Hundred. Around 10:00 A.M., Smith and his staff settled in on the little steamer *Metamora*, seamen hoisted the flag, and the Eighteenth Corps was off. Most of the fleet had navigated the Pamunkey and York rivers by evening and anchored for the night near Fort Monroe.[54]

THE DISAPPEARANCE of the entire Union army from Cold Harbor caught Lee by surprise. During the night of June 12–13, Confederate pickets had detected sounds of heightened activity behind Union lines. Not until morning, however, did they discover that the enemy had left for parts unknown. Lee sent out scouting parties, but the northerners were nowhere to be found. "Even Marse Robert, who knew everything knowable, did not appear to know what his old enemy proposed to do or where he would be most likely to find him," a Confederate later remarked.[55]

Barringer's reports that Federals were crossing at Long Bridge provided a partial clue to Grant's whereabouts: bluecoats were swarming across the Chickahominy, and Union elements—Chapman's and Warren's men— were advancing toward Richmond along Long Bridge Road. Whether Grant meant to launch his main attack there or continue over the James was not at all clear to Lee, but the Confederate moved immediately to block the approaches to Richmond. Riddell's Shop intersection had to remain in southern hands.

Reductions in Lee's manpower during the previous week severely curtailed the Confederate commander's ability to react to Grant's move. On June 7, Maj. Gen. John C. Breckinridge's division—more than 2,000 soldiers—had left Cold Harbor to counter Hunter's growing Union menace in the Shenandoah Valley. The next day, two of Lee's cavalry divisions had ridden off to oppose Sheridan's mounted incursion against the Virginia Central Railway. And at 3:00 A.M. on June 13, as the last of Grant's infantry started toward the James, Lt. Gen. Jubal A. Early's entire Confederate Second Corps—yet another 8,000 men—departed to bolster the Rebel numbers in the Valley. To meet Grant's shift toward the James, Lee could muster only two infantry corps, a division recently borrowed from the Petersburg defenses, and six cavalry regiments, totaling at most 40,000 men.

With most of his cavalry absent, Lee lacked the horsemen necessary to scout out the enemy's position. Assuming that Chapman's and Crawford's advance out Long Bridge Road presaged a general Union attack along that axis, Lee directed Lt. Gen. Ambrose P. Hill's Confederate Third Corps to cross the Chickahominy at Alexander's Bridge, pass through Savage's Station, and hurry as quickly as possible toward Riddell's Shop to intercept the Federals. Lt. Gen. Richard H. Anderson's First Corps trailed behind Hill, followed by Maj. Gen. Robert F. Hoke's division. Midmorning, aside from a scattering of pickets, orderlies, and cavalrymen, the Confederate entrenchments at Cold Harbor stood empty, looking across at the vacant Union lines.[56]

A mile past Savage's Station, Hill's lead division under Maj. Gen. Cadmus M. Wilcox met a courier from Gary. Federals, the man reported, already held Riddell's Shop and were pushing west. Increasing his pace—a participant called the advance a "forced march"—Wilcox struck Charles City Road a short distance west of the critical intersection. Backed by a company from the 14th South Carolina Infantry, Confederate sharpshooters advanced, "cheering lustily, and driving the Federal dismounted cavalry before them," a southerner recounted. "We held them as long as we could," a Vermonter wrote, "and then fell back in 'middling good order' without much loss to the edge of the woods, and then to our horses in the open field, where we mounted up expeditiously as possible, and drew saber."[57]

While Wilcox pounded Chapman at Riddell's Shop—it was now about four o'clock in the afternoon, and Wilson and his staff were enjoying a "first class dinner" in the woods—another of Hill's divisions under Maj. Gen. Henry Heth joined Barringer at White Oak Swamp and took up "about the best position we had seen during the campaign," a Rebel recorded. Crawford responded to Heth's appearance by dispatching Col. Peter Lyle's brigade to assist Bates. Approaching White Oak Bridge, Lyle's troops came under fire from the Confederate fort. "The first shell struck the road before it reached our column," an officer in the 39th Massachusetts remembered, noting that "the men opened to the right and left, and the shell

Grant's Disengagement from Cold Harbor

ricocheted down between them." Deploying next to Bates, Lyle's troops repelled a determined charge by Heth's Rebels. Half an hour later, Heth's soldiers attacked again, only to be repulsed once more, and combat on the White Oak Swamp front settled into a long-range shooting match across the stream.[58]

Sparring at Riddell's Shop, however, was far from over. Near dark, Wilcox's Rebels overran the right of Chapman's line and drove the Union horsemen back through Carle's supporting brigade. "The cavalry broke and ran through our infantry," observed the staffer Maj. Washington A. Roebling, who watched in horror as the riders stampeded past, pursued by Confederates. "Get your cavalry out of the way or we will fire into them," a trooper heard Crawford shout. "Get your infantry out of the way or we will run over them," Wilson allegedly hollered back. Fitzhugh's guns saved the day, sweeping Wilcox's ranks "with grape and canister," a Federal recalled, and driving the southerners back.[59]

Carle's retreat left Lyle surrounded by Confederates. After nightfall, Lyle summoned his officers and outlined an escape plan. "He also told us to tell our men of our position," Lt. John H. Dusseault of the 39th Massachusetts remembered, "also that no orders above a whisper should be given, and, that if we heard so much as a tin dipper jingling upon a man's haversack, to cut it off." At the appointed hour, Lyle's troops stole quietly through a grain field. "The men," an officer recalled, "knowing our position and being anxious to get out, kept increasing their pace and rattling the grain, so that it was necessary to halt them and to start them again from time to time until we had cleared the grain field." Lt. James B. Thomas of the 107th Pennsylvania Infantry declared the movement "the most successfully done [withdrawal] of any line I ever saw."[60]

By midnight, Crawford and Chapman were marching to rejoin the Fifth Corps, having safeguarded the Union army's passage and promoted the facade of a Union offensive north of the James. "It was necessary that some small portion of the army should make this demonstration and occupy the attention of the enemy while the chief part of it should be crossing to the Petersburg side of the James," wrote Lieutenant Dusseault. "It was thought to be our turn to take the risk which attended it. General Warren is said to have remarked that he never expected to see us again."[61]

Lee meanwhile went into camp near Riddell's Shop, waiting for the enemy's next move. The Army of Northern Virginia was now fully below the Chickahominy and arrayed from White Oak Swamp to Malvern Hill, Hill's Corps on the left, Anderson's on the right, and Hoke's division in the rear. "The way our men build fortifications beats the world," a Confederate wrote his wife. "In three hours we had a capital line of works."[62]

Losses for both sides in the battle of Riddell's Shop, as the engagement came to be called, were light. Wilcox estimated his casualties at slightly more than a hundred men, and Heth's losses were likely of the same order. Crawford's subtractions were about fifty, as were Chapman's—the 8th New York Cavalry lost nine men, the 3rd Indiana sixteen. Gary never submitted an official tally, but his casualties must have approximated those of his Union counterpart. Compared to the previous month's bloodlettings, the actions at Riddell's Shop and White Oak Bridge were but minor skirmishes. Strategically, though, they had accomplished a great deal. The Army of the Potomac would complete its march to the James undisturbed, and Lee would remain in the dark over his enemy's plans.[63]

DURING HOT AND DUSTY June 13, while Crawford and Chapman held the Army of Northern Virginia at bay, Grant and Meade accompanied Hancock's corps to the James. Meade's staff, riding behind Barlow, marveled over the provost guard's efficiency as it rounded up stragglers and prodded laggards at bayonet point. "Their tempers do not improve with heat and hard marching," the aide Lyman observed. The column wound past Edna Mills to Samaria Church—often called St. Mary's Church in Union reports—and on through Ladd's Store, Ware's, Walker's, and Wadill's, reaching the James River Road near Wilcox's Landing around 5:30 P.M. Road-worn warriors gaped in awe at the grand waterway set amid fields of wheat, oats, and clover. "To appreciate such a sight you must pass five weeks in an almost unbroken wilderness, with no sights but weary, dusty troops, endless wagon-trains, convoys of poor wounded men, and hot, uncomfortable camps," Lyman wrote home. "Here was a noble river, a mile wide, with high green banks, studded with large plantation houses. In the distance, opposite, was Fort Powhatan, below which lay two steamers; and, what seemed strangest of all, not a Rebel soldier to be seen anywhere!"[64]

Concerned that Confederates might overwhelm the Union column's rearguard at White Oak Swamp, the engineer Michler laid out a defensive line north of Wilcox's Landing. Hancock's troops, who had marched twenty-seven miles since leaving Cold Harbor, displayed little enthusiasm for the work. "Of course everyone is out of humor," a surgeon observed, "and a good deal of grumbling and no little swearing is the consequence." To everyone's relief, headquarters decided that the digging was unnecessary and ordered it suspended.[65]

Grant's Disengagement from Cold Harbor

"General Grant's Campaign—Transportation of Hancock's Corps across the James at Wilcox's Landing." William Waud included two key officers in his work: Grant on horseback to the right of the large tree and Winfield Scott Hancock seated to the right of the commanding general. Much of the army used pontoon bridges to get across the James, noted accompanying text, but "the crossing at this point was effected by transports." *Harper's Weekly*, July 9, 1864, 436, 442.

Settling into quarters at the Clarke home near Wilcox's Landing, Grant notified Butler that he intended to commence crossing the James by ten the next morning. Butler was to sink vessels loaded with stones upriver from City Point to prevent Rebel gunboats from interfering with the crossing. Instructions also went out to Meade to find a suitable gathering point on the southern bank and to send cavalry toward Malvern Hill to probe Lee's new position. The army's soldiers remained quizzical. "When will wonders cease," a lieutenant wrote in his diary. "Thirty six hours ago the Army of the Potomac was within nine miles of Richmond, and now we are forty miles distant."[66]

Union engineers prepared two crossing sites. One was near the Second Corps encampment, where laborers repaired Wilcox's Landing and built two new wharves across the river at Windmill Point to receive transports ferrying troops across the river. A more ambitious project involved the construction of a pontoon bridge a few miles downstream connecting Weyanoke Point to Fort Powhatan. Under the supervision of Butler's engineer Weitzel, laborers prepared a road to Weyanoke Wharf, corduroyed it, and toiled through the night to complete a 500-foot causeway and a pier. The bridge approaches were finished by 9:45 A.M. on June 14, "a quarter of an hour before the time indicted by General Grant," Weitzel later preened.[67]

While the Union high command laid their plans at Wilcox's Wharf, Warren's troops bid farewell to the Chickahominy and started for Samaria Church, following a short cut discovered by the staffer Roebling. Warren and his staff reached the church near midnight and went into camp. The rest of the Fifth Corps infantry doggedly continued on to join them. The troops had suffered through their share of night marches, and this one proved every bit as grueling as its predecessors. A soldier christened the marching "'steady by jerks,' wearisome and painful." A surgeon remembered the trek as "very tedious, mostly through long lanes of trees flanked by swamps." Soldiers lighting cook fires set the undergrowth aflame, giving a "species of purgatorial grandeur to the scenes on this night march," the surgeon remarked. The 20th Maine's colonel noted that swamp magnolia was in bloom, and its scent filled the heavy night air. "The men trudged on, patiently, but in the silence of weariness," he observed.[68]

THE ARMY OF THE POTOMAC'S disengagement from Cold Harbor and march to the James had been a success. By midnight on June 13, Hancock had encamped at Wilcox's Landing and was ready to begin crossing the James the next morning; Warren was close behind at Samaria Church, poised to follow in Hancock's footsteps and reach Wilcox's Landing mid-morning; Wright and Burnside were encamped at Jones' Bridge, a few hours' march from Charles City Court House; and Smith's Eighteenth Corps was well under way, its transports due to arrive at Bermuda Hundred during the afternoon of June 14. At the cost of only a few casualties, the Union commander had transferred his entire force to the James and stood poised to launch a two-pronged offensive against Petersburg with vastly superior numbers.

Equally important, Grant's well-executed movement had positioned the Federals to assail Petersburg before Lee could shift a single soldier to the beleaguered city's assistance. While Grant's rapid southward progress had suggested to the Confederate commander that the Federals contemplated a thrust toward Petersburg, the strong Union cavalry and infantry probe at Riddell's Shop militated in favor of a Federal movement north of the James, against Richmond. Uncertain about Grant's objective and hamstrung by the absence of most of his own cavalry, Lee remained immobile near Riddell's Shop, protecting Richmond from an attack that Grant had no intention of making. Once again, as had happened frequently in the campaign, Lee had no choice but to forfeit the initiative to his opponent.

The ensuing days, however, saw Grant and his generals commit a series of errors that dashed their hopes of quick victory and dulled the luster of their withdrawal from Cold Harbor to the James. By morning on June 15, Smith's Eighteenth Corps, augmented by troops and cavalry from Butler, was marching from Bermuda Hundred toward Petersburg, only seven miles away. Logistical mistakes, however, kept most of the Potomac army from joining Smith's foray. At Wilcox's Wharf, only a few ships had arrived to ferry Hancock's troops, slowing the Second Corps to a snail's pace and leaving the Fifth Corps to stand idly by. Ships carrying pontoons for the bridge at Weyanoke did not arrive from Fort Monroe until the evening of the 14th—"through inexcusable tardiness, and more than culpable neglect of duty," Weitzel later complained—delaying completion of the great pontoon bridge until midnight. Pontoons used to span the Chickahominy at Long Bridge might have provided an alternate source of bridging material on the James, but Major Ford had taken those pontoons to Coles Ferry to construct a crossing for the army's wagon train. "Our army lost a day by that," Warren's staffer Roebling caustically observed. "In other words, rather than run the very remote risk of losing a wagon train, they run the very positive risk of losing Petersburg, as the success of the whole movement depended on one day."[69]

Because of these mishaps, only Hancock's corps was available to cooperate with Smith, and the triumphant advance on Petersburg degenerated into a dismal tale of ambiguous orders, faulty coordination, misleading maps, and bungled ration deliveries, frittering away the advantages gained by the movement to the James.

In later years, aging warriors regarded Grant's disengagement from Cold Harbor as a high point of the Union commander's generalship. The historian Thomas L. Livermore praised Grant's withdrawal to the James as "one of the boldest and most brilliant [movements] of modern wars." No less an authority than Brig. Gen. Edward P. Alexander, commanding the Confederate First Corps artillery, concurred, proclaiming the maneuver "the most brilliant stroke in all the Federal campaigns of the whole war" and "the most brilliant piece of logistics of the war." The theme was taken up more recently by Clifford Dowdey, who observed that of all Grant's operations, "none demonstrated a more complete mastery of the mechanics and logistics of moving a large, oversupplied army than the march which began secretly out of the Cold Harbor lines on the night of June 12–13th."[70]

Grant's withdrawal from Cold Harbor was certainly capably planned and executed, but the praise of later historians overstates the accomplishment. In retrospect, the Federal high command committed a serious oversight by failing to ensure that means for crossing the river were in place when the army reached Charles City Court House. Although the Union force reached the James on schedule, the delayed bridging and transports threw the entire maneuver out of kilter. Rather than launching an irresistible sweep toward Petersburg with the Army of the Potomac and the Eighteenth Corps, Grant had to settle for a more modest offensive involving only two corps. Equally damaging to the larger operation's success was Grant's and Meade's decision to remain near Charles City Court House to supervise the crossing of the rest of the army. Lacking a superior officer to coordinate their movements, the Second and Eighteenth Corps were left to operate on unfamiliar ground with no overall coordination. As a consequence, the Cockade City held, and the war continued for another ten months.

Notes

1. Francis A. Walker, *History of the Second Army Corps in the Army of the Potomac* (New York: Scribner's, 1886), 514; Asa W. Bartlett, *History of the Twelfth Regiment New Hampshire Volunteers in the War of the Rebellion* (Concord, N.H.: Ira C. Evans, Printer, 1897), 207; William P. Derby, *Bearing Arms in the Twenty-Seventh Massachusetts Regiment of Volunteer Infantry during the Civil War, 1861–1865* (Boston: Wright and Potter Printing Co., 1883), 306–7; James A. Emmerton, *Record of the Twenty-third Regiment Mass. Vol. Infantry in the War of the Rebellion, 1861–1865* (Boston: William Ware and Co., 1886), 208–9; D. Augustus Dickert, *History of Kershaw's Brigade* (Newberry, S.C.: Elbert H. Aull, 1899), 375–76.

2. Horace Porter, *Campaigning with Grant* (New York: Century, 1897), 188; Andrew A. Humphreys, *The Virginia Campaign of '64 and '65: The Army of the Potomac and the Army of the James* (New York: Scribner's, 1883), 199.

3. Grant's plan and the risks inherent in it are rehearsed in Grant to Halleck, June 5, 1864, in U.S. War Department, *The War of the Rebellion: A Compilation of the Official Records of the Union and Confederate Armies*, 127 vols., index, and atlas (Washington, D.C.: Government Printing Office, 1880–1901), ser. 1, 36(3):598 (hereafter cited as *OR*; all references are to ser. 1); Ulysses S. Grant, *Personal Memoirs of U. S. Grant*, 2 vols. (New York: Charles L. Webster, 1885), 2:279–81; Adam Badeau, *Military History of General Ulysses S. Grant, from April, 1861, to April, 1865*, 3 vols. (New York: Appleton, 1881), 2:339–42; and Humphreys, *Virginia Campaign*, 199.

4. Ulysses S. Grant, *The Papers of Ulysses S. Grant*, ed. John Y. Simon and others, 32 vols. to date (Carbondale: Southern Illinois University Press, 1967–), 2:32 (hereafter cited as *PUSG*); Porter, *Campaigning with Grant*, 187–88. On June 9, Butler almost undid Grant's plan with an ill-conceived attempt to take Petersburg. Receiving confirmation that no more than 2,000 Confederates manned Petersburg's earthworks, Butler decided—apparently without notifying Grant—to send a mixed expedition of cavalry and infantry to capture the place. The attack fizzled, however, and served only to put the Rebels on alert. Fortunately for Grant's intended offensive, there was little that the Confederates could do to act on their concerns and augment Petersburg's garrison. Lee was tied up facing Grant, and Beauregard was occupied protecting the Richmond and Petersburg Railroad from Butler.

5. Grant to John J. Abercrombie, and John A. Rawlins to Abercrombie, June 7, 1864, in *PUSG*, 11:28–29; Abercrombie to Rawlins, June 12, 1864, in *OR* 36(3):768.

6. Henry W. Benham to Seth Williams, June 4; Benham to Benjamin F. Butler, June 6; Grant to Henry W. Halleck, June 10; Benham to Williams, June 12, 1864, in *OR* 36(3):593, 662, 722, 772; *PUSG*, 11:20. Benham received conflicting orders from Meade and Halleck with respect to the New York bridging and the bridging from Port Royal. See Benham to Williams, and Benham to Butler, both June 5, 1864, in *OR* 36(3):632–33.

7. Orders, June 11, 1864, in *OR* 36(3):747–49.

8. Grant to George G. Meade, June 8, 1864, in *OR* 36(3):695; Nathaniel Michler's report, in *OR* 36(1):302.

9. Andrew A. Humphreys to Warren, 7:30 P.M., June 10, and Special Orders, June 10, 1864, in *OR* 36(3)730–31.

10. Washington A. Roebling's report, June 11, 1864, in Gouverneur K. Warren Collection, New York State Library and Archives, Albany (repository hereafter cited as NYSLA); Order, June 10, 1864, in *OR* 36(3):731.

11. Order, June 12, and Gouverneur K. Warren to Charles Griffin, June 12, 1864, both in *OR* 36(3):763.

12. Meade to Williams, Williams to Winfield S. Hancock, Horatio G. Wright to Williams, and Charles H. Morgan to David B. Birney, all June 10, 1864, in *OR* 36(3):728–30.

13. Wesley Brainerd, *Bridge Building in Wartime: Colonel Wesley Brainerd's Memoir of the 50th New York Volunteer Engineers*, ed. Ed Malles (Knoxville: University of Tennessee Press, 1997), 242.

14. Circular, June 12, 1864, in *OR* 36(3):759–60.

15. Ibid. Later, Second Corps headquarters considered having Barlow and Gibbon continue past Wicker's to other roads that struck Dispatch Station Road farther east. Whether Barlow and Gibbon continued along this alternative route is not apparent from the record. See Circular, June 12, 1864, in *OR* 36(3):760.

16. Humphreys, *Virginia Campaign*, 201–2.

17. Order, June 11, and Order, June 12, 1864, in *OR* 36(3):750, 764.

18. George A. Armes, *Ups and Downs of an Army Officer* (Washington, D.C.: n.p., 1900), 101; Order, June 10, 1864, in *OR* 36(3):732; J. Warren Keifer's report, John W. Horn's report, and Aaron W. Ebright's report, in *OR* 36(1):735, 740, 750–51.

19. Order, June 12, 1864, in *OR* 36(3):747–49.

20. Order, June 11, 1864, in *OR* 36(3):748.

21. Porter, *Campaigning with Grant*, 189.

22. Grant to Herman Biggs, Abercrombie to Rawlins, and Perley P. Pitkin to Montgomery C. Meigs, all June 12, 1864, in *OR* 36(3):768–69; Grant's report, in *OR* 36(1):95.

23. Weitzel's report, in *OR* 36(1):676.

24. Charles A. Page, *Letters of a War Correspondent* (Boston: L. C. Page, 1899), 111; Theodore Lyman, *Meade's Headquarters, 1863–1865: Letters of Colonel Theodore Lyman from the Wilderness to Appomattox*, ed. George R. Agassiz (Boston: Atlantic Monthly Press, 1922), 156; Theodore Lyman, *Meade's Army: The Private Notebooks of Lt. Col. Theodore Lyman*, ed. David W. Lowe (Kent, Ohio: Kent State University Press, 2007), 201.

25. Charles S. Wainwright, *A Diary of Battle: The Personal Journals of Colonel Charles S. Wainright, 1861–1865*, ed. Allan Nevins (New York: Harcourt, Brace, and World, 1962), 414–15.

26. The 22nd New York had joined Chapman's brigade on June 5 and the 1st New Hampshire Cavalry on June 9. See George H. Chapman's report, in *OR* 36(1):901, and Roebling's report, in Gouverneur K. Warren Collection, NYSLA.

27. Lyman, *Meade's Headquarters*, 157.

28. James H. Wilson, *Under the Old Flag: Recollections of Military Operations in the War for the Union, the Spanish War, the Boxer Rebellion, etc.*, 2 vols. (New York: Appleton, 1912), 1:398–99; Roebling's report, Gouverneur K. Warren Collection, NYSLA. Wilson claimed that he saw Warren the next day and was surprised to learn that Warren did not remember the incident. Wilson wrote that he later told Grant of Warren's rudeness and that Grant replied, "Well, I'll take care of Warren anyhow" (Wilson, *Under the Old Flag*, 1:401). In his biography of Warren, *Happiness Is Not My Companion: The Life of General G. K. Warren* (Bloomington: Indiana University Press, 2001), David M. Jordan sides with Warren and questions whether the incident reported by Wilson ever occurred. However, Wilson's diary entry for June 12 notes, "Intolerance of Warren" (James H. Wilson diary, Library of Congress, Washington, D.C. [repository hereafter cited as LC]).

29. "From the Eighth Cavalry, near Harrison's Landing, June 16, 1864," *Rochester Daily Union and Advertiser*, June 23, 1864; "From the Eight New York Cavalry, near Prince George Court House Virginia, June 20, 1864," *Seneca County Courier*, June 30, 1864. For the identity of the Confederate cavalry contesting the crossing, see Paul B. Means, "Additional Sketch Sixty-Third Regiment," in Walter Clark, ed., *Histories of the Several Regiments and Battalions from North Carolina in the Great War, 1861–'65*, 5 vols. (Goldsboro, N.C.: Nash Brothers, 1901), 3:609.

30. James H. Wilson's report and Chapman's report, in *OR* 36(1):883, 901–2; Ira Spaulding's report, in *OR* 40(1):296. The newsman Page claimed that twenty Union cavalrymen died storming the Confederate rifle pits, but his account was secondhand and unsubstantiated; see Page, *Letters of a War Correspondent*, 120–21.

31. Chapman's report, in *OR* 36(1):901; Spaulding's report, in *OR* 40(1):296; Wilson to Humphreys, June 12, 1864, in *OR* 36(3):767.

32. Roebling's report, in Gouverneur K. Warren Collection, NYSLA; Robert Tilney, *My Life in the Army: Three Years and a Half with the Fifth Army Corps, Army of the Potomac* (Philadelphia: Ferris and Leach, 1912), 93–94; *New York Daily Tribune*, June 18, 1864.

33. Daily Memoranda, in *OR* 40(1):316; Robert Keating, *Carnival of Blood: The Civil War Ordeal of the Seventh New York Heavy Artillery* (Baltimore: Butternut and Blue, 1998), 162, 168; Lemuel A. Abbott, *Personal Recollections and Civil War Diary, 1864* (Burlington, Vt.: Free Press Printing Co., 1908), 80; St. Clair A. Mulholland, *The Story of the 116th Regiment Pennsylvania Volunteers in the War of the Rebellion* (Philadelphia: F. McManus Jr. & Co., 1899), 263.

34. John Ramsey's report and John C. Tidball's report, in *OR* 36(1):461, 422.

35. Lafayette Church to dear family, June 21, 1864, transcribed by Bob Bowman and Janet Kondziela, in Clark Historical Library, Central Michigan University, Mount Pleasant.

36. Theodore F. Vaill, *History of the Second Connecticut Volunteer Heavy Artillery* (Winsted, Conn.: Winsted Printing Co., 1868), 70; Lewis Bissell to father, June 18, 1864, in Lewis Bissell, *The Civil War Letters of Lewis Bissell*, comp. Mark Olcott (Washington, D.C.: Field School Educational Foundation Press, 1981), 260; Alanson Haines, *History of the Fifteenth Regiment New Jersey Volunteers* (New York: Jenkins and Thomas Printers, 1883), 214–15; "Diary of Movements of the 3rd Division 6th Army Corps, June 12, 1864," Manassas National Military Park Library, Manassas, Va.

37. Abraham J. Palmer, *The History of the Forty-Eighth Regiment, New York State Volunteers in the War for the Union, 1861–1865* (Brooklyn, N.Y.: Charles D. Dillingham, 1885), 153.

38. L. O. Merriam, "Personal Recollections," 47, Fredericksburg and Spotsylvania National Military Park Library, Fredericksburg, Va. (repository hereafter cited as FSNMP); Leander W. Cogswell, *A History of the Eleventh New Hampshire Regiment Volunteer Infantry in the Rebellion War* (Concord, N.H.: Republican Press Association, 1891), 375–76; Orlando B. Willcox to Ambrose E. Burnside, June 13, 1864, in *OR* 40(2):10–11.

39. Order, June 11, 1864, in *OR* 36(3):747–49.

40. Horace K. Ide, *History of the First Vermont Cavalry Volunteers in the War of the Great Rebellion* (Baltimore: Butternut and Blue, 2000), 180; "Barringer's North Carolina Brigade of Cavalry," *Raleigh (N.C.) Daily Confederate*, February 22, 1865; Wilson to Andrew A. Humphreys, June 13, 1864, in *OR* 40(2):8.

41. "From the Eighth Cavalry, near Harrison's Landing, June 16, 1864," *Rochester Daily Union and Advertiser*, June 23, 1864; "From the Eight New York Cavalry, near Prince George Court House Virginia, June 20, 1864," *Seneca County Courier*, June 30, 1864; Wilson's diary, June 13, 1864, LC; Robert J. Trout, *Galloping Thunder: The Stuart Horse Artillery Battalion* (Mechanicsburg, Pa.: Stackpole, 2002), 504–5.

42. Benjamin F. Cook, *History of the Twelfth Massachusetts Volunteers (Webster Regiment)* (Boston: Twelfth [Webster] Regiment Association, 1882), 135; *Annual Circular of the Secretary of the Regimental Association (Twelfth Webster Regiment)*, no. 7, 1902, 10; Isaac Hall, *History of the Ninety-Seventh Regiment New York Volunteers (Conkling Rifles) in the War for the Union* (Utica, N.Y.: Press of L. C. Chiles & Son, 1890), 200; Arthur A. Kent, ed., *Three Years with Company K: Sergt. Austin C. Stearns, Company K, 13th Mass. Infantry* (Rutherford, N.J.: Fairleigh Dickinson University Press, 1976), 282; John D. Vautier, *History of the 88th Pennsylvania Volunteers in the War for the Union* (Philadelphia: Lippincott, 1894), 189; Wilson to Humphreys, June 13, 1864, in *OR* 40(2):10.

43. Chapman's report, in *OR* 40(1):644; Ide, *History of the First Vermont Cavalry*, 80; William G. Hinson Diary, *South Carolina Historical Magazine* 75 (January 1974): 18–19; W. E. Doyle, "Gary's Fight at Riddell's Shop," *Confederate Veteran* 39 (January 1931): 19–20.

44. Chapman's report, in *OR* 40(1):644; R. E. McBride, "The Bucktails," *National Tribune*, February 12, 1885, 3; Wilson to Humphreys, June 13, 1864, in *OR* 40(2):11–12.

45. Wilson, *Under the Old Flag*, 1:452; Samuel J. B. V. Gilpin diary, June 13, 1864, LC.

46. John W. Haley, *The Rebel Yell and the Yankee Hurrah: The Civil War Journal of a Maine Volunteer*, ed. Ruth L. Silliker (Camden, Me.: Down East Books, 1985), 169–70; Edwin B. Houghton, *Campaigns of the Seventeenth Maine* (Portland, Me.: Short and Loring, 1866), 198–99; Thomas Smyth diary, May 12–13, 1864, Delaware Public Archives, Dover; William Child, *A History of the Fifth Regiment, New Hampshire Volunteers, in the American Civil War* (Bristol, N.H.: R. W. Musgrove, 1893), 255; Daily Journal, in *OR* 40(1):316; Charles H. Banes, *History of the Philadelphia Brigade* (Philadelphia: Lippincott, 1876), 276.

47. Keating, *Carnival of Blood*, 171; Nelson Armstrong, *Nuggets of Experience: Narratives of the Sixties and other Days, with Graphic Descriptions of Thrilling Personal Adventures* (San Bernardino, Calif.: Times-Mirror P. and B. House, 1904), 55; John Gibbon to Hancock, June 13, 1864, in *OR* 40(2):5.

48. John F. L. Hartwell, *To My Beloved Wife and Boy at Home*, ed. Ann H. Britton and Thomas J. Reed (Madison, N.J.: Fairleigh Dickinson University Press, 1997), 238; Oliver Wendell Holmes Jr., *Touched with Fire: Civil War Letters and Diary of Oliver Wendell Holmes, Jr., 1861–1864*, ed. Mark De Wolfe Howe (Cambridge, Mass.: Harvard University Press, 1946), 144–45; Wilbur Fisk, *Hard Marching Every Day: The Civil War Letters of Private Wilbur Fisk*, ed. Emil and Ruth Rosenblatt (1983; reprint, Lawrence: University Press of Kansas, 1992), 229–30; George T. Stevens, *Three Years in the Sixth Corps: A Concise Narrative of Events in the Army of the Potomac, from 1861 to the Close of the Rebellion, April, 1865* (Albany, N.Y.: S. R. Gray, 1866), 355; James L. Bowen, *History of the Thirty-Seventh Regiment Mass. Volunteers, in the Civil War of 1861–1865* (Holyoke, Mass.: Clark W. Bryan & Co., 1884), 338.

49. Burnside to Humphreys, June 13, 1864, in *OR* 40(2):9.

50. Wright to Meade, June 13, 1864, in *OR* 40(2):9.

51. William P. Hopkins, *The Seventh Regiment Rhode Island Volunteers in the Civil War, 1862–1865* (Boston: Providence Press, 1903), 189–90; Spaulding's report, in *OR* 40(1):197; Hartwell, *To My Beloved Wife and Boy at Home*, 239; Haines, *Fifteenth New Jersey*, 216; Fisk, *Hard Marching Every Day*, 229–30; Henry C. Houston, *The Thirty-Second Maine Regiment of Infantry Volunteers* (Portland, Me.: Press of Southworth Brothers, 1903), 254–55; E. K. Russell to mother, June 19, 1864, FSNMP.

52. Berea M. Willsey, *The Civil War Diary of Berea M. Willsey: The Intimate Daily Observations of a Massachusetts Volunteer in the Union Army, 1862–1864*, ed. Jessica H. DeMay (Westminster, Md.: Heritage Books, 1995), 156; "Letter from the 2nd Connecticut Artillery," in *Winstead (Connecticut) Herald*, July 1, 1864; Wright to Burnside, June 13, 1864, in *OR* 40(2):10.

53. John A. Brady's Dispatch, June 14, 1864, in *New York Herald*, June 17, 1864; Millett S. Thompson, *Thirteenth Regiment of New Hampshire Volunteer Infantry in the War*

of the Rebellion, 1861–1865: A Diary Covering Three Years and a Day (Boston: Houghton Mifflin, 1888), 374–75.

54. Emmerton, *Twenty-third Regiment*, 215; 115th New York Scrap Book, 45, Sarasota Springs Public Library, Sarasota Springs, N.Y.; John A. Brady's Dispatch, June 14, 1864, *New York Herald*, June 17, 1864.

55. John R. Zimmerman diary, June 13, 1864, Lloyd House, Alexandria, Va.; Robert Stiles, *Four Years under Marse Robert* (New York: Neale, 1903), 308.

56. Cadmus M. Wilcox's report, Lee Headquarters Papers, Virginia Historical Society, Richmond (repository hereafter cited as VHS); E. J. Hale's report, July 19, 1864, in James Lane Papers, Auburn University, Auburn, Alabama; Moxley Sorrel memorandum, June 13, 1864, in *OR* 40(2):647.

57. Wilcox's report, Lee Headquarters Papers, VHS; J. F. J. Caldwell, *The History of a Brigade of South Carolinians, Known First as "Gregg's," and Subsequently as "McGowan's Brigade"* (Philadelphia: King and Baird Printers, 1866), 160; James Conner, *Letters of General James Conner*, ed. Mary Conner Moffett (Columbia, S.C.: privately printed, 1950), 135; William S. Dunlop, *Lee's Sharpshooters; or, the Forefront of Battle: A Story of Southern Valor that Never Has Been Told* (Little Rock, Ark.: Tunnah and Pittard Printers, 1899), 101–2; Chapman's report, in *OR* 40(1):,644; Ide, *History of the First Vermont Cavalry*, 180.

58. Thomas J. Luttrell diary, FSNMP; Charles R. Jones, "Historical Sketch, 55th North Carolina," *Our Living and Our Dead*, April 22, 1874, 2; Dunlop, *Lee's Sharpshooters*, 101–2; Wilcox's Report, Lee Headquarter Papers, VHS; Chapman's report, in *OR* 40(1):644; James B. Thomas to Lucy, June 15, 1864, in James B. Thomas, *The Civil War Letters of First Lieutenant James B. Thomas, Adjutant, 107th Pennsylvania Volunteers*, ed. Mary Warner Thomas and Richard A. Sauers (Baltimore: Butternut and Blue, 1995), 192–93; Alfred S. Roe, *The Thirty-Ninth Regiment Massachusetts Volunteer Infantry* (Worcester, Mass.: Thirty-Ninth Regiment Veteran Association, 1914), 217; Charles E. Davis Jr., *Three Years in the Army: The Story of the Thirteenth Massachusetts Volunteers, from July 16, 1861, to August 1, 1864* (Boston: Estes and Lauriat, 1894), 370.

59. Chapman's report, in *OR* 40(1):644; Ide, *History of the First Vermont Cavalry*, 180; Roebling's report, in Gouverneur K. Warren Collection, NYSLA; R. E. McBride, "The Bucktails," *National Tribune*, February 12, 1885; "From the Eighth Cavalry, near Harrison's Landing, June 16, 1864," *Rochester Daily Union and Advertiser*, June 23, 1864; "From the Eight New York Cavalry, near Prince George Court House Virginia, June 20, 1864," *Seneca County Courier*, June 30, 1864; Graham Daves, "Twenty-Second Regiment," in Clark, *Histories of the Several Regiments*, 2:173.

60. Roe, *Thirty-Ninth Regiment*, 216–17.

61. Ibid., 217.

62. Wilcox's report, Lee Headquarters Papers, VHS; Conner, *Letters of General James Conner*, 135; Moxley Sorrel's journal, June 13, 1864, in Museum of the Confederacy, Richmond, Va.

63. *Philadelphia Inquirer*, June 18, 1864.

64. Lyman, *Meade's Headquarters*, 158.

65. Michler's report, in *OR* 40(1):289; Mulholland, *Story of the 116th Regiment*, 266;

J. Franklin Dyer, *The Journal of a Civil War Surgeon*, ed. Michael B. Chesson (Lincoln: University of Nebraska Press, 2003), 168.

66. Grant to Butler, Butler to Grant, Rawlins to Butler, and Grant to Meade, all June 13, 1864, in *OR* 40(2):4, 12, 13, 3; Elisha Hunt Rhodes, *All for the Union: The Civil War Diary and Letters of Elisha Hunt Rhodes*, ed. Robert Hunt Rhodes (1985; reprint, New York: Orion, 1991), 161.

67. Weitzel's report, in *OR* 40(1):676–77.

68. Philemon Halsted Fowler, *Memorials of William Fowler* (New York: A. D. F. Randolph, 1875), 90–91; Francis J. Parker, *The Story of the Thirty-Second Regiment Massachusetts Infantry* (Boston: C. W. Calkins, 1880), 466; Lewis H. Steiner diary, June 13, 1864, in Maryland Historical Society, Baltimore; Ellis Spear, *The Civil War Recollections of General Ellis Spear*, ed. Abbott Spear (Orono: University of Maine, 1997), 121.

69. Weitzel's report, in *OR* 40(1):676–77.

70. Thomas L. Livermore, "Failure to Take Petersburg, June 15, 1864," in *Papers of the Military Historical Society of Massachusetts*, 14 vols. (Boston: Historical Society of Massachusetts, 1881–1918), 5:46; Edward Porter Alexander, *Fighting for the Confederacy: The Personal Recollections of General Edward Porter Alexander*, ed. Gary W. Gallagher (Chapel Hill: University of North Carolina Press, 1989), 419; Edward Porter Alexander, *Military Memoirs of a Confederate: A Critical Narrative* (New York: Scribner's, 1907), 547; Clifford Dowdey, *Lee's Last Campaign: The Story of Lee and His Men against Grant—1864* (Boston: Little, Brown, 1960), 317.

We Will Finish the War Here
Confederate Morale in the Petersburg Trenches, June and July 1864

⇥ M. KEITH HARRIS ⇤

The men of the Army of Northern Virginia faced troubling odds as spring 1864 gave way to summer. Heavy fighting in May and the first half of June had cost Gen. Robert E. Lee's army dearly. Suffering as many as 35,000 casualties, including a significant portion of their command structure, Confederates confronted a staggering disadvantage in manpower as well as an aggressive Union commander in Lt. Gen. Ulysses S. Grant, who had vowed to fight to the finish and seemed determined to make good on his promise.[1] The Army of the Potomac's recent movements only intensified an urgent situation. By mid-June, Federals had crossed the James River and maneuvered around the Confederate capital at Richmond to lay siege to Petersburg, a transportation hub and important supply and industrial center on the Appomattox River. And although the Rebel army was well entrenched in a formidable defensive position, a siege would almost certainly not bode well for the Confederacy. The fall of Vicksburg, Mississippi, the year before served as a sobering lesson. Even Lee sensed the dire situation, reportedly remarking to a subordinate that a siege probably meant that only a "mere question of time" stood between an encircling host of Yankees and Confederate demise.[2]

Despite the tremendous odds, diaries and correspondence written that summer show that many soldiers in the Army of Northern Virginia expected a victory over the "Yankee hordes" was imminent. While some looked simultaneously to the battlefields of Georgia, Maryland, and the Shenandoah Valley with optimism and anxiety, most were eager to reignite the fray to their immediate front, destroy the enemy, and secure independence. Tracing the letters and diaries of a sampling of officers and men from Virginia, Mississippi, Alabama, and Maryland, as well as a few who divulged neither their rank nor state of origin, one can observe a hopeful spirit in the early siege period. In fact, optimism and high morale pervaded the Rebel lines in the early summer of 1864. Soldiers in the Army of Northern Virginia, despite an expected number of skulkers, naysayers, and pessimists within the ranks, believed that victory was not only certain but close at hand.

A problematic "road to Appomattox" assumption hangs like an ill-omened cloud over much of the scholarship dedicated to the Confederate war effort during this period. This approach supposes that Confederates steadily lost their will to fight beginning in the summer of 1863 when decisive defeats at Gettysburg and Vicksburg sapped the nascent country's fighting spirit. Many historians tend to see despondency and a downward trend in morale after that troubling summer.[3] Such a viewpoint figures the Petersburg siege as a futile waiting game for Confederates: the early months in the trenches merely initiated a long period of stagnation in the Eastern Theater, punctuated occasionally by short-lived moments of hopefulness. James M. McPherson, in his Pulitzer Prize–winning history of the war, *Battle Cry of Freedom*, follows this analytical tack. He suggests that "in the long run . . . Lee and the South could not withstand a siege." Still, McPherson notes that initially "time was on the Confederacy's side," arguing that soldiers focused on the war in Georgia and the elections in the North rather than their immediate front. In Virginia, McPherson argues, "the Rebels were holding out for time." Confederate soldiers did complain incessantly of the heat, the cramped quarters, the constant shelling, and their inactivity. A few of the most disconcerted even turned their grumblings into forecasts of doom. Yet typical sentiment suggested steadfast devotion to cause and country as well as an optimistic outlook for the future.[4]

If this optimism reflected the enthusiasm prevalent earlier in the war, it multiplied during the new stage. A hopeful spirit, even under the duress of siege, persisted during the first weeks of summer and endured so long as Lee effectively could maintain a functioning field army. This counters the notion held by many who retrospectively underscore the siege as certainly the last chapter of the Confederate war effort. Such skepticism would have surprised entrenched Confederates in the Petersburg defenses. They believed they had never been defeated and anxiously looked forward to the moment when they could deliver the final blow to the Army of the Potomac and secure their independence.

Sentiments either complaining or foretelling disaster were unusual in Confederate diaries and correspondence during this period, though there surely were dissenting voices. Testimony from soldiers in all Civil War armies and theaters reveals that at least some in the ranks had had enough of war, and Confederate soldiers sweltering in the "ditches" at Petersburg in the early summer of 1864 were no exception. Selections of testimony reveal unmistakable elements of discontent among those in the trenches, and their complaints of extreme hardships are scattered throughout letters and diaries. Richmond native John Hampden Chamberlayne, an officer who had seen action as a soldier in the 21st Virginia Infantry and endured several months as a prisoner of war before he took command of an artillery battery in 1864, complained often of boredom and discomfort. "The army still lies inactive sweltering in the sun & waiting for something to turn up," he wrote his mother in mid-July, and "the monotony of this hot & dusty life is irksome to the last degree." Others were troubled that their nation was at risk of failure. Creed Thomas Davis's wartime diary, for example, suggests greater concerns than mere unpleasant conditions. While serving as a private in the Second Company of the Richmond Howitzers, Davis saw his world crumbling around him. "Indeed our affairs do look gloomy," he confessed on June 15 as the siege became apparent. Five days later he admitted that "if [he] had a mind, [he] might desert" to the encircling Yankees. By June 25, the news was even more disconcerting: "Genl Grant still entrenches himself before Petersburg, he will no doubt capture the place." In retrospect, Davis's discouraging forecast seems prophetic. Reminded of Vicksburg, troubled Confederate nationalists feared that a Yankee siege in the East would drain the lifeblood from their nation.[5]

John Herbert Claiborne, a surgeon with the 12th Virginia Infantry, worried somberly about Grant's next move. "I fear [Grant] has sat down for a summer's siege & if so—oh how wearisome to us all who wait our destiny in this campaign," he wrote his wife on June 12. "I begin to think most any thing is better than suspense. . . . We must possess our souls in patience." Lt. Thomas Tileston Greene of the 61st Alabama Infantry expressed a similar sentiment in a letter home. "In all probability the siege of [Richmond] will be a second Vicksburg," he wrote, "I hope without its fatal termination. The enemy can take the Rail Roads running South and shut us off from the world completely I hope this may not be so but dread it and have reason to fear it."[6]

Pessimists notwithstanding, the prospects for victory appeared bright to many. John Chamberlayne, while gripped by monotony and discomfort, did not seem to believe Confederate prospects for victory were in danger. Writing in May, while still on active campaign, he assured his mother, "Mr. Grant is a thoroughly whipped man." The passage of time only boosted Chamberlayne's convictions. After an interview with several Federals captured outside Petersburg, he informed those at home that Yankee conscripts had no stomach for further fighting. "Their presence in the army shows that their services are at last low," he wrote, concluding, "I believe all the danger is taken out of Grant's people." Although an enemy far greater in number hemmed in Confederate defenders, Chamberlayne predicted the end of the northern will to fight—reinforcing the notion that numbers alone mattered little to confident Rebels. Soldiers presumed that they would meet Grant's army with success, no matter where it moved or what it did. Capt. Joseph Banks Lyle, an officer in the 5th South Carolina Infantry, wrote in a similar vein in early June—shortly before the Confederate army entrenched outside Petersburg. "Three days ago the enemy withdrew from our front and centre," he observed; "we do not understand this movement, but are quietly awaiting the development of his plans. All are satisfied that Lee will meet and be ready for him wherever he may show himself."[7]

Grant's initial movements against Petersburg—those to which Captain Lyle referred—commenced between June 9 and 15 under forces commanded by Union generals Benjamin F. Butler and George Gordon Meade. From the onset, Confederate confidence pervaded the ranks. On the day the first movements toward a siege took place, James Montgomery Holloway, a surgeon with the 11th Mississippi Infantry, wrote to his wife from the Chimborazo Hospital, near Richmond. "Strange to say whilst I feel some anxiety," he commented, "I dont really believe that an army double the size now encamped against us—would prevail—You would be struck with the fortitude, confidence & trust depicted upon the countenances of almost every one you meet in the streets. . . . The news this evening is that Grant is moving towards the James with the view of crossing and if true Lee will be forced to make a corresponding move." Holloway conceded that a major defeat south of the James would doom Richmond but ended on a positive note: "Why do I indulge in ifs? How can I forget for a moment that our cause is a righteous one. . . . We have an invincible army—it has never been defeated."

Holloway, by implication, rejects the idea of a Confederate defeat at Gettysburg, roughly a year earlier. Like many across the Confederacy, Holloway's argument suggests that Lee's withdrawal from Pennsylvania in July 1863 did not represent the devastating defeat or "turning point" that future analyses would embrace. Ten days into the siege, Holloway wrote again, remarking, "You would be surprised to see how composedly the whole people contemplate it—it has not as yet interfered in the slightest degree

We Will Finish the War Here

with the comfort of anyone. I dont believe Grant can take Richmond. . . . Whenever the enemy strikes a blow he suffers and our army is in as good condition as it was at the onset of the campaign."[8]

Such optimism was reminiscent of testimony from May, when the Army of Northern Virginia pummeled the Federals during the Overland campaign. Rebel confidence gained a great deal of ground during that month of near-constant fighting. The army inflicted tens of thousands of casualties on the Army of the Potomac at the battles of the Wilderness, Spotsylvania, and Cold Harbor—fights that yielded one of the Union war's lowest points in morale both at home and in the ranks. Illustrating a sense of optimism among Confederates, Gary W. Gallagher, in an essay on the Wilderness campaign, suggests Lee's soldiers saw their role that spring as crucial and singles out the many soldiers who believed confidently that success in "this part of Virginia" would lead to independence.[9]

This sentiment did not fade as the Overland campaign reached its climax. Virginia cavalryman Richard Henry Watkins, anticipating the certainty that Grant would next move on the Confederate capital, wrote his wife on June 1, in the midst of battle at Cold Harbor, that "Genl RE Lee has recd large reinforcements. His army is thoroughly organized well equipped well fed in fine spirits & if Grant enters Richmond [Lee] will certainly display more skill and his troops more courage than I think [Grant's soldiers] possess." Later that month, with the Petersburg siege well under way, Watkins continued, "tis amazing to know that Grant has thus far been foiled in all of his plans, and thus is nothing to discourage or to lessen the confidence of the Army in Genl Lee." Insisting that his fellow Confederates were "well & cheerful," whether campaigning in the field or reporting on a siege, Watkins's confidence seemed unshakable. Even rumors early in July that Grant was poised for a major assault on Richmond caused little stir in the Army of Northern Virginia. As Watkins announced on July 4, "This was the day fixed by Grant for his grand entry into Richmond. Hardly think he will get there."[10]

Lee's leadership was often the centerpiece of Confederate confidence. Col. William Ransom Johnson "Willy" Pegram, brother of Confederate general John Pegram and a talented young artillery officer, wrote his sister late in July, "My confidence in Genl Lee still increases, & I think our cause more than ever, under Providence, dependent on him. He should certainly have control of all of operations through out the Confederate States. In fact I should like to see him King or Dictator. He is one of the few great men who ever lived, who could be trusted."[11]

M. KEITH HARRIS

Some in the Army of Northern Virginia were so sanguine regarding their army's capabilities that any further Federal attack seemed unlikely. For example, Joseph Lyle issued a nonchalant dismissal of the enemy in early July, noting, "no general assault [is] looked for by us. . . . I think enemy fears to attempt it." Roughly two weeks later, Lyle noted, "many believe that [Grant] will not attempt an assault upon our lines here, that he will shift operations to some other field & that he is even now sending off some of his forces." Lyle's testimony indicates some soldiers thought Union offenses in the Virginia theater were faltering in the face of impenetrable Rebel defenses. Confident that Lee's works ultimately would wear their adversary down, John Chamberlayne turned to the Napoleonic wars for a comparison. "Lee is cutting his mark of Grant now," he observed in late July; "the lines of Petersburg without a mountain gap will make Lee known as Torres Vedras Wellington."[12]

Reports of the "third invasion" of the North were another reason for optimism in the ever-expanding trenches around the Petersburg–Richmond front. After driving Federals under Maj. Gen. David Hunter away from Lynchburg during the third week of June, Lt. Gen. Jubal A. Early and his small army of 15,000 Rebels advanced down the Shenandoah Valley under orders from General Lee to clear the area of the enemy and, if possible, threaten Washington, D.C. With skill and audacity, Early proceeded to do exactly that. By early July, he had maneuvered Hunter's troops out of the Valley, defeated a force under Maj. Gen. Lew Wallace at the battle of Monocacy south of Frederick, Maryland, and positioned his force within shelling distance of the U.S. capital. Late in the month, troops under Early's command made forays into Pennsylvania, where they burned much of the town of Chambersburg on July 30. Confederate soldiers in the trenches around Petersburg welcomed news of Early's successes with hope and relief. John Herbert Claiborne expressed great joy at the possibility that relief from the worsening conditions in Petersburg were near. "It is perhaps—this City—the most disagreeable human habitation that is left upon this sin stricken earth," Claiborne informed his wife in an intense bout of private protest: "Yet we are cheerful & determined and you hear no word of complaint. I hope Early's advance into Pennsylvania act as a deviation . . . & the war may soon be carried to their own doors again."[13]

Soldiers in the Petersburg trenches followed Early's advances with extreme interest, entering details in their diaries—particularly as reported by the northern press—as the drama unfolded. "Great excitement in Yankeedom," Joseph Lyle jotted in his diary while hopefully observing, "some

"Rebels Destroying the Chesapeake and Ohio Canal." Soldiers in Lee's army would have enjoyed the woodcuts in *Harper's Weekly* that showed how Jubal Early's invading force had laid a heavy hand on parts of Maryland. Four such illustrations, including this one, appeared about two weeks after Early withdrew to Virginia, leaving behind "as the traces of its devastation desolated homes, empty roosts and stables, and broken communications." *Harper's Weekly*, July 30, 1864, 481, 484.

of the enemy's forces have been sent away from our front" to assist in the defense of Washington. Between July 9 and 26, Lyle detailed Early's victories and anticipated possible attacks on northern cities. "Early defeats the enemy under Lew Wallace at Monocacy Bridge, new Frederick," he noted and cheerfully continued, "our forces are said to be pushing towards Baltimore & Washington." He also reported on widespread joy among the citizens of Petersburg. A brief comment on July 14 described a "visit [to] the city" where he happily concluded, "all exultant—our forces within 3 miles of Washington—many believe that Early will endeavor to take the City."[14]

Others similarly welcomed news of Early's operations north of the Potomac. Maryland native Lt. Samuel Johnson McCullough of the 2nd Maryland Infantry noted in his diary on July 12 that "a Corps of Grant's forces is supposed to have left our front & more are thought to be going. They all predict another Pennsylvania campaign." Perhaps expecting to join his fellow Marylanders fighting with General Early, and certainly hoping for relief from the constant enemy shelling, McCullough shared rosy expectations for the overall war effort. "The news from Early is of the most exciting character," he acknowledged, "the 'Sentinel Extra' of this afternoon reporting him to have completely routed the enemy at Manasas bridge with great loss. . . . Early is reported marching on Baltimore."[15]

Hope that Early's exploits would offer relief to those under siege conditions appeared frequently in letters home. James Holloway's letter of July 7 to his wife typified this sentiment. "There is exciting news from Grant's Army to night—it is said that he has left the front at Petersburg—where he has gone is not yet known—all agree that he has gone somewhere," Holloway announced before adding, "There is a rumor to night that Early—with Ewell's Corps has whipped the Yankees at Martinsburg. . . . This seems very reliable and if true is cheering news. It looks rather strange that whilst Grant—according to Northern accounts has Lee hemmed up and starving in Richmond—forces can be spared from his army to go so far off and disperse the enemy." Richard Watkins agreed, noting, "News reached us last evening that Genl Early is within a short distance of Baltimore with Ewell's corps—Hope he will create such a diversion as will render it necessary for Grant to change his base to the other side of the Potomac. I don't like his shelling Petersburg."[16]

Willy Pegram expressed a similar concern for relief but was eager to finish the fight in a pitched battle. "You are all . . . very much elated, I suppose, by the news from Early," he wrote somewhat cautiously. "I regard it as a very brilliant & successful 'raid' so far," he continued, "but hope Early may meet with no disaster in getting back, after having penetrated so far into the enemy's country." Overall Pegram, who had forged a reputation for great gallantry and aggressiveness during the Army of Northern Virginia's earlier campaigns, would have preferred that Early "had done less, in the way he has done, provided he had drawn Grant away from here. Not that I think Richmond or Petersburg in any danger, but I would like to have this kind of warfare broken up, and to get to field fighting once more."[17]

We Will Finish the War Here

Artillerist and engineer Peter Guerrant grew excitable about reports of Early's activities in mid-July. "We heard a lady say a short two hours ago," he recorded in his diary, "that she saw a paper of yesterday which said Genl Early had liberated the prisoners . . . at Point Lookout. I hope it may be true." Guerrant noted stories of even grander accomplishments in the North: "I heard a gentleman who had see an extra say that Washington had fallen into our hands & that Genl Early had mounted all of his men & was recrossing the Potomac. I do not know whether it was or not, I am anxious to see the papers."[18]

Such rumors of Early's exploits far exceeded his actual accomplishments in July. Wishful thinking inspired a stream of reports that Early had captured Baltimore or Washington City. James Holloway learned in mid-July, for example, that "a rumor is current to day that Baltimore is occupied by our forces and that a large body of the Rebel sympathizers have organized and give to our assistance." The dubious report brought out a vindictive strain in Holloway's writing. Wishing that "every [person] in the North could be made to feel the terror [of war]," he watched the news with great anticipation.[19]

The day after describing the terror in the North, Holloway envisioned the potential of the invasion. "The most exciting rumor is however, that Early is marching in Washington City with Ewell's Corps & Cavalry," stated Holloway, who shared a craving for retribution common in the Confederacy. "Would it not be a rich joke if he could slip into the Capital & burn it? The moral effect would be crushing to the prospects of the North—and would—I think, tend to shorten the war." Also speaking to the power of rumor, others grew equally excited by hearsay reports. On July 15, Samuel McCullough wrote in his diary, "The news from Maryland is of a more exciting character than ever, the Confederates being reported to be in possession of Baltimore. Fifteen thousand men are also said to have surrendered. Grant still remains inactive & everything is quiet save the occasional booming of a gun."[20]

Other soldiers viewed engagements in the Shenandoah Valley, Maryland, and Pennsylvania with skepticism, or cautious optimism at best. After learning of Early's "endeavors to take [Washington] City," Joseph Lyle reflected that he could not "believe such a thing." Although he held fast to his "great confidence," he nevertheless envisioned Early's rumored attack far too grand to be realistic.[21] And on July 15, the usually optimistic Richard Watkins confessed to his wife, "All sorts of sensation rumor and extravagant uproar about Genl Early's Maryland raid. Much is expected from him by some but I very much fear that he will accomplish but little. Genl Early has heretofore been slow & I reckon will continue so to be." A day later, after relating the excitement of a possible capture of Baltimore, James Holloway admitted, "I dont believe one word of it—Maryland is too well subdued for any organized demonstration on the part of our friends." Finally, after his expectations had risen only days before, John Claiborne began to question the good that would come of an invasion of the North: "Early is carrying everything before him and it rejoices us to know that he is meting out to them the same that they measure for us. I confess however that I doubt the wisdom of the diversion. . . . We have not the men to lose." Even some of those campaigning with Early in the Valley grew suspicious of inflated claims. Writing from Winchester on July 14, Thomas Greene informed his sister, "If all the news we hear in this little village be true the War is over, but I only believe half and think that part slightly exaggerated, though I always hope for the best." Better judgment tempered attitudes and expectations in the trenches around Petersburg. Although many soldiers grew optimistic at news of Early's successes, they ultimately believed the burden of victory lay on the army around Petersburg.[22]

Coinciding expressions of confidence and skepticism also sprang from battles then raging around Atlanta. Many in the Petersburg trenches looked expectantly to Confederate generals Joseph E. Johnston and John Bell Hood. While soldiers in the Army of Northern Virginia saw themselves as the primary national army and centerpiece of the Confederate military effort, at least a few thought the war might conclude victoriously in Georgia. Late in July, Holloway revealed his feelings regarding the battles outside Atlanta soon after the aggressive Hood, who had fought effectively as a division commander under Lee, replaced the more defensive-minded Johnston as commander of the Confederate Army of Tennessee and faced off against Maj. Gen. William Tecumseh Sherman's forces. "The excitement is intense this evening," wrote Holloway, "over the news from Hood. . . . The complete success in that direction will go farther to end the war than any thing else. . . . Now—with Grant in his present position and Sherman retreating Lincoln's chance for re-election will be much lessened and his newest call for 800,000 men will remain unanswered." The same day, John Claiborne similarly directed a hopeful gaze far to the south of Petersburg. Describing the death of Union general James B. McPherson during the fighting at Atlanta and the "enemy's retreat in confusion," he professed that "if Sherman can be smashed out there we shall be relieved here. I await the result with anxiety."[23]

We Will Finish the War Here

Gen. Joseph Eggleston Johnston. Public reaction to Johnston in the spring and summer of 1864 highlights the degree to which Lee commanded unmatched respect in the Confederacy. Although popular among many Confederates, Johnston inspired almost none of the unwavering devotion directed toward Lee. Many Rebels thought Johnston too passive in his generalship. "I must confess that I am not as much of a Johnston man as I have been," one of his soldiers wrote in July. "He is too cautious, is not willing to risk a battle until he is satisfied he can whip it." National Archives, image number 111-B-1782.

Willy Pegram, on the other hand, saw the struggle for Atlanta as potentially problematical and raised pointed questions about the decisions of Confederate president Jefferson Davis. "The removal of Genl. Johnston has caused great indignation against the President in this army," sputtered Pegram. "If he is removed, because he refused holding Atlanta, I am very glad of it. He can certainly be better sacrificed than Atlanta." But the feud between the president and Johnston was well known, and Pegram suspected personalities might have entered the equation of Johnston's dismissal from army command: "If he is removed from the influence of Bragg, and prejudice of the President, my confidence in the latter will be entirely lost. I shall not only cease to admire him, but to believe him not a patriot. No man who would sacrifice a General, & thereby the good of the cause, to his prejudice, can be a patriot." Placing similar emphasis on the fight in Atlanta, Joseph Lyle claimed, "All looking to Ga with great anxiety—complete success there for us, will give us peace—disaster will give us four years more of war." When writing of Early's successes, Lyle feared misplaced enthusiasm. "The wrong ox has been gored—fear that Atlanta is doomed."[24]

Yet few soldiers in the Petersburg lines likely believed the war would end in Georgia. Most thought the Army of Northern Virginia would deal the death blow against invading Federals. On August 3, John Chamberlayne wrote home requesting information on the Atlanta campaign. "I hope you will write me fully of matters. If they will whip Sherman, we will finish the war here—for Grant is at a dead lock." James Peter Williams, a Virginia artillerist in the Confederate trenches relating war news to his aunt, seemed thankful that the army finally had settled into position for what he expected to be the decisive battle. Earlier in March, he had confessed, "I wish the war could be carried out without so much moving & marching about"; by late June, he gladly proclaimed, "I think everything is going as well as we could wish & have no doubt that this campaign will wind up this cruel war."[25]

The feeling that Grant was simply leading his men to slaughter suggested a sense of confidence among many Confederate soldiers in the trenches. Though Grant ultimately had subdued Confederate defenders at Vicksburg roughly a year prior, a series of stinging Rebel "victories" in the East over the previous few weeks convinced those in Virginia that they would not meet the same fate. Rebels had repulsed repeated Union assaults throughout May and June, including a costly series between June 15 and 18 resulting in more than 11,000 Union casualties. Pvt. Joseph D. Stapp, serving with the 41st Alabama Infantry, wrote his mother from Petersburg on July 8 about the futility of further Union attacks. "The yankies are all on the East side of this place," he informed her. "Our trenches and theirs, are in sight of each other & the pickets are very near they have charged our works several times but have been repulsed every time." When Samuel McCullough anticipated heavy action in mid-June, he illustrated great confidence in the Army of Northern Virginia. On June 20, he told an acquaintance, "Grant's main army is in our front & we will probably soon have some heavy fighting. Our loss is not over 1000 since the new base of operations, whilst the Yankees have lost at least 4 or 5 times as many. The men are all in good spirits and ready for the fight."[26]

It was the battle of the Crater on July 30 that convinced many Confederates—especially those who saw the Federal attack as an act of Union desperation—victory was close at hand. Earlier in the month, Pennsylvania miners under the command of Lt. Col. Henry Pleasants had dug an underground shaft toward a salient in the Confederate line occupied by a regiment of South Carolinians. Pleasants's diligent soldiers packed the tunnel with enough explosives to blow a hole in the Confederate line, whereby Union forces could exploit the breach and thus render Lee's defenses untenable. The explosion on July 30, while horrifically destructive, did little to forward the Union cause. Last-minute changes in the order of battle—white soldiers replaced a division of United States Colored Troops originally designated to lead the attack—and poor leadership contributed to a gruesome slaughter. Confederates under the command of Brig. Gen. William Mahone quickly repulsed attacking Federals and sealed the gap caused by the explosion.[27]

In reality, both Grant and the commander of the Army of the Potomac, Maj. Gen. George Gordon Meade, had detected little strategic potential in Pleasants's plan and lost interest during the mine's construction. Lee's Confederates, however, interpreted the Union fiasco as a last-ditch, futile effort by Grant that resulted in a resounding Confederate victory over a force several times their size. Union killed, wounded, and missing numbered nearly 3,800; the Confederates lost fewer than half this number. While many soldiers only noted the slaughter of Union troops, others described the scene in vivid detail, including their reading of the events as a prelude to imminent Confederate victory. Pvt. Matthew Wood Allen entered into his diary on July 30 a typical, if somewhat lackluster, description of the actions at the Crater: "The Yankees sprung a mine and charged through our works but were driven back with great slaughter. A great many prisoners were captured, among them some Negroes."[28]

John Hampden Chamberlayne wrote to his mother soon after the explosion in much greater, and grimmer, detail. "Their whole force was concentrated & that days attempt was doubtless the grand affair," he began. "There was a gloomy look out for some two hours after which we clear them out retaking the guns, killing upwards of 700 outright; wounding many more & taking 11 to 1200 prisoners." Overall, concluded Chamberlayne, it had been a "brilliant & important victory achieved by 1/3 of our force & with comparatively light loss: a month of mining, his whole force concentrated, & his own time & place selected enabled him only to lose from 4500 to 5000 men & gain nothing—for we hold every foot of ground—& they have not advanced one inch."[29]

Federal operations during the first days of August suggested to entrenched Confederates that the Army of the Potomac was growing more desperate with the passing weeks. In dismissive style, Richard Henry Dulany of Loudoun County, Virginia, an officer in the Laurel Brigade, wrote from Brig. Gen. Thomas Lafayette Rosser's headquarters on August 3, "The yanks made a desperate assault upon Petersburg on Saturday morning . . .

blowing up our advance earthworks. . . . A gentleman told Genl Lee that the enemy had blown up a battery and had captured our outer works and he did not even get up out of his chair but simply said to one of Beauregard's staff, go and tell Genl Beauregard to drive those people out of our works It is not hard to imagine such calmness, and such perfect confidence in troops."[30]

Rebels perceived the use of black troops in the attack as both an outrage and an indication of Union desperation. Thomas A. Smith, a soldier corresponding with his sister throughout the Petersburg siege, observed, "Such is the character of the enemy with whom we have to deal—bringing our own slaves against us—surely there will be a day of retribution (justice) for such vandalism when they will own and acknowledge the justice of their punishment." Smith believed the Federals had not given up on "their digging propensities—a deserter came in yesterday and revealed the secret of other places being mined by the enemy—but little can be made of this mode of operation, as Mr. Grant has found out by his last trial."[31]

Willy Pegram seemed to pity the black troops but saw their demise as a boon to Confederate soldiers. "It seems cruel to murder them in cold blood," he explained, "but I think the men who did it had very good cause for doing so. . . . I have always said that I wished the enemy would bring some negroes against this army. I am convinced, since Saturday's fight, that it has a splendid effect on the men." He also described how the victory had boosted Confederate morale. "On the whole, Saturday was, through the merciful kindness of an all & ever merciful God, a very brilliant day to us," he concluded with obvious pride. "The enemy's loss was, at the lowest figures, three to our one, but the moral effect to our arms was very great, for it shows that he cannot blow us out of our works; or, at least, that he cannot hold a breach after making it."[32]

On July 31, the day following the unsuccessful Yankee attack, Joseph Lyle predicted that the Union cause was on its last legs. "Several companys of these regts were blown up & lost entirely," he noted with a sense of triumph. The Federals "entered the breach in our works—attempted to make progress but were driven from our lines with great slaughter. . . . Our loss about 1000—that of the enemy from four to five times that number." Just three Confederate divisions "beat back Grant's whole army, sappers, miners, negroes, powder & all." Lyle ended on a personal note directed toward the Union commander: "Grant, your cause is ruin—you go the way of your predecessor."[33]

Optimism persisted within the ranks throughout the summer of 1864.

Confederate soldiers on the Petersburg line anticipated conclusive battles against the investing Union army—and their role in the prospective victory. Yet the weeks and months dragged on beyond their ability to sustain such optimism and ultimately undermined their ability to withstand Grant's encircling forces. No set-piece battle drove the Yankees from their front, and time worked to favor the Union as Lee had predicted. In addition, news of the fall of Atlanta in early September, Early's later shattering defeats in the Shenandoah Valley between mid-September and mid-October, the reelection of Abraham Lincoln, Sherman's subsequent march through Georgia, and finally the loss of Savannah compromised morale in the Petersburg trenches. By early 1865, Grant's lengthening lines had extended Confederate resources beyond an effective defense. A final Rebel attempt to break the siege at Fort Stedman on March 25 yielded little more than heavy casualties. But these realities should not distract from the point that for much of the summer of 1864, Confederate soldiers in the Army of Northern Virginia presumed inevitable victory. They had no way of knowing the siege would last until April 1865, when the evacuations of Petersburg and Richmond led to a quick succession of events that finally closed the books on the Confederate States of America.

Notes

1. Cheers resounded throughout the United States when U. S. Grant vowed to "fight it out on this line if it took all summer." By mid-June, the transition from active campaigning to a siege had taken place. The "line" thus became the vast trench works defending Petersburg and Richmond. Although the war now wearied many in the North who saw little progress in Grant's actions, unlike his predecessors, the Union commander had no intention of withdrawing from the Petersburg-Richmond front. See James M. McPherson, *Battle Cry of Freedom: The Civil War Era* (New York: Oxford University Press, 1988), 734, and Ulysses S. Grant, *Personal Memoirs of U.S. Grant* (2 vols., 1885; reprint in 1 vol., New York: Da Capo, 1982), 454–60.

2. Douglas Southall Freeman, the most famous of Lee's many biographers, notes that this remark to Jubal A. Early on the eve of the Petersburg siege was the first time Lee had hinted at such an outcome; see Freeman, *R. E. Lee: A Biography*, 4 vols. (New York: Scribner's, 1934–35), 3:397–98. Conveying a sense of "Lee as a powerless god," one scholar hyperbolically suggests he "already sensed the outcome" and experienced a "frisson of terror" (Robert Hendrickson, *The Road to Appomattox* [New York: John Wiley and Sons, 1998], 45). Lee's foreshadowing ultimately proved correct. For nearly ten months, between June 1864 and April 1865, opposing armies engaged in trench warfare interspersed with a series of battles until the exhausted Army of Northern Virginia was forced to withdraw from its fortifications and evacuate Peters-

M. KEITH HARRIS

burg and Richmond. In physical terms, the siege was trying for Lee's Confederates. Men complained incessantly of heat, vermin, unsanitary conditions, boredom, lack of food, and constant shelling that nearly always put them in harm's way. Over the course of the siege, Grant's army grew to more than twice the size of Lee's. In time, Union forces constructed entrenchments extending from east of Richmond to south and west of Petersburg. Determined, well supplied, and heavily outnumbering their foe, the Federals mounted assaults at places such as Deep Bottom and the Crater late in July, Boydton Plank Road in October, and Hatcher's Run in February that did not break the siege. Yet by spring 1865, Confederates faced intimidating odds. On March 25, Lee attempted a breakout at Fort Stedman. This failed effort cost him far more than he could afford to lose and set the stage for the abandonment of the Petersburg line.

3. Richard E. Beringer, Herman Hattaway, Archer Jones, and William N. Still Jr., *Why the South Lost the Civil War* (Athens: University of Georgia Press, 1986), 424–25, 300, 425; Bell Irvin Wiley, *The Road to Appomattox* (Memphis: Memphis State College Press, 1956), 34, 70–71. For an exploration of Confederates who maintained a belief in possible victory until late in the conflict, see Jason Phillips, *Diehard Rebels: The Confederate Culture of Invincibility* (Athens: University of Georgia Press, 2007).

4. McPherson, *Battle Cry of Freedom*, 743. On widespread Confederate despair and the frustrations on the Petersburg-Richmond front throughout 1864, see J. Tracy Power, *Lee's Miserables: Life in the Army of Northern Virginia from the Wilderness to Appomattox* (Chapel Hill: University of North Carolina Press, 1998), 286, 288, 302–3.

5. John Hampden Chamberlayne to "My Dear Mother," July 11, 1864, section 4, Chamberlayne Family Papers, Mss1C3552b49–109, Virginia Historical Society, Richmond (repository hereafter cited as VHS); Diary of Creed Thomas Davis, Mss5:1D2914:1, VHS.

6. John Herbert Claiborne to "My Dear Wife," June 12, 1864, Letters of John Herbert Claiborne, MSS 3633, Albert and Shirley Small Special Collections Library, University of Virginia, Charlottesville (repository hereafter cited as UVA); Thomas Tileston Greene to Elise Glenn Skinner, May 23, 1864, folder 1, section 17, MssG8368a62–141, Greene Family Papers, VHS.

7. John Hampden Chamberlayne to "My Dear Mother," June 23, 1864, Chamberlayne Family Papers, VHS; Joseph Banks Lyle to Medora Caroline McArthur, June 9, 1864, section 1, Joseph Banks Lyle Papers, Mss1L9881a1–110, VHS.

8. James Montgomery Holloway to Annie Wilcox Holloway, June 12–13, 23, 1864, folder 7, section 1, Holloway Papers, Mss1H7286a111–127, VHS. As Holloway's comments suggest, the surrender at Vicksburg, following a six-week siege, had loomed much larger to many Confederate citizens than Lee's defeat at Gettysburg. For testimony on this point, see Kate Stone, *Brokenburn: The Journal of Kate Stone, 1861–1868*, ed. John Q. Anderson (Baton Rouge: Louisiana State University Press, 1955), 168–70, 229–30, 233. See also Gary W. Gallagher, "'Lee's Army Has Not Lost Any of Its Prestige': The Impact of Gettysburg on the Army of Northern Virginia and the Confederate Home Front," in Gallagher, ed., *The Third Day at Gettysburg and Beyond* (Chapel Hill: University of North Carolina Press, 1994), 1–30.

9. Gary W. Gallagher, "Our Hearts Are Full of Hope: The Army of Northern Virginia in the Spring of 1864," in Gary W. Gallagher, ed. *The Wilderness Campaign* (Chapel Hill: University of North Carolina Press, 1997), 42.

10. Richard Henry Watkins to Mary Purnell Watkins, June 1, 22, 28, July 4, 1864, folder 6, section 1, Watkins Papers, Mss1W3272a291–349, VHS.

11. W. J. [William Ransom Johnson] Pegram to Mary Evans [Pegram] Anderson, July 21, 1864, folder 2, section 1, Pegram-Johnson-McIntosh Papers, MssP3496a16–30, VHS.

12. Joseph Banks Lyle to Medora Caroline McArthur, July 2, 15, 1864, Joseph Banks Lyle Papers, VHS; John Hampden Chamberlayne to My Dear Mother, July 28, 1864, Chamberlayne Family Papers, VHS.

13. John Herbert Claiborne to "My Dear Wife," July 11, 1864, Letters of John Herbert Claiborne, UVA. For a day-by-day account of Early's advance down the Valley, see Joseph Judge, *Season of Fire: The Confederate Strike on Washington* (Berryville, Va.: Rockbridge Publishing Co., 1994). For a brief postwar account of Early's actions in the Valley and a critique of Early's generalship, see John B. Gordon, *Reminiscences of the Civil War* (1903; reprint, Baton Rouge: Louisiana State University Press, 1993), 317–18.

14. Diary of Joseph Banks Lyle, section 2, Joseph Banks Lyle Papers, Mss1L9881a111, VHS.

15. Diary of Lt. Samuel Thomas McCullough, Jed Hotchkiss Papers, MSS 2907, UVA.

16. James Montgomery Holloway to Annie Wilcox Holloway, July 5–8, 1864, Holloway Papers, VHS; Richard Henry Watkins to Mary Purnell Watkins, July 7, 1864, Watkins Papers, VHS.

17. W. J. [William Ransom Johnson] Pegram to Virginia Johnson [Pegram] McIntosh, July 14, 1864, Pegram-Johnson-McIntosh Papers, VHS.

18. Diary of Peter Guerrant, July 1–August 15, 1864, Mss1G9375a330, VHS.

19. James Montgomery Holloway to Annie Wilcox Holloway, July 14–18, 1864, Holloway Papers, VHS.

20. James Montgomery Holloway to Annie Wilcox Holloway, June 16, 1864, Holloway Papers, VHS; Diary of Samuel Thomas McCullough, Lt. Samuel Thomas McCullough Papers, UVA.

21. Diary of Joseph Banks Lyle, Joseph Banks Lyle Papers, VHS.

22. Richard Henry Watkins to Mary Purnell Watkins, July 15, 1864, Watkins Papers, VHS; James Montgomery Holloway to Annie Wilcox Holloway, July 14–18, 1864, Holloway Papers, VHS; John Herbert Claiborne to "My Dear Wife," June 12, 1864, Letters of John Herbert Claiborne, UVA; Thomas Tileston Greene to Elise Glenn Skinner, July 14, 1864, Greene Family Papers, VHS.

23. James Montgomery Holloway to Annie Wilcox Holloway, July 23, 1864, Holloway Papers, VHS; John Herbert Claiborne to "My Dear Wife," July 23, 1864, Letters of John Herbert Claiborne, UVA.

24. W. J. [William Ransom Johnson] Pegram to Mary Evans [Pegram] Anderson, July 21, 1864, Pegram-Johnson-McIntosh Papers, VHS; diary of Joseph Banks Lyle, Joseph Banks Lyle Papers, VHS.

25. John Hampden Chamberlayne to "My Dear Mother," August 3, 1864, Cham-

berlayne Family Papers, VHS; James Peter Williams to "Dear Aunt Mary," March 22, June 28, 1864, Papers of James Peter Williams, folder 1861–1865, box 3, MSS 490, UVA.

26. Joseph D. Stapp to "Dear Mother," July 8, 1864, folder 1, Joseph D. Stapp Papers, Mss2St275b, VHS; Samuel Thomas McCullough to "Dear Sam," June 20, 1864, Papers of Lt. Samuel Thomas McCollough, UVA.

27. Grant did not take a personal interest in overseeing the constructing of the mine shaft, leaving the work to Pleasants and his Pennsylvanians under the supervision of Maj. Gen. Ambrose E. Burnside, commander of the Union Ninth Corps. He did, however, in retrospect, "approve heartily" of the plan of attack. See Grant, *Personal Memoirs*, 462–66. On the failures of Union leadership at the Crater, see Alan Axelrod, *The Horrid Pit: The Battle of the Crater, the Civil War's Cruelest Mission* (New York: Carrol and Grap, 2007). On The battle of the Crater and Civil War memory, see Kevin M. Levin, *Remembering the Battle of the Crater: War as Murder* (Lexington: University Press of Kentucky, 2012).

28. Journal of Matthew Wood Allen, Matthew Wood Allen Papers, Mss5:1A1543:1, VHS.

29. John Hampden Chamberlayne to "My Dear Mother," August 3, 1864, Chamberlayne Family Papers, VHS.

30. Richard Henry Dulany to Mary Ann [DeButts] Whiting, August 3, 1864, section 13, DeButts Family Papers, MssD35454a476510, VHS.

31. Thomas A. Smith to "Dear Lizzie," August 2, 1864, folder 1862–1864, Thomas A. Smith Letters to His Family, MSS 6846-ct, UVA.

32. W. J. [William Ransom Johnson] Pegram to Virginia Johnson [Pegram] McIntosh, August 1, 1864, Pegram-Johnson-McIntosh Papers, VHS.

33. Diary of Joseph Banks Lyle, Joseph Banks Lyle Papers, VHS.

A War Thoroughfare

Confederate Civilians and the Siege of Petersburg

⊰ CAROLINE E. JANNEY ⊱

By early July 1864, Petersburg resident Charles Campbell could scarcely believe the devastating effects the nearly month-long siege was having on his beloved city. The insufferable whistle and thunderous explosions of shells filled the air day and night. In the eastern portions of the city, most houses that had not been demolished by projectiles had been razed by ravaging flames. Business at the city's factories and stores had largely been suspended, from both want of merchandise and the dangerous proximity to Federal guns. Most terrifying of all, several civilians had been killed by Union shells and others had been severely wounded, prompting many of the town's residents to flee the pandemonium. It "looks like a deserted city," Campbell observed in his journal; "the people move away by a sort of contagious instinct of danger." "On every side" he wrote, "one sees & hears war, war." Confederate surgeon John H. Claiborne concurred with Campbell's assessment, writing to his wife that Petersburg "is perhaps . . . the most disagreeable human habitation that is left upon this sin stricken earth."[1] In the once grand city, there was no longer a distinction between home front and battlefront.

When the Federal bombardment of their city began in mid-June 1864, Petersburgers believed they were experiencing a brutal and uncivilized war in which the Union army deliberately targeted civilians.[2] Historians and popular culture most often point to Maj. Gen. William T. Sherman's march through Georgia and the Carolinas or Maj. Gen. Philip H. Sheridan's operations in the Shenandoah Valley as evidence of a Union policy of hard war in which the property of noncombatants was destroyed in order to undermine Confederate morale.[3] Prior to these campaigns, however, Confederate civilians already had experienced the bombardments of Fredericksburg, Vicksburg, Charleston, and Atlanta. But it was Petersburg that endured the longest period of unannounced shellings, mounting civilian casualties, and increasing deprivations. Motivated by their belief that Union soldiers and the northern populace took pleasure in targeting noncombatants and sustained by a deep faith in the Confederate cause, throughout June and July 1864 the city's white residents endured the early siege with firm resolve, setting a pattern that would continue for another eight months. The bombardment did not undermine Petersburg civilians' faith in the Rebel cause but, rather, confirmed their belief that they were fighting a barbaric foe and strengthened the determination of Confederates both within and beyond the city's borders.[4]

On the eve of the Civil War, the Cockade City was a bustling manufacturing and transportation hub situated on the south bank of the Appomattox River just twenty-two miles below Richmond. In 1860, it claimed a population of 18,266, which included 5,680 slaves and 3,644 freedmen, giving it the highest proportion of free African Americans in any southern city. By all accounts it was a modern city replete with gas-fueled streetlights, brick sidewalks, a municipal water system, several daily newspapers, eight banks, four volunteer fire companies, and more than 150 grocers. The second-largest municipality in Virginia, its five railroads radiated from the city shipping products from its cotton and flour mills, ironworks, and tobacco manufacturers, as well as human commodities via its slave trade. Confederates understood that Petersburg's link between Richmond and supplies to the west and south made it the gateway to the southern capital and a prime target for Union armies. As such, the defense of Petersburg was the defense of Richmond. If the former fell, the latter was sure to follow.[5]

During the first three years of war, life in Petersburg resembled that of many other southern communities at war. Troops arrived and departed along the railroad lines, ladies organized sewing and aid societies to support the troops, and industrial warehouses served as eleven hospitals and three military prisons. But life also proceeded as usual for many: actors still took the stage at Phoenix Hall on Bollingbrook Street, farmers continued to bring their fresh vegetables to the market, and children played in the streets, often pretending to scout for Yankee soldiers. By the spring of 1864, however, the pressures of war had wrought significant changes on the industrial city. The railroads remained active, but the Confederate army had commandeered the trains for military use, and the Union navy had implemented a blockade on the Appomattox River, thus disrupting much trade. With the exception of food markets, there was little to no retail trade. Most of the tobacco factories had closed their doors, and many of the ironworks were following suit. The cotton and flour mills, however,

A War Thoroughfare

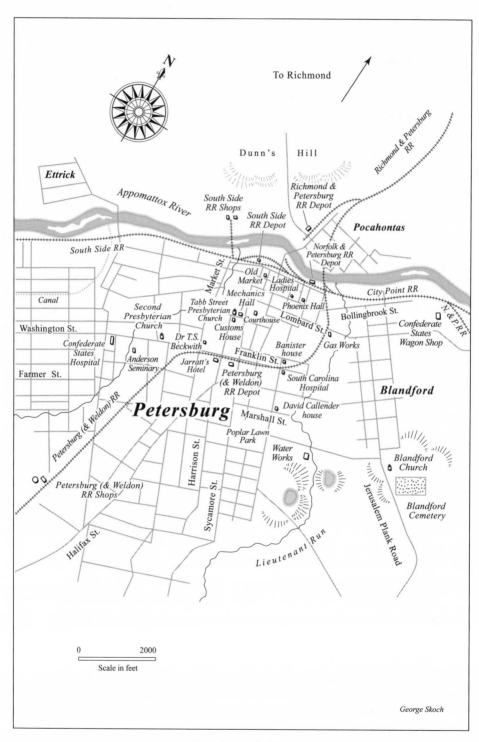

Petersburg, Virginia

Dr. John H. Claiborne, whose letters provide invaluable testimony about operations in and around Petersburg in 1864. Virginia Historical Society, Richmond, Virginia.

continued to operate. With large government contracts to supply flour as well as canvas for tents, sheets, and other materials, the mills remained open through the labor of women, children, and older men.[6]

The war's mounting toll on the city's population between 1861 and 1864 was no less significant as a constant stream of soldiers and civilians moved in and out of town. In April 1861, six Petersburg militia companies had mustered into active service. By the third year of war, seventeen companies of local men had enlisted in the regular Confederate army even as overcrowding in Richmond forced families to relocate to Petersburg. In early May 1864, when Federal troops under the command of Maj. Gen. Benjamin F. Butler landed at Bermuda Hundred (eight miles from Petersburg), a wave of refugees from Prince George and the eastern part of Chesterfield counties began to flood into the city bringing their slaves and wagons piled high with household goods. Throughout the month, more refugees, primarily women and children, arrived from areas north and west of Richmond as Lt. Gen. Ulysses S. Grant and Gen. Robert E. Lee moved south and east during the battles of the Overland campaign. Such an influx only added to the scarcity of goods: everything from crucial pins and needles necessary for repairing clothes to more luxurious items such as ice from Maine.[7]

But conditions were about to turn markedly worse. On Thursday morning, June 9, Confederate surgeon John Herbert Claiborne, executive officer in charge of the city's military hospitals, penned a letter to his wife, Sarah. "The enemy have landed on the south side of the James and Appomattox,"

A War Thoroughfare

he wrote, "and are this morning in what force I do not know at our breast works 2–1/2 miles from the city on the City Point Road." Such news, he informed his wife, who had taken refuge with family in North Carolina, had aroused a great state of excitement throughout the city. Around nine o'clock that morning, General Butler's forces attacked Petersburg along the Jerusalem Plank Road south of the city. As the bell of the courthouse and then church bells began to clang, approximately 125 "grey-haired men, and beardless boys" of the second-class militia rushed to the city's defenses. These volunteers included the last remaining men in the city, those younger than seventeen and older than fifty who worked in the iron foundries, the cotton mills, and the railroads. After approximately two hours of fighting, the Union forces retreated leaving fifteen dead, eighteen wounded, and another forty-five captured.[8]

The list of those who had fallen in defense of their city included a professor of French in the Petersburg Female College, a prominent druggist, and the son of the late postmaster. Also among the dead was the elderly and nearly deaf William Banister. His teenaged daughter later recalled the painful scene when her uncle arrived at their home bearing her father's lifeless body. He had been "shot through the head, his gray hair dabbled in blood." "My precious mother stood like one dazed," she remembered, "but in a few seconds she was kneeling by my father in such grief as I had never seen before." Thirty-two-year-old Bessie Callender proclaimed the following day "the saddest that ever dawned in Petersburg," as families held services for their fallen loved ones throughout the day. But such "was only the beginning of the horrors we were to go through," Anne Banister later observed.[9]

On the night of June 12, Dr. Claiborne sat down to write another letter to Sarah. "We are still in the dark in reference to Grant's movements and until they are developed we shall not know our fate," he informed her. But Claiborne, like many other Petersburg residents, recognized that this was not to be short lived. "I feel he has sat down for a summer's siege and if so— oh how wearisome to us all who wait our destiny in this campaign." Two days later, Grant and the Army of the Potomac began to cross the James River and soon began a siege that would last significantly longer than Claiborne's optimistic hopes of a few months. At 7:00 A.M. on June 15, the city bells commenced warning anxious residents that Union forces lay just east of the city. Petersburgers from schoolgirls to old men clamored to view the action, racing to the top of the iron port building on Sycamore Street to look through spyglasses. To the northeast they could see large plumes of smoke rising from farmhouses that had been struck by gunboats on the Appomattox. But more important, from their lofty vantage point they saw Confederate reinforcements marching toward the city.[10]

At daybreak the following morning, June 16, Union artillery launched the first shells toward the city. The bombardment initially centered on the Old Market section of the city because of its proximity to the railroad depot and the Federal belief that the missiles landing there would hit Confederate soldiers. Other shells were launched toward the South Carolina hospital on Bragg's Hill. "But the guns soon enlarged their operations," one resident reported, "sweeping all the business part of the city, and then invading the residential region." A few minutes before eight o'clock that morning, the residents of Bollingbrook Street were "startled by the unannounced arrival of a three inch shell," which passed through the granite coping of Wilcox's cellar but did little damage. Other shells were more destructive. One "came shrieking diagonally across the Court House," striking the home of baker Charles Brown on Sycamore Street. The shell burst through the east wall, leaving a hole as big as a person and sending a brick fragment flying into a Mrs. McGregor's head, causing her to bleed profusely. Yet another shell exploded in Blandford, hitting two slave children belonging to James Hall who had been asleep in their bed. The explosion left the four-year-old girl's left arm broken and her temporal artery cut. Her six-year-old brother fared much worse, his right leg requiring amputation between the knee and ankle. Even with such casualties, the guns did not abate. Instead the rapid cannonading continued at regular intervals throughout the day and well into the night. "I lay quietly until nearly one o'clock listening to the bursting shells when one exploded so near that the light flashed in my face," Fanny Waddell remembered.[11]

With Grant's forces applying pressure just two miles east of Petersburg, on Friday evening, June 17, Confederate soldiers and local men labored to dig a new line of defenses. That night, panic spread through the town, many persons convinced it was "certainly to fall into the hands of the Yankees." But salvation arrived the following morning, June 18, amid a cloud of dust as General Lee and veteran units from the Army of Northern Virginia marched into the city. Petersburg's residents soon learned that their local boys, the 12th Virginia Infantry, were among the reinforcements. Crowds of onlookers and anxious family members rushed downtown, filling every available corner along Sycamore Street. From his wagon, Reuben Ragland poured coffee into the canteens of the thirsty soldiers while another man tossed plugs of tobacco to the weary veterans. "It was pathetic to witness

A War Thoroughfare

the meeting of wives & husbands, mothers and sons, and quite refreshing the greetings between beaux and lovely lasses," recalled Sgt. James E. Whitehorne.[12] Some of the soldiers looked so rough and sunburned that their friends and loved ones had trouble recognizing them. "It made one's heart ache to look at them," one mother remembered. But despite the men's gaunt faces and dusty uniforms, the residents were overjoyed and comforted to have their men so near.[13]

The arrival of Confederate troops did not stop the bombardment. Instead, the cannonading intensified. Shells continued to fall in the heart of the city throughout the day on Saturday, claiming both buildings and human casualties.[14] One mortar round entered George Bain's backyard, striking his four-year-old son in the stomach and rendering him immediately insensible.[15] On Sunday, June 19, a shell burst over the Second Presbyterian Church, the steeple having provided an irresistible target, just as the Reverend John Miller finished a prayer. The parishioners fled the church, leaving Miller to disarm the shell. Thirty-two-year-old Bessie Callender, whose home on Marshall Street in the southeast corner of the city was near much of the initial shelling, took her three children and a slave, along with a bedstead and some beds for pallets, a table, and a few chairs, to a room on Washington Street out of range of the shells. The sight of the ambulances bringing in the wounded and the notion that the city would be surrendered so frightened her that she asked her husband for a glass of whiskey—without sugar—to calm her nerves. Callender was not alone in her terror amid a cacophony of explosions simultaneously unimaginable and horrific. As one woman later explained, "To persons unfamiliar with the infernal noise made by the screaming, ricocheting, and bursting of shells, it is impossible to describe the terror and demoralization which ensued."[16]

Although historians overwhelmingly agree that Federals did not engage in a "total war," that is, deliberately employ the use of military force against the enemy's noncombatant population, the citizens of Petersburg felt otherwise.[17] In their perception, the "barbaric Yankees" were deliberately destroying the city and harming its residents. After all, churches and residences, not merely military infrastructure such as railroads, proved to be the targets of Union guns. But more important, they believed that Union commanders had explicitly, and without compassion, ordered the shelling of a city occupied primarily by women and children. "How frightful this is!" exclaimed resident Georgiana Walker from the safety of England, "that even ladies are to fall victims to the cruel barbarity of our foe." The *Charleston Mercury* likewise was appalled that the Union would resort to

CAROLINE E. JANNEY

the "barbarous practice of shelling a city" occupied primarily by "defence-less women and children."[18]

Although the laws of war held that fortified cities could be subject to bombardment without notification, Confederates in Petersburg and throughout the South argued that the most reprehensible aspect of the bombardment was the Union army's failure to warn the residents before shelling the town.[19] Petersburg's Sara Pryor observed that "they opened on our city without the slightest notice, or without giving opportunity for the removal of non-combatants, the sick, the wounded, or the women and children." Catherine Edmondston of North Carolina concurred, complaining angrily that "without warning or note of their intention, they advanced in force & commenced an indiscriminate shelling of the town." But given what Confederates perceived as the Yankees' earlier ruthless behavior at Fredericksburg and Vicksburg, many were not surprised. Fiery secessionist Edmund Ruffin, whose daughter-in-law resided in the city, noted bitterly that it was "needless to say" that the Yankees had commenced firing "without warning the women and children to move." A Richmond newspaper claimed that none "but the most dastardly race on the face of the earth would engage in a business so supremely contemptible, as well as inexpressibly villainous." A South Carolina newspaper was especially enraged by the bombing of churches but offered a possible solution: "For every person—white or black—injured by these shells the general commanding should cause a Yankee prisoner to be put to death." "Such barbarous practices," the writer maintained, "should meet with desperate remedies."[20]

Most Union soldiers, in contrast, maintained that the bombardment was a military necessity rather than an assault on a civilian population. Numerous early reports commented that the guns had succeeded in their goal of stopping communication between Richmond and points south of Petersburg. Moreover, many Federals believed that they were firing only on enemy troops, "all the white people" having evacuated the city during the June 9 attack. Several weeks later, rumors circulated through the Federal camps that Grant had issued an order that all women and children were to leave the city. Indeed, by early July the Union provost marshal noted that "the town was nearly deserted," a report that had been largely confirmed by African Americans from town.[21]

It is entirely possible that the soldiers in blue believed the city had been evacuated, thus explaining their matter-of-fact assessment of the bombardment. On Saturday evening, June 18, Col. John C. Tidball, commanding the 4th New York Heavy Artillery, reported that his guns had "opened fire on the city." Receiving no reply from Confederate guns, at midnight he ordered another bombardment. Two days later, he issued yet another order to shell the town and its bridges. Lt. Jacob Federhen, commanding a battery of Massachusetts light artillery, reported similar activity, his guns having expended four solid shot on the town on the night of June 19 and eight solid shot at the depot the following night. Although solid shot would have posed less danger to civilians than explosive rounds, neither commander reported any cause for hesitation due to the presence of noncombatants. The following morning, however, Maj. Gen. George G. Meade, the Army of the Potomac's commander, questioned the military necessity of shelling the town. Maj. Gen. David Bell Birney responded that "shelling the town seems to compel the enemy to cease firing." Satisfied with Birney's response, Meade pronounced bombardment a "legitimate military operation" that might be "resorted to whenever necessary."[22]

Despite insistences on the strategic importance of bombing the city, there is evidence throughout the siege that some Union artillerists and soldiers deliberately targeted churches and residences. At least one battery celebrated July 4th by firing at the city's steeples. Commanding a battery at Fort Willcox in mid-July, Bvt. Maj. Jacob Roemer instructed one of his lieutenants to "climb that tree and give me by signals, the proper direction and elevation for sending our shells into the most thickly populated and most important residential portion of Petersburg." In August, General Birney directed his chief of artillery to "open on the town of Petersburg all available guns from 7:30 to 9:30 this evening." "The 13-inch mortar will be fired upon [the] court-house as rapidly as it can be handled," he noted. The following month Birney ordered his artillery chief to "concentrate on the middle steeple" in the city. Union soldiers seem to have worried about potential casualties only when they observed eight railroad cars of troops "apparently dressed in blue uniforms" at the depot. "Is it possible that these are our men to be put there to prevent the shelling of the city?" Maj. Gen. William F. "Baldy" Smith telegraphed Grant's headquarters.[23]

On the northern home front, reaction to shelling a city still occupied by noncombatants was mixed. Like many soldiers, numerous Union newspapers presumed that the inhabitants had fled the city or understood that bombardment was a military necessity.[24] At least several newspapers, however, interpreted the shelling as retributive justice. In late June, the Democratic *New York Herald* correspondent noted that the 30-pounder Parrott shells "now have perfect range and when our guns open they will prove anything but mirthful to the inhabitants." The paper reported soon there-

"General Grant's Campaign—View of Petersburg from Captain Davis's Battery,
First Connecticut Artillery." William Waud gave readers of *Harper's Weekly* a Federal
perspective on the shelling of Petersburg. The brief description of the sketch included
no indication of concern for the residents of the city. *Harper's Weekly*,
August 13, 1864, 517, 520–21.

after that "many of the inhabitants of Petersburg have been injured by our
shells." After one shot struck the office of the *Petersburg Express* and killed a
man working there, the Republican *Philadelphia Press* pointed out that the
Petersburg paper had become "singularly notorious as being one of the
most vile and rampant in its editorials" of the North. The *Press* supposed
that a shell bursting into this "corrupt sanctum" seemed to be "a voice from
on high, to warn that the day of vengeance is at hand." In the *Press*'s esti-
mation, Petersburg residents seemingly deserved the hell in which they
were living.

Many northerners likewise believed that if women often proved to be
the casualities of the Union guns, it was a product of their own doing.[25]
At the beginning of the war, noted one northerner, Petersburg's women
"formed a mounted company of sixty armed with carbines and revolvers."
Such reports of Confederate women's defiant and unfeminine behavior
had permeated the northern army and home front throughout the war.

A War Thoroughfare

These accounts pointed out the ways in which southern white women deviated from accepted (i.e., northern) gender norms. But they also suggested that the city's women *were* in fact active participants in the conflict, thereby enlarging the very definition of who was a combatant. Well before General Sherman implemented his hard war policy on the Georgia home front, some Unionists had already begun suggesting that the boundary between civilian and combatant—at least in the Confederacy—was nonexistent.[26]

If the town's citizenry was in part to blame for the bombardment, argued some Unionists, the Confederate leadership was equally liable for placing noncombatants in harm's way. One northern correspondent charged that Gen. P. G. T. Beauregard had constructed his Confederate works with "recklessness and inhumanity . . . in close contiguity with the dwellings of inhabitants." The reporter believed that as he had done at Charleston, Beauregard would not remove the nonmilitary dwellers from the city in an effort to "claim exemption from our fire."[27]

By Monday morning, June 20, Petersburg's streets were chaotic. In the words of one local resident, the city had become "a war thoroughfare." Wagons, soldiers, and horsemen headed east along Washington Street to the front lines while the city's residents scrambled west amid a suffocating cloud of dust to escape the range of incoming shells.[28] Recognizing that the Union artillery was not likely to cease its bombardment, the city's Common Council sent representatives to discuss the matter with General Beauregard. Failing to speak directly with the commanding general, the council offered its own plan of action, recommending that "people as individuals exercise their best judgment in taking care of their families by going into their cellars and along the slopes of the hills in the event of a heavy shelling." Few residents, however, needed a city proclamation to convince them that it was in their best interest to either find new places of residence or leave the besieged city altogether.[29]

Some families from the eastern portions of town elected to move in with family and friends in safer districts. Others thought such locales would still be too close to Union guns and relocated to the surrounding countryside, seeking to ensure their safety while remaining close enough to visit the market and see loved ones. Bessie Callender, whose husband, David, remained in the city to run the cotton mills, moved in with friends in Chesterfield, nearly twenty miles from Petersburg, so that she might return to town several times a week to check on her home, to accompany her father on his visits to the factories, and to attend church every Wednes-

CAROLINE E. JANNEY

day and Sunday. Many Petersburgers, however, felt compelled to remove themselves even farther from the besieged city. Callender's widowed sister, Charlotte Ruffin, and her children moved fifty miles northwest to reside with her father-in-law, Edmund Ruffin. Other women and children crowded trains to North Carolina, taking with them harrowing tales of "the brutal shelling" from their "Christian brethren."[30]

Lacking the resources to become refugees, the city's destitute residents improvised. "These people are camped and bivouacked in every form and manner in the surrounding country as far as ten miles," Dr. Claiborne wrote his wife. With no other means to escape the bombardment, many had erected tent cities beyond the range of the Union guns on the western edge of town and in the woods on the other side of the Appomattox River. Some had constructed tents of canvas, but frequently the shelters consisted of little more than blankets draped over poles or bush arbors designed to offer some relief from the hot sun and infrequent rain. Many had taken their furniture, beds, trunks, and tables; still others were merely "sitting on logs and eating out of all sorts of plates and drinking out of gourds." The challenges of camp living were overwhelming. Because the summer's incessant drought had burned up the vegetables in gardens and sapped the wells dry, obtaining food and fresh water proved nearly impossible. Prices at the local market were exorbitant, ranging from $1 per egg to $3 for a quart of blackberries, hardly fees the poor could afford.[31]

As both the tent dwellers and those who relocated learned, the decision to become a refugee did not guarantee one's comfort or safety. For many, it meant separating from family. Bessie Callender was close enough to visit her father and husband on a regular basis, but her sister and mother were far away. The Dunlop family likewise endured the pain of separation, as daughter Mattie opted to move to North Carolina while her mother and two sisters persisted in remaining at Petersburg "rather than endure the miseries of refuge-ism." Many quickly realized that their new abodes were not necessarily more secure than their last. One woman and her daughter sought refuge with a family in the country only to be caught between Confederate cavalry "and some Yankee raiders," prompting them to return to the shell-infested city.[32]

Even as many residents scrambled to leave the besieged city, others rushed into its confines believing it safer than their homes along Union lines. "The whole town is in a sort of transmigration state," observed Charles Campbell on June 29. Houses would be vacated and then filled by newcomers, he claimed, resulting in a metamorphosis of "families which gives rise to many strange combinations." A correspondent for the *New York Herald* traveling with the Federal army similarly reported that "almost every house we come to is entirely deserted," their occupants having hastily evacuated to the city. "From intelligence just received from Petersburg," the reporter wrote, "we learn that the former occupants of these country places have gone into the city, where, in some instances, several families are crowded into one house." This constant ebb and flow of residents into and out of the city continued throughout the summer. Claiborne informed his wife in mid-July that "most everybody is out of the lower part of Town and I believe 2/3 of the population of the whole city." Life as residents had known it before June 1864 ceased to exist. As Campbell somberly noted, "We now have war at the door."[33]

Despite such foreboding commentary, civilians who opted to remain in the city began devising new means to withstand the constant shelling. Impoverished residents often slept in churches beyond reach of shells or begged for vacant beds at the general hospitals. Anne Banister's family, whose home sat "in exact range of shells from the Yankee's Fort Stedman and Battery No. 5," moved into their basement, where they tended to her bedridden brother. Thomas Branch piled sandbags around his house; others used cotton bales to barricade their homes against shells or prepared subterranean spaces where they might take shelter at a moment's notice—including the cellars of Tabb Street Church and Anderson Seminary, where Charles Campbell placed benches and mattresses for the city's orphans.[34]

Just as the soldiers encircling their city entrenched themselves in the earth, Union officials reported that Petersburg residents were "digging caves in and about town" roughly five to six feet deep, which they subsequently covered with timbers and dirt. Trying to describe the unearthly scene to his wife in late July, Dr. Callender reported that Mr. Hinton had a bombproof in the garden that he would scramble into when the shelling became too intense. Such was not an unusual sight in the besieged city, as one Confederate officer reported "nearly every house had a bomb proof in the yard, or cellar."[35]

As the pervasive shelling continued throughout July, the townspeople adapted not only by constructing bombproofs but also by adjusting their daily rhythms of life. Residents became acutely aware of one 13-inch heavy mortar in particular, avoiding town during the early morning hours. "We called it the Petersburg Express, as it was fired every morning until it got so hot at midday they stopped," Bessie Callender recollected; "then persons would pass along Bollingbrook and lower Sycamore Street." Not only were new schedules the order of the day, but new locales were as well. "The post office has been removed to Dunlop Street not far from the basin," Charles Campbell reported on July 5, and "the telegraph office has been transferred to the head of Old Street." Numerous other businesses and many factory offices relocated west to Ettrick Street. Still others were forced to close their doors. The Confederate Army Wagon Shop in Old Blandford and Tappey and Lumsden's Southern Foundry closed, as did the Lead Works after the Virginia and Tennessee Railroad could no longer deliver ore. The flour and cotton mills, however, continued to operate because they were beyond the range of Union guns. Only two houses of worship remained open, forcing individuals to attend different congregations or forgo services altogether; however, Federal batteries had ceased to fire during church hours.[36]

In mid-July, a Confederate soldier passing through the streets observed that it was "a pretty town indeed" but had been "shelled to pieces a great deal now." The Directors' Room at the Exchange Bank had been smashed and two iron foundries were destroyed, while the *Express* office at the Pocahontas Depot, the Ladies' Hospital on Bollingbrook Street, two other buildings, and numerous residences had been destroyed by fire. Many residents were terrified that flames would prove the ultimate annihilation of the city. On July 17, Dr. Claiborne nervously wrote his wife that the Union had knocked the gas pipes into piles and "we have no gas now." He believed that the Yankees were not yet aware of their success but remained "afraid they will shell the water works next—if so they can burn the city at their leisure." One visiting Confederate officer remarked that "the destructive work of the shells was visible on every hand. Here a chimney was knocked off, here a handsome residence was deserted, with great rents in its walls, and the windows shattered by explosion; here stood a church tower mutilated, the church yard filled with new-made graves." Such a scene he found "exceedingly depressing."[37]

Despite Confederate surgeon Spencer Welch's reassurance to his wife in early July that "the shells do very little harm and have killed but few," the Union guns continued to inflict some civilian casualties. In the southeastern section of the city, a shell crashed into Andrew Dunn's house, injuring Dunn, on July 21. Others were not so lucky, especially during the first three weeks of the bombardment. June 25 had proven to be an especially deadly day. A shell exploded at attorney John Lyon's home near the Custom House, killing a woman; a Blandford woman died when a shell

The caption on the negative of this image reads, "Bombarded House,
Petersburg, Va." Taken after the fall of the city in April 1865, it shows the rear
of the Dunlop house on Bollingbrook Street. Library of Congress Prints and
Photographs Division, LC-DIG-cwpb-02652.

fragment struck her in the head; and a slave man belonging to Dinwiddie
Grigg was killed by a Union shell. Five days later, Charles Campbell described an even more horrific scene: "A negro woman was killed today by
a shell: her head cut off: It is said that she was holding a child, that escaped
unhurt." The following week another slave woman, belonging to Dr. T.
Beckwith, was killed at a residence on Market Street.[38]

Although the cannonading was deadly, many residents could not help
but comment on its spectacular sights and sounds. Sara Pryor recalled how
"the shells made a fluttering sound as they traversed the air, descending
with a frightful hiss, to explode or be buried in the earth. When they exploded in midair by day, a puff of smoke, white as an angel's wing, would
drift away, and the particles would patter down like hail." The shells reminded her of Fourth of July rockets, "except that they were fired not

A second study of ruins taken in April 1865, with "Interior, Colonial Mansion on Bollingbrook St., Petersburg," marked on the negative. Library of Congress Prints and Photographs Division, LC-DIG-cwpb-02267.

upward, but in a slanting direction." Writing years later, Pryor claimed that she "never felt afraid of them!" Another resident, too, related the otherworldliness of the shells. "During the last week the scene at night was sometimes grand and to highest degree sublime. Those who from a point of safety witnessed the shelling told me that they could sometimes count six or seven mortar shells in the air at once, with their trailing fuse on fire—some seeming to ascend to the very clouds before bursting or coming down." Observing from the roof of Union headquarters, northern reporter L. A. Hendrick likewise considered it a "grand and fearful spectacle." "The fiery paths," he noted, were "like so many charging meteors shooting athwart of the sky—of hissing shells."[39]

Despite these spectacular demonstrations, the damage inflicted by the incoming missiles combined with the summer's drought took a toll

Sara Pryor, from a miniature painted in Rome about a decade before the siege of Petersburg. Mrs. Roger A. Pryor, *Reminiscences of Peace and War* (New York: Macmillan, 1904), frontispiece.

on the shrinking wallets and stomachs of Petersburg's citizens. "For five miles around the country is but one camp," Claiborne wrote his wife in late July; "you have no conception of it—and every thing to eat is or will soon be consumed." Already expensive, the cost of food continued to rise during the summer as the siege persisted. At the local farmers' market, tomatoes sold for $5 per quart, small green corn nubbins for $6 per dozen, and eggs for $10 a dozen. Even with such outrageous prices, most residents found ways of coping. Some sent their children to pick up corn that had spilled from the quartermasters' bags. The Common Council continually increased aid to the city's poorest residents, hoping to alleviate their increasingly dire conditions. Sara Pryor insisted that her family was never forced to eat rats, mice, or mule meat (as she suggested many of the black residents were doing). Instead, they subsisted on peas, bread, and sorghum and managed to buy a little milk.[40]

By early July, the city had not seen a drop of rain in seven weeks while temperatures soared to well above 100 degrees on several occasions. Claiborne described a summer of "heat not often equaled at this latitude— dust such as has never been surpassed anywhere—a dried and parched vegetation." Not only did the residents worry that their gardens would fail to produce, but the town also had begun to experience an increase in robberies. The local newspaper reported that vegetables, hogs, cows, calves, watermelons, flour, bacon, lard, and poultry had all become common targets for criminals. Two African Americans, one a slave and the other a free woman, were found guilty of stealing sugar from the Confederate army.

But thievery was a two-way street. Hungry soldiers frequently stole from residents' gardens and pilfered from people in the woods and fields surrounding the city. "The soldiers, it appears, go every where & like the locusts of Egypt eat everything—even blackberries," complained Charles Campbell on July 21, after he had taken his children in search of the ripe summer fruit. "Between the drought & the soldiers," he observed, "there is a bad prospect of getting vegetables to live on."[41]

For all his grumbling about food, neither Campbell nor any of the other residents who left written accounts indicated that they felt demoralized by the siege or lost faith in the Confederate cause. Instead, after the initial shock of bombardment in mid-June, residents' fear turned to anger, and their support for Lee's Army of Northern Virginia and the Confederacy surged.[42] Rumors that Grant was to storm and torch the city on July 4, the anniversary of Vicksburg's surrender the previous year, especially fueled resistance among the townspeople. "The proposition that Grant is going to capture Petersburg on the 4th seems to take for granted that Gen. Lee will be quite passive in the case," Campbell optimistically declared. But the day came and went with little more than the usual shelling, yet again reassuring residents that their army could protect them. Days later Confederate assistant secretary of war John Tyler Jr. observed the town folks' strong resolve, declaring that the "inhabitants prefer that their houses should be destroyed sooner than surrender, and have quite made up their minds to the result. I have never known a braver or more patriotic people." Had they read northern accounts confirming that the Federal artillery were purposely firing on the city's steeples in celebration of July 4th, their determination might have been further impassioned.[43]

Throughout the stifling summer, many civilians continued to donate time and aid to the Confederate soldiers in their midst. Some sent their cows to the Fairgrounds Hospital to graze so that the wounded soldiers might have fresh milk. The children of Anderson's Seminary spent their days cutting strips of newspaper and stitching on wooden handles to craft fly fans for the invalid soldiers. Even with the market's exorbitant prices, the city's wealthier women showered General Lee with gifts, including a nice set of shirts, vegetables, bread, milk, ice cream, and a peach—the first he had seen in two years. The most tenacious testimonial of support, however, came from Dr. Claiborne. In a letter to his wife on July 14, he declared that if the siege continued through winter, "this will be a city of desolation." But that would not matter because "happy in ruins, yet saved in honor, will she be in comparison with Norfolk, Vicksburg, and New

Orleans." He claimed not to have heard one cry for peace but, rather, for "war—blood for blood—let us perish and our little ones—but let the fight go on." "I for one," he declared, "am ready to see the last brick thrown down rather than the city surrender."[44]

Confederates' disgust with what they considered uncivilized Union tactics around Petersburg continued unabated. Even as Maj. Gen. David Hunter commenced raids against Lynchburg and in the Shenandoah Valley and as General Sherman clashed with Gen. John Bell Hood on the outskirts of Atlanta, Brig. Gen. Henry A. Wise complained that "Grant is doing the meanest sort of fighting" around Petersburg. "He is shelling this city now with barbarous inhumanity, without regard to age or sex, God or man." Noting that women and children were the chief targets of Grant's shells, a Richmond woman sarcastically rejoined, "But what matters it? They are rebels—what difference does it make about their lives or limbs?" Lest they think otherwise, the *Richmond Enquirer* reminded northerners that "the disturbing of women and children, does not conquer soldiers in the field."[45]

Confederate soldiers and officers repeatedly praised the civilians, women in particular, for their stoic behavior in the face of constant enemy fire. Surgeon Welch informed his wife that he often encountered "young ladies sitting on their porches reading quietly while shells were occasionally bursting near by." Brig. Gen. Edward Porter Alexander recalled similarly that "the citizens got accustomed to the shells in a surprising way. I have seen ladies walking the streets, & on their front porches, when, about once in ten minutes, a shell would fall somewhere." Lee's artillery chief William Nelson Pendleton observed that the "people of the place, ladies and all, bear this outrage upon their pleasant homes with great fortitude and dignity." Yet another soldier marveled at seeing "ladies pass coolly along the streets as though nothing unusual was transpiring while the 160-pound shells were howling like hawks of perdition through the smoky air and busting in the very heart of the city."[46] Such defiance implied white women's confidence that Lee's army would not allow their city to be taken. Moreover, their behavior seems to have reassured Confederate men of their womenfolk's steadfast belief in the cause.[47]

Just as Union shells did not differentiate between Confederate combatants and noncombatants, neither did they discriminate by race. The city's enslaved population had no choice as to whether to flee the city or to endure the bombardment. Former slave Fanny Berry recalled that along with her master, "we left Petersburg when de shellin' commenced an' went to

Pamplin in box cars, gettin' out of de way." "Dem were scared times too," she recollected, "cause you looked to be kilt any minute by stray bullets." Others were not so lucky to escape the ravages of shells. By late July, at least two slaves had been killed by the projectiles and another four were severely wounded. Members of Petersburg's free black community likewise had little to no choice in protecting themselves. Some managed to move their families west out of town, where they hollowed out small spaces from the earth in which to live. But most of the free African American community resided on the eastern edges of town in neighborhoods especially prone to shelling, enduring it as best as possible.[48]

Even with the continual threat of bombardment, many of Petersburg's black residents did not perceive northern soldiers as uncivilized barbarians.[49] Slaves had run away from their masters to Union lines throughout the war, evidenced by frequent advertisements from frustrated owners in the local newspapers, and the siege created even more such opportunities.[50] Black refugees sought primarily to escape bondage but frequently provided invaluable intelligence to the Union army. "We have received from a detachment of the Cavalry Corps . . . near Reams' Station, a party of contrabands, fifteen in number—men, women, and children," reported Col. George H. Sharpe. Although they did not provide much new intelligence, they confirmed that Maj. Gen. George E. Pickett remained in town and that General Beauregard had moved his headquarters closer to General Lee's. Intelligence was not the only service they rendered: by mid-July, Grant ordered that "every negro that comes in is now taken into service, the best specimens physically being enlisted in companies already organized, and the others are employed as laborers in some of the departments or sent north."[51]

Some slaves who elected not to flee likewise acted as informants. Such was the case with an unidentified slave belonging to James Ennis, a farmer residing five miles outside Petersburg. After a week of hauling wheat into the city, the slave reported to Union officials that Confederates were repairing the Weldon Railroad and that trains arrived and departed the city day and night. Protecting one's family often served as the primary motivation for slaves to put themselves in such a precarious situation. One such individual, in an effort to get his wife and family through the lines, provided Col. T. M. Bryan Jr. valuable intelligence. "I have promised him protection if he does," Bryan assured his superiors.[52]

Freedmen and freedwomen also shared valuable information with the Union army. A black woman living within sight of the railroad regularly

A War Thoroughfare

reported the movement of Confederate troops along the tracks to Federal officials. William Henry rode out of Petersburg in late June and was presumed by Confederates to be in search of stock feed. Instead, he headed for Union lines, where he reported that "he passed very few troops; that the main part of the enemy's force was withdrawn yesterday morning from the front of the Second and Sixth Corps," and on the location of General Lee's headquarters. Several days later, either Henry or another freedman identified by Union officials only as "our agent" returned from Petersburg reporting that the Weldon Railroad had been repaired and the first train had run the previous evening. The agent hastened to inform the U.S. soldiers that "the noncombatants are engaged ... in making willow baskets for the sharpshooters (probably fascines)" that would be filled with dirt.[53] Such reports confirmed what many Union soldiers believed: the city's white civilian population *was* directly involved in the war effort and thus should not be considered innocent victims.

Black families who sought the protection of the Federal army all too often discovered that many Union soldiers were not sympathetic to their plight; after all, most northern white men had not enlisted because of abolitionist sympathies.[54] African American women across the war's landscape were sometimes subject to physical assault from soldiers who viewed them as "the legitimate prey of lust." In South Carolina, for example, one northern missionary reported that "no colored woman or girl was safe from the brutal lusts of the [white] soldiers—and by soldiers I mean both officers and men." As historian Jacqueline Campbell points out, few African American women left any record of their treatment by the white troops, forcing historians to rely on testimony from white witnesses. One instance on the outskirts of Petersburg reveals that Union soldiers committed atrocities against black women during the siege. In midsummer, Col. George H. Sharpe "rejoiced" to report that supposed outrages committed upon white residents had not occurred but did admit "there were excesses with the negro women there." No doubt many black women were subjected to such abuse.[55]

Partial relief from the shelling, if not from the oppressive heat, came in late July for both white and black residents of the city. All is "quiet along our lines," Dr. Claiborne wrote his wife on July 27. "Fewer shot have been fired in the last three days since Lee's army came amongst us. I do not know what this unusual stillness bodes. It really seems strange to hear no cannon, no shell bursting and not puttering of musketry." Edmund Ruffin agreed that the shelling occurred at a slower pace than usual but noted rumors

CAROLINE E. JANNEY

from Union deserters that the enemy had begun mining under Confederate lines. Despite such an ominous report, the combination of empty stomachs and less-frequent shelling encouraged many of those who had pitched tents just outside the city to begin returning. Claiborne lamented that "some are returning to the city saying that they had as soon be killed by shell as to perish by starvation." He cautioned against such optimistic behavior, warning that "the foe is only sleeping." But news from Hood's army in Georgia buoyed morale. "If Sherman can be smashed out there," one resident wrote, "we shall be relieved here."[56]

Despite the alleged good news from Atlanta, Claiborne had been correct in distrusting the quiet along the lines. "A little after four in the morning the city was roused by the most awful thunder—like nothing I can imagine, except, perhaps, the sudden eruption of a volcano," recalled Sara Pryor. For nearly a month, the 48th Pennsylvania Infantry, a regiment from the northeastern coal regions of that state, had been tunneling under the Confederate line. On the morning of July 30, the Federals exploded 8,000 pounds of black powder that sent "fragments of earth . . . at once flying in every direction, making a rent in the lines of some thirty or forty yards." Simultaneously, Union batteries opened fire on the city, dropping between twenty and thirty shells per minute. For nearly two hours, the local paper reported, shells "fairly rained upon our streets." The townspeople, however, had not a clue as to what was happening. "Instantly the unhappy residents of the town poured into the street and out on the road," Pryor recollected, "anywhere to escape what we supposed to be an earthquake." Anne Banister remembered that "it seemed as if the very earth would open and swallow us up. Window panes were shattered and the whole air was filled with rumbling noises which terrified and deafened one. We could not hear each other when we spoke, the din was so great." "Could it be the end of all things?" she wondered. Despite the doomsday prediction, the only civilian casualty proved to be Robert Green, chief engineer of the city's fire department, whose finger was cut off by a shell.[57]

While the Crater explosion was shocking in itself, the Army of Northern Virginia's first encounter with United States Colored Troops was perhaps even more alarming for both Confederate soldiers and Petersburg's civilians. "The poor wretches advanced shouting, 'No quarter! Remember Fort Pillow!'" recollected soldier Joseph Waddell. Petersburg resident and private in the 12th Virginia Henry Bird remembered similarly: "The negros' charging cry of 'no quarter' was met with a stern reply of 'amen,'" wrote Bird, "and without firing a single shot we closed with them. . . . Southern

A War Thoroughfare

bayonets dripped with blood and after a brief but bitter struggle the works were ours." Confederate general Edward Porter Alexander later reported that "some of the Negro prisoners, who were originally allowed to surrender by some soldiers, were afterward shot by others, & there was, without a doubt, a great deal of unnecessary killing of them."[58]

In town, some white residents exhibited paternalistic pity toward the African American soldiers. Dr. Claiborne wrote his wife that in the "hand to hand fight with a negro Brigade," the "poor Blacks suffered dreadfully." Others sought reassurance that the slaves in their midst would remain loyal to their white masters. One popular story that circulated throughout the town and the entire South told of a slave who had run away from Alabama (or Mississippi), joined the Union army, and subsequently recognized his former master during the battle at the Crater. Allegedly, the soldier dropped his musket and ran to his former master during the thickest of fighting, shouting, "You shall not hurt my young Master!" Miraculously, the former slave reached the Confederate soldier just in time to deflect a bullet. Numerous former slaves were killed in battle that day, but according to popular Confederate accounts, this particular slave was spared because of his rediscovered loyalty to his master.[59]

Many townspeople rejected this faithful slave myth, instead revealing the intensity of their animosity toward the African American troops. When Lt. Gen. Ambrose Powell Hill paraded a mixed group of black and white prisoners from the Crater through the city, residents rushed to their windows and doors and into the streets to witness the scene. One white Union officer remembered, "We were assailed by a volley of abuse from men, women, and children that exceeded anything of the kind that I ever heard." As the prisoners crossed onto Merchant Island in the Appomattox River, the city's white men "berated the Federals for arming their slaves against them." Noting that the white officers and black soldiers had been confined together, the *Petersburg Daily Express* sarcastically quipped, "Our authorities will not be so cruel as to separate such bosom and deeply sympathizing friends in their captivity."[60] In the absence of direct evidence from Petersburg's slaves and freedpeople, one can only imagine how they felt during those hot August days.

The weeks after the Union's failed attack at the Crater witnessed a slackening pace of Union firing and growing confidence among Confederates throughout Virginia.[61] The *Richmond Enquirer* reported that "the occasional shelling of the city has lately only accumulated bricks and other building materials in the streets, without seriously harming anybody." Still, shells had done considerable damage to civilian property, "smashing into smithereens stout cornices and fragile ornaments, making all furniture a mass of fragments, and stripping the walls to the lattice and joints." Pantries had been invaded, libraries demolished, and children left "hungry from the lack of intellectual pabulum." But Lee and his army had not given up Petersburg and thus continued to protect Richmond. From his residence just west of the besieged city, Edmund Ruffin wrote that the Union could and probably would "very effectually destroy the principal part of the town" but insisted this would "not bring them nearer to the object of capturing the town" or "induce its surrender." He had not heard "of a voice being raised, or a secret wish entertained" for surrender from Bessie Callender, her sister Lottie Ruffin, or their mother. The *Staunton Vindicator* reported that Grant was sending away his troops and "removing his heavy guns from the front," indicating "an evacuation of his present position." The paper optimistically predicted that "there will be no more fighting of any magnitude around Petersburg. The next grand battle between Lee and Grant may probably be fought on northern soil." But should Grant elect to remain outside the city, the *Vindicator* remained confident that he would "find Gen. Lee, as ever, ready to foil him at every point."[62]

Contrary to the Confederate confidence, in mid-August the Union guns commenced shelling Petersburg more intensely than in June or July. "Yesterday morning, between nine and eleven o'clock, shells were sent to the number of some fifty or sixty," a Richmond paper reported, hastening to add that "the citizens are the only sufferers, the army being well supplied." The renewed bombings claimed the lives of two more residents near the Old Market, and a woman in the Old Market district was struck by a shell fragment that ripped her arm from its socket.[63] Dr. Claiborne reassured his wife that such deaths were infrequent but remained especially concerned about the numbing effect the continual shelling was having on the residents. "Many people have become so used to the danger that they go about the streets as if nothing was wrong. . . . I fear more accidents will happen now than formerly," he wrote. Six days later, upon hearing that Atlanta had capitulated to Sherman, he remained confident that Petersburg would not fall because it was protected by the Confederacy's foremost hero, Robert E. Lee. "Our supplies are abundant and our hopes high," he informed his wife.[64]

The Union artillery's unrelenting bombardment and the exodus of civilians continued throughout the autumn.[65] In early October, rumors that the city was to be evacuated prompted the frenzied departure of many

A War Thoroughfare

families. And yet some citizens appear to have adjusted to the disruptions of war by attempting to resurrect a sense of normality in their lives. Several schools reopened in the southern neighborhoods of the city, passenger trains on Southside and the Petersburg and Richmond Railroads resumed their schedules, and the library lent books to the city's avid readers despite the damage to the periodicals room. Regular mail and telegraph service recommenced, and the city water system remained in operation. Towns-people likewise managed to find time for entertainment, enjoying a vocal and instrumental concert for the benefit of the city's free schools and a traveling minstrel show. Weddings continued as well, Sgt. R. P. Scarbrough recounting that "a great many of the soldiers are marrying around and in Petersburg, some for life, some for the war and some for one winter only."[66]

The cooler temperatures of November brought both the news of Lincoln's reelection and a hiatus in the shelling for the first time in more than four months. "Grant agreed to cease shelling the city if General Lee would agree to keep all government property out of it," Spencer Welch reported to his wife. Grateful that the bombardment had slackened, a local news-paper reported that at least 90,000 shells had been thrown into the city, between fifteen and twenty persons had been killed, and approximately double that number were wounded. In the surrounding countryside, the deep boom of the artillery had been superseded by the clatter of axes as troops built shelters for the impending winter. Many residents soon determined it was safe to move back into town. Bessie Callender and her family returned permanently to their home on Marshall Street, pleasantly surprised to find that it had not been touched by shells. But Grant's policy of strangling the city was succeeding as food and supplies remained incredibly scarce, the prices now higher than in Richmond. Callender splurged and bought rough country shoes at the Old Market for $200, "with leather strings and no lining for the children, Mammy, [and] Mary our cook."[67]

As feeding the mouths of their hungry children became an increasing problem, Petersburg residents began to ponder the merits of maintaining their slaves. In August, John Claiborne had hoped that at least three of his slaves would run away. "I sincerely wish that she [Rachel] and Anniss and Lizzie would go to the yankees voluntarily and relive me of their care and responsibility of further providing for them," he had written his wife. By September, he had elected to keep one slave woman, Fanny, who washed and mended for him, but freed the others to relieve some of his burden. Three months later, he wrote to Sara that he was considering sending her two female slaves so that she might hire them out for extra cash.

Ultimately, he decided against sending any male slaves, as he believed he could get higher prices for their labor from the Confederate government. "I can probably get from 40 to 80 dolrs. per month for the boys and have them fed—with privilege of buying clothes at Gov. prices," he wrote. He noted that he would not "be surprised at their being purchased and eventually freed [by the Confederate government]. I think the days of slavery are numbered in this State if not in the Confederacy—and that is another reason why I would not take more trouble to keep mine than is required by duty."[68]

During the winter months, cold rains lashed the city in what seemed a much-delayed response to the parched summer. The rain-soaked streets and roads were only part of the misery. Hundreds of acres around the city had been stripped of tree and shrub, creating a shortage of firewood for the winter. By January, citizens could only acquire wood on order from the military, limiting some families to one fire in the house. Food was even scarcer. The Callenders managed to subsist on a dinner of bacon that Bessie had cured and a quantity of peas, a little rice, and stewed dried applies sweetened with sorghum. She was fortunate enough to have six hogs killed and put in the smoke house to cure, but given the dire straits of food in the city, she adamantly refused to give any to the quartermaster for the army. For the poor, the situation was predictably much worse. The First Baptist Church opened a soup house to provide for the destitute, sometimes feeding more than 600 famished people a day. One resident recalled that "flocks of pigeons would follow the children who were eating bread and crackers." But the pigeons soon disappeared, having become food themselves.[69]

Bessie Callender's reluctance to share her food with the army did not indicate a damping of faith in the Confederacy. Indeed, she chose to reveal her support in other ways. Several soldiers kept their clothes at Callender's home rather than in their tents. Along with her slaves, Bessie washed, ironed, and mended the garments. She likewise helped at the local hospitals, preparing lemonade for the invalid soldiers but also tending to the wounded men and assisting with an occasional amputation. And Bessie was not alone in her continued allegiance to the Confederate cause. In December, the city's fathers voted to provide $12,000 to the 12th Virginia Infantry so that the men might purchase shoes. The owner of Jarratt's Hotel offered free meals to soldiers in want of food. Town residents raised funds to purchase a new mount for Brig. Gen. David A. Weisiger, "commander of an infantry brigade in which many Petersburg sons served." By early January, residents had subscribed between $35,000 and $40,000 (of inflated currency) to furnish the soldiers with a New Year's dinner, and the Common Council appropriated another $2,000 to furnish thirty pairs of shoes for Company E of the 3rd Virginia Infantry. Maj. Gen. John B. Gordon reported that "there was scarcely a home within its corporate limits that was not open to the sick and wounded of Lee's army. Its patriotic citizens denied themselves all luxuries and almost actual necessaries in order to feed and strengthen the hungry fighters in the trenches."[70]

On March 9, 1865, Dr. Claiborne reported to his wife that Petersburg had not been evacuated. The "people seem pretty cheerful," as did the soldiers, even though rations remained small and desertions were frequent. Still, the citizenry continued to contribute "very freely of their means both in provisions and money." On March 25, the first major military action of the spring commenced when Lee attacked Fort Stedman. The following day, Claiborne assured his wife yet again that the "people seem to be cheerful and hoping for the best." But as Lee and Grant's forces clashed south of the city at the battle of Five Forks on April 1, few civilians knew what was happening beyond the siege lines. All of that was about to change. At ten o'clock that evening, "nearly 150 Union cannon opened from positions east, south, and southwest of the city." Three hours later, the firing abated and an uncomfortable silence fell over the region.[71]

The following day, General Lee wrote Secretary of War John C. Breckinridge that it was now "absolutely necessary that we should abandon our position tonight or run the risk of being cut off in the morning." By midnight, even if they still had faith in Lee and his army, many of Petersburg's residents were bracing for the worst. Bombproofs had been reinforced and whiskey distributed among the residents to calm nerves. At 4:40 A.M., Grant's offensive began in earnest. Bessie Callender remembered that "it was four o'clock in the morning when some soldiers, running, came across our yard." By 10:40 A.M., Lee had decided to evacuate the city, ordering his troops to set the tobacco warehouses on fire as they fled. Early on the morning of April 3, the Army of the Potomac marched into Petersburg as the mayor and two members of the Common Council waited to surrender. Not long thereafter, the United States flag was unfurled above the Cockade City.[72] For months the town's citizens had endured and come to expect the shrill whistle of a shell or the crack of a musket. But "the stillness that settled down upon us after this was appalling!" Marie Morrison later declared.[73]

Certainly not all of Petersburg's residents felt the same overwhelming sense of loss and defeat. As the Union soldiers marched into town on

April 3, the city's African American residents emerged from their shelters and homes. They crowded into the streets, some grasping the hands of Union soldiers and singing praises of the triumphant army. "Exclamations of wonder and astonishment were heard constantly, as something strange or new met their gaze. And the colored troops, especially, came in for a large share of attention," reported one northern paper. Union soldiers likewise recounted the "enthusiastic welcome given to the Yanks by the negroes." Such devotion to the Union cause was shown "by the exertions they made to save the bridge across the Appomattox, which had been fired by the retreating rebels. Great credit is due them for quenching the flames."[74]

As they marched into the surrendered town, Federal soldiers took stock of the damage rendered by the ten-month bombardment. In later years, William Endicott of the 10th Massachusetts Battery recollected that he and his comrades "were pleased to see that many of the houses had great gaps in their walls, made by the passage of our shells." "We were fortunate enough to pass by the church [actually the courthouse] whose clock it was the fashion of our men to set their watches . . . until a three-inch shot tore through it." "The citizens looked rather black as we pointed up to it," he recalled, "but our guard only laughed." Most Unionists writing in 1865, however, were quick to dispel notions that the army had egregiously attacked innocent civilians or ravaged the city. One paper reported that "the city presents a very cleanly and respectable appearance," except for the lower portion of the city, which had been injured by shot and shell the previous summer. "Not so much injury has been done to the place by our artillery," noted soldiers from the 37th Wisconsin Infantry and the 8th Michigan Veteran Volunteers (although a Union survey of the city that summer would count 625 structures that had been damaged). The soldiers noted that the upper and western part of the town had been scarcely touched and asserted that "business in that part of the town has gone on apparently as usual, only with a necessarily diminished prosperity." "Not many dwelling houses in that region have been touched," they claimed. "The greatest real damage to the City," the Federals were quick to point out, "was done by the Confederate soldiers."[75]

In the coming weeks and months, northerners would describe and document the physical destruction of the city and countryside, prompting curious visitors to stream to the Cockade City. But most Federals maintained that Confederate accounts vastly overestimated the number of civilian casualties. The *New York Herald* sharply dismissed reports from Richmond newspapers alleging that inhabitants had been injured by shells as "wholly without foundation." In fact, the paper claimed that not a single white person had been slain.[76] While there are no accurate statistics, evidence suggests that between six and twenty civilians had been killed and at least nine others severely injured by the shells. Given the length of the bombardment, this number may seem low—a fact one wartime newspaper suggested was "a special blessing from Providence." But it surpassed the number killed during the December 1862 bombardment of Fredericksburg (estimated by historian George Rable as "probably no more than four people") and was in line with the estimate that fewer than twelve citizens perished during the six-week siege of Vicksburg.[77] The precise number of civilian deaths will never be known, but the body count did not preoccupy Confederates. The fact that there were any confirmed their assumptions about their ruthless and uncivilized foe.

Although they laid down their guns and agreed to take oaths of loyalty in the spring of 1865, most white Petersburgers continued to harbor deep and painful memories of the horrors through which they had lived. Years later they vividly recalled the infernal noise of screaming shells and the panic they felt as they rushed to extinguish flames that seemed destined to engulf the town. They recounted their frenzied efforts to slip into bombproofs at a moment's notice and never forgot the sheer terror of the morning the mine exploded creating the infamous Crater.[78] And they remembered that hundreds of buildings, including numerous homes and most of the city's churches, had been damaged or destroyed by Union shells and that a number of noncombatants, white and black, women and children, had become casualties.[79]

Northerners and some later historians insisted that during the Civil War, military force had not been employed against the enemy's noncombatant population, but the bombardment of the city confirmed Confederates' convictions of Yankee barbarity. White southerners always would believe that the enemy had subjected them to inhumane and uncivilized treatment. Perhaps most important, these tales of Yankee atrocities would become a powerful weapon in the coming years as northerners and southerners fought the postwar battle over the war's memory. Passed down for generations by Petersburg's white residents, stories of the Union's malevolence helped foster a continued pride and reverence for the city's Confederate past and hindered efforts of sectional reconciliation.[80]

CAROLINE E. JANNEY

The author would like to thank Gary W. Gallagher, Andrew Janney, and Robert Janney for their helpful comments and careful reading of this essay, as well as James H. Blankenship Jr. and Emmanuel Dabney at Petersburg National Battlefield for their assistance with sources.

1. Charles Campbell Diary, June 17, July 2, 3, 1864, Special Collections, College of William and Mary, Williamsburg, Va. (item hereafter cited as CCD without reference to repository); *New York Herald*, April 6, 1865; John Claiborne to his wife, Sarah Alston Claiborne, July 11, 1864, Letters of John Herbert Claiborne, 1864–1865, accession #3633, Albert and Shirley Small Special Collections Library, University of Virginia, Charlottesville (repository hereafter cited as UVA; all letters from Claiborne are in this collection).

2. Historians have distinguished between total and hard war. On total war, see Mark E. Neely Jr., "Was the Civil War a Total War?" *Civil War History* 37 (March 1991): 5–28; Charles Royster, *The Destructive War: William Tecumseh Sherman, Stonewall Jackson, and the Americans* (New York: Knopf, 1991); Lance Janda, "Shutting the Gates of Mercy: The American Origins of Total War, 1860–1880," *Journal of Military History* 59 (January 1995): 7–26; and Jacqueline Glass Campbell, *When Sherman Marched North from the Sea: Resistance on the Confederate Home Front* (Chapel Hill: University of North Carolina Press, 2003), 55–56. On hard war, see Mark Grimsley, *The Hard Hand of War: Union Military Policy toward Southern Civilians, 1861–1865* (New York: Cambridge University Press, 1995), and Grimsley, "Conciliation and Its Failure, 1861–1862," *Civil War History* 39 (December 1993): 317–35.

3. For historians who concentrate primarily on Sherman and Sheridan, see Neely, "Was the Civil War a Total War?"; Campbell, *When Sherman Marched North*; Royster, *Destructive War*; and John Bennett Walters, *Merchant of Terror: General Sherman and Total War* (New York: Bobbs Merrill, 1973).

4. For the argument that common suffering on the home front strengthened rather than diminished Confederate resolve, see Gary W. Gallagher, *The Confederate War* (Cambridge, Mass.: Harvard University Press, 1997); William A. Blair, *Virginia's Private War: Feeding Body and Soul in the Confederacy, 1861–1865* (New York: Oxford University Press, 1998); Campbell, *When Sherman Marched North*; and William A. Blair, "Barbarians at Fredericksburg's Gate: The Impact of the Union Army on Civilians," in *The Fredericksburg Campaign: Decision on the Rappahannock*, ed. Gary W. Gallagher (Chapel Hill: University of North Carolina Press, 1995), 142–70.

5. Noah Andre Trudeau, *The Last Citadel: Petersburg, Virginia, June 1864–April 1865* (Boston: Little, Brown, 1991), 4; Heidi Campbell-Shoaf, "Life in the Trap," *Civil War Times*, August 2004, 36; A. Wilson Greene, *Civil War Petersburg: Confederate City in the Crucible of War* (Charlottesville: University of Virginia Press, 2006), 8; *Chicago Tribune*, June 23, 1864; James G. Scott and Edward A. Wyatt IV, *Petersburg's Story: A History* (Petersburg, Va.: Titmus Optical Company, 1960), 171; *New York Herald*, June 18, 1864. To protect such a vital rail center, in the summer of 1862 Confederates constructed a ten-mile line of fortifications below the Appomattox River east, south, and west of the city complete with fifty-five artillery batteries.

6. Scott and Wyatt, *Petersburg's Story*, 172; Campbell-Shoaf, "Life in the Trap," 38; Sara Rice Pryor, *Reminiscences of Peace and War* (1908; reprint, Freeport, N.Y.: Books for Library Press, 1970), 252; William D. Henderson, *Petersburg in the Civil War: War at the Door* (Lynchburg, Va.: H. E. Howard, 1988), 101; Bessie Callender Papers, "Personal Recollections of the Civil War," Petersburg National Battlefield, Petersburg, Va. (item hereafter cited as Callender, "Recollections," without reference to repository).

7. Henderson, *War at the Door*, 101–2; Scott and Wyatt, *Petersburg's Story*, 170; Campbell-Shoaf, "Life in the Trap," 38; *The Cockade City of Union: Petersburg, Virginia* (n.p.: n.p., 1906), 3.

8. Claiborne to wife, June 9, 1864, UVA; Henderson, *War at the Door*, 108–10; Greene, *Civil War Petersburg*, 177–80; Anne E. Banister, "Incidents in the Life of a Civil War Child, 1864–1865," unpaginated manuscript, accession #4792, UVA.

9. Callender, "Recollections," 16; *Petersburg Daily Express*, June 9, 10, 1864; Banister, *Incidents*.

10. Claiborne to wife, June 12, 1864, UVA; CCD, June 15, 1864.

11. *Richmond Enquirer*, June 21, 1864; CCD, June 16, 17, 1864; Pryor, *Reminiscences*, 279; Trudeau, *Last Citadel*, 91.

12. CCD, June 18, 1864; John C. Waugh, *Surviving the Confederacy: Rebellion, Ruin, and Recovery—Roger and Sara Pryor during the Civil War* (New York: Harcourt, 2002), 219; CCD, June 18, 1864; Whitehorn quoted in Greene, *Civil War Petersburg*, 188.

13. Callender, "Recollections," 18; Greene, *Civil War Petersburg*, 188.

14. According to James H. Blankenship Jr., historian at Petersburg National Battlefield, the shells most likely came from Union siege guns (anything larger than a 20-pounder Parrott), all located to the east of the city. The exact locations of the guns, however, are unknown.

15. *Charleston Mercury*, June 23, 1864.

16. Henderson, *War at the Door*, 115; Waugh, *Surviving*, 220–22; Callender, "Recollections," 17–18; Pryor, *Reminiscences*, 279–80.

17. For those who argue against a Union policy of total war, see Neely, "Was the Civil War a Total War?" 27; Grimsley, *Hard Hand of War*, 2–5; and Campbell, *When Sherman Marched North*, 55–56. For the argument that the Union did employ total war, see Janda, "Shutting the Gates of Mercy."

18. Georgiana Freeman Gholson Walker, *Private Journal of Georgia Freeman Walker, 1862–1865: With Selections from the Post-War Years, 1865–1876*, ed. Dwight F. Henderson (Tuscaloosa, Ala.: Confederate Publishing, 1963), 106, accessed through the North American Women's Letters and Diaries Database, http://alexanderstreet.com/products /nwld.htm (hereafter cited as NAWLD); *Charleston Mercury*, June 23, 1864.

19. Section 1, Article 19, of the Lieber Code (prepared by Francis Lieber and promulgated as General Orders No. 100 by President Lincoln in 1863) stated that "Commanders, whenever admissible, inform the enemy of their intention to bombard a place, so that the noncombatants, and especially the women and children, may be removed before the bombardment commences. But it is no infraction of the common law of war to omit thus to inform the enemy. Surprise may be a necessity" (U.S. War Department, *The War of the Rebellion: A Compilation of the Official Records of the Union*

and Confederate Armies, 127 vols., index, and atlas [Washington, D.C.: Government Printing Office, 1880–1901], ser. 3, 3:150 [hereafter cited as *OR*]).

20. Pryor, *Reminiscences*, 279; Catherine Ann Devereux Edmondston, *"Journal of a Secesh Lady": The Diary of Catherine Ann Devereux Edmondston, 1860–1866*, ed. Beth Gilbert Crabtree and James W. Patton (1979; reprint, Raleigh, N.C.: Division of Archives and History, Department of Cultural Resources, 1995), 579 (entry for June 18, 1864); Edmund Ruffin, *The Diary of Edmund Ruffin*, ed. William Kauffman Scarborough, 3 vols. (Baton Rouge: Louisiana State University Press, 1972–89), 3:468 (entry for June 18, 1864); *Richmond Enquirer*, July 4, 1864, reprinted in *New York Times*, July 7, 1864; *Charleston Mercury*, June 23, 1864.

21. *OR*, ser. 1, 40(2):27; *Philadelphia Press*, June 27, 1864; *Agitator* (Wellsboro, Pa.), June 29, 1864; *OR*, ser. 1, 40(3):76, 132.

22. *OR*, ser. 1, 40(2):239, 423–25, 515.

23. Edward P. Weston, ed., *The Northern Monthly: A Magazine of Original Literature and Military Affairs* (Portland, Me.: Bailey and Noyes, 1864), 429; *OR*, ser. 1, 42(2):584, 830; L. A. Furney, ed., *Reminiscences of the War of the Rebellion, 1861–1865 by Bvt-Maj. Jacob Roemer* (Flushing, N.Y.: Estate of Jacob Roemer, 1897), 228; Ulysses S. Grant, *The Papers of Ulysses S. Grant*, ed. John Y. Simon and others, 32 vols. to date (Carbondale: Southern Illinois University Press, 1967–), 11:164.

24. *New York Times* quoted in *Chicago Tribune*, June 23, 1864. For examples of newspapers ignoring the shelling of civilians or justifying it as a military necessity, see the *Democratic Watchman*, *Huntington Globe*, *New York Herald*, *Tioga County (Pa.) Agitator*, and *Erie (Pa.) Observer*, June–October 1864.

25. *Philadelphia Press*, June 25, 1864.

26. *New York Herald* quoted in *Chicago Tribune*, July 1, 1864; *New York Herald*, June 30, July 7, 1864; *Philadelphia Press*, June 29, July 8, 1864. For discussion of southern white women deviating from accepted gender roles in the postwar period, see Nina Silber, *The Romance of Reunion: Northerners and the South, 1865–1900* (Chapel Hill: University of North Carolina Press, 1993), 19.

27. *Philadelphia Press*, June 25, 1864.

28. CCD, June 20, 25, 1864.

29. Petersburg Common Council Minutes (hereafter cited as PCCM), June 20, 1864, Office of the Clerk of City Council, City of Petersburg, Va.

30. CCD, June 17, 1864; Callender, "Recollections," 18; Ruffin, *Diary*, 3:472 (entry for June 22, 1864); Edmondston, *"Journal of a Secesh Lady,"* 579 (entry for June 19, 1864). Charlotte "Lottie" Ruffin eventually returned to be with her sister.

31. Claiborne to wife, July 11, 1864, UVA; CCD, June 19, July 4, 13, 14, 1864; Callender, "Recollections," 22; Trudeau, *Last Citadel*, 92; Henderson, *War at the Door*, 128.

32. Edmondston, *"Journal of a Secesh Lady,"* 597 (entry for July 30, 1864); CCD, July 11, 1864; Claiborne to wife, July 14, 1864, UVA.

33. *New York Herald*, June 26, 1864; Claiborne to wife, July 11, 1864, UVA; CCD, June 22, 29, 1864.

34. Henderson, *War at the Door*, 126; Banister, *Incidents*; CCD, June 27, July 3, 6, 1864. According to James Blankenship, the shells in range of the Banister home proba-

bly did not come from Fort Stedman, where Federals only had 12-pounder Napoleons whose range was less than a mile. The 30-pounder Parrotts at former Confederate Battery No. 5 (renamed Battery No. 4 when the Union re-faced it) might have been in range of High Street.

35. *OR*, ser. 1, 40(3):436; Claiborne to wife, July 27, 1864, UVA; Waugh, *Surviving*, 222–23; Pryor, *Reminiscences*, 280–81; Edward Porter Alexander, *Fighting for the Confederacy: The Personal Recollections of General Edward Porter Alexander*, ed. Gary W. Gallagher (Chapel Hill: University of North Carolina Press, 1989), 474.

36. Callender, "Recollections," 19; Trudeau, *Last Citadel*, 291; CCD, July 5, 1864; Henderson, *War at the Door*, 119; Waugh, *Surviving*, 222.

37. Richard J. Johnson to "Cousin," July 14, 1864, from Petersburg, accession #4695, UVA; CCD, July 9, 12, 1864; Edmondston, *"Journal of a Secesh Lady,"* 587 (entry for July 11, 1864); Claiborne to wife, July 17, 1864, UVA; Confederate officer quoted in Trudeau, *Last Citadel*, 91.

38. Greene, *Civil War Petersburg*, 221; Spencer Glasgow Welch, *A Confederate Surgeon's Letters to His Wife* (New York: Neale, 1911), 127 (entry for July 6, 1864), accessed through the American Civil War: Letters and Diaries Database, http://www.alexander street2.com/cwldlive/index.html (hereafter cited as ACWLD); *Charleston Mercury*, June 23, 1864; CCD, June 26, 30, July 7, 22, 1864.

39. Pryor, *Reminiscences*, 282; Claiborne to wife, September 4, 1864, UVA; *New York Herald*, August 2, 1864.

40. Claiborne to wife, July 21, 1864, UVA; *Petersburg Daily Express*, July 23, 1864; CCD, June 24, July 18, 1864; Greene, *Civil War Petersburg*, 173, 216; Pryor, *Reminiscences*, 283.

41. Claiborne to wife, July 11, 1864, UVA; *Petersburg Daily Express*, July 23, August 1, 1864; CCD, July 2, 21, 1864.

42. For a similar argument regarding Georgia and the Carolinas during Sherman's March, see Campbell, *When Sherman Marched North*, 6, 33. For a discussion of morale as dynamic, see James M. McPherson, *For Cause and Comrades: Why Men Fought in the Civil War* (New York: Oxford University Press, 1997), 88–89. For the argument that Robert E. Lee and his Army of Northern Virginia became the most important national institution in the Confederacy, see Gallagher, *Confederate War*, 8–12, 163.

43. CCD, July 3, 1864; Ruffin, *Diary*, 3:487–88 (entry for July 5, 1864); *OR*, ser. 1, 40(3):758; Lucy Muse Walton Fletcher Diary, July 3, 1864, Perkins Library, Duke University, Durham, N.C.; Weston, *Northern Monthly*, 429; Robert Tomes and Benjamin G. Smith, *The War with the South: A History of the Great American Rebellion*, 3 vols. (New York: Virtue and Yorston, 1867), 3:455.

44. CCD, June 25, July 14, 1864; J. William Jones, *Life and Letters of Robert E. Lee, Soldier and Man* (1906; reprint, Harrisonburg, Va.: Sprinkle, 1986), 318; Claiborne to wife, July 14, 17, 1864, UVA.

45. Wise quoted in Greene, *Civil War Petersburg*, 197; Judith White Brockenbrough McGuire, *Diary of a Southern Refugee during the War* (Richmond, Va.: J. W. Randolph, 1889), 304 (entry for July 24, 1864), NAWLD; *Richmond Enquirer*, July 4, 1864, reprinted in the *New York Times*, July 7, 1864.

46. Welch, *Confederate Surgeon's Letters*, July 6, 1864, 102; Alexander, *Fighting for the Confederacy*, 474; soldier quoted in Trudeau, *Last Citadel*, 92.

47. For the argument that most Confederate women lost faith in the war effort, see Drew Gilpin Faust, *Mothers of Invention: Women of the Slaveholding South in the American Civil War* (Chapel Hill: University of North Carolina Press, 1996), 234–47, and George C. Rable, *Civil Wars: Women and the Crisis of Southern Nationalism* (Urbana: University of Illinois Press, 1989), 73–90. For an interpretation that most Confederate women did not abandon nationalistic feelings, see Campbell, *When Sherman Marched North*, and Gallagher, *Confederate War*, esp. 75–80.

48. Federal Writers' Project, *Born in Slavery: Slave Narratives from the Federal Writers' Project, 1936–1938*, Virginia, interview of Mrs. Fannie Berry, February 26, 1937, 6; Greene, *Civil War Petersburg*, 195; Pryor, *Reminiscences*, 283; CCD, June 26, 1864.

49. On the varied response of African Americans to Union soldiers, see Campbell, *When Sherman Marched North*, 47; Leslie A. Schwalm, *A Hard Fight for We: Women's Transition from Slavery to Freedom in South Carolina* (Urbana: University of Illinois Press, 1997), 116–44; and Ira Berlin, Barbara J. Fields, Thavolia Glymph, Joseph P. Reidy, and Leslie S. Rowland, eds., *Freedom: A Documentary History of Emancipation, 1861–1867*, ser. 1, vol. 1, *The Destruction of Slavery* (New York: Cambridge University Press, 1985), 5–6, 9, 49–50.

50. On slaves making their way to Union lines and sharing information, see Glenn David Brasher, *The Peninsula Campaign and the Necessity of Emancipation: African Americans and the Fight for Freedom* (Chapel Hill: University of North Carolina Press, 2012). For examples of advertisements for runaways, see *Petersburg Daily Express*, October 24, 1861, January 18, May 9, 26, October 7, 1862, July 31, September 21, 1863, February 6, March 26, June 4, August 1, 30, 1864. The frequency of advertisements increased dramatically in the spring and summer of 1864.

51. *OR*, ser. 1, 40(3):334, (2):464.

52. *OR*, ser. 1, 40(3):75, 161. Despite his heroic attempt to aid the Union cause, John C. Babcock dismissed the man as "unintelligent" because he could "give not definite information of what he saw in Petersburg."

53. *OR*, ser. 1, 40(3):98, 133, (2):403–4.

54. Gary W. Gallagher, *The Union War* (Cambridge, Mass.: Harvard University Press, 2011), 75–118.

55. Northern missionary quoted in Campbell, *When Sherman Marched North*, 46; *OR*, ser. 1, 40(2):601; Schwalm, *Hard Fight for We*, 102–4. Sharpe dismissed the attacks, noting that "they rested upon evidence which I considered secondary and conflicting."

56. Claiborne to wife, July 14, 23, 27, 1864, UVA; CCD, July 16, 1864; Ruffin, *Diary*, 3:507, 512 (entries for July 21, 27, 1864).

57. *Charleston Mercury*, August 4, 1864; *Petersburg Daily Express*, August 1, 1864; Pryor, *Reminiscences*, 290; Banister, *Incidents*.

58. *Petersburg Daily Express*, August 1, 1864; diary of Joseph Addison Waddell, August 2, 1864, in *Valley of the Shadow: Two Communities in the American Civil War*, Virginia Center for Digital History, University of Virginia, http://valley.vcdh.virginia.edu; *Petersburg Daily Express*, August 1, 1864; Bird quoted in Greene, *Civil War Petersburg*, 208; Alexander, *Fighting for the Confederacy*, 462.

59. Claiborne to wife, July 30, 1864, UVA; *Staunton Vindicator*, August 12, 1864; Edmondston, *"Journal of a Secesh Lady,"* 600 (entry for August 3, 1864).

60. Union officer quoted in Greene, *Civil War Petersburg*, 209–10; *Petersburg Daily Express*, August 1, 1864.

61. *Erie (Pa.) Observer*, August 18, 1864. On the cessation of shelling, see *Petersburg Daily Express*, August 5, 1864. For a discussion of the plunge in northern morale because of the stalemate in Atlanta and failure at the Crater, see James M. McPherson, *Battle Cry of Freedom: The Civil War Era* (New York: Oxford University Press, 1988), 750–56.

62. *Richmond Enquirer* quoted in *New York Times*, August 15, 1864; Ruffin, *Diary*, 3:527 (entry for August 7, 1864); *Staunton Vindicator*, August 12, 19, 1864.

63. *Richmond Enquirer*, August 30, 1864; Claiborne to wife, August 28, 1864, UVA; John Bratton, *Letters of John Bratton to His Wife*, ed. Elizabeth Porcher Bratton (n.p.: privately published, 1942), 206, ACWLD; Greene, *Civil War Petersburg*, 215. Sara Pryor, for example, had endured enough and moved her family three miles outside the city to her brother-in-law's farm; see Pryor, *Reminiscences*, 296–97.

64. Claiborne to wife, August 28, September 4, 1864, UVA; CCD, August 16, 1865.

65. Ruffin, *Diary*, 3:566 (entry for September 15, 1864); McGuire, *Diary of a Southern Refugee*, 304; Claiborne to wife, September 18, 1864, UVA. For accounts of individuals leaving the city, see Greene, *Civil War Petersburg*, 215.

66. Ruffin, *Diary*, 3:599 (entry for October 8, 1864); John B. Jones, *A Rebel War Clerk's Diary*, 2 vols. (Philadelphia: Lippincott, 1866), 2:300 (entry for October 5, 1864); *Petersburg Daily Express*, October 17, November 9, 1864; Greene, *Civil War Petersburg*, 216–17; Scarbrough quoted in Campbell-Shoaf, "Life in the Trap," 41.

67. Welch, *Confederate Surgeon's Letters*, 114, 116 (November 3, 28, 1864); *Republican Compiler* (Gettysburg, Pa.), December 19, 1864; David Lane, *A Soldier's Diary: The Story of a Volunteer, 1862–1865* (Jackson, Miss.: privately published, 1905), 228 (entry for November 1864), ACWLD; Henderson, *War at the Door*, 131; Callender, "Recollections," 23.

68. Claiborne to wife, August 7, September 18, 21, December 21, 1864, UVA.

69. Callender, "Recollections," 23–27; Campbell-Shoaf, "Life in the Trap," 41.

70. Callender, "Recollections," 28, 35; PCCM, December 1, 1864, January 2, 1865; Greene, *Civil War Petersburg*, 224–25; *Charleston Mercury*, January 3, 1865; John B. Gordon, *Reminiscences of the Civil War* (1903; reprint, Baton Rouge: Louisiana State University Press, 1993), 414.

71. Claiborne to wife, March 9, 26, 1865, UVA; Greene, *Civil War Petersburg*, 243.

72. Jones, *Life and Letters of Robert E. Lee*, 363; Callender, "Recollections," 40; PCCM, April 2, 1865; Greene, *Civil War Petersburg*, 246, 252; *Chicago Tribune*, April 6, 1865.

73. Callender, "Recollections," 40; Marie Morrison, "Evacuation of Petersburg," April 3, 1902, accession #10839, UVA.

74. *New York Herald*, April 6, 1865; *Chicago Tribune*, April 6, 1865; *Grant's Petersburg Progress*, April 5, 1865.

75. John D. Billings, *The History of the Tenth Massachusetts Battery of Light Artillery in the War of the Rebellion* (Boston, Mass.: Arakelgan Press, 1909), 451; *Chicago Tribune*, April 6, 1865; *New York Herald*, April 6, 1865; *Grant's Petersburg Progress*, April 5, 1865; *New York Observer and Chronicle*, August 24, 1864.

CAROLINE E. JANNEY

76. *Grant's Petersburg Progress*, April 5, 1865; *New York Herald*, April 6, 1865.

77. Noah Trudeau argues that "although no comprehensive count was ever made, it seems that less than half a dozen citizens died as a result of the siege" (Trudeau, *Last Citadel*, 422). My estimate comes from compilations of accounts found in diaries, newspapers, and letters, as well as Edmund Ruffin's estimates as of November 1864 as described in Greene, *Civil War Petersburg*, 221. For example, one newspaper noted that "only four white persons have been killed, and not more than ten or twelve colored persons and twice as many of each race wounded" (*Wilmington Journal*, December 1, 1864). For numbers on civilian deaths in Fredericksburg, see George C. Rable, *Fredericksburg! Fredericksburg!* (Chapel Hill: University of North Carolina Press, 2002), 166. Stephen Davis discusses a Macon, Georgia, newspaper that compared figures from Petersburg and Atlanta, noting, in Davis's words, that the "low casualities represented a special blessing from Providence." He points out that estimates of the number of civilian deaths during the one-and-a-half-month bombardment of Atlanta ranged from 19 to a "gross exaggeration" of nearly 500 (Stephen Davis, *What the Yankees Did to Us: Sherman's Bombardment and the Wrecking of Atlanta* [Macon: Mercer University Press, 2012], 243–47).

78. Banister, *Incidents*; Pryor, *Reminiscences*; Callender, "Recollections."

79. Henderson, *War at the Door*, 141–42; Trudeau, *Last Citadel*, 422. For a comprehensive list of damage sustained by buildings within Petersburg, see National Archives, RG 393, Records of the U.S. Army, Continental, 1821–1920, pt. 4, entry 1712, Letters Received by Provost Marshal, Petersburg, Va., 1865 (copies of letters from the NA supplied by James H. Blankenship Jr., historian at Petersburg National Battlefield).

80. For a similar argument about Fredericksburg, see Blair, "Barbarians at Fredericksburg's Gates," 163.

The Devil Himself Could Not Have Checked Them

Fighting with Black Soldiers at the Crater

⊰ KEVIN M. LEVIN ⊱

On July 9, 1864, *Frank Leslie's Illustrated Newspaper* featured on its front page a dramatic image of the 22nd United States Colored Troops (USCT) carrying the first line of Rebel works as part of the initial assaults on June 15 by the Army of the James against the city of Petersburg, Virginia. The image depicts the men hauling off a captured Confederate cannon while two dead soldiers serve as a reminder of the sacrifice paid for this prize. It is a moment of triumph that the artist, E. F. Mullen, did not want readers to think went unnoticed on the field of battle. In the backdrop, white Ohioans doff their hats, wave regimental flags, unsheathe swords, and cheer in an open display of support for their black comrades.

The accompanying article highlighted the assault of the "colored troops" in Brig. Gen. Edward Hinks's Third Division, Eighteenth Army Corps. "The majority of the whites expected that the colored soldiers would run," wrote the reporter, "but the sable forces astonished everybody by their achievements." Once inside the enemy's works, "Numbers of them kissed the gun they had captured with extravagant satisfaction and a feverish anxiety was manifested to get ahead and charge some more of the rebel works." The corps commander praised Hinks's men in a "congratulatory order" and stated confidently that "Such honor as they have won will remain imperishable."[1]

A few weeks after this story appeared, black men serving in the Army of the Potomac were once again utilized against Confederate works outside of Petersburg, this time unsuccessfully. Writing from Bermuda Hundred a few days following what became known as the battle of the Crater, a soldier from New York informed his family that "Everybody here is down on the niggers."[2] Even a cursory glance at the available archival record suggests that this man's sentiments were representative of many white soldiers in the Army of the Potomac. This assessment of African American men in the two brigades of Brig. Gen. Edward Ferrero's Fourth Division, who bore the brunt of blame for the decisive Union defeat on July 30, 1864, stands

"Hinks's Division of Negro Infantry Bringing in the Guns Captured from the Confederates at Baylor's Farm, near Petersburg, Va., June 15th, 1864."
Frank Leslie's Illustrated Newspaper, July 9, 1864, 241.

in sharp contrast to the response a few weeks previous and represents the nadir of white Union soldiers' perceptions of their black comrades in uniform during the Petersburg campaign.

In recent years, historians have explored how the presence of USCT men at the Crater reinforced Confederate commitment to an independent nation based on white supremacy and why Confederates enthusiastically participated in or supported the massacre of black soldiers following the

The Devil Himself Could Not Have Checked Them

battle. Unfortunately, scholars have not sufficiently probed how white Union soldiers assessed the performance of their black comrades following the battle—beyond emphasizing their overtly racist language and concluding that men who served in the Army of the Potomac represented a cross section of a broader society steeped in racism.[3]

Our preoccupation with the racial attitudes among men in the Army of the Potomac, and others serving in the Virginia theater, runs the risk of overlooking salient aspects of their first experience fighting alongside black soldiers that can be found in their personal correspondence. First and foremost, while the scapegoating of black soldiers at the Crater was widespread, it was only temporary. It did not lead to a concerted call from among the white rank and file to remove USCT men from the army entirely. Many Union soldiers acknowledged the bravery of African Americans fighting at the Crater—even some who could not resist revealing their own racial prejudices. The result of the battle did little to challenge a growing consensus among white enlisted men that African Americans could and should contribute militarily and share in the sacrifices necessary to defeat the Confederacy. White soldiers insisted, however, that the deployment of "colored" units be done in a way that avoided the interracial mixing that ensued at the Crater. The issue was not whether blacks should be part of the army, but rather the conditions under which white men were willing to serve alongside them in the shared goal of preserving the Union. This framework proved to be the foundation of a collective experience among white and black soldiers that continued to resonate through the postwar period. The pull of sectional reconciliation failed to prevent many white veterans, including those who served directly with black soldiers, from openly and positively acknowledging the African Americans' performance at the Crater as well as their role in saving the Union.

The spring campaign started off with much promise as Maj. Gen. George G. Meade's Army of the Potomac—now under the watchful eye of Lt. Gen. Ulysses S. Grant—once again engaged Gen. Robert E. Lee's army in central Virginia. Even without a decisive Union victory in and around the Wilderness in early May, the men cheered as Grant shifted the army southward rather than retreat across the Rapidan River. Within a matter of weeks, the army had absorbed tens of thousands of casualties as it continually pounded the Army of Northern Virginia and edged closer to the Confederate capital of Richmond. Following the bloody battle of Cold Harbor on June 3, Grant shifted his army once again, this time in a bold move

south of the James River toward the crucial transportation hub at Petersburg, roughly twenty-eight miles below Richmond. The move caught Lee off guard; however, the initial assaults against the city failed to break its defenses and provided Confederates with sufficient time to transfer the
bulk of their force to what was quickly becoming the new focal point of fighting in Virginia.[4]

With both armies strained as the result of the constant fighting and weary of further frontal assaults, men on both sides commenced digging earthworks. Soldiers welcomed the respite from hostilities but worried about their possibilities for future success. "I see no prospect of our being any more expeditious in reducing this place than McClellan was, in front of Yorktown," lamented John W. Haley, an officer in the Union Fifth Corps. On the nation's independence day, Haley could not help but remind his family "that this is the day General Grant promised to eat his dinner in Richmond. There seems to be a hitch somewhere." Most men, however, maintained a stoic resolve, as did a soldier in the 51st New York Infantry, who remained confident that "success will attend the *next effort* I make."[5]

By early July, that "next effort" was already in the planning stages. Constant Union digging resulted in a forward position in a sector occupied by Brig. Gen. Robert B. Potter's division of Maj. Gen. Ambrose E. Burnside's Ninth Corps. A regiment of Pennsylvanians under the command of Lt. Col. Henry Pleasants speculated that a tunnel could be extended under a Confederate salient occupied by Brig. Gen. Stephen Elliott's South Carolina brigade and a 4-gun artillery battery. The plan called for the mine to be packed with explosives, then detonated, creating a gap in the Rebel line that could be exploited by a coordinated assault. Beginning in the last week of June and continuing through the end of July, the men of the 48th Pennsylvania constructed a tunnel roughly 500 feet long that contained, in galleries extending under the Confederate position, 320 kegs of gunpowder totaling 8,000 pounds.[6]

With the tunnel close to completion, the Union high command formulated a plan to exploit what promised to be an impressive and destructive explosion. Burnside proposed using Brig. Gen. Edward Ferrero's division, which included two brigades of USCT troops, to spearhead the attack and widen what many believed would be a significant gap in the Confederate position. Ferrero's division was to push into the remains of the fort and swing left and right, sweeping the Confederate lines, followed by the other three divisions in Burnside's corps. The objective of the assault was a cemetery atop a ridge, some 600 yards beyond the point of explosion, that overlooked Petersburg. If all went as planned, armed black men stood a chance of being the first Union soldiers to enter the city of Petersburg.[7]

Burnside's decision to utilize Ferrero's division fundamentally altered the character of the planned assault by bringing it into line with the Lincoln administration's decision to utilize African Americans in its war for Union. Although black soldiers had been deployed extensively and even successfully in other theaters of war, apart from the assaults outside of Petersburg the previous month, they were strangers to combat with white comrades in the Army of the Potomac. In Burnside's corps, roughly two-thirds of the men were new recruits, which likely exacerbated the suspicions of, and resistance to, the service of black men in the army. In demonstrating their manhood and bravery to the nation, the USCT men would have to surmount a war weary and discriminatory army and skeptical home front, as well as their own government. Indeed, Ferrero's men only recently had been informed that after close to a year of protest they finally would earn pay equal to that of white soldiers.[8]

Burnside decided to use Ferrero's division to lead the assault because it was fresh compared to his other three divisions, which had been worn down by the fighting through Virginia and the monotony of life in the trenches. However, the physical condition of the black division did not render it ready for battle. The 39th USCT was first armed in April while passing through the capital, and its men, according to one officer, were struggling to determine "whether the explosive part of the cartridge is the powder or the ball." Basic training took a back seat to the numerous tasks assigned to the division between May and mid-July, from guarding wagon trains to defending the army's rear against possible Confederate cavalry raids to digging earthworks near Petersburg. Each new assignment left the division temporarily detached from its parent corps until July 22—a little more than a week before powder in the mine was to be detonated.[9]

Burnside's intention to utilize Ferrero's division as the vanguard of the Federal assault remained in place until the afternoon prior to the attack, when Meade vetoed the use of black units. Meade already harbored doubts about the "colored troops," preferring to utilize them as laborers instead of in combat roles. In this case, with a presidential election looming in November, he also worried that the public might accuse the army of needlessly sacrificing black men if the assault failed. Burnside was instructed to use his more experienced white divisions—with Ferrero's in support—to push straight through the breach in the Confederate lines and head for Cemetery Hill.[10]

Burnside was a competent commander when given specific instructions, but he found it difficult to improvise. Forced to make major revisions at the eleventh hour, he instructed his other three division commanders to draw lots from a hat to determine who would lead the assault. Brig. Gen. James H. Ledlie came up short and received the assignment—even though he already had shown signs of incompetence, cowardice, and drunkenness. The two divisions commanded by Potter and Brig. Gen. Orlando B. Willcox were to follow. The final plan called for Ledlie's division to move into and through the crater with Willcox following on the left and Potter on the right to prevent Confederates from counterattacking. The explosion of the mine and assault were set for the early hours of July 30.[11]

Col. Stephen Minot Weld of the 56th Massachusetts Infantry, of Ledlie's division, described the explosion as "the grandest spectacle I ever saw." Within seconds, he noticed "a huge mass of earth and flame rising some 50 or 60 feet in the air, almost slowly, majestically, as if a volcano had just opened, followed by an immense volume of smoke rolling out in every direction." From the beginning, nothing went right for Burnside's four divisions. The sight of a smoldering hole measuring 125 feet long, 50 feet wide, and 20–30 feet deep cost precious time as attackers gazed at the destruction wrought by four tons of black powder and worked to uncover members of Elliott's South Carolina brigade who had been positioned directly above the blast. By 7:00 A.M., three Union divisions were crammed tightly within the confines of the Crater itself or were bogged down in the complex chain of rifle pits, traverses, and bombproofs that extended outward. Several attempts to push forward beyond the Crater allowed scattered units to secure some ground, but Confederate forces, including well-positioned artillery, quickly responded to prevent a breakout.[12]

At approximately 8:00 A.M., two brigades in Ferrero's Fourth Division were ordered into the mix. The First Brigade, under the command of Lt. Col. Joshua K. Sigfried, led with Col. Delavan Bates's 30th USCT in the vanguard. Once beyond Federal lines, the brigade made its way over roughly 150 yards of open ground, all the while taking enfilading fire from Confederate rifles and artillery. Front elements of the brigade passed to the right of the Crater and into a confusing series of Confederate rifle pits and entrenchments; the rest of the brigade was forced into the horror of the pit itself, which quickly became a cauldron of death. Col. Henry G.

The Devil Himself Could Not Have Checked Them

Thomas faced the challenge of advancing the Second Brigade away from the escalating bloodbath inside the Crater, managing to organize some of his men for an advance. Together, Thomas and Sigfried moved elements of their commands—all the while yelling, "Remember Fort Pillow" and "No Quarter"—into the chain of rifle pits, trenches, and covered ways. Once in position, both Sigfried's and Thomas's brigades, along with scattered units from the other divisions, made an attempt to gain ground against stiff Confederate resistance.

Any opportunity for a concerted push by units that were now scattered and racially mixed slipped away quickly as Confederate Brig. Gen. William Mahone's division arrived around 9:00 A.M. Mahone promptly ordered the 800 Virginians of Brig. Gen. David A. Weisiger's brigade into battle, and two additional brigades from the division eventually entered the action and helped retake the salient before fighting died down in the early afternoon. Union casualties numbered 3,798, all but 300 of them from Burnside's Ninth Corps. Ferrero's Division accounted for more than one-third of all Union casualties. Confederates losses numbered approximately 1,400.[13]

The scale of violence at the Crater fit into the broader narrative of a war that had surpassed what many believed possible in 1861, but the presence of United States Colored Troops constituted a fundamental shift in the conflict for men in both Lee's Army of Northern Virginia and the Army of the Potomac. In the days and weeks following the battle, Union soldiers sorted out who was to blame for their defeat.

Soldiers shared their frustrations with family members back home by threatening not to re-enlist or by promising to vote for the Democratic nominee in the upcoming presidential election. More specifically, soldiers in the three white divisions in the Ninth Corps, as well as many comrades throughout the Army of the Potomac, directed their frustrations at the Union high command, including Generals Meade, Grant, and Burnside. A soldier in the 35th Massachusetts Infantry was convinced "there were men enough to eat the Rebs up if they had been put in" but concluded that jealousy prevented Meade from fully supporting Burnside's attack. Another soldier observed that "with Grant in command we have been in front of Petersburg as long, aye longer than McClellan sat in front of Richmond." Compared to Grant, this soldier opined that McClellan was a "humane general and tried to avoid useless slaughter of his men."[14]

Eventually the brunt of blame from within the ranks focused on the black soldiers. They were easy targets for the obvious reasons related to race, but they were also clearly observed by many to have fallen back in confusion following Mahone's counterattack. "The colored troops," according to Edward Whitman, "had become panic-stricken dropped their arms and fled without dealing a blow." A soldier in the 117th New York Infantry recalled that "the Rebs gave one volley and a yell, and such a skedaddle you never heard of!" A Pennsylvania soldier simply noted, "the devil himself could not have checked them." The vast majority of accounts that fasten responsibility for the defeat on retreating black men fail to mention that the Confederate attack also sent just as many (if not more) white troops into a full stampede.[15]

Not all Union soldiers placed the blame on the "colored troops," and even those who did were able to acknowledge their initial advance around the Crater as well as the bravery exhibited on the battlefield. Writing from Bermuda Hundred, Orrin S. Allen shared with his wife reports that "they fought like heroes. I saw them and I talked with soldiers who has always been down on them before but said they never seen men fight better." A member of Burnside's staff recorded in his journal that "Gen. Ferrero's colored troops advanced with the most determined bravery."[16]

Not surprisingly, the most vocal support came from officers within the Fourth Division. Capt. James A. Rickard, who served in the 19th USCT, asserted that "The charge of Ferrero's division . . . and temporary capture of their interior works . . . is a record to win back the previously prejudiced judgment of the president, cabinet generals, and officers of the Army of the Potomac, who up to this time had thought negroes all right for service in menial capacity." "They went up as well as I ever saw troops," recalled Col. Henry G. Thomas, but even he could not ignore what was apparent to many: "They came back very badly. They came back on the run, every man for himself."[17]

The collapse of elements of the Fourth Division alone would have been sufficient to attract attention from those looking to isolate blame for the defeat on July 30, but the rout placed white soldiers in a situation they had never before faced on a Virginia battlefield. The scattered white and black units that collapsed in the face of Mahone's countercharge fell back on positions held by their own men. These defenders, desperately trying to hold their ground, found themselves being stampeded by black and white comrades with incensed Rebels in close pursuit. The Confederates instantly had been transformed by their first sight of a large number of black men in uniform. "It had the same affect upon our men that a red flag had upon a mad bull," was the way one South Carolinian who survived the initial explosion described the reaction of his comrades. Fighting at the Crater took place just beyond an area densely populated by white civilians and African Americans (enslaved and free), triggering among the former long-standing fears of slave rebellions, both real and imagined. Reports that the black men advanced shouting "Remember Fort Pillow" and "No Quarter," as well as numerous accounts that USCT had refused to take prisoners following their earlier assaults outside Petersburg, only fueled Confederate rage. Counterattacking Rebel soldiers at the Crater almost immediately determined to make an example of the USCT men they faced.[18]

Evidence of the massacre of black soldiers is overwhelming in the surviving letters and diaries of Confederates who were present on the battlefield or nearby. Jerome Yates of the 16th Mississippi Infantry freely admitted that "Most of the Negroes were killed after the battle," as did James Verdery, who described the encounter as a *"Bloody Sight a perfect Massacre nearly* a Black flag fight." Artillery colonel William Ransom Johnson Pegram shared with his family that the presence of black soldiers "has a splendid effect on our men." Pegram concluded that though "it seems cruel to murder them in cold blood," the men who did it had "very good cause for doing so."[19] Whether that "cause" included a handful of reports that black soldiers executed Confederate prisoners during their initial charge is unknown, but what cannot be denied is that the battle quickly took its place in what historian William Dobak has described as a "cycle of atrocity and vengeance."[20]

In addition to the otherworldly nature of the landscape caused by the explosion of the mine and the close-quarter fighting, white Union soldiers holding defensive positions on July 30 found themselves at the center of a rapidly disintegrating situation. They responded by trying to slow down the retreating soldiers. Edward Cook of the 100th New York Infantry feely admitted that "white troops 'fired' into the retreating niggers." An officer in the 4th New Hampshire Infantry used his saber "freely on the cowards." Others recalled having "to fix Baonetts [*sic*] to stop them."[21] This was a desperate moment for the men of the Fourth Division, but the other three divisions also coped with the added element of an enraged enemy likely to treat them as accomplices in inciting former slaves to servile insurrection.

Mahone's countercharge and the collapse of the Fourth Division left both white and black Union soldiers trapped in the Crater and adjacent earthworks. Writing for *Century* magazine in the mid-1880s, George Kilmer vividly recalled the panic that seized white soldiers and the fear "that the enemy would give no quarter to negroes, or to the whites taken with them." "It has been positively asserted," continued Kilmer, "that white men bayoneted blacks who fell back in to the crater . . . in order to preserve the whites from Confederate vengeance." The retreating blacks, according to Alonzo Rich of the 36th Massachusetts Infantry, "mixed them up so that they [Confederates] didn't show white men any mercy att [*sic*] all." The three white divisions had spent the morning holding precariously to earthworks in and around the Crater, but now black comrades unintentionally had placed them in an even more desperate spot.[22]

As a result of a failure to agree to the terms of a truce, it was not until August 1 that the dead and wounded could be collected from the battlefield. By then there were few survivors. Body parts littered the ground, and numerous corpses showed the effects of having been trampled upon. One Pennsylvanian recalled that "The wounded were fly-blown and the dead were all maggot-eaten. So we had to lift them with shovels." The condition of the bodies was enough to sicken even the most stoic soldier, and realization that one "could not tell the white from the black by their hair" likely added to white soldiers' emotional pain and disgust with their black comrades.[23]

On August 1, while Union burial parties pursued their grim work, Confederates staged a parade of approximately 1,500 white and black prisoners through the streets of Petersburg on their way to prison camps farther south. Confederate general A. P. Hill ordered that the prisoners be organized interracially. As they were marched and countermarched, Union captives felt the sting of numerous taunts from the civilian population. "See the white and nigger equality soldiers" and "Yanks and niggers sleep in the same bed!" could be heard from the street level and verandas. Organizers of the parade used this unusual scene primarily to highlight how defeat in the war might compromise the Confederacy's racial hierarchy; however, it also served to humiliate the white Union soldiers. Brig. Gen. William Francis Bartlett, who was taken prisoner during the battle after having lost his prosthetic leg, informed his family that they were being "treated worse, on account of being taken with them."[24]

The experience of white Union soldiers fighting alongside blacks at the Crater sheds light on immediate post-battle assessments. For a select few whites, outrage over the performance of the black troops remained a vibrant theme in their personal accounts. The day after the battle, Charles J. Mills of the 56th Massachusetts Infantry admitted that "the niggers, tho' excellent to charge, were not worth a straw to resist" and "ran like sheep." Three days later, Mills confided to his mother, "They cannot be trusted for anything, and are, in short, a hideous mistake, I fear." As late as the end of September, Mills continued to exercise little restraint in his letters home over what he saw as the abysmal performance of USCT soldiers.[25]

While many white soldiers echoed Mills's frustrations over what Grant would later describe as a "stupendous failure," relatively few embraced his conclusion that USCT participation was a "hideous failure" or called outright for an end to the government's policy of recruiting black soldiers. Rather, the experience of fighting with black soldiers helped to clarify white soldiers' opinions about how best to employ USCT units in battle. Many white veterans likely would have agreed with Alonzo Rich, who earlier commented on the implications of whites being "mixed up" with blacks: "I am willing the niggers should fight but I say put them all in together and let them fight. If not keep them out and let the white men do it." For Rich, the battle reinforced the belief that if blacks were going to be used militarily they should act independently of whites to avoid the kinds of problems experienced at the Crater.

Within a matter of weeks after July 30, morale recovered within the Army of the Potomac owing to Sherman's taking of Atlanta and additional offensive operations around Petersburg that met with limited success. The presence of the Fourth Division within the Ninth Corps, however, continued to be problematical for men in the three white divisions. Confederates singled out Burnside's interracial corps with artillery demonstrations and constant harassment by sharpshooters. In November, as if acknowledging the sentiments of men such as Alonzo Rich, the Fourth Division was transferred to Benjamin Butler's Army of the James, in which all black units fighting in Virginia eventually were consolidated. The Fourth Division had served roughly six months with the Army of the Potomac. Once Confederates learned of the transfer, trading between pickets proceeded and life generally improved for the rest of the corps.[26]

It is difficult to gauge the extent to which the white rank and file were willing to look beyond their initial perceptions of black comrades that had been forged on July 30. One day after the battle, Col. Alvin C. Voris of the 67th Ohio Infantry noted, as did so many others, "All join in saying the 'nigger' did verry badly and had no excuse for it." By November, Voris had been promoted to brigadier general and given temporary command of a black unit. The experience left him with a very different assessment of attitudes toward the USCT men. "To the people at home who through this campaign have heard the negro question harped upon with so much zeal than any other subject ever agitated," he observed, "it would be astonishing to learn that in the army the prejudice heretofore existing against the negro has almost entirely died out. Officers return the salute of the colored soldier with cordiality, and treat them with kindness, and the soldiers are glad to welcome them as comrades in arms." Voris did not go so far as to claim white soldiers reached out to black comrades as "their social associates, but they are not ashamed to recognize them as fellow soldiers and entitled to all the honors of veterans."[27]

Voris's distinction between "social associates" and "fellow soldiers" is crucial to understanding the evolution of racial attitudes among the enlisted white soldiers toward their black counterparts. Few of the former fought the war simply to abolish slavery and even fewer were engaged in a fight for civil rights and equality. Yet by 1864 a growing number acknowledged the shared sacrifice and bravery of their black comrades on battlefields from Virginia to Louisiana in pursuit of preserving the Union. For men in the Army of the Potomac, this acknowledgment may have surfaced more easily following the consolidation of black units into one corps. That organizational move provided sufficient space to acknowledge the contributions of black comrades without having to worry about being placed in the kind of position that, in the heat of battle at the Crater, had fueled widespread expressions of profound prejudice.[28]

How veterans remembered the role of USCT men in the battle of the Crater unfolded as a complicated postwar story. For a number of reasons, black and white veterans of the Fourth Division never had the opportunity to return to Petersburg to help shape the public memory of the battle. Neither was African American participation in the action on July 30, 1864, remembered by white veterans from other units in the Ninth Corps who met with Confederate veterans in the city after the war.

Yet the story of the USCT men was not entirely forgotten. Even the push toward sectional reconciliation by the early twentieth century, which was strong among one-time enemies, did not prevent Union veterans from honoring the bravery and sacrifice of black comrades. For example, white veterans sometimes lauded black troops in the pages of regimental histories. The history of the 45th Pennsylvania Infantry did not focus on how some black soldiers abandoned their positions early in the fighting, instead praising the USCT men who "Kept up a heavy fire of musketry on the advancing enemy compelling them to take shelter." And while this author acknowledged his unit was forced back into the confines of the Crater itself, "the Negroes kept up a heavy fire against the Rebels outside the fort." An even more favorable assessment can be found in the regimental history of

The Devil Himself Could Not Have Checked Them

the 36th Massachusetts Infantry, whose author suggested that the Fourth Division should have been allowed to lead the assault. "Many who saw their advance on the 30th were satisfied," remembered the author, "that if they had been permitted to lead the assault, they would have secured the crest of Cemetery Hill and achieved a brilliant victory."[29]

Recognition of black gallantry and bravery also could be found in a wide array of postwar newspapers and magazines. Victory and the passage of years helped veterans achieve a certain detachment from the emotion and prejudice that welled up in so many white soldiers immediately after the battle. Two white veterans writing in the *National Tribune*—the official organ of the Grand Army of the Republic—illustrate this phenomenon. A. H. C. Jewett, a first lieutenant in the 4th New Hampshire Infantry, argued that black soldiers fell victim to poor planning and leadership, which placed them in a situation "that no soldiers, black or white, could contend successfully." USCT units performed no better or worse than the "average white regiments." A few months later in the same publication, another eyewitness to the battle sought further to clarify the performance of the USCT by challenging Jewett's mistaken assertion that the black division led the failed assault.[30]

The African American veterans of the Fourth Division stood the best chance of being remembered by their former white officers, who collectively also proved to be their greatest advocates. The officers' postwar accounts reflect both the shared experience of the battlefield and the continuing gulf between the two races. Some white officers wrote about the bravery of USCT units as an extension of their own ongoing work, often with African Americans, to uplift the black race and promote equal justice. Most simply could not fully credit their own war experience and acts of bravery without referencing former "colored" comrades.[31]

One of the earliest accounts, and arguably the most important, was Henry G. Thomas's article in *Century* magazine in 1877. The popularity of *Century*'s series on the war, and republication of this article in the fourth volume of *Battles and Leaders of the Civil War*, guaranteed that a wide popular audience would read about the bravery of the men under his command, whom he believed deserved the "respect of every beholder." Thomas began his account by conveying the optimism that pervaded the ranks on the eve of their first opportunity to "show the white troops what the colored division could do." The decision to replace the division just before explosion of the mine not only left the reader wondering what might have been had the original plan been adhered to, but it also absolved the officers and men of responsibility for the disaster.[32]

Writing in 1907 in the *National Tribune*, Capt. D. E. Proctor of the 30th USCT recalled the heroism of the men under his command, reminding readers of the debt still owed. "It's the white man's burden to settle the question whether a man is a man," observed Proctor, "without regard to race, color or previous condition." The former captain then predicted: "In God's own time it will be settled rightly, but we feel that those who were participants in the great war for the preservation of the Union, and incidentally the freedom of the slave, will never see that day."[33]

No two former officers of the Fourth Division were more supportive of the black men under their command than Col. Delavan Bates and Lt. Col. Freeman S. Bowley, both from the 30th USCT. Bates authored one of the most extensive accounts of black troops at the Crater, published in late January 1908 in *The National Tribune*. While Bates did not pass over the opportunity to highlight his own participation in the battle, the article focused on the performance of the men in the regiment. More unusual, however, was his commitment to sharing a more personal profile of these men with his readers. Bates recalled on the eve of battle a scene involving the men of Co. H, who were gathered to listen to one of their own noncommissioned officers, who before the war served as a preacher:

> My deah bredern, dis am gwine to be er gre't fite de gre'tes' we'uns hab eber seen if we'uns tek Petrsburg mos' likly we'l tuk Richmun, and derstroy Mars Gin'ul Lee's big ahmy and den clos de wah. Ebery man hed orter lif up hiself in praher fur er strong hyart. O, bredern, 'member de pore cullud fokses ober yer in bondage. En 'member Marse Gin'ul Grant, en Marse Gin'ul Burnside, en Marse Gin'ul Meade, en all de uder ob de gre't Gin'uls ober yunner watch'n yer, en, moreover, de fust nigger dat goes ter projeckin' es gwine ter git dis byarnut inter him. 'Fore Gawd, hits sho nuff trufe Ise tellin' yer.[34]

Bates's decision to render in the original dialect what he remembers hearing, while somewhat jarring within an early twenty-first-century context, gives voice to the black veterans of the Crater in a way that they could not do themselves owing to their lack of access to publications. What emerges is a strong bond built around a shared history of slavery and the hope that their actions on that day would spell its doom. The failure of the attack did nothing to diminish their bravery. According to Bates, "one thing that has been proven, viz, the colored troops dared meet not only in open field the best troops of the Confederacy, but they also dared attack them behind breastworks almost impregnable, and as to results the best standard by which to test the qualities of an army is this: The number killed on the battlefield."[35]

Freeman Bowley authored four accounts of the battle between 1870 and 1899, which differ in detail but collectively highlight his own brave conduct on the field as well as that of the men under his command. The failure on the part of the nation to acknowledge his men, as well as Bowley's own failure to secure a Medal of Honor, threatened his sense of honor as a soldier and challenged his conviction that the war had given rise to new freedoms and civil rights for African Americans.[36] Like Bates, Bowley also gave voice to the men in his command, placing himself alongside them in the heat of battle to face the same dangers and exhibit a common strength to resist the Confederate tide and risk possible death. "Of the men of my regiment who had rallied with me," wrote Bowley, "all but one, a Sergeant, lay dead or dying. As he stood at my elbow, loading and firing, I said to him, 'Sergeant, things are looking very bad for us.' . . . 'Yes, Lieutenant,' he answered, 'dey is sho'ly lookin' powerful bad. I reckon, sah, we has to die right yere, sah!' And this was said not in a spirit of bravado, nor in a tone of regret, but as a matter of fact our duty had called us to this place, and it was a part of that duty 'to die right yere,' and there was no thought of shirking the responsibility."[37]

Even after his capture and imprisonment, Bowley refused to distance himself from his command. Unlike some of his fellow officers, he acknowledged to his captors directly when asked to identify his command: "Thirtieth United States Colored Infantry." Throughout his captivity between Petersburg and Columbia, South Carolina, Bowley withstood the taunts and abuses of white southerners, who believed that he and the rest of the Union army were "all a miserable lyin' set of thieves, come down yere to steal we'uns niggers." Bowley's memory of these encounters strengthened his own conviction that his service in the USCT was part of a much larger commitment to emancipation and the betterment of the black race. While his postwar accounts are sprinkled with stories of reconciliation and reunion, Bowley never backed away from accounting for the execution of large numbers of his men once surrendered. In contrast to former USCT officers who "never had an interest in the black race" or had at some point abandoned their commitment to reform, by 1900 Bowley was one of the few USCT officers who remained committed to challenging a collective memory of the war that had moved noticeably, but not completely, away from honoring the service of black soldiers and their role in saving the Union.[38]

African American veterans in the Grand Army of the Republic fully embraced the opportunity to remind their communities and the nation of their service in the war. As members of both segregated and integrated posts throughout the North and South, black men took part in marches at GAR encampments, Memorial Day events, and especially Emancipation Day ceremonies. The GAR's commitment to racial inclusivity and recognition of African Americans' role in preserving the Union and eradicating slavery did not, however, translate into a concerted push for black civil rights by white members. Comradeship across racial lines was based overwhelmingly on having fought together on the same battlefields and experienced the same hardships and sacrifice in pursuit of a common cause.[39]

References to the Crater figured prominently in the stories told by black veterans, but their performance was also the subject of numerous addresses by white comrades. In his lecture to the James M. Warner Post of the GAR in Morrisville, Vermont, Frank Kenfield reflected on the battle that left him a prisoner until the end of the war. In the middle of his description of Mahone's countercharge, Kenfield abruptly shifted his focus. "I wish to say one word here in regard to the colored troops," he told his audience, "they fought like heroes and many a rebel bit the dust from their unerring bullets, and as the rebels charged in upon us I heard the order given 'save the white men but kill the damn niggers.' And I saw them run their bayonets through many a colored man showing him no mercy." In often recalling this scene, Kenfield confessed, "a cold shudder goes through me as I think of how those poor colored men were butchered in cold blood."[40]

It is unknown whether there were any black veterans present in the audience that evening, but Kenfield's listeners likely embraced his memory of the USCT men as integral to their broader memory of the war. Such stories reflected a commitment to the principle that service to and sacrifice for the Union rose above the color of a man's skin.

By the early twentieth century, public memory of the battle of the Crater was predominantly in the hands of white southerners who stamped the battlefield site with an interpretation that celebrated Mahone's famous countercharge as one of the final stands in the Confederacy's Lost Cause. When the National Park Service gained control of the site in 1936, it inherited an interpretation of the battle that all but ignored the presence of United States Colored Troops. Challenges to this institutional memory

The Devil Himself Could Not Have Checked Them

and a push for a more inclusive interpretation that acknowledged the performance of black soldiers emerged with an increased sense of urgency in the late 1970s. At the center of this new counter-memory could be found a historical record of the men of the Fourth Division that had been shaped first by the fear and hatred of racism and later by the acknowledgment of a shared record of service and sacrifice for a cause that left all Americans with a more perfect Union.

Notes

1. *Frank Leslie's Illustrated Newspaper*, July 9, 1864, 247.

2. Edward L. Cook letter, August 4, 1864, Michael C. Cavanaugh Collection, Historical Society of Schuylkill County, Pottsville, Pa. (repository hereafter cited as HSSC).

3. Noah Andre Trudeau, *Like Men of War: Black Troops in the Civil War, 1862–1865* (New York: Little, Brown, 1998); Richard Slotkin, *No Quarter: The Battle of the Crater, 1864* (New York: Random House, 2009); Earl J. Hess, *Into the Crater: The Mine Attack at Petersburg* (Columbia: University of South Carolina Press, 2010). Though not specifically about the Crater, Chandra Manning offers a more sophisticated if unconvincing interpretation of evolving racial attitudes in the Union army in 1864. For Manning, the racist accusations that poured forth in the wake of the battle against the "colored soldiers" constituted a retreat from sentiments of "racial justice and equality" that originated early in the war and grew steadily through the successful campaigns of 1863. Whether Manning correctly interprets changing racial attitudes within the army as a whole has been questioned, but it is highly doubtful that the battle altered any individual soldier's racial outlook one way or the other. See Chandra M. Manning, *What This Cruel War Was Over: Soldiers, Slavery, and the Civil War* (New York: Knopf, 2007), 155–56.

4. For a good overview of the campaign, see Mark Grimsley, *And Keep Moving On: The Virginia Campaign, May–June 1864* (Lincoln: University of Nebraska Press, 2002).

5. Charles S. Wainwright, *A Diary of Battle: The Personal Journals of Colonel Charles S. Wainright, 1861–1865*, ed. Allan Nevins (New York: Harcourt, Brace, and World, 1962), 429; John W. Haley, *The Rebel Yell and the Yankee Hurrah: The Civil War Journal of a Maine Volunteer*, ed. Ruth L. Silliker (Camden, Me.: Down East Books, 1985), 178; John M. Jackson to Betsy Jackson, July 5, 1864, John M. Jackson Letters, Rare Books and Special Collections, Notre Dame University, South Bend, Ind.

6. On the planning and construction of the mine, see Hess, *Into the Crater*, 11–25.

7. Ibid., 53–62; Slotkin, *No Quarter*, 67–77.

8. Noah Andre Trudeau, "A Stranger in the Club: The Army of the Potomac's Black Division," in *Slavery, Resistance, Freedom*, ed. Gabor S. Boritt and Scott Hancock (New York: Oxford University Press, 2007), 96–117; William A. Dobak, *Freedom by the Sword: The U.S. Colored Troops, 1862–1867* (Washington, D.C.: Center of Military History, 2011), 358–59; Trudeau, *Like Men of War*, 91–93, 252–55.

9. On the question of the training of the Fourth Division for the assault, see Hess,

Into the Crater, 54–55; Slotkin, *No Quarter*, 96–102; Dobak, *Freedom by the Sword*, 357–58; and William Glenn Robertson, "From the Crater to New Market Heights: A Tale of Two Divisions," in John David Smith, ed., *Black Soldiers in Blue: African American Troops in the Civil War Era* (Chapel Hill: University of North Carolina Press, 2002), 179–82.

10. Hess, *Into the Crater*, 55–57.

11. William Marvel, *Burnside* (Chapel Hill: University of North Carolina Press, 1991), 393–95. On James H. Ledlie, see Grady McWhiney and Jack J. Jenkins, "The Union's Worst General," *Civil War Times Illustrated* 34 (June 1995): 30–39.

12. Stephen Minot Weld, *War Diary and Letters of Stephen Minot Weld, 1861–1865* (1912; reprint, Boston: Massachusetts Historical Society, 1979), 353. On the explosion and initial advance, see Slotkin, *No Quarter*, 181–95.

13. On the advance by the Fourth Division, see Robertson, "From the Crater to New Market Heights," 183–86; Trudeau, *Like Men of War*, 236–43; and Edward A. Miller Jr., *The Black Civil War Soldiers of Illinois: The Story of the Twenty-Ninth U.S. Colored Infantry* (Columbia: University of South Carolina Press, 1998), 66–73.

14. Cleveland Fisher letter, August 8, 1864, HSSC; Haley, *Rebel Yell and the Yankee Hurrah*, 193.

15. Harry F. Jackson and Thomas F. O'Donnell, *Back Home in Oneida: Hermon Clarke and His Letters* (Syracuse, N.Y.: Syracuse University Press, 1965), 150; Hamilton R. Dunlap letter, August 1, 1864, HSSC.

16. Orrin Sweet Allen letter, August 3, 1864, Virginia Historical Society, Richmond (repository hereafter cited as VHS); William S. Hess diary, July 30, 1864, VHS.

17. Accounts from Dudley Cornish, *The Sable Arm: Black Troops in the Union Army, 1861–1865* (New York: Longmans, Green, 1956), 277–78.

18. Robert J. Stevens, *Captain Bill* (Richburg, S.C.: Chester District Genealogical Society, 1985), 58. On how Confederates interpreted the presence of black soldiers, see Kevin M. Levin, *Remembering the Battle of the Crater: War as Murder* (Lexington: University Press of Kentucky, 2012), 25–32.

19. Jerome B. Yates to his wife, August 3, 1864, in Robert G. Evans, ed., *The 16th Mississippi Infantry: Civil War Letters and Reminiscences* (Jackson: University Press of Mississippi, 2002), 281; James Paul Verdery to sister, July 31, 1864, Eugene and James Paul Verdery Papers, Special Collections, Duke University, Durham, N.C. (repository hereafter cited as DU); William Ransom Johnson Pegram letter in Andrew Carroll, ed., *War Letters: Extraordinary Correspondence from American Wars* (New York: Scribner's, 2001), 100.

20. Dobak, *Freedom by the Sword*, 353. Additional analysis of Confederates massacring black soldiers can be found in Levin, *Remembering the Battle of the Crater*, 25–28; Slotkin, *No Quarter*, 234; and Hess, *Into the Crater*, 217–18.

21. Edward L. Cook letters, July 30, 1864, HSSC; Louis H. Bell letter, August 12, 1864, HSSC.

22. George L. Kilmer, "The Dash into the Crater," *Century*, September 1887, 775–76; Alonzo Rich letter, July 31, 1864, Manuscript Collection, Petersburg National Battlefield, Petersburg, Va.

23. Hamilton R. Dunlap diary, letter to his brother, August 1, HSSC.

24. On the parade, see Levin *Remembering the Battle of the Crater*, 1, and Francis

Winthrop Palfrey, *Memoir of William Francis Bartlett* (Boston: Houghton, Osgood and Co., 1878), 122.

25. Charles J. Mills letters, July 31, August 3, September 26, 1864, HSSC.

26. Warren Wilkinson, *Mother, May You Never See the Sights I Have Seen: The Fifty-Seventh Massachusetts Veteran Volunteers in the Last Year of the Civil War* (New York: Harper and Row, 1990), 309–10.

27. Alvin C. Voris to [?], November 10, 1864, in Jerome Mushkat, *A Citizen-Soldier's Civil War: The Letters of Brevet Major General Alvin C. Voris* (DeKalb: Northern Illinois University Press, 2002), 205, 233.

28. On the changing racial attitudes in the Union army, see Randall C. Jimerson, *The Private Civil War: Popular Thought during the Sectional Conflict* (Baton Rouge: Louisiana State University Press, 1988), 104–11; James M. McPherson, *For Cause and Comrades: Why Men Fought in the Civil War* (New York: Oxford University Press, 1997), 126–28; and Manning, *What This Cruel War Was Over*, 147–66.

29. Allen Diehl Albert, *History of the Forty-fifth regiment Pennsylvania Veteran Volunteer Infantry, 1861–1865* (Williamsport, Pa.: Grit Publishing, 1912), 157; *History of the Thirty-Sixth Regiment Massachusetts Volunteers, 1862–1865* (Boston: Press of Rockwell and Churchill, 1884), 241.

30. Quoted in Andre M. Fleche, "'Shoulder to Shoulder as Comrades Tried': Black and White Union Veterans and Civil War Memory," *Civil War History* 51 (June 2005): 188–89.

31. Joseph T. Glatthaar, *Forged in Battle: The Civil War Alliance of Black Soldiers and White Officers* (New York: Free Press, 1990), 231–64.

32. Henry G. Thomas, "The Colored Troops at Petersburg," *Century*, September 1887, 777–82.

33. D. E. Proctor, "The Massacre in the Crater," *National Tribune*, October 17, 1907.

34. Delavan Bates, "A Day with the Colored Troops," *National Tribune*, January 20, 1908.

35. Ibid.

36. On Bowley's view of the war, see the introduction to Keith Wilson, ed., *Honor in Command: Lt. Freeman S. Bowley's Civil War Services in the 30th United States Colored Infantry* (Gainesville: University Press of Florida, 2006), 1–41.

37. Wilson, *Honor in Command*, 139.

38. Ibid., 137 (on the massacre of USCT, see 152–56); Glatthaar, *Forged in Battle*, 259.

39. On the GAR, see Barbara A. Gannon, *The Won Cause: Black and White Comradeship in the Grand Army of the Republic* (Chapel Hill: University of North Carolina Press, 2011).

40. Frank Kenfield, "Captured by Rebels: A Volunteer at Petersburg, 1864," *Vermont History* 36 (Autumn 1968): 233.

The Battle of the Crater in Recent Fiction

⇥ STEPHEN CUSHMAN ⇤

People who saw Anthony Minghella's 2003 film version of Charles Frazier's 1997 best-selling novel *Cold Mountain* found themselves confronted in its opening minutes by vivid images of the battle of the Crater. Despite the inevitable inaccuracies of Minghella's representation (he both wrote the screenplay and directed the film), many but not nearly all of which several web users have meticulously detailed with varying degrees of sympathy, the twenty seconds of screen time devoted to the actual explosion of the mine constructed by Lt. Col. Henry Pleasants and the 48th Pennsylvania Infantry (at one point we can see the shiny metallic number 48 on the hat of the soldier who lights the fuse) are as powerfully rendered and memorable as any twenty seconds of battle reenactment in any Civil War film.

Here is the paragraph in Frazier's novel that corresponds to Minghella's film version:

> What he told Veasey was about the blowup at Petersburg. His regiment had been situated directly beside the South Carolina boys that got exploded by the Federal tunnelers. Inman was in the wattled trenches parching rye to make a pot of what they would call coffee when the ground heaved up along the lines to his right. A column of dirt and men rose into the air and then fell all around. Inman was showered with dirt. A piece of a man's lower leg with the boot still on the foot landed right beside him. A man down the trench from Inman came running through and hollering, Hell has busted![1]

Whatever one's ultimate feeling about the relative worth of pictures and words or of films and novels, Minghella's explosion, with, for instance, its brief image of a soldier's clothing getting blown off his body by the force of the blast, considerably intensifies Frazier's somewhat flat, perfunctory narration.

This intensification raises productive questions, and these questions point in turn to larger ones about how recent American fiction, specifically Richard Slotkin's *The Crater* (1980) and Duane Schultz's *Glory Enough for All* (1993), have represented historical events and conditions leading up to and away from July 30, 1864, in Petersburg, Virginia.[2] What aspects of these events and conditions has a particular novelist chosen to enlarge? Which has he chosen to ignore or reduce? How does he treat historical documents and earlier historical narratives? What do these choices and treatments tell us about the nature of Civil War narrative in general and narratives of the battle of the Crater in particular?

Returning briefly to Minghella's cinematic intensification of Frazier's narration, sooner or later one must reckon with the question, Why does Minghella open his film with extensive representation of the battle of the Crater when Frazier's novel gives it only a couple of understated paragraphs about a third of the way through? The one battle Frazier represents at any length, using the familiar conventions of what John Keegan, in his 1976 study *The Face of Battle*, calls "the battle piece," is Fredericksburg, which, as Inman recollects it, takes up four of the first nine pages of *Cold Mountain*.[3] Since the novel opens with Inman recovering from his wound, and since he received that wound at Petersburg, perhaps Minghella thought he should simplify the story by unraveling chronology and showing Inman's wounding in its original place and context. Or perhaps Minghella wanted to start his film with an attention-grabbing bang, and he felt the explosion at Petersburg would give him a literal one in a concentrated form, whereas the stone wall on Marye's Heights at Fredericksburg would not. Or perhaps the choice of the explosion at Petersburg reflects, at some disputable level of consciousness, the new prominence of sudden, unforeseen explosions in the awareness of American filmgoers after the attacks of September 11, 2001, which fell between the publication of Frazier's novel and the release of Minghella's film.

For both Frazier and Minghella the battle of the Crater serves as a brief backdrop. Neither is particularly concerned with the larger contours and consequences of the battle. Frazier, for example, makes no mention of the presence or role of black soldiers at Petersburg, and Minghella, who features a Native American Confederate in his reenactment, briefly shows that Confederate, in an oddly complex moment, locked in hand-to-hand combat with a single black Yankee, who along with his adversary does a brief double take, as the racial irony of their struggle appears to dawn on him. By contrast, both Richard Slotkin and Duane Schultz build their novels around the battle of the Crater, treating it not as backdrop but as the central subject of their respective narratives. In doing so, they offer students of the battle multiple opportunities for thinking about a complicated chain of causes and effects, as they select and fashion historical materials into coherent stories. Having begun with the most recent representation of Petersburg, Minghella's 2003 film, and worked backward to its 1997 antecedent, I will continue the retrograde pattern and follow with Schultz's 1993 novel before turning to Slotkin's 1980 one.

Duane Schultz's version of the explosion detonated under the South Carolina regiments of Brig. Gen. Stephen Elliott's brigade on the last Saturday of July 1864 at 4:45 A.M., an hour and fifteen minutes late, anticipates several features of Frazier's description at the same time that it flourishes its distinct signature:

> A column of earth, smoke, and flame leapt two hundred feet in the air, all gray and black and rent with jagged red and yellow fire. At its summit, a black cloud spread like the cap of a giant mushroom. For an instant, it hung immobile in the sky, as if time itself had stopped, until, to the horror of thousands of spellbound spectators, a macabre rain of debris fell toward the ground: gun barrels, rocks, clods of dirt and clay as big as houses, artillery wheels, fluttering remnants of tents, shattered timbers—and men, and parts of men, arms, legs, heads, torsos, all burned black and lifeless.[4]

Where Frazier understates, perhaps to suggest the stoically laconic indirect discourse of his battle-jaded main character, Schultz embellishes his explosion with vivid verbs and dramatic, even gothic, adjectives, such as "macabre." Both Frazier and Schultz identify the explosion with the most common of all Civil War images, amputated body parts, but Schultz, who has also written novels about World War II, adds the finishing touch of the "fiery mushroom cloud" (290).[5]

Schultz detonates his version of the Petersburg mine roughly four-fifths of the way through his novel, a fraction that reflects his decision to make the story of the battle of the Crater largely the story of Henry Pleasants and the 48th Pennsylvania. Pleasants appears on the second page of the novel as "a slim, dapper man of average height," whom some might have called "a dandy, but not to his face" (2). Many other characters, both fictional and historical, populate *Glory Enough for All*, some more believably than others, and many other points of view take center stage at different times. But for Schultz, Pleasants's point of view remains the dominant one throughout, and Pleasants's story, including the loss of his wife, Sallie Bannan, and his later engagement in 1863 to the much younger Anne Shaw while the members of the 48th were serving as provost guards in Lexing-

"General Grant's Campaign—The Explosion of the Mine and Assault on Cemetery Hill, before Petersburg, July 30, 1864." The two major illustrated newspapers in the United States gave extensive coverage to the battle of the Crater. A. R. Waud's sketch in *Harper's Weekly*, drawn from behind Union lines, depicts the mushroom cloud rising from the Rebel works. *Harper's Weekly*, August 20, 1864, 536–37.

ton, Kentucky, shapes and filters the mass of historical material involving the battle of the Crater. Pleasants and his plucky, colorful, fictional subordinates, whose challenges and triumphs constitute the best parts of the novel; Pleasants and his infuriating confrontations with the meddling Maj. James C. Duane (whose last name, coincidentally the same as Schultz's first one, the novelist gives throughout his book as "Dunne"),[6] Maj. Gen. George G. Meade's chief engineer and Pleasants's chief antagonist; Pleasants and his encounters with his sometimes helpful, sometimes unhelpful superiors, Brig. Gen. Robert B. Potter, Burnside, Meade, and Lt. Gen. U. S. Grant; Pleasants and his acquaintance with Lt. Ezra Boyce, a white officer serving with the Ninth Corps Fourth Division, who helps give Schultz narrative access to black soldiers; Pleasants and his letters to and from Anne Shaw, which occasionally break up Schultz's narrative and one of which figures prominently in Pleasants's solution of the problem of ventilating the mine (153–54): these are the raw materials of Schultz's story of the Crater.

STEPHEN CUSHMAN

"Siege of Petersburg—The Ninth Corps Charging on the Enemy's Works after the Explosion of the Mine." *Frank Leslie's* version of the Union attack placed the crater created by the explosion in the center background. Paul F. Mottelay and T. Campbell-Copeland, eds., *The Soldier in Our Civil War*, 2 vols. (New York: Stanley Bradley Publishing Company, 1893), 2:294–95.

And a very attractive story it is, too, as it becomes the story of a particularly capable individual, who despite many severe obstacles, both personal and professional, does his job exceedingly well and, despite other people's awful, overshadowing blunders, ultimately receives recognition for his work from no less an authority than Grant himself, who first credits Pleasants in conversation with Meade (243) and finally, after he has become president, congratulates Pleasants in person on the penultimate page (359), where his gracious tone has little in common with the matter-of-fact one in which he only briefly mentions the Pennsylvania miner in his *Personal Memoirs*.[7] Although they are very different novels in many ways, Michael Shaara's *Killer Angels* (1974) suggests an antecedent to *Glory Enough for All*, as Joshua Lawrence Chamberlain, another volunteer colonel, is to the former what Henry Pleasants is to the latter. For all the venomous irony of Schultz's title, which repeats the words of the spectacularly incompetent and culpable Brig. Gen. James H. Ledlie, in fact the novel does glorify

Lt. Col. Henry Pleasants. In testimony before a congressional committee, Pleasants detailed how little support he received from the army's upper command in digging the mine shaft: "The only officers of high rank, so far as I learned, that favored the enterprise were General Burnside, the corps commander, and General [Robert B.] Potter, the division commander." Robert Underwood Johnson and Clarence Clough Buel, eds., *Battles and Leaders of the Civil War*, 4 vols. (New York: Century, 1887), 4:546.

Pleasants, who, like Chamberlain, emerges as a respectable candidate for hero worship.

But for students of the battle of the Crater, Schultz's decision to place Pleasants squarely at the center of the story has some inescapable consequences. Many readers may feel, for example, that Confederate points of view remain significantly underrepresented throughout the novel. Schultz does introduce us to the character of a South Carolina sharpshooter, Caleb Caffee, fairly early on (39–41), and Caffee figures in the action by taking a shot at Pleasants while the latter makes measurements of the Confederate position with a theodolite, as well as by hearing the underground sounds of the Pennsylvania miners working. But his remains the only somewhat developed southern interior. Gen. Robert E. Lee does not make his first appearance in the novel until two-thirds of it has gone by (224–27), and Brig. Gen. William Mahone enters only after the mine has exploded, occupies two pages (306–7), and then returns briefly during the subsequent action.

Writers of Civil War novels labor under no obligation to give equal time to both sides, as the examples of Stephen Crane and Margaret Mitchell quickly show, and if Schultz chose to spend the bulk of his narrative time on northern thoughts and perceptions, his only literary obligation was to do so fruitfully. But the limitations of his aesthetic choices become clearer when we shift our attention from the scarcity of southern points of view to his circumscription of black ones. Because Henry Pleasants emerges as the narrative center, to and from which most narrative roads lead, Schultz's representations of the United States Colored Troops (USCT) in Ferrero's Fourth Division necessarily depend on Pleasants and consequently have little imaginative autonomy or depth. *Glory Enough for All* opens quite effectively with six pages describing the execution of a black soldier for killing one drunken Union cavalryman and wounding another after they tried to run him down and beat him with their sabers. But how things look to that black soldier or to any of his 4,300 fellow soldiers in the First and Second Brigades of the Fourth Division we can only guess when the condemned man begins to sing a spiritual and more than 4,000 other soldiers spontaneously join him. The only spoken commentary on this memorable scene comes from Pleasants, who, "clenching and unclenching his fists," refers to the condemned soldier as "Poor dumb bastard" (2) and turns away from the spectacle, muttering, "I've got to find a way to end this goddamn war" (6).

Subsequent representations of blacks also lack depth. At one point Schultz refers to Robert, Burnside's "black servant from the Indian fight days in New Mexico," and delivers the noteworthy sentence, "Every night of the campaign at Petersburg, with tent flaps closed against the outside world, Ambrose Burnside, major general, commander of fifteen thousand troops, shared a meal and bared his soul to an aging, semiliterate former slave" (78). If Schultz can shift his focus even momentarily from Pleasants to the Confederate sharpshooter Caffee, then presumably he could also do so in the case of Robert, perhaps during one of Burnside's soul-baring sessions. Likewise, when Pleasants goes to call on Lieutenant Boyce and finds himself challenged by a black sentry and subsequently questioned by the black Corporal of the Guard, the only thoughts and reactions we get are those of the white visitor: "Pleasants was impressed. This was right out of the manual. If these colored troops could fight as well as they did guard duty, then the rebs were surely in for trouble" (84).

As in the case of southern points of view, when Schultz signed his contract with St. Martin's, he did not bind himself to represent black ones, and if it feels to some as though he missed several rich opportunities for fictional innovation, others might argue that a novelist has to make choices and that Schultz's choice, to give Pleasants the leading role and relegate others to mute walk-on status or, in the case of famous generals, cameo appearances, is one of novelistic expediency rather than of imaginative nearsightedness. At least he represents black soldiers at all, the argument might go, and if his choices deny those soldiers full narrative recognition, no one book can do everything, and a student of the battle of the Crater always has other resources available. After all, the imperatives guiding a commercial novel writer and those motivating a rigorous student of history may overlap, and often do, but they are not identical.

Ways in which those imperatives differ become clearer when we consider Schultz's treatment of certain kinds of historical narrative and his apparent attitude toward Civil War historiography. Consider, for example, Schultz's staging of a conversation between Grant and Meade, one in which he has Grant tell his subordinate a famous story:

> "By the way, did you hear what happened to Mr. Lincoln yesterday when he went to see Early's men in action?"
>
> Grant continued without pause, not wanting to give Meade the chance to object. [Here follow several paragraphs about Early's invasion of the suburbs of Washington and Lincoln's going out to watch the action from Fort Stevens on July 12, 1864.]
>
> "General Wright was beside himself with worry that he would go down in history as the man who got the President shot. Try as he might, he could not persuade Lincoln to take cover. Old Abe seemed to be enjoying himself. . . . Then that bright young captain from the Sixth, the writer's son, Oliver Wendell Holmes, Jr., he got into the act. He claims he didn't recognize the President, but that hardly seems credible. He shouted, 'Get down, you damn fool, before you get shot.'" (214–15)

What hardly seems credible, of course, is that such a conversation could have taken place between Grant and Meade, the former treating the latter as though he had no access to information, official or anecdotal, and as though he needed, any more than Grant himself, the little glosses, such as "the writer's son, Oliver Wendell Holmes, Jr.," which are clearly intended for members of a general audience reading over Meade's shoulder.

We might call passages such as the one above, and they are not rare in *Glory Enough for All*, the Shakespearean Background Speech, since their sole function is to slip an unknowing reader or audience member a bolus of historical narrative, a bolus such as the one at the beginning of *Hamlet*, when Marcellus asks someone to tell him why the Danish sentries keep such strict watch, while other people make cannons and still others buy weapons, concluding, "Who is't that can inform me?" Horatio obligingly answers, "That can I," and proceeds to deliver a long speech describing the motivations of young Fortinbras of Norway for invading Denmark. Although Marcellus would have to be living at Elsinore in a state of sensory deprivation not to know what Horatio tells him, members of an Eliza-

STEPHEN CUSHMAN

bethan audience needed this information, as do we, and the convention of delivering it to us in unrealistic speeches does not violate our sense of dramatic decorum. But in the case of supposedly realistic conversation between historical figures in a Civil War novel, and between generals at that, we have a very different matter.

One could argue in Schultz's defense that he is writing for a lay audience, not for an audience of knowledgeable Civil War students, who do not require, for example, the early definitions of "abatis" and "chevaux-de-frise" (20, 21), and if he wants his lay readers to grasp that the Union army "'learned at Cold Harbor that the defense has the advantage in trench warfare and that superior numbers don't count for much,'" why not put that sentence into Grant's mouth (130), even if the real Meade, to whom the sentence gets spoken, presumably did not need the lecture? When it comes to another sentence, however, one that Schultz puts into Grant's mouth near the end of *Glory Enough for All*, the nature of his method and its implications for serious students of the war become transparent. Once again the novel is filtering the action through the perspective of Henry Pleasants when he, along with the rest of Potter's Second Division, moves forward through the breach in the Confederate fortifications. Having advanced to the lip of the Crater and seen for himself the chaos there, he decides to return to the Union lines to try to find Burnside in order to talk with him about the fiasco: "But before Pleasants had gotten halfway across the field, he spied an old man in a private's uniform walking toward him, pushing his way through the fleeing mob" (312). Contrary to the historical record, which does not describe the lieutenant general advancing beyond the Union lines, this old man turns out to be Grant, and, predictably, he and Pleasants engage in conversation, during which Pleasants tells Grant that Burnside "'picked that drunken coward Ledlie to lead the attack'" (313), whereupon Grant, who had not heard this news before, responds this way:

> "This is the saddest affair I have witnessed in this entire war. Such an opportunity for breaking through fortifications I have never seen, and I do not expect to ever see again. The entire opportunity has been lost. There is now no chance of success. These troops must be withdrawn. It is simply slaughter to leave them there." (313)

The first two sentences of this speech, after slight modifications, do in fact come from the real Grant. The first one, reading in its original form, "It was the saddest affair I have witnessed in the war," is a famous sentence, one that appears throughout the historiographical record of the battle of the

The Battle of the Crater in Recent Fiction

Crater. Schultz himself uses it as one of three epigraphs at the beginning of his novel, although he misquotes it as "It is the saddest affair I have witnessed in this war." The sentence constitutes what I have called elsewhere "a memorable line," and memorable lines function, along with plot summary, analysis, anecdotes, and battle pieces, as stock ingredients of much Civil War history and fiction.[8] What makes this particular example of a memorable line significant is that Schultz has transposed it from the written record into speech. In their original form Grant's sentences appeared in a message to Chief of Staff Henry W. Halleck, dated August 1, 1864, and subsequently published in the *Official Records* (*OR*).[9] Although no law exists that prohibits a novelist's lifting something written and changing it to something spoken, even a casual reader can hear the change in key from the elegant inversion of direct object and predicate in the written sentence, "Such an opportunity for breaking through fortifications I have never seen, and I do not expect to ever see again" (again slightly modified from the original), and the four short, simple, subject-verb, Hemingwayesque sentences that follow.

An earlier instance of Schultz's transposing from writing to speech is even more telling and reveals the self-consciousness of his method. In a seven-page scene close to the center of the novel, Meade and Burnside are quarreling about the feasibility of Pleasants's mine, about Burnside's request for 12,000 pounds of gunpowder, about the combat value of colored troops, and about the jurisdiction of command in the operations after the mine explodes. The peevish Meade quickly turns on Burnside, demanding to know if the latter lacks confidence in his ability to lead the army. At that point the following thoughts pass through the mind of the subordinate commander: "It was time to eat crow, to apologize for something he had neither said nor intended, and he framed his reply carefully, as though dictating a letter that would enter the army's endless files and remain there for future historians to read. If Burnside had to grovel, he would do so expertly" (169). Burnside's expert groveling then follows:

"Perhaps I spoke in haste, General, and in my excitement exercised
a poor choice of words. I assure you, sir, in all candor, that I never
dreamt of implying a lack of confidence in your ability to do all that
is necessary in any movement that may be undertaken by my corps
in your army. Were you personally to direct such an attack as I have
in mind from my line, I would express nothing but confidence in the
outcome. I would serve in my subordinate capacity with cheerfulness,

as I have done since you assumed command of the Army of the Potomac." (169)

What makes this passage so delicious is that Burnside speaks it in anything but "all candor," as he confirms one of Ambrose Bierce's great dicta, found in his story "One Kind of Officer," "It is one of the important uses of civility to signify resentment."[10] But delicious as it is, the passage, in which Burnside wields the language with skill and dexterity he rarely showed when wielding troops in the field, clearly belongs to the deliberate realm of dictated letters, not to that of spoken vernacular, such as "eat crow." Burnside's original apology to Meade, which Schultz has changed slightly, appeared in a message dated July 4, 1864, a message that has entered the army's endless files and has been read by subsequent historians in the *OR*.[11] In effacing the difference between written and spoken language, and in tipping us the nod that he knows we know he is doing so ("as though dictating a letter"), Schultz makes a revealing decision about how to treat his sources and how to represent this most elegantly written of written records.

The gap between the language of written records and the language of actual speech, as we imagine it, is one of the defining features of Civil War study. Just as photography made the war both uncannily familiar and unfamiliar, showing us sharp images of things we recognize immediately but always showing them to us in black-and-white abstraction from the colorful world we actually inhabit, so the extensive written records left us by participants and witnesses make them at once familiar and unfamiliar, giving us the actual words they wrote down but also distancing us from the actual words they spoke. Not until Edison's inventions in the later nineteenth century would it become possible to record spoken words directly. Until then the recording of speech depended on writing alone, and writing inevitably reflects the prevailing conventions of decorum and rhetoric. As any reader of Civil War memoirs soon learns, some writers, such as Grant, use much simpler language than others. But even the simplest written language from the Civil War, especially when published by a general, is only at best a distant cousin of the language that general spoke in the field, particularly at moments of extreme pressure.

Spending any time with historical dictionaries of American slang soon teaches us that most of the more pungent phrases and words characteristic of soldiers' speech as recorded in Vietnam, for example, also flourished in the nineteenth century. The absence of those phrases and words from the written record, even in the private journals and letters of soldiers, testifies to a code of written behavior that literary modernism would begin to challenge after World War I, and even then it would take most of the twentieth century to narrow the gap between writing and actual speech, not always to the enhancement of the former. But the difference between writing and speech does not rest solely on the presence or absence of pungent words and phrases. The basic rhythms of the two modes also differ drastically, those of writing depending primarily on the grammatical and syntactical patterns of complete, often complex sentences such as this one, those of speech depending primarily on much shorter, and often ungrammatical, phrasal units. Just as soldiers did not fight the Civil War in black and white, they did not fight it in long, polished, complete sentences.

Schultz's decision to treat the written record of the *OR* as a resource to be mined for the speech of his characters is a decision to bridge the language gap that characterizes experience of the Civil War for students of the conflict. Perhaps this bridging was precisely his aim, and enthusiastic readers of his novel might point approvingly to its attempt to overcome the estranging effects of writing, particularly writing from an earlier century. If so, fair enough. After all, many readers may welcome having their experience of history simplified for them. Somewhat more suggestive, though, is the way Schultz bridges the gap between his own writing and that of earlier historical writing. In this case, it is not a matter of making a character speak words actually written by his historical original; in this case, it is a matter of one's attitude toward sources and the boundaries between books.

Take, for example, this sentence from *Glory Enough for All*, one spoken to Burnside by "a highly agitated Meade" (261): "'We have eighty fieldpieces, eighteen giant ten-inch mortars, twenty-eight of the Coehorn mortars, and eighteen four-and-a-half-inch siege guns'" (262). This sentence comes almost verbatim from Bruce Catton's *A Stillness at Appomattox*: "A powerful mass of artillery had been quietly moved up into position during recent nights—eighty field pieces, eighteen huge 10-inch mortars, twenty-eight of the lighter coehorn mortars, and eighteen 4½-inch siege guns, all dug in where they could sweep the Confederate position."[12] Here the fictional Meade speaks not as the historical Meade wrote; he speaks the written script of Bruce Catton, whose sentence echoes the answers of Henry Hunt, Army of the Potomac chief of artillery, to questions posed by the judge advocate during the inquiry after the battle: "There were eighteen siege guns in the line, eighteen large mortars, and twenty-eight Coehorns along in the lines in front, and some eighty field pieces."[13]

STEPHEN CUSHMAN

In reeling off Catton's catalog of artillery pieces, derived from Hunt's testimony, the fictional Meade not only delivers another Shakespearean Background Speech; he also shows us that his author, whose book does not include any bibliographical note on the sources he used, values a seamlessly transparent, continuous, self-contained representation of the battle of the Crater that attempts to render invisible its connections to both primary documents and Civil War historiography. In borrowing nearly verbatim from an eminent historian, Schultz does nothing many writers have not also done, among them Shakespeare, who lifted liberally throughout his career from Raphael Holinshed's *Chronicles of England, Scotland, and Ireland* (1577), for example. Most readers of historical fiction are prepared to grant works of the imagination a license to proceed without footnotes, bibliographies, and the armature of formal scholarship. If they were not, they would not be reading that fiction. But in granting this license, the grantors do not necessarily forfeit the right to point to the Wizard-of-Oz, pay-no-attention-to-the-man-behind-the-curtain quality of the workmanship, as well as to the attitude toward the written archive it reflects.

Richard Slotkin's approach to the battle of the Crater could not be more different. In *The Crater* he does not merely acknowledge the connections between his book and earlier writing; he places those connections front and center, and in doing so he makes them one of the subjects, implicit or explicit, of his pioneering, ambitious novel. Whereas Schultz's book works for a seamless, transparent, self-contained picture of the Rebel of the Crater, Slotkin's puts all its seams, opacities, and debts fully on view. Take, for example, Slotkin's version of the famous explosion:

Booker saw his own hazy shadow fall forward out of the embrasure. He looked behind him.

Above the parapet of the blackened battery, the thin dome of the sun bulged, an eyelid-peep of fire.

He heard a *bump* like a machine starting up below the floor of a factory loft.

The ground bumped.

He turned and looked across the field. The gray fields were flat, the long black horizontal of the rebel lines, the line of brush in the ravine.

Bulged.

A black sound muscled the strata up and aside like the shoulders of a giant, *a firehead bulged out of the black*, a roar, a black wind, and he covered his head to shut out the black roaring of the air and saw behind

The Battle of the Crater in Recent Fiction

his eyelids the firehead bulging out of the black folded earth, a head
of fire, a birth, a death.[14]

Some may feel that the final four words of this excerpt, "a birth, a death,"
perhaps strain toward rhetorical portentousness, which this extraordinary passage hardly needs. But even with this slight excess Slotkin master-
fully anticipates both the laconic understatement of Frazier's description
in *Cold Mountain* and Schultz's more highly wrought description in *Glory
Enough for All*.

Booker is Major Judah Booker, a German Jew originally born Bookser,
a veteran of the war in Kansas, and now an officer in the 43rd USCT, First
Brigade, Fourth Division, Ninth Corps. Slotkin's simile likening the sound
of the mine beginning its explosion to "a machine starting up below the
floor of a factory loft" suits Booker's point of view especially well, since in
his youth he worked as an apprentice iron molder with his father in the
Sinclair Factory in St. Louis, and it connects to Slotkin's ongoing representation of nineteenth-century labor struggles in the United States.[15] Like
Frazier's character Inman, Booker has seen plenty of war, and like Inman's
his point of view has little use for gratuitous overstatement. Short, simple
sentences like "The ground bumped," along with the minimal sentence
fragment "Bulged," annotate his steady-nerved perceptions adequately.
But when the explosion comes, the prose changes, and lyric intensifica-
tions of language usually associated with poetry suddenly dominate, with
synesthesia ("black sound"), simile ("like the shoulders of a giant"), meta-
phor ("firehead"), and rhythmic repetition (of "black," "firehead," "roar")
all enriching the description. Especially inventive is Slotkin's merging of
Booker's perception of the sunrise with his perception of the explosion,
an uncanny blending of the familiar and unfamiliar.[16]

What makes this moment much more than a verbal tour de force, however, is its placement within a narrative sequence of discontinuous moments,
a series of quick cuts, each identified by a time of night, or early morning,
on July 30, 1864. The sequence begins twenty pages earlier with Lincoln in
Washington at midnight, and it jumps quickly in successive short sections
among characters in the 48th Pennsylvania, the 14th New York Heavy Artillery, various regiments of USCT in the Fourth Division, Ferrero's headquarters, Meade's headquarters, and a field hospital in the First Division
bombproof before the explosion occurs. Then, after Booker witnesses the
explosion, the quick-jumping sequence continues, now widening out to
include still more figures, among them Confederates in Pegram's Salient

African American soldiers in the works at Petersburg eight days after
thousands of USCT troops fought at the Crater. Library of Congress,
Prints and Photographs Division, LC-DIG-cwpb-01232.

and the headquarters of Maj. Gen. Bushrod Johnson. In other words, whereas Schultz's narrative approach to the battle of the Crater has one dominant center, that of Henry Pleasants, Slotkin's spreads itself among many centers, Union and Confederate, black and white.

Even more effective is the distribution among the successive sections of actual excerpts from the *OR*. Slotkin introduces the first excerpt from the *OR* a few pages into *The Crater*, a sentence from Burnside to Meade, asking him on June 21, 1864, "Do you care to consider a proposition for an assault on the enemy in front of our lines?" (18), and he continues this technique, which establishes the distinctive rhythm of his narrative, until nearly the end of his 559-page novel.[17] In a final note Slotkin refers to and comments on his use of the *OR*:

> *The Crater* is a work of fiction based on history. I have attempted to make the narrative follow as closely as possible the historical sequence of events, and the historical record as it concerns those events and the individuals who figured prominently in them. Most of the dispatches in the text are taken verbatim from the *Official Records of the War of the Rebellion*. However, several have been either invented or significantly altered; and in some cases I have altered or interpolated words, dates, or names of fictional characters for the sake of clarification or of narrative consistency. (559)

Inventing or significantly altering the historical record is the privilege of "fiction," which comes from a Latin verb meaning to touch, form, or mold. When, for example, Slotkin includes Special Orders No. 152 and the reprimand by the provost marshal general of Lt. Lemuel D. Dobbs, 19th USCT, for beating a Union cavalryman who struck and killed a black sentry (169), he is altering the historical record by inserting one of his own fictional characters into it. In making this kind of fictional alteration, Slotkin does nothing that Schultz does not also do.

The difference, of course, is that Slotkin, who unlike Schultz is an academic scholar, wants to give his fiction the texture of the archive, of the written record that historians read. In adopting what we might call a documentary technique, Slotkin builds into the form of his novel the same kinds of gaps and disjunctions that characterize study of the Civil War. Instead of absorbing and synthesizing a range of sources, which he then presents in a mostly continuous, homogenized form, as Schultz does, Slotkin preserves the discontinuous and heterogeneous, placing his reader in the position of the historian face to face with primary sources, which often tell stories that differ. Whereas Schultz's readers passively receive his digested research in its fictionalized form, Slotkin's readers reenact a version of the author's research and reading. As a result, Slotkin's readers do not read, or do not read for long, under the illusion that they have transparent access to events leading up to and beyond July 30, 1864; they read with the self-consciousness that they are witnessing events through the mediation of documents and that the fictional version of those events depends on interpretation of the documents that record them.

Take the matter of the language gap between written records, especially those preserved in the *OR*, and the actual speech of nineteenth-century soldiers as we might imagine it. Whereas Schultz's tendency is to bridge this gap and level out the differences between writing and speaking, Slotkin preserves and dramatizes the gap. Consider, for example, the gritty but usually unmentioned details of thousands and thousands of men living in the same place for months while they follow the natural routines of their bodies. Here is Schultz, a few pages into his novel, on the subject:

> A stench hit them as soon as they neared the front. The trenches were foul, open, stagnant sewers simmering in the heat. They stank of sweat, unwashed bodies, urine and excrement, rotting food, and decaying, purulent corpses, bloated and unburied, lying just beyond the deep scars scratched out of the red Virginia soil. (15)

These are good sentences, vivid and unflinching, well crafted and rhythmically muscular. But the use of "purulent," for example, a Latinate word that few of Schultz's readers have used recently and most would have to look up (it means containing or secreting pus) reflects his decision to avoid one end of the language spectrum by sticking to the other, the end characterized by education and formality.

Compare Slotkin on the same subject on the first page of his story:

> Rees turned a corner of the trench where a covered way slanted back towards the rear, and the stink of someone's shit smacked him across the face like an insult. . . . Sergeant Rees's rage swelled in him like a gigantic bubble, which blew up, filling the air with a rich profanity of Welsh and English curses, a rage against trenches in the earth, with a lid of stone-stunning sun and pain; and damned rebel snipers; and most particularly against the godddamned, nest-fouling, potato-eating, egg-stealing Irish Mick sons of bitches that would shit like an

The Battle of the Crater in Recent Fiction

animal or a nigger right where they were living rather than walk three feet to the privy like a human being. (3–4)

As the stink hits Rees's nose (Slotkin drops the final "e" from the name of Sergeant Henry Reese, an actual, and very important, soldier in the 48th Pennsylvania), so this passage hits the eye, and through the eye, the sensibilities of his reader. Like Schultz in the passage above, Slotkin narrates here from an omniscient point of view, but unlike Schultz he tinges his omniscience with idiomatic indirect discourse, coloring his language, which also deploys un-Reesian punctuation (semicolons) and lyricism ("a lid of stone-stunning sun and pain"), with the profanity and racism he attributes to his character.

This bracing passage does several things at once. With the image of Rees's gigantic rage bubble blowing up, Slotkin foreshadows the exploding of the mine 377 pages later, after Rees himself, in accordance with the historical record, has descended bravely into the mine to fix the fuse that has gone out (Schultz has two fictional characters perform this repair); with the references to "Irish Mick sons of bitches" and "an animal or a nigger," he introduces notions of ethnicity, race, and racism, which will be central to his story throughout; and with his salty diction, he stakes out the soldierly end of the language spectrum, so that when his reader comes later to the excerpts from the *OR*, particularly to the messages from the verbally elegant and formal Burnside, Rees's corps commander, the contrast and incongruity between them will glare even more.

Multiple narrative centers and a frankly represented language gap are not all that distinguish Slotkin's treatment of the battle of the Crater from Schultz's. Whereas Schultz leaves unspoken his connections to, and dependency on, earlier narratives of the battle, Slotkin declares them unambiguously: "I want to acknowledge my debt to the historical studies of slavery and Afro-American culture by Herbert Gutman, Willie Lee Rose, Lawrence Levine, and Eugene Genovese; the Civil War histories of Bruce Catton and Shelby Foote; and the studies of labor struggles in the 1860s and 1870s by Wayne Broehl, Herbert Gutman and Robert V. Bruce" (559). A sentence like this does not merely demonstrate the professional behavior of the Olin Professor of English Emeritus at Wesleyan University, who has produced both fiction and scholarship; it reflects the historical sensibility operating behind his novel, a sensibility that informs his vision of both the battle of the Crater in particular and Civil War historiography in general.

To test the soundness of this large claim, let us take two of the most memorable of memorable lines in all writing about the battle of the Crater, historical or fictional:

> We looks like men a-marching on,
> We looks like men a war!

Slotkin introduces these lines, spontaneously composed by Private Johnson Number Five (who also appears in Catton's *A Stillness at Appomattox*, 231) and taken up by the soldiers of the 19th USCT, right after the soldiers learn the news that they have been selected by Burnside to lead the assault after the mine explodes. Meade, backed by Grant, will subsequently overrule Burnside's decision, citing political risks and, as it turns out, significantly increasing the odds of failure. But for the moment the lines express the exultation of the black troops over the long-delayed recognition of them as men and soldiers. True to the narrative rhythm of *The Crater*, an excerpt from the *OR*, in which Henry Halleck writes to Grant about a delay in paying the army, immediately follows the last repetition of these lines.

Schultz evidently liked these lines, too, and made use of them thirteen years later in *Glory Enough for All*. But more to the immediate point are Slotkin's sources. Working backward in time, we come first to the third volume of Shelby Foote's *The Civil War* and this sentence: "'We looks like men a-marching on, We looks like men of war,' they sang as they came up in the wake of the other three divisions, which were scarcely to be seen, having vanished quite literally into the earth."[18] In his eight pages on the battle of the Crater, Foote does not have much more to say about the black soldiers, although he asserts unequivocally that the decision not to have them lead the assault "was provoked by racism; racism in reverse" (534). But he does name, in a bibliographical note that must be among the most elegant and eloquent in recent Civil War historical writing (1063–65), his many sources, among them Catton's *A Stillness at Appomattox*. Returning to this book, we find Private Johnson Number Five's memorable lines (put into his mouth by Slotkin, not by Catton) appearing near the end of a ten-page meditation on black soldiers (234), a meditation Catton introduces with this remarkable short paragraph:

> The difficulty was that an imponderable entered into things here, deep as the ocean and unpredictable as a tornado at midnight. Ferrero's division was made up entirely of colored soldiers. (226)

Although it is not clear how a tornado at midnight churns any more unpredictably than one in broad daylight, it is clear that Catton, a native

Michigander for whom both unpredictable tornados and deep oceans may have figured more as poetic images than as immediate realities, knows that, writing in the early 1950s with segregation firmly in place and without widespread historiographical precedent for discussing the role of black soldiers, he has reached a special rhetorical moment and must elevate his own rhetoric accordingly. Not all of Catton's statements about "Ferrero's dark battalions" (228) will make contemporary readers comfortable, as when he muses, "Somewhere, far back in dim tribal memories, there may have been traditions of war parties and fighting and desperate combat" (226–27). But they testify to his deep interest in black soldiers, an interest that includes his reading of Thomas Wentworth Higginson's *Army Life in a Black Regiment*, which Catton describes in an endnote as "one of the most fascinating books, incidentally, in Civil War literature" (414).[19]

Higginson's ninth chapter, titled "Negro Spirituals" (187–213) and an early example of what would now be called ethnomusicology, is Catton's source for all but one of the songs he quotes, among them "I Know Moonrise," which Schultz borrows for the opening execution scene of *Glory Enough for All* (5–6), and "My Army Cross Over," which Slotkin quotes just before turning to "We looks like men a-marching / We looks like men a war!" (112). As it turns out, Catton's source for this last and most often quoted pair of lines is not Higginson writing about the 1st South Carolina Volunteers, later the 33rd USCT; it is Henry Goddard Thomas's "The Colored Troops at Petersburg," published in the *Century Illustrated Monthly Magazine* in September 1887 and subsequently collected in *Battles and Leaders of the Civil War*.[20] In Thomas's article the lines appear along with their musical setting as "'We-e looks li-ike me-en a-a marchin' on, we looks li-ike men-er war,'" the hyphenated forms of the words suggesting the cadences of the singing itself.

In *The Crater* Henry Goddard Thomas figures prominently, appearing first as colonel of the Second Brigade, Fourth Division, "about forty, a vigorous man, with a clear and lovely fair complexion, smooth cheeks above a rich brown beard" (44), and finally as a brevet major general returning to Petersburg on July 30, 1877, to attend a reunion of the combatants, Union and Confederate. Slotkin gives Thomas the last section of his novel, as the veteran remembers Lt. Christopher Pennington (based on the actual Lt. Christopher Pennell), who was killed dramatically during the battle, and he brings his narrative to a close by representing Thomas in the process of gathering material for the *Century* article (554). In pointing to this incipient narrative within his narrative, in finishing his own historical fiction by representing the beginning of an earlier act of historical writing, Slotkin confirms once again the deep bond between the former and the latter, and he establishes an important analogy for reading his Civil War novel: as the tracing of textual connections back through a genealogy of his sources to an original moment of writing (Slotkin to Foote to Catton to Higginson or Thomas) constitutes both a recovering of different writers' contributions and an honoring of those contributions, so writing a fictional history of black soldiers at the battle of the Crater, which combines extensive historical research with imaginative reenactment, constitutes both a recovering of those soldiers' contributions and an honoring of them. As Slotkin's borrowings from earlier sources inevitably memorialize those sources, along with the people behind them, so his account of the battle of the Crater memorializes the people who fought there, particularly those who have not been memorialized previously.[21]

In writing about black soldiers, Slotkin must imagine nearly everything, especially when he attempts to enter their interior worlds, as he does so effectively in the cases of Sgt. Cato Ezekiel Randolph (55–61) and Pvt. James Johnson Number Five, formerly Dayson's Chaney (220–25), since his sources cannot help him where the historical record is nearly silent. The large achievement of *The Crater* shows itself even more clearly when we recall that its composition preceded both the publication of the multi-volume *Freedom: A Documentary History of Emancipation, 1861–1867* by the Freedmen and Southern Society Project, beginning in 1982, and the release of Edward Zwick's film *Glory* in 1989.[22] But even if Slotkin had had the former on which to draw or the latter as a precedent for representing the interior worlds of black soldiers (like Catton's *A Stillness at Appomattox*, *Glory* draws on Higginson's *Army Life in a Black Regiment* in order to tell its version of Robert Gould Shaw and the 54th Massachusetts Infantry), he still would have had to depend primarily on his imagination, since even these sources mostly filter the speaking of black soldiers through the writing of white officers or officials.

As *The Crater* makes abundantly clear, Slotkin's sympathetic representations of black soldiers reflect an acute awareness of the dangers inherent in a white writer's performing black speech and song. The precedents of minstrelsy are never far away, and Slotkin's consciousness of their proximity manifests itself in references to minstrelsy throughout his novel.[23] Early on, for example, on the same page that introduces Henry Goddard Thomas, Ferrero, who before the war "'had kept a hotel near West Point and taught the cadets to dance,'" recalls how his assuming command of the

Ninth Corps colored troops led some to nickname his division "Ferrero's Minstrels and Dixie Cut-ups" (44). Then, in another example forty-five pages later, Major Booker blackens his face as he prepares to lead some of his soldiers in capturing a Confederate prisoner at night:

> "All right," said Booker, "one more thing." He broke a piece of charcoal in his hand, spat on it. Then he rubbed it over his cheeks. The men watched him, their faces inscrutable. "When I spent time out West," he said, "I stayed with the Indians awhile. Whenever they went out to fight, they blacked up their faces some. Good spirits, they figured; and your face don't shine in the moonlight. You all have your warpaint on already." That got grins all around. (89)

The grins of the black soldiers, first described here with the familiar adjective "inscrutable," may merge with the inward smile of many a reader, who can release a little racial tension, thanks to Booker's joke. But that tension flickers throughout *The Crater*.[24] Here, for instance, Booker traces his blackface to time he spent with the Crow Indians (121–24); yet the unspoken reference is to the blacking-up of white performers in nineteenth-century minstrel shows.

To Slotkin's enduring credit, he never shies from or denies this tension, turning it instead into one of the significant motifs of his novel, most explicitly in a nearly thirty-page section that alternates passages in which Ferrero, who has gone to Washington with his wife to see about reconfirmation of his commission, watches a performance of Daltrey's Ethiopian Delineators at Carey's Theater with passages representing soldiers from both sides of the line back at Petersburg (300–328). At one point in the performance, Corn Meal Man, a white performer in blackface with another "layer on layer" (317) of white flour on top of that, dances and sings "Jump Jim Crow," which includes this verse:

> I whip my weight in wildcats,
> I eat an alligator
> I drink de Mississippi up!
> O I de very cratur! (318)

Almost 300 pages earlier, Slotkin shows the young Lincoln, during his trip down the Mississippi to New Orleans, thinking about this same song and these same lines (32), but even more complex than this "layer on layer" is the triple exposure of cratur-creator-crater, which causes us to reexamine Slotkin's title and hear it as both *The Crater* and *The Creator*.

STEPHEN CUSHMAN

In the context of "Jump Jim Crow" the cratur-creator is God, irreverently figured as the folk hero of a western tall tale, but in the context of Slotkin's title the crater-creator is the novelist himself, who in undertaking the representation of a battle in which black soldiers figured prominently but, as far as the historical record shows, almost silently, except for a little timely singing, undertakes the tricky task of endowing them with speech without caricaturing them into mere spectacle, without reducing the language gap to cheap entertainment. In fact more than a tricky task, Slotkin's is in many ways an impossible one, a point that the repeated pun on cratur-creator-crater, with its origin in minstrel performance, seems to acknowledge. Just as Booker's blackface, despite the unassailable motives and integrity of the white man leading black soldiers into the possibility of wounding and death, has a minstrelsy component to it, so, too, does Slotkin's blackface, despite the unassailable motives and integrity of the white man devoting years to researching and writing a story that seeks to illuminate many historical and political injustices, racial and economic.

Whatever the tendencies of his readers to want to read *The Crater* politically, Slotkin himself, in an essay titled "Fiction for the Purposes of History," describes his undertaking in explicitly political terms:

> Historical novels are always political in their implications—that is a given of the form. But the politics is of two kinds. There is of course the politics of content, the political perspective and values that shape the writer's choice of subject and mode of treatment. Fenimore Cooper used his fiction to project a historical myth of racial nationalism; I use mine to project a myth in which racism is undone, and ideas of justice are questioned and redefined.[25]

Few readers of *The Crater*, which James McPherson calls in his foreword to the novel "the best account I have ever read" of the battle of the Crater (xvi) and which Gary Gallagher lists among his ten "superior examples of Civil War fiction," could question the truth of this last statement.[26]

Slotkin does not stop with the politics of content, however:

> But there is also a politics implied in the choice of the novel form. Novels don't read well without strong characters, and the emphasis on character implies a theory of historical causation that contemporary historians find suspect: a "heroic" theory, which emphasizes the agency of more or less powerful persons as shapers of events. (231)

The Battle of the Crater in Recent Fiction

Although we have no evidence that Schultz would describe his choice of the novel form this way, the centrality he gives to Henry Pleasants in *Glory Enough for All* would suggest that he believes just as much as Slotkin in a heroic theory of the historical novel, since his depiction of Pleasants represents him as a more or less powerful person who shapes events. The main difference between *Glory Enough for All* and *The Crater* is that the latter represents the battle of the Crater, and by implication the larger war of which it formed only a small part, as an event or cluster of events shaped by many, many more or less powerful people, especially those not previously recognized as such. The politics of Slotkin's form includes not just the presentation of strong characters, who reflect the novelist's faith "in political action to produce change and realize ideals of social justice" and his desire "to assist in forming the critical consciousness that makes such action possible" (231), but in his treatment of language, narrative point of view, and earlier historical writing. It is in these features of his novelizing as much as in his depiction of strong characters that Slotkin demonstrates the generic differences between Civil War fiction and Civil War historiography at the same time that he affirms their close and inescapable kinship.

Notes

1. Charles Frazier, *Cold Mountain* (New York: Atlantic Monthly, 1997), 123–24. Frazier could have found the detail about the soldier yelling "Hell has busted!" in many places, and his final page (358) acknowledges many sources from which he drew, but the earliest important source is Maj. Gen. William Mahone's *The Battle of the Crater* (Petersburg, Va.: Franklin Press Co., n.d.), 5. (Mahone went into the battle a brigadier general but was promoted by Lee on July 30, 1864, for his performance during it.) Although this little twelve-page booklet, which measures five and a quarter by four and seven-eighths inches, shows no date of publication, the catalog entry for it in the University of Virginia Special Collections gives the date as 1864, placing it among the earliest published reminiscences of the battle of the Crater.

2. Since the release of Minghella's film and the publications of both Slotkin's and Schultz's novels, there has been a spate of historical scholarship on the battle of the Crater, including most recently John F. Schmutz, *The Battle of the Crater: A Complete History* (Jefferson, N.C.: McFarland, 2009); Richard Slotkin, *No Quarter: The Battle of the Crater, 1864* (New York: Random House, 2009); Earl J. Hess, *Into the Crater: The Mine Attack at Petersburg* (Columbia: University of South Carolina Press, 2010); and Kevin M. Levin, *Remembering the Battle of the Crater: War as Murder* (Lexington: University Press of Kentucky, 2012). A useful earlier account is that of Michael A. Cavanaugh and William Marvel, *The Petersburg Campaign: The Battle of the Crater, "The Horrid Pit," June 25–August 6, 1864* (Lynchburg, Va.: H. E. Howard, 1989).

3. John Keegan, *The Face of Battle* (New York: Viking, 1976), 30, 36–46, 62–68.

STEPHEN CUSHMAN

4. Duane Schultz, *Glory Enough for All: The Battle of the Crater* (New York: St. Martin's, 1993), 290. Subsequent references to this edition will appear parenthetically in the text, as will references to other one-volume works after first citations.

5. Henry Pleasants Jr., who was the cousin of the lieutenant colonel of the 48th Pennsylvania, also uses the image of the mushroom-shaped cloud in *The Tragedy of the Crater* (Boston: Christopher Publishing House, 1938), 76: "The great smoke cloud now spread out like a gigantic mushroom." Since *The Tragedy of the Crater* purports to synthesize the Pleasantses' recollections of the battle, the original comparison to a mushroom in fact may have originated with the man who actually saw the explosion. But Hiroshima and Nagasaki made the phrase "mushroom cloud" idiomatic, and, consequently, Schultz's use of the phrase cannot help sounding anachronistic to contemporary ears. Using another anachronism, Schultz describes the astonished reaction of regimental commanders in Brig. Gen. James H. Ledlie's First Division to Burnside's choice of that division as "shock troops" (274), a phrase that first appeared many years later during World War I. Richard Slotkin also uses this anachronism at least once (363; for full citation see n. 14 below).

6. The consistent substitution of "Dunne" for "Duane" could be a mistake, in which case it is a serious one, or it could be a deliberate gesture meant for insiders, who might appreciate the resonances behind a statement on the copyright page that *Glory Enough for All* is "A Thomas Dunne book." Unfortunately, other evidence suggests that it is most likely a mistake, since Schultz also misspells Brig. Gen. Edward Ferrero's last name throughout as "Ferraro," as does Henry Pleasants Jr. in *The Tragedy of the Crater*.

7. Ulysses S. Grant, *Personal Memoirs of U. S. Grant* (2 vols., 1885; reprint in 1 vol., New York: Penguin, 1999), 495.

8. Stephen Cushman, *Bloody Promenade: Reflections on a Civil War Battle* (Charlottesville: University Press of Virginia, 1999), 192.

9. U.S. War Department, *The War of the Rebellion: A Compilation of the Official Records of the Union and Confederate Armies*, 127 vols., index, and atlas (Washington, D.C.: Government Printing Office, 1880–1901), ser. 1, 40(1):17 (hereafter cited as *OR*; all references are to ser. 1).

10. William McCann, ed., *Ambrose Bierce's Civil War* (New York: Wing Books, 1996), 193. (Originally published in *Can Such Things Be?* [New York: Cassell, 1893].)

11. Burnside's apology to Meade appears twice in the *OR*: 40(1):162 and 40(2):629.

12. Bruce Catton, *A Stillness at Appomattox* (Garden City, N.Y.: Doubleday, 1953), 237. For another borrowing, compare Schultz's "walking two and three abreast the way they had done for weeks, colliding with the scores of stragglers, walking wounded, and couriers heading in the opposite direction" (310) with Catton's "wide enough for no more than two or three men abreast, colliding with stragglers, walking wounded, couriers, and other persons" (246).

13. *OR* 40(1):96.

14. Richard Slotkin, *The Crater*, foreword by James M. McPherson (1980; reprint, New York: Henry Holt, 1996), 380.

15. See, for example, Slotkin's paragraph containing the pithy formulation near the end of *No Quarter*: "The irony for the Union is that in winning its war for free

labor, it created a new financial and industrial order in which free labor principles no longer applied" (346).

16. According to the Astronomical Applications Department of the United States Naval Observatory, sunrise in Petersburg, Va., on July 30, with no adjustment for Daylight Saving Time, which did not exist during the Civil War, is 5:13 A.M., or twenty-eight minutes after the mine exploded. See, as of January 6, 2014, http://aa.usno.navy.mil/cgi-bin/aa_rstablew.pl.

17. For the original sentence, see *OR* 40(2):283. Slotkin has modified it slightly from "on the front of our lines" to "in front of our lines."

18. Shelby Foote, *The Civil War: A Narrative*, vol. 3, *Red River to Appomattox* (New York: Random House, 1974), 537.

19. Although Catton cites an edition of 1900, the first edition of *Army Life in a Black Regiment* was published in 1870 (Boston: Fields, Osgood, and Co.). Sections of the book first appeared in the *Atlantic Monthly* from October 1864 through January 1865. See Christopher Looby, ed., *The Complete Civil War Journal and Selected Letters of Thomas Wentworth Higginson* (Chicago: University of Chicago Press, 2000), 7 n. 11.

20. *Century Illustrated Monthly Magazine*, September 1887, 777–82; collected in Robert Underwood Johnson and Clarence Clough Buel, eds., *Battles and Leaders of the Civil War*, 4 vols. (New York: Century, 1887), 4:563–67 (subsequently reprinted in several editions, including one in New York by Thomas Yoseloff in 1956).

21. That memorializing the neglected service of United States Colored Troops at the battle of the Crater is one of Slotkin's main interests becomes explicit in the final sentence of *No Quarter*: "There is no monument [at Petersburg National Battlefield] to the memory of the African American troops who fought and died in the crater" (353). In 1993, a monument to USCT units at Petersburg was dedicated on part of the battlefield where black soldiers fought on June 15, 1864. The inscription reads:

IN MEMORY OF
THE VALOROUS SERVICE OF REGIMENTS
AND COMPANIES
OF THE U.S. COLORED TROOPS
ARMY OF THE JAMES
AND ARMY OF THE POTOMAC
SIEGE OF PETERSBURG
1864–1865.

22. Ira Berlin, Barbara J. Fields, Steven F. Miller, Joseph P. Reidy, and Leslie S. Rowland, eds., *Free at Last: A Documentary History of Slavery, Freedom, and the Civil War* (New York: New Press, 1992), provides a rich, one-volume introduction to *Freedom: A Documentary History of Emancipation*.

23. For an excellent recent discussion of minstrelsy, see Eric Lott, *Love and Theft: Blackface Minstrelsy and the American Working Class* (New York: Oxford University Press, 1993).

24. At the outset of *No Quarter*, Slotkin has this to say about his motive for studying the battle of the Crater: "Above all, the Battle of the Crater is worth a closer look because the flash of its explosion illuminates the centrality of *race* in the tangle of

social and political conflicts that shaped American life as the Civil War approached its climax" (xiii).

25. Richard Slotkin, "Fiction for the Purposes of History," *Rethinking History* 9 (June/September 2005): 231.

26. Gary W. Gallagher, "The Civil War 200: 100 More of the Best Civil War Books Ever Published," *Civil War: The Magazine of the Civil War Society* 55 (February 1996): 43.

⇥ BIBLIOGRAPHIC ESSAY ⇤

The best source for published primary material on the period May–July 1864 is U.S. War Department, *The War of the Rebellion: The Official Records of the Union and Confederate Armies*, 127 vols., index, and atlas (Washington, D.C.: Government Printing Office, 1880–1901), ser. 1, vol. 36, pts. 1–3, and vol. 40, pts. 1–3. Coverage of the respective armies is unbalanced, with far more Federal than Confederate reports and correspondence. Additional documents are in *Supplement to the Official Records of the Union and Confederate Armies*, ed. Janet B. Hewett and others, 95 vols. and 5-vol. index (Wilmington, N.C.: Broadfoot, 1994–2001), ser. 1, vol. 6, and ser. 3, vol. 7.

For the Union high command, volumes 10–11 of *The Papers of Ulysses S. Grant*, ed. John Y. Simon and others, 32 vols. to date (Carbondale: Southern Illinois University Press, 1967–) are essential regarding the general in chief's decisions and actions. *Personal Memoirs of U. S. Grant*, 2 vols. (New York: Charles L. Webster, 1885), a monument of American literature, presents the general's postwar interpretations. For a convenient modern edition, with some correspondence added, see Ulysses S. Grant, *Memoirs and Selected Letters*, ed. Mary Drake McFeely and William S. McFeely (New York: Library of America, 1990). George Gordon Meade, *The Life and Letters of George Gordon Meade*, 2 vols. (New York: Scribner's, 1913), tracks Meade's accommodation to a reduced role as Grant increased his influence on the Army of the Potomac during the Overland campaign and at Petersburg.

Robert E. Lee's letters and other documents can be found in *The Wartime Papers of R. E. Lee*, ed. Clifford Dowdey and Louis H. Manarin (Boston: Little, Brown, 1961). Closest to a memoir from Lee are his postwar conversations with William Allan, William Preston Johnston, and Edward Clifford Gordon, published as "Testimony of R. E. Lee" in Gary W. Gallagher, ed., *Lee the Soldier* (Lincoln: University of Nebraska Press, 1996). Walter Taylor, *Lee's Adjutant: The Wartime Letters of Colonel Walter Herron Taylor, 1862–1865* (Columbia: University of South Carolina Press, 1995), offers an excellent perspective from Confederate headquarters through the eyes of a member of Lee's staff. Of the Confederate corps commanders in

June 1864, only Jubal Early wrote about the campaign. *A Memoir of the Last Year of the War for Independence, in the Confederate States of America* (1867; reprint, Columbia: University of South Carolina Press, 2001), allocates the first part of the text to the period before Early left for the Shenandoah Valley in mid-June.

Three books stand out among general narratives by well-placed participants. Edward Porter Alexander's *Military Memoirs of a Confederate: A Critical Narrative* (New York: Scribner's, 1907) and *Fighting for the Confederacy: The Personal Recollections of General Edward Porter Alexander*, ed. Gary W. Gallagher (Chapel Hill: University of North Carolina Press, 1989), dissect military operations with the eye of a superb engineer and artillerist— the Georgian was the best gunner in the Confederacy—and the instincts of a scholar. Andrew A. Humphreys, who served as chief of staff to George G. Meade and later as commander of the Second Corps, contributed *The Virginia Campaign of '64 and '65: The Army of the Potomac and the Army of the James* (New York: Scribner's, 1883), a book of lasting value that used records from the War Department as well as correspondence with officers from both sides.

Among Union letters, diaries, and reminiscences, *A Diary of Battle: The Personal Journals of Colonel Charles S. Wainwright, 1861–1865*, ed. Allan Nevins (New York: Harcourt, Brace, and World, 1962), and *The Civil War Letters of General Robert McAllister*, ed. James I. Robertson Jr. (New Brunswick, N.J.: Rutgers University Press, 1965), are indispensable. Like Porter Alexander, Theodore Lyman bequeathed students of the war two superior titles: *Meade's Headquarters, 1863–1865: Letters of Colonel Theodore Lyman from the Wilderness to Appomattox*, ed. George R. Agassiz (Boston: Atlantic Monthly Press, 1922), and *Meade's Army: The Private Notebooks of Lt. Col. Theodore Lyman*, ed. David W. Lowe (Kent, Ohio: Kent State University Press, 2007). *"Fear Was Not in Him": The Civil War Letters of Major General Francis C. Barlow*, ed. Christian G. Samito (New York: Fordham University Press, 2004), provides insights into the Union division commander. Superb views from the ranks include John W. Haley's *The Rebel Yell and the Yankee Hurrah: The Civil War Journal of a Maine Volunteer*, ed. Ruth L. Silliker (Camden, Me.: Down East Books, 1985), and Wilbur Fisk's *Hard Marching Every Day: The Civil War Letters of Private Wilbur Fisk, 1861–1865*, ed. Emil and Ruth Rosenblatt (Lawrence: University Press of Kansas, 1992 [originally published privately as *Anti-Rebel: The Civil War Letters of Wilbur Fisk*]). Frank Wilkeson's unvarnished *Recollections of a Private Soldier in the*

Army of the Potomac (New York: Putnam's, 1887) counters all romantic notions of Civil War military service.

On the Confederate side, J. Tracy Power's *Lee's Miserables: Life in the Army of Northern Virginia from the Wilderness to Appomattox* (Chapel Hill: University of North Carolina Press, 1998) quotes extensively from a mass of unpublished manuscripts to detail the actions and attitudes of Confederate soldiers. George S. Bernard's *War Talks of Confederate Veterans* (1892; reprint, Dayton, Ohio: Morningside, 1981) and *Civil War Talks: Further Reminiscences of George S. Bernard and His Fellow Veterans*, ed. Hampton Newsome, John Horn, and John G. Selby (Charlottesville: University of Virginia Press, 2012), contain extensive material on the Crater.

Five multivolume sets include valuable postwar testimony that, as with all retrospective evidence, should be used with some caution. *Southern Historical Society Papers*, ed. J. William Jones and others, 52 vols. (1876–1959; reprint, with 3-vol. index, Wilmington, N.C.: Broadfoot, 1990–92), and *Confederate Veteran*, 40 vols. (1893–1932; reprint, with 3-vol. index, Wilmington, N.C.: Broadfoot, 1984–86), are foundational for Confederate topics. Equivalent Union material resides in the *Papers* of the Military Order of the Loyal Legion of the United States, 66 vols. and 3-vol. index (Wilmington, N.C.: Broadfoot, 1991–96). Read before the state commanderies of the MOLLUS, many of these papers illuminate aspects of operations in June and July 1864. Union and Confederate veterans contributed to volumes 4 and 5 of *Papers of the Military Historical Society of Massachusetts*, 14 vols. (1895–1918; reprint in 15 vols. with a general index, Wilmington, N.C.: Broadfoot, 1989–90), and volume 4 of *Battles and Leaders of the Civil War*, ed. Robert Underwood Johnson and Clarence Clough Buel, 4 vols. (New York: Century, 1887).

For firsthand views from behind the lines, readers can select from among a huge number of titles. Two of the most quotable are *"Journal of a Secesh Lady": The Diary of Catherine Ann Devereux Edmondston, 1860–1866*, ed. Beth Gilbert Crabtree and James W. Patton (Raleigh: North Carolina Division of Archives and History, 1979), which is the best published woman's diary, Union or Confederate, and volume 3 of *The Diary of George Templeton Strong*, ed. Allan Nevins and Milton Halsey Thomas, 4 vols. (New York: Macmillan, 1952), a monument among nineteenth-century American diaries.

General historical narratives that contain significant coverage of June and July are Noah Andre Trudeau's undocumented but trustworthy *Bloody*

Roads South: The Wilderness to Cold Harbor, May–June 1864 (Boston: Little, Brown, 1989) and Clifford Dowdey's engagingly written and openly pro-Confederate *Lee's Last Campaign: The Story of Lee and His Men against Grant—1864* (Boston: Little, Brown, 1960). Shorter and more recent is Mark Grimsley's *And Keep Moving On: The Virginia Campaign May–June 1864* (Lincoln: University of Nebraska Press, 2002).

Individual battles have received detailed attention. Gordon C. Rhea's four-volume study of the Overland campaign dominates the literature on the topic. The third and fourth volumes, which reflect their author's impressive research and careful analysis, are pertinent here: *To the North Anna River: Grant and Lee, May 13–25, 1864*, and *Cold Harbor: Grant and Lee, May 26–June 3, 1864* (Baton Rouge: Louisiana State University Press, 2000, 2002). For the fighting at Petersburg on June 15–18, Thomas J. Howe, *The Petersburg Campaign: Wasted Valor, June 15–18, 1864* (Lynchburg, Va.: H. E. Howard, 1988), remains the only full-length study. Also in the H. E. Howard series, Michael A. Cavanaugh and William Marvel, *The Petersburg Campaign: The Battle of the Crater, "The Horrid Pit," June 25–August 6, 1864* (1989), provides a clear tactical overview of the most famous military action at Petersburg. Three books that appeared in just a two-year period examine the tactical story of the Crater in greater detail. Richard Slotkin's *No Quarter: The Battle of the Crater, 1864* (New York: Random House, 2009) is grippingly written and especially strong on USCT participation, while Earl J. Hess's *Into the Crater: The Mine Attack at Petersburg* (Columbia: University of South Carolina Press, 2010) is measured, built on sound research, and persuasive. Less impressive but still useful is John F. Schmutz's *The Battle of the Crater: A Complete History* (Jefferson, N.C.: McFarland, 2009). Kevin M. Levin's *Remembering the Battle of the Crater: War as Murder* (Lexington: University Press of Kentucky, 2012) deals effectively with the much-contested memory of the battle.

Three recent specialized studies merit close attention from serious students. Earl Hess analyzes the evolution of field works in *Trench Warfare under Grant and Lee: Field Fortifications in the Overland Campaign* and *In the Trenches at Petersburg: Field Fortifications and Confederate Defeat* (Chapel Hill: University of North Carolina Press, 2007, 2009). Alfred C. Young III brings order to the tangled question of Confederate casualties in *Lee's Army during the Overland Campaign: A Numerical Study* (Baton Rouge: Louisiana State University Press, 2013).

A pair of classic military biographies by master stylists introduce readers to Grant and Lee. Bruce Catton's *Grant Takes Command* (Boston: Little,

Brown, 1969) and Douglas Southall Freeman's *R. E. Lee: A Biography* (4 vols., New York: Scribner's, 1934–35) showcase what happens when gifted historians write about compelling subjects. Other biographical studies include Freeman Cleaves's workmanlike *Meade of Gettysburg* (Norman: University of Oklahoma Press, 1960), William Marvel's revisionist *Burnside* (Chapel Hill: University of North Carolina Press, 1991), David M. Jordan's *Winfield Scott Hancock: A Soldier's Life* (Bloomington: Indiana University Press, 1988), and James I. Robertson Jr.'s *General A. P. Hill: The Story of a Confederate Warrior* (New York: Random House, 1987).

For photographs, readers should consult William A. Frassanito, *Grant and Lee: The Virginia Campaigns, 1864–1865* (New York: Scribner's, 1983). Although it offers fewer iconic photographs than the author's earlier books on Gettysburg and Antietam, this one also juxtaposes modern photographs alongside period views of numerous sites and provides a useful analytical text. For more illustrative material, including color reproductions of paintings, see Gregory Jaynes and the Editors of Time-Life Books, *The Killing Ground: Wilderness to Cold Harbor*, and William C. Davis and the Editors of Time-Life Books, *Death in the Trenches: Grant at Petersburg* (Alexandria, Va.: Time-Life Books, 1986).

The experiences of both Richmond and Petersburg during the summer of 1864 have received careful attention from scholars. A. Wilson Greene's *Civil War Petersburg: Confederate City in the Crucible of War* (Charlottesville: University of Virginia Press, 2006), chapters 6–8, does a fine job of melding military and nonmilitary history. For Richmond, Emory M. Thomas's *The Confederate State of Richmond: A Biography of the Capital* (Austin: University of Texas Press, 1971), part 4, and Ernest B. Furgurson's *Ashes of Glory: Richmond at War* (New York: Alfred A. Knopf, 1996), chapters 21–23, explore the city's complex story from political, social, and military perspectives.

A trio of books completes this short review of worthwhile literature. For the broadest strategic picture of the war in the summer of 1864, readers should go first to Herman Hattaway and Archer Jones, *How the North Won: A Military History of the Civil War* (Urbana: University of Illinois Press, 1983). Parts of trilogies by Bruce Catton and Douglas Southall Freeman continue to engage those hoping for fine narrative treatments. The third volume of Freeman's *Lee's Lieutenants: A Study in Command* (3 vols., New York: Scribner's, 1942–44) describes and analyzes Confederate leaders, and Bruce Catton's *A Stillness at Appomattox* (Garden City, N.Y.: Doubleday, 1953) employs his usual distinguished writing to cover the Army of the Potomac's activities.

BIBLIOGRAPHIC ESSAY

⊰ CONTRIBUTORS ⊱

KEITH S. BOHANNON is a member of the Department of History at the University of West Georgia and teaches courses on the Civil War and the history of Georgia. He is the author of a number of essays and articles in scholarly journals and popular magazines and coeditor of *Campaigning with "Old Stonewall": Confederate Captain Ujanirtus Allen's Letters to His Wife* (Louisiana State University Press, 1998).

STEPHEN CUSHMAN is Robert C. Taylor Professor of English at the University of Virginia. He has written several volumes of poetry and literary criticism, as well as *Bloody Promenade: Reflections on a Civil War Battle* (University Press of Virginia, 1999), which focuses on the battle of the Wilderness, and *Belligerent Muse: Five Northern Writers and How They Shaped Our Understanding of the Civil War* (University of North Carolina Press, 2014) which examines the narrative artistry of Abraham Lincoln, Walt Whitman, William T. Sherman, Ambrose Bierce, and Joshua Lawrence Chamberlain.

GARY W. GALLAGHER is John L. Nau III Professor in the History of the American Civil War at the University of Virginia and past president of the Society of Civil War Historians. His recent books include *The Union War* (Harvard University Press, 2011) and *Becoming Confederates: Paths to a New National Loyalty* (University of Georgia Press, 2013).

M. KEITH HARRIS is an independent scholar in Los Angeles, California. A contributor to scholarly journals and creator of two historical blogs, he is the author of *Across the Bloody Chasm: The Culture of Commemoration among Civil War Veterans* (Louisiana State University Press, 2014).

CAROLINE E. JANNEY is professor of history at Purdue University and president of the Society of Civil War Historians. She is the author of *Burying the Dead but Not the Past: Ladies' Memorial Associations and the Lost Cause* and *Remembering the Civil War: Reunion and the Limits of Reconciliation* (University of North Carolina Press, 2008, 2013).

ROBERT E. L. KRICK, a Richmond-based historian, was reared on the Chancellorsville battlefield. He has written extensively on the Confederate military effort and specializes in the Army of Northern Virginia. His books include *Staff Officers in Gray: A Biographical Register of the Staff Officers in the Army of Northern Virginia* (University of North Carolina Press, 2003).

KEVIN M. LEVIN, a specialist in the memory of the Civil War, has published articles in numerous magazines and journals as well as contributing to volumes of essays. He writes the blog *Civil War Memory* (http://cwmemory .com/) and is author of *Remembering the Battle of the Crater: War as Murder* (University Press of Kentucky, 2012).

KATHRYN SHIVELY MEIER is assistant professor of history at Virginia Commonwealth University. Her first book, *Nature's Civil War: Common Soldiers and the Environment in 1862 Virginia* (University of North Carolina Press, 2013), explores how Civil War soldiers adapted to the mental and physical challenges of their wartime environments using survival techniques and informal networks of care.

GORDON C. RHEA is an attorney who resides in Mount Pleasant, South Carolina. A frequent lecturer on military history across the United States and participant in television documentaries, he has published four volumes on the Overland campaign, most recently *To the North Anna River: Grant and Lee, May 13–25, 1864,* and *Cold Harbor: Grant and Lee, May 26–June 3, 1864* (Louisiana State University Press, 2000, 2002).

JOAN WAUGH, a professor in the Department of History at UCLA, researches and writes about nineteenth-century America, specializing in the Civil War, Reconstruction, and Gilded Age eras. She has published many essays and books on Civil War topics, including *The Memory of the Civil War in American Culture* (with Alice Fahs; University of North Carolina Press, 2004) and *U. S. Grant: American Hero, American Myth* (University of North Carolina Press, 2009).

INDEX

Index

compared to Washington, xiii, 1–2; confidence of, xi, 178; at the Crater, 227 (n. 27), 274, 287, 291–92, 301; crossing the James, xiv–xv, 177–78, 179, 180 (ill.), 185–86, 187, 200 (ill.), 202, 203, 214, 232; evaluated, xv, 1, 10, 23, 201, 202; foreign observers on, xiii, 1, 15; and Lee, 4–5, 15–16, 22, 25, 130, 153; and Lincoln, xii, 13–14, 23; and McClellan, 13; and Meade, 155, 301; and Overland campaign, 33–34, 115, 118, 125, 151, 154, 266–67; and Petersburg, xiv–xv, 158, 160, 162, 177–78, 213, 224, 232–34, 245, 251, 252; and politics, 2, 6, 7, 9, 10; as president, 167; and the press, xiii, 1, 7–11, 12, 21; promotion of, 3, 25 (n. 25); reputation of, xiii, 1, 3–4, 17, 23–24; strategy of, x, 23, 157–58, 176, 178, 179; and Warren, 205 (n. 28); in the West, 4, 6. *See also* Army of the Potomac

Great Seal of the Confederacy, 1

Greeley, Horace, 8

Green, J. E., 129

Green, Robert, 249

Greene, A. Wilson, 171 (n. 32)

Greene, Thomas, 219

Greene, Thomas Tileston, 84, 212

Gregg, John, 19

Griffin, Charles, 182, 183, 190

Grigg, Dinwiddie, 242

Grimsley, Mark, 257 (n. 2), 280 (n. 4)

Guinea Station, Va., 117

Hagood, Johnson, 63 (n. 4), 119

Haley, John West, 81, 84, 108 (n. 92), 163, 267

Hall, James, 233

Halleck, Henry W., xi, 292, 301

Hamill, H. M., 48, 71 (n. 61)

Hamlet, 290–91

Hammell, John S., 184

Hancock, Winfield Scott, x, xiv, 79, 94, 125, 151, 152 (ill.), 154–55, 162, 173

(n. 67), 181, 183, 184, 200 (ill.), 201; and Barlow, 158–59

Hanna, William F., 172 (n. 47)

Hanover Junction, Va., 36, 37, 115

Hansell, Charles P., 50, 54

Hardaway, Robert A., 127

Hardeman, Isaac, 114

Hard war, 238; defined, 228

Harper's Weekly, 7–8, 10, 21, 27 (n. 15), 160, 167–68, 174 (n. 84), 200, 216, 237, 286

Harris, Henry H., 117, 128, 136 (n. 51)

Harris, M. Keith, xv

Harrisburg, Pa., 151

Harrison's Landing, Va., 144

Hart, Patrick, 192

Harvard University, 140, 141, 146, 149, 169 (n. 6)

Harvey, Eleanor Jones, 175 (n. 89)

Haskell, Alexander C., 53

Hatch, John, 90

Hatcher's Run, battle of, 225 (n. 2)

Hatton, John W. F., 77

Haw's Shop, battle of, 49–51, 52, 54, 56

Hawthorne, Nathaniel, 171 (n. 31)

Hay, John, 14

Hazard, John G., 190

Henagan, John W., 55

Hendrick, L. A., 243

Henry, William, 248

Hervé, Edouard, 22

Hess, Earl J., 79, 84, 106 (n. 67), 109, 126, 130, 132 (n. 8), 174 (n. 76), 280 (n. 6), 280–81 (n. 9), 281 (n. 20), 306 (n. 2)

Heth, Henry, 19, 123, 197–98, 199

Higginson, Thomas Wentworth, 302, 303

Higgins's place, Va., 183, 184

Hildreth, James W., 89–90

Hill, Ambrose P., 24, 113, 131, 197, 250, 273

Hill, Daniel Harvey, 133 (n. 19)

Hinks, Edward, 264

Hinrichs, Oscar, 115

Hinson, William G., 53